THE LAW & POLIT
C000124866

The Law & Politics of Brexit

Edited by
FEDERICO FABBRINI

OXFORD
UNIVERSITY PRESS

OXFORD
UNIVERSITY PRESS

Great Clarendon Street, Oxford, OX2 6DP,
United Kingdom

Oxford University Press is a department of the University of Oxford.
It furthers the University's objective of excellence in research, scholarship,
and education by publishing worldwide. Oxford is a registered trade mark of
Oxford University Press in the UK and in certain other countries

© The Several Contributors 2017

The moral rights of the authors have been asserted

First Edition published in 2017

All rights reserved. No part of this publication may be reproduced, stored in
a retrieval system, or transmitted, in any form or by any means, without the
prior permission in writing of Oxford University Press, or as expressly permitted
by law, by licence or under terms agreed with the appropriate reprographics
rights organization. Enquiries concerning reproduction outside the scope of the
above should be sent to the Rights Department, Oxford University Press, at the
address above

You must not circulate this work in any other form
and you must impose this same condition on any acquirer

Crown copyright material is reproduced under Class Licence
Number C01P0000148 with the permission of OPSI
and the Queen's Printer for Scotland

Published in the United States of America by Oxford University Press
198 Madison Avenue, New York, NY 10016, United States of America

British Library Cataloguing in Publication Data
Data available

Library of Congress Control Number: 2017950759

ISBN 978-0-19-881043-8

Links to third party websites are provided by Oxford in good faith and
for information only. Oxford disclaims any responsibility for the materials
contained in any third party website referenced in this work.

Table of Contents

Foreword

Danuta Hübner

It is undeniable that the referendum of 23 June 2016 opened a new stage in European, as well as British politics, marred by uncertainty and, possibly, varying degrees of expectations, both on the part of the EU and the UK. The negotiations concerning the terms of leaving the Union by one of its important members will be complex and challenging.

Although ostensibly focused on intricate points of law, they will not be detached from the vagaries of politics. For it is quite obvious to everybody that recourse to a referendum did not appear as a result of immaculate conception, but was an outcome of political calculation on the part of the Conservative Party and Prime Minister David Cameron. It turned out that what was to be just a ploy in the internal British game became a historical fact that is about to change the political landscape of the United Kingdom as well as that of the European Union for generations to come.

As someone said: "Be careful what you wish for. Wishes are brutal, unforgiving things".

And now, one year after that fateful decision, here we are, in the unforgiving world of Brexit and its unpredictable politics, beginning the most difficult negotiations of contemporary history. Their outcome is highly uncertain for the EU, the UK and, most importantly, our citizens. And yet the parties should be wary of entering the negotiations with trepidation and ill-feeling, because this would diminish their ability to lead the process in an orderly fashion. The process itself is complex enough and no additional burden need be added to it.

Both the EU and the UK must do everything to reduce the uncertainty that will accompany the difficult negotiations ahead.

On this point, it is of prime importance that everything should be done to protect the interests of all who are or will be affected by the negotiations. I mean here, first and foremost, the citizens of both the EU and the UK. The Union is the Union of citizens. They should not live in fear of losing their rights—also their right to transparent negotiations that would have consequences for them and their families.

One year on, apart from putting our minds to the difficult task of negotiating ahead, coming out of the initial shock and starting to absorb its consequences, is the right moment to begin to understand why Brexit did actually happen, what led to it, as well as to look at what lies before us. Negotiations are one thing, and complex enough. But also, in the EU, Brexit challenges us with developing a quite new set of constitutional questions, and a necessity of finding further possible paths for national and European development and integration.

Brexit, thus, as a *sui generis* phenomenon, is not only a brutal political reality, but also an inviting object of multi-faceted scholarly investigation in the areas of British and European politics, economics, law, as well as cultural studies. In time, certainly many volumes will appear on the causes, motives, and (mis)calculations that led to Brexit, as well as on the negotiating process itself.

The book that you have in your hands is the first comprehensive study that makes it easier for the reader to comprehend the complexity of the law and politics of Brexit. It is an indispensable compendium of knowledge on all key substantial issues that will impinge on the new post-Brexit settlement in Britain and in the European Union.

Leading political scientists, lawyers, and economists, under the capable editorship of Professor Federico Fabbrini, have taken up the task of explaining why Brexit happened, what are the prospects for the negotiations, what are the regional and European ramifications, and what all this means for the future of Europe, beyond Brexit.

There is a wealth of expertise here, which will certainly turn out to be a treasure trove for all scholars, students, and practitioners of European and British politics, its past, present, and future.

Acknowledgments

This volume is the result of a research project I have undertaken since my appointment as a Full Professor of Law at the School of Law & Government of Dublin City University (DCU)—ironically, on the day of the Brexit referendum. Special thanks are due to Alex Flach and his team at Oxford University Press—Natasha Flemming, Natalie Patey, and Liz Davey—for making sure the publication of this volume could happen in record time. The book chapters were first presented at a Conference hosted at DCU on April 20–21, 2017. The Conference was opened by Charles Flanagan (then Minister for Foreign Affairs and Trade of Ireland) and concluded by Danuta Hübner (President of the Constitutional Affairs Committee of the European Parliament)—who honored us by kindly agreeing to write the Foreword to the volume. The DCU Conference was made possible by the generous sponsorship of a number of partners: the Bertelsmann Stiftung in Gütersloh, Germany; the Centro Studi sul Federalismo in Turin, Italy; the Reinholdt W Jork og Fond in Copenhagen, Denmark; and Matheson Law Firm, in Dublin, Ireland. A special thank you goes to Joe Beashel, Flavio Brugnoli, Katharina Gnath, Tim Scanlon, and Stefani Weiss for their trust and engagement. My friends Graham Butler, from the University of Aarhus and Matteo Scotto from Villa Vigoni (the Italian-German Center of European Excellence) also contributed materially and immaterially to the event at DCU, and I want to thank them warmly here.

I am particularly grateful to DCU and my colleagues there for supporting the Conference project out of which the book stems. The President and Deputy President, Brian MacCraith and Daire Keogh, kindly agreed to introduce the Conference, and the Dean of the Faculty of Humanities John Doyle and the Head of the School of Law & Government Gary Murphy continuously supported the idea of inviting a large crowd of international speakers to discuss Brexit at DCU. Moreover, a number of colleagues from the School of Law & Government and DCU contributed to the Conference, either by acting as panel chairs and papers discussants, or by assisting in the organization and the marketing of the event. Their participation was valuable and I want to name them here, in alphabetical order: Eimear Brady, Michael Breen, Monica Cappelletti, Ronan Condon, Stephen Coutts, Brenda Daly, Aisling De Paor, Karen Devine, John Doyle, Robert Elgie, James Gallen, Katy Halpin, Tom Hickey, Ken McDonagh, Iain McMenamin, Tanya Ni Mhuirthile, Gary Murphy, Roderic O'Gorman, Eoin O'Malley, John Quinn,

Diarmuid Torney, Gezim Visoka, and Carol Woods. Many of the LLM students of my "EU Law" module also actively assisted and enthusiastically attended the event—confirming that the future of Europe remains a matter of great concern for the new generations.

Given the result of the Conference and the publication of this book, DCU has now decided to constitute a permanent observatory on Brexit—the "Brexit Institute", which I have the honor to direct. A special thank you is due to the President of DCU Brian MacCraith for believing in this initiative, and deciding to invest in this idea. While this book aims to provide a first comprehensive analysis of the law and politics of Brexit, further research and new policy analyses on Brexit will be necessary, and the Institute aims to establish itself as a central venue to this end. Anyone interested in investigating further the manifold challenges posed by the withdrawal of the United Kingdom from the European Union is therefore welcome and encouraged to get in touch with us at: www.dcubrexitinstitute.eu. Brexit creates fissure lines across Europe. But having worked in multiple universities across this continent—first at Tilburg Law School, in the Netherlands, and then at iCourts (the Center of Excellence for International Courts) at the University of Copenhagen, in Denmark—I know how academic linkages create strong transnational bonds, a de facto solidarity that no national border can trump. This book is therefore dedicated to all my colleagues and institutions, past and present, for their contribution in uniting Europe.

Table of Cases

UNITED KINGDOM

EUROPEAN UNION

GERMANY

Table of Cases

Table of Legislation

List of Abbreviations

AFSJ	Area of Freedom, Security, and Justice
AMR	Alert Mechanism Report
BEPG	Broad Economic Policy Guidelines
CAP	Common Agricultural Policy
CJEU	Court of Justice of the European Union
CMU	Capital Markets Union
CSRs	country-specific recommendations
DG FISMA	Directorate General of Financial Services and Markets
DUP	Democratic Unionist Party
EAW	European Arrest Warrant
EBA	European Banking Authority
ECB	European Central Bank
Ecofin	Economic and Financial Affairs Council
ECRIS	European Criminal Records Information System
EDP	Excessive Deficit Procedure
EEA	European Economic Area
EFSF	European Financial Stability Facility
EFSM	European Financial Stability Mechanism
EIOPA	European Insurance and Occupational Pensions Authority
EIP	Excessive Imbalances Procedure
EIS	Europol Information System
EMIR	European Market Infrastructure Regulation
EMS	European Monetary System
EMU	Economic and Monetary Union
ERM	Exchange Rate Mechanism
ESCB	European System of Central Banks
ESMA	European Securities and Markets Authorities
ESRC	Economic and Social Research Council
EU(W)B	European Union Withdrawal Bill
FTAs	free trade agreements
GDP	gross domestic product

IDR	in-depth review
JHA	justice and home affairs
JITs	joint investigation teams
JMC(E)	Joint Ministerial Committee (Europe)
JMC (EN)	Joint Ministerial Committee (European Negotiations)
LCM	legislative consent motion
MFF	multiannual financial framework
MIP	Macroeconomic Imbalances Procedure
MPU	minimum price per unit
NCA	National Crime Agency
NTBs	non-tariff barriers
PNR	Passenger Name Record
QMV	qualified majority voting
SDLP	Social Democratic and Labour Party
SGP	Stability and Growth Pact
SIS II	Schengen Information System
SRM	Single Resolution Mechanism
SSM	Single Supervisory Mechanism
UKCE	UK in a Changing Europe
UKSC	United Kingdom Supreme Court
UUP	Ulster Unionist Party

List of Contributors

Catherine Barnard is Professor of EU Law and Employment Law at Trinity College, University of Cambridge

Michele Chang is Professor of Political Economy at the College of Europe, Bruges

Eileen Connolly is Professor of International Politics at the School of Law & Government of Dublin City University

Paul Craig is Professor of English Law at St John's College, University of Oxford

Deirdre Curtin is Professor of European Law at the European University Institute

Sionaidh Douglas-Scott is Anniversary Professor of Law at Queen Mary University, London and special legal adviser to the Scottish Parliament European and External Affairs Committee

John Doyle is Professor of International Conflict Resolution, and Dean of the Faculty of Humanities and Social Sciences at Dublin City University

Federico Fabbrini is Professor of European Law at the School of Law & Government of Dublin City University and Principal of the DCU Brexit Institute

Danuta Hübner, a Professor of Economics, is a Member of the European Parliament and Chairwoman of the European Parliament Constitutional Affairs Committee

Kalypso Nicolaïdis is Professor of International Relations at St Antony's College, University of Oxford

Uwe Puetter is Professor of European Public Policy & Governance at Central European University

Giorgio Sacerdoti is Professor Emeritus of International Law at Bocconi University and former Chairman of the WTO Appellate Body

Stephen Tierney is Professor of Constitutional Theory at the University of Edinburgh

Marlene Wind is Professor of EU Politics at the University of Copenhagen

1

Introduction

Federico Fabbrini

1. Introduction

On June 23, 2016, the United Kingdom (UK) voted to leave the European Union (EU).[1] Brexit represents arguably the most important political event in Europe since the fall of the Berlin wall. Whereas discussion had occurred in the past whether an EU Member State could withdraw from the EU,[2] the Treaty of Lisbon of 2009—rescuing a provision of the defunct Treaty establishing a European Constitution of 2003—explicitly enshrined an exit clause in EU primary law. According to Article 50 Treaty on European Union (TEU), "Any Member State may decide to withdraw from the Union in accordance with its own constitutional requirements." However, the idea that a Member State would leave the EU was largely regarded as an impossible happening. In fact, according to Giuliano Amato, the main drafter of Article 50 TEU, this clause was never actually meant to be used.[3] The decision of the UK to withdraw from the EU sent shock-waves throughout Europe and the world.[4] Culminating a period in which Europe has been increasingly questioned,[5] Brexit upset consolidated assumptions on the finality of the EU, and simultaneously opened new challenges—both in the EU institutional fabric,

---

[1] The Electoral Commission, *EU Referendum Results* http://www.electoralcommission.org.uk/find-information-by-subject/elections-and-referendums/past-elections-and-referendums/eu-referendum/electorate-and-count-information.

[2] See Joseph H. H. Weiler, "Alternatives to Withdrawal from an International Organization: The Case of the European Economic Community" (1985) 20 *Israel Law Review* 282.

[3] See Christopher Hooton & Jon Stone, "Brexit: Article 50 Was Never Actually Meant to Be Used, Says Its Author" *Independent* (July 26, 2016).

[4] See Timothy Garton Ash, "Is Europe Disintegrating?" *The New York Review of Books* (January 19, 2017).

[5] See Sarah Hobolt, *Europe in Question* (OUP 2009).

Introduction. First edition. Federico Fabbrini © Federico Fabbrini 2017. Published 2017 by Oxford University Press.

and in the constitutional settlements reached within the UK, *e.g.* in Scotland and Northern Ireland.

While the withdrawal process is still unfolding, and many uncertainties remain, a first comprehensive legal and political analysis of how Brexit impacts on UK and the EU appears of the utmost importance. This Introduction maps the key issues, which are then examined in depth throughout this book. As such, sections 2 to 5 summarize the law and politics of Brexit, while sections 6 to 10 outline the content of the other chapters of this volume. Specifically, section 2 sets the context of the Brexit referendum. Section 3 analyzes the follow-up to the referendum and the ensuing litigation. Section 4 discusses the UK notification of withdrawal and section 5 examines the start of the negotiations and its uncertainties. Section 6 then moves to over-view the book's structure. Section 7 dwells on the politics, process, and pros-pects of Brexit. Section 8 examines Brexit's implications on the internal UK constitutional structure. Section 9 focuses conversely on its implications on the internal EU system, and, finally, section 10 considers the long-term effect that Brexit may have on the future of Europe.

2. The Road toward the Brexit Referendum

The decision of the UK to leave the EU found its roots in the idiosyncratic approach of the UK vis-à-vis the project of European integration—but was catalyzed by the hasty moves of two Prime Ministers.[6] Since joining the EU in 1973, the UK remained a wary member of the EU—resisting most steps forward in European integration, and securing for itself a number of opt-outs from measures endorsed by most other Member States: Hence, when the EU created a common currency in 1992, the UK (with Denmark) was exempted from joining the euro;[7] when the EU incorporated the Schengen free border system in 1997, the UK (with Ireland) opted out of the abolition of internal border controls;[8] and when the EU enacted documents in the area of social rights—first through a Social Rights Protocol in 1992 and then through a Charter of Fundamental Rights in 2000—the UK (in the latter case, with Poland) secured an exception aimed at excluding it from the new common European rules.[9] Moreover, despite proclaiming its support for the stabiliza-tion of the euro, the UK did not join the efforts to strengthen the Eurozone

---

[6] See Paul Craig, "Brexit: A Drama in Six Acts" (2016) 41 *European Law Review* 447 and Patrick Birkinshaw & Andrea Biondi (eds.), *Britain Alone* (Kluwer 2016).
[7] Protocol No. 15.   [8] Protocol No. 20.   [9] Protocol No. 30.

undertaken in the aftermath of the Euro crisis, being the only country (with the Czech Republic) which did not sign the Fiscal Compact in 2012,[10] and resisting forms of financial assistance to Eurozone countries in fiscal stress.[11]

In fact, opposition toward the EU entrenched within UK politics, and particularly within the Conservative Party—reaching its apex during the governments led by David Cameron. In order to tame the Eurosceptic fringe, in 2011 the UK government adopted the EU Act,[12] which committed the government to call a referendum to authorize any further expansion of EU powers. Moreover, in 2012 the UK government launched a balance of competences review, designed to assess areas where competences ought to be repatriated from the EU to the national sphere:[13] while the assessment ultimately concluded in 2014 that the division of powers between the UK and the EU was proper, Prime Minister Cameron expressed his intention to renegotiate British membership in the EU. Running for parliamentary elections in 2015, the Conservative Party committed to call a referendum on membership in the EU. Winning an unexpected majority in Westminster, Prime Minister Cameron spelled out his demands for a new deal between the UK and the EU: While Parliament approved the EU Referendum Act 2015, empowering the government to call a referendum on EU membership,[14] on November 10, 2015 the Prime Minister outlined in a letter to the President of the European Council its request for a re-negotiation of the status of the UK in the EU—in the field of economic governance, competitiveness, sovereignty, and migration.[15]

Political bargaining between the UK and its European partners took place for several months under the leadership of the President of the European Council Donald Tusk and concluded in February 2016, when the European Council reached a legally binding agreement outlining a new settlement for the UK in the EU.[16] The new deal was codified in a series of documents,

---

[10] Treaty on Stability, Coordination and Governance in the Economic and Monetary Union (March 2, 2012) http://www.eurozone.europa.eu/media/304649/st00tscg26_en12.pdf.

[11] See Council Regulation (EU) No. 2015/1360 of 4 August 2015, amending Council Regulation (EU) No. 407/2010 establishing a European financial stabilization mechanism OJ 2015 L 210/1.

[12] European Union Act 2011, c. 12 (UK) on which see Paul Craig, "The European Union Act 2011: Locks, Limits and Legality" (2011) 48 *Common Market Law Review* 1915.

[13] Foreign & Commonwealth Office, "Review of the Balance of Competencies" (December 12, 2012) https://www.gov.uk/guidance/review-of-the-balance-of-competences.

[14] European Union Referendum Act 2015, c. 36 (UK) on which see Kenneth Armstrong, *Brexit Time* (CUP 2017).

[15] Letter of Prime Minister David Cameron to European Council President Donald Tusk (November 10, 2015).

[16] See European Council Conclusions (February 19, 2016) EUCO 1/16, Annex I ("A New Settlement for the United Kingdom within the European Union").

including a decision of the heads of state and government of the EU Member States—technically an international treaty concluded by the leaders of the twenty-eight EU countries on the margin of the meeting of the European Council.[17] The new deal accommodated in legally binding terms several of the British requests. Among others, it set up special protections (to be later incorporated in the main text of the EU treaties) for the status of non-Eurozone Member States like the UK, introduced an emergency break procedure that would have authorized the UK to suspend free movement of people when inward migration passed a critical threshold, and even exempted the UK from participating in the future to the process of "ever closer union."[18] In certain ways, therefore, the agreement struck by the President of the European Council went quite far in sacrificing foundational EU principles to appease the British requests.[19] Based on this deal, therefore, Prime Minister Cameron called a referendum in June 2016 and campaigned to remain in the EU.

As is well known, however, on June 23, 2016 the British people voted to leave the EU,[20] rendering the new settlement between the UK and the EU null and void.[21] With 72% of the British population casting a ballot, 52% of voters favored leaving the EU, and 48% remaining in the EU. Nevertheless, the vote was highly uneven. While England and Wales supported Brexit, 62% of voters in Scotland and 55% in Northern Ireland cast their vote to remain in the EU. As statistical analysis following the referendum emphasized,[22] voters in urban areas like the London metropole largely favored Remain, while voters in rural or de-industrialized areas in the South and North of England overwhelmingly supported Leave. Highlighting a growing generational cleavage, moreover, electors younger than 50 years old heavily cast their ballot in favor of remaining in the EU—with the outcome of the referendum largely driven by the voting pattern of older generations: Arguably this reflected how several decades of continuing Brussels-bashing by British politicians and opinion-makers from all sides of the political spectrum had left a deep distrust vis-à-vis the EU, which a few months of electoral campaigning in favor of Europe could not cure. Moreover, the Remain camp mostly advanced economic reasons in favor of the EU, while Leave astutely played the voters'

---

[17] ibid.   [18] TEU, Preamble.
[19] See Eva-Maria Poptcheva and David Eatock, "The UK's 'New Settlement' in the European Union: Renegotiation and Referendum", European Parliament Research Service in-depth analysis (February 2016) PE 577.983.
[20] See n. 1.
[21] See Statement of the EU Leaders and the Netherlands Presidency on the Outcome of the UK Referendum (June 24, 2016) PRESS 381/16.
[22] See Sarah Hobolt, "The Brexit Vote: A Divided Nation, A Divided Continent" (2016) 23 *Journal of European Public Policy* 1259.

emotions with arguments about sovereignty and control of migration, which ultimately won the day.

3. The Implementation of the Brexit Referendum

The Brexit referendum precipitated one of the most dramatic constitutional crises the UK had ever faced. Following the resignation of David Cameron, and the formation of a government led by Theresa May, the new Prime Minister committed to carry out the will of the British people.[23] Yet, if her predecessor had miscalculated electoral politics, she failed to anticipate constitutional constraints.[24] While the government planned to trigger Article 50 TEU and initiate the process of withdrawal from the EU autonomously, litigation started on the need to obtain parliamentary approval before doing so. In November 2016, the High Court of England and Wales ruled that the government could not invoke its royal prerogatives to notify Article 50 TEU,[25] since the effect of that decision would be ultimately to deprive UK citizens of EU rights originally attributed to them by Parliament through the approval of the European Communities Act (ECA) 1972, which gave effect to UK membership to the EU. In a separate case in Northern Ireland, instead, the High Court rejected the argument that the devolved legislatures had to give their consent to UK withdrawal from the EU, and while emphasizing the importance of the Good Friday Agreement, denied that the people of Northern Ireland had to approve by majority withdrawal because of the special status of the region.[26]

Cases were consolidated on appeal and heard by the UK Supreme Court (UKSC). In January 2017, the UKSC ruled 8 to 3 that the government could not trigger Article 50 TEU without parliamentary legislation, but it unanimously held that consent by the devolved legislatures was not needed.[27] The UKSC summarized the constitutional background to the dispute,[28] and emphasized how "Parliamentary sovereignty is a fundamental principle of the UK constitution."[29] It clarified that: "[t]he Royal prerogative encompasses the residue of powers which remain vested in the Crown, and they are exercisable

---

[23] See Prime Minister Theresa May, speech at the Conservative Party Conference, Birmingham (October 5, 2016).

[24] See also the report of the House of Commons, Public Administration and Constitutional Affairs Committee, "Lessons Learned from the EU Referendum," (March 7, 2017) HC 496 (chastising the Cameron Government for failing to prepare contingency plans for the eventuality of a victory of the Leave vote).

[25] See *Miller* [2016] EWHC 2768.   [26] See *Agnew* [2016] NIQB 85.

[27] *Miller* [2017] UKSC 5.   [28] ibid para. 40.   [29] ibid para. 43.

by ministers, provided that the exercise is consistent with Parliamentary leg-islation."[30] According to the UKSC, however, while the UK government enjoyed prerogative powers in foreign affairs,[31] because of the principle of dualism[32] only Parliament could give domestic effect to treaties within the UK.[33] As it explained, the ECA 1972 represented a statute of "constitutional character"[34] since it served as the "conduit pipe"[35] to incorporate within UK law all EU law—a body of norms with direct effect and supremacy over other sources of UK law.[36] The UKSC thus affirmed the High Court judgment that an act of the executive could not displace rights and privileges accorded to UK citizens by an act of Parliament, when the latter enacted the ECA 1972.[37]

According to the majority of the UKSC, neither the ECA 1972 nor sub-sequent legislation justified the government's view that it could notify with-drawal from the EU without parliamentary approval. As it stated, "by the 1972 Act, Parliament endorsed and gave effect to the [UK]'s membership of [the EU] in a way which is inconsistent with the future exercise by ministers of any prerogative power to withdraw from such Treaties."[38] In fact, "a com-plete withdrawal ... will constitute as significant a constitutional change as that which occurred when EU law was first incorporated in domestic law by the 1972 Act. .. It would be inconsistent with long-standing and fundamen-tal principle for such a far-reaching change to the UK constitutional arrange-ments to be brought about by ministerial decision or ministerial action alone. All the more so when the source in question was brought into existence by Parliament through primary legislation, which gave that source an overrid-ing supremacy in the hierarchy of domestic law sources."[39] Moreover, the UKSC rejected the view that subsequent legislation—and notably the EU Referendum Act 2015—could have endowed the government with a royal prerogative it did not possess when ECA 1972 was enacted.[40] As it pointed out, "[w]here, as in this case, implementation of a referendum result requires a change in the law of the land, and statute has not provided for that change, the change in the law must be made in the only way in which the UK consti-tution permits, namely through Parliamentary legislation."[41]

Hence, the UKSC made a relevant clarification on the nature of the June 2016 referendum—confining it to the sphere of the political: "[t]he referen-dum of 2016 did not change the law in a way which would allow ministers to withdraw the United Kingdom from the European Union without legisla-tion. But that in no way means that it is devoid of effect. It means that, unless

[30] ibid para. 47.   [31] ibid para. 54.   [32] ibid para. 55.   [33] ibid para. 57.
[34] ibid para. 67.   [35] ibid para. 65.   [36] ibid para. 60.   [37] ibid para. 69.
[38] ibid para. 77.   [39] ibid para. 81.   [40] ibid para. 102.   [41] ibid para. 121.

and until acted on by Parliament, its force is political rather than legal. It has already shown itself to be of great political significance."[42] Otherwise, the UKSC also minimized the legal impacts of constitutional conventions in the UK system. Answering the questions coming from Norther Ireland, it rejected the view that the Northern Ireland Act 1998, read in conjunction with the Good Friday Agreement, required consent from the devolved legislature,[43] or by the people of Northern Ireland,[44] before the UK government could trigger Article 50 TEU since "within the [UK], relations with the [EU], like other matters of foreign affairs," are left to the UK government.[45] Moreover, it also excluded that it could enforce the so-called Sewel Convention, according to which the UK Parliament will not normally legislate with regard to devolved matters without the consent of devolved legislatures.[46] As the UKSC ruled, judges "are neither the parents nor the guardians of political conventions; they are mere observers."[47] Hence, without underestimating the role that constitutional conventions play in the operation of the UK constitution,[48] the UKSC concluded that "the policing of its scope and the manner of its operation does not lie within the constitutional remit of the judiciary."[49]

4. The Notification of Withdrawal

The judgment of the UKSC in *Miller* slightly complicated the UK government plan to start the official withdrawal from the EU. While the House of Commons had already agreed in December 2016 to a resolution calling on the executive to activate Article 50 TEU before March 31, 2017,[50] the UKSC was crystal clear that if "ministers cannot give Notice [of withdrawal] by the exercise of prerogative powers, only legislation which is embodied in a statute will do. A resolution of the House of Commons is not legislation."[51] Nevertheless, Brexit was never put into question by the UKSC. In fact, just days ahead of its ruling, on January 17, 2017, Prime Minister May had outlined her strategy for withdrawal in a major speech, where she had expressed the government's intention to take the UK out not only from the EU but also from the single market.[52] Two days after *Miller*, on January 26, 2017 the UK government introduced a 134-word bill in Parliament with a

---

[42] ibid para. 124.   [43] ibid para. 130.   [44] ibid para. 135.
[45] ibid para. 129.
[46] See now also the Scotland Act 2016, c. 11 (UK), Sec. 28(7)–(8).
[47] *Miller* (n. 27) para. 146.   [48] ibid para. 151.   [49] ibid.
[50] House of Commons resolution (December 7, 2016).   [51] *Miller* (n. 27) para. 123.
[52] See Prime Minister Theresa May, speech, Lancaster House (January 17, 2017).

view toward keeping the timeframe it had anticipated, of notifying Article 50 TEU to the European Council before the end of March 2017. The operative part of the government bill simply stated that "the Prime Minister may notify, under Article 50(2) [TEU] the United Kingdom's intention to withdraw from the EU."[53]

The House of Commons swiftly approved the bill with no amendments on February 8, 2017, sending the draft legislation to the House of Lords. On March 7, 2017, the House of Lords also approved the bill—proposing two amendments.[54] On the one hand, the Lords asked to insert in the bill a clause protecting the status of the EU citizens residing in the UK at the time of Brexit. On the other, they called for an amendment that would give Parliament a final say over any withdrawal agreement. The UK government, however, rejected the amendments by the House of Lords on the argument that this would unduly constrain its negotiating position. Called again to vote on the text, the House of Commons on March 13, 2017 swiftly voted the Brexit bill exactly in its original wording—and the House of Lords, pursuant to UK constitutional practice,[55] eventually acquiesced, approving the bill in the afternoon of the same day. On March 16, 2016, the EU Notification of Withdrawal Act 2017 received royal assent, becoming law.[56] On March 29, 2017, therefore, the UK government eventually triggered Article 50 TEU by notifying in a letter addressed to the President of the European Council the British decision to withdraw from the EU and the European Atomic Energy Community (Euratom).[57] The letter, which requested to negotiate jointly the terms of the withdrawal and those of a new deep and special partnership between the UK and the EU, started the two-year exit time-frame set in Article 50 TEU.[58]

---

[53] See EU (Notification of Withdrawal) Bill, HC 132.

[54] Since the Brexit referendum the House of Lords also engaged in a thorough analysis of the implications of UK withdrawal from the EU, resulting in several detailed and well-research reports. See *e.g.* "The Invoking of Article 50," (September 13, 2016) HL 44; "Brexit and Parliamentary Scrutiny," (October 20, 2016) HL 50; "Brexit: UK-Irish Relations," (December 12, 2016) HL 76; "Brexit: the Options for Trade," (December 13, 2016) HL 72; "Brexit and Acquired Rights," (December 14, 2016) HL 82; "Brexit and Financial Services," (December 15, 2016) HL 81; "Brexit: Future UK-EU Security Cooperation," (December 16, 2016) HL 77; "Brexit: UK-EU Free Movement of People," (March 6, 2017) HL 121.

[55] See Meg Russell, *The Contemporary House of Lords: Westminster Bicameralism Revisited* (OUP 2013).

[56] See EU (Notification of Withdrawal) Act 2017, c. 9 (UK).

[57] Letter of Prime Minister Theresa May to European Council President Donald Tusk (March 29, 2017).

[58] See TEU, Article 50(2) (indicating that the notification of withdrawal starts a two-year negotiating time-frame which can only be extended by unanimous agreement of the members of the European Council).

The notification of Article 50 TEU shifted the ball on the EU camp. The European Commission[59] and the European Parliament[60] had already appointed their chief negotiators for Brexit, and the European Council had agreed that the Commission would undertake the negotiations with the UK on behalf of the EU, subject to the supervision of a European Council task-force.[61] Yet, the EU institutions and the Member States had until then faithfully abided to the commitment undertaken after the Brexit referendum of abstaining from any negotiation before notification.[62] Following the trigger-ing of Article 50 TEU, on March 31, 2017 the President of the European Council Donald Tusk published the draft guidelines for the negotiation with the UK, summarizing the proposed EU approach in handling first, the divorce with the UK, and then the new relations with it.[63] On April 5, 2017 the European Parliament gave its input on the strategy, identifying its red-lines, and stressing that Article 50 TEU gave it the power to withhold its consent to any agreement with the UK.[64] On April 29, 2017, the European Council, meeting at twenty-seven without the UK, approved the political guidelines of the Brexit negotiations.[65] Finally, on May 3, 2017 the European Commission published its negotiating directives, detailing the European Council guide-lines with a view toward starting negotiations with the UK,[66] which were duly approved by the General Affairs Council on May 22, 2017.[67]

While the European Council guidelines and the Commission direc-tives reaffirmed negotiating objectives that had been already voiced in

[59] See European Commission press release, "President Juncker appoints Michel Barnier as chief negotiator," (July 27, 2016) IP/16/2652.

[60] See European Parliament press release, "Parliament appoints Guy Verhofstadt as representative on Brexit matters," (September 8, 2016).

[61] See Informal Meeting of the Heads of State and Government of 27 Member States, as well as the Presidents of the European Council and the European Commission (December 15, 2016).

[62] See Informal Meeting of 27, Statement (June 29, 2016) para. 2.

[63] See General Secretariat of the Council, Draft guidelines following the United Kingdom's Notification under Article 50 TEU (March 31, 2017) XT 21001/17.

[64] See European Parliament resolution of 5 April 2017 on negotiations with the United Kingdom following its notification that it intends to withdraw from the European Union, P8_TA(2017)0102.

[65] See European Council Guidelines (April 29, 2017) EUCO XT 20004/17.

[66] See European Commission, Recommendation for a Council Decision authorizing to open negotiations on an agreement with the UK setting out the arrangements for its withdrawal from the EU (May 3, 2017) COM(2017) 218 final.

[67] See Council Decision (EU/Euratom) of 22 May 2017 authorizing the opening of negotia-tions with the United Kingdom setting out the arrangements for its withdrawal from the European Union, Doc. XT21016/17. See also Council Decision (EU) 2017/900 of 22 May 2017 concerning the establishment of the ad hoc Working Party on Article 50 TEU OJ [2017] L138/138.

Brussels[68]—including maintaining the unity of the twenty-seven, providing clarity to citizens and business, and solving the problem of the Irish border—they were also very explicit in signaling a tough stance. They excluded any talk on the future bilateral relations before sufficient progress has been achieved on withdrawal, underlined the expectation that the UK would fully settle its financial obligations before leaving, foreclosed any possibility for the UK to access the EU single market through a free trade deal, and reaffirmed the role of the European Court of Justice (ECJ) in any future agreement. In fact, German Chancellor Angela Merkel clearly warned the UK against illusions about post-Brexit ties.[69] It is arguably in anticipation of the difficult negotiations ahead that on April 18, 2017 Prime Minister May surprised all by calling for snap elections to consolidate her parliamentary majority in view of negotiations with the EU.[70]

5. The Negotiations and the Challenges Ahead

Nevertheless, Prime Minister May's bet for early elections turned into a boomerang. On June 8, 2017, Conservative Party lost its majority in the House of Commons,[71] and was thus forced to enter into a confidence and supply agreement with the Democratic Unionist Party (DUP) of Northern Ireland in order to form a government.[72] The result of the British parliamentary elections, therefore, shed further uncertainties on the beginning of the negotiations with the EU, which eventually started on June 19, 2017 – almost a year after the Brexit referendum. In fact, while talks between EU Chief Negotiator Michel Barnier and UK Secretary of State for Exiting the EU David Davis are now underway – on the issues of citizens' rights, the border between Ireland

---

[68] See *e.g.* Michel Barnier, Speech at the Committees of the Regions (March 22, 2017) as well as European Commission nonpaper on key elements likely to feature in the draft negotiating directives (April 2017).

[69] See Angela Merkel, Speech at the Bundestag (April 27, 2017).

[70] See Theresa May, Speech at 10 Downing Street (April 18, 2017). The decision by the Prime Minister to call early elections was approved by a resolution of the House of Commons voted by more than two thirds of its members, as required by the Fixed-term Parliament Act 2011, c. 14 (UK).

[71] The Electoral Commission, *UK General Election 2017*, https://www.electoralcommission.org.uk/find-information-by-subject/elections-and-referendums/upcoming-elections-and-referendums/uk-general-election-2017

[72] See Confidence and Supply Agreement between the Conservative and Unionist Party and the Democratic Unionist Party (June 26, 2017) https://www.gov.uk/government/publications/conservative-and-dup-agreement-and-uk-government-financial-support-for-northern-ireland/agreement-between-the-conservative-and-unionist-party-and-the-democratic-unionist-party-on-support-for-the-government-in-parliament

and Norther Ireland, and the financial settlement – major challenges loom large on Brexit's prospects. First, there are a number of questions that still accompany the process of withdrawal. Despite the willingness of the EU to phase the negotiations, it is unclear to what extent the EU and the UK may succeed in even just reaching a withdrawal agreement in less than two years. Given the contentious nature of some of the issues to be dealt with—particularly money[73]—it is possible that a cliff-edge scenario may materialize, with the UK leaving in March 2019 with no deal.[74] To avoid this from happening, the European Council may unanimously extend the negotiating deadline. In fact, in August 2017 the UK government has flagged the possible need for a transitional agreement, that may allow the UK to phase out of the EU in a longer time-frame, while preparing the terrain for a new partnership between the EU and the UK.

Second, there are uncertainties on how Brexit will be carried out within the UK. In March 2017 the UK government unveiled a "Great Repeal Bill," vowing to ensure an orderly transition of the UK legal system out of the EU, and in July 2017 it introduced in Parliament the EU Withdrawal Bill, designed to domesticate large chunks of EU laws after exit.[75] However, in light of the results of the June 2017 elections, and the ensuing political instability, it is possible that institutional tensions may worsen within the UK. Given the very different electoral outcomes in the Brexit referendum across the nations of the UK, pressure has been mounting in the devolved governments to renegotiate their positions within the UK. The Scottish executive presented its proposal to maintain Scotland's place in the EU single market;[76] the Northern Irish First and Deputy First Ministers demanded that the specificities of Northern Ireland be taken into account in the negotiations;[77] and even Wales asked for greater autonomy.[78] While both the UK government and the European Council have shown sensitivity for the Northern Irish situation,[79]

[73] Compare the report of the House of Lords European Union Committee, "Brexit and the EU Budget," (March 4, 2017) HL 125 with the working paper of the European Commission Task Force for the Preparation of the Negotiations with the United Kingdom under Article 50 TEU, "Essential Principle on Financial Settlement" (May 24, 2017) Doc no 2.

[74] See the report of the House of Commons Foreign Affairs Committee, "Article 50 Negotiations: Implications of 'No Deal,'" (March 12, 2017) HC 1077.

[75] See the White Paper of the UK Government Department for Exiting the European Union, "Legislating for the United Kingdom's Withdrawal from the European Union," (March 30, 2017) Cm 9446 and European Union (Withdrawal) Bill, HC 5.

[76] See Scottish Government, "Scotland's Place in Europe," (December 2016).

[77] See Northern Irish Executive Office, Letter to the Prime Minister (August 10, 2016).

[78] See Welsh Government, "Securing Wales' Future" (January 2017).

[79] Compare Letter of Prime Minister Theresa May to European Council President Donald Tusk (March 29, 2017) with European Council Guidelines (n. 65) para. 11.

the agreement between the Conservative Party and the DUP may weaken
the power-sharing arrangement in place in Northern Ireland, and the EU has
made clear that if Northern Ireland re-united with Ireland it would automatically become part of the EU (as did East Germany after the Fall of the Berlin
Wall). Moreover, centrifugal pulls are in action in Scotland. Objecting to the
idea of being taken out of the EU against its will, the Scottish government in
March 2017 opened a new front for the UK government by calling for a new
Scottish independence referendum[80]—designed to revisit the results of the
2014 referendum and end the 1707 Union between Scotland and England.[81]

Third, there are also questions on the effects that Brexit may produce on
the functioning of the EU. Since the Brexit referendum, the only formal
effect of the UK withdrawal decision on the EU has been to produce a change
in the order of the rotating presidency of the Council[82]—with the UK waiv-
ing its turn for the second half of 2017—and the resignation of the UK
Commissioner, who was promptly replaced by a new one (although with a
re-shuffling of the Commission's portfolios).[83] In fact, the European Council
has affirmed its intention that "negotiations with the [UK] will be kept separate from ongoing Union business and shall not interfere with its progress."[84]
Nevertheless, this may be wishful thinking as it seems likely that the Brexit
negotiations will absorb a significant amount of EU resources. Moreover,
the Brexit negotiations may seed tensions between the EU institutions, and
among the EU Member States. On the one hand, arm-wrestling may occur
between the European Commission, which is competent in conducting the
withdrawal negotiations, and the European Council, which aims to maintain political control on the withdrawal process. On the other hand, disa-
greements may arise among the EU Member States—on the question where
to relocate the two EU agencies currently housed in the UK, the European
Medicines Agency and the European Banking Authority (EBA), but also on
more important issues, like concessions to be made to the UK.[85]

[80] See Scottish Parliament Motion S5M-04710 (March 28, 2017).
[81] See Aileen McHarg *et al.*, *The Scottish Independence Referendum* (OUP 2016).
[82] See Council Decision (EU) 2016/1316 of 26 July 2016, amending Decision 2009/908/EU,
laying down measures for the implementation of the European Council Decision on the exercise of
the Presidency of the Council OJ 2016 L 208/42.
[83] See European Commission statement on the Decision of Commissioner Lord Hill to Resign
from the Commission and on the Transfer of the Financial Service Portfolio to Vice-President
Dombrovskis (June 25, 2016) 16/2332; and Council of the EU, press release, "Julian King
appointed new commissioner for security union," (September 19, 2016).
[84] European Council Guidelines (n. 65), para. 27
[85] See European Council Conclusions (June 22, 2017), EUCO 8/17, Annex: I ("Procedure
Leading up to a Decision on the Relocation of the European Medicines Agency and the European
Banking Authority in the Context of the United Kingdom's Withdrawal from the Union").

In fact, last but not least, there are also questions about how the Brexit negotiations will interplay with the debate on the future of Europe. Following the decision of the UK to withdraw from the EU the heads of state and government of the twenty-seven EU Member States and the leaders of the EU institutions outlined in Bratislava, in September 2016, a roadmap to relaunch the EU.[86] This plan was reaffirmed on March 25, 2017 in a Declaration to celebrate the 60th anniversary of the Treaties of Rome.[87] Also in spring 2017, the European Commission has published a whitepaper on the future of Europe,[88] and the European Parliament has approved several resolutions delineating a vision for the Union at twenty-seven.[89] Notwithstanding the differences in the degree of ambition, all these initiatives call for further steps forward in the project of European integration. Nevertheless, it is unclear to what extent the unity of the twenty-seven may be tested not only by Brexit— but also by the leftovers of the multiple crises that the EU has recently faced, including the euro-crisis, the migration-crisis and the rule of law crisis. In this context, it will be interesting to see whether the UK withdrawal will be leveraged to tackle other structural issues in the EU—or whether, particularly after the election of new French President Emmanuel Macron, experiments with multispeed integration will be set in motion by a group of states (for instance the Eurozone countries) to reach a new constitutional deal for the EU.[90]

***

6. The Structure of the Book

This book brings together the contributions of leading academics from top universities across Europe to explore the constitutional challenges that Brexit poses in regional and European perspectives. By blending the analyses of lawyers, political scientists, and political economists the book aims to provide a first, interdisciplinary assessment of some of the most pressing issues raised by Brexit. In fact, the book claims that neither a formalistic legal analysis nor a simple political reportage suffices to explain a process such as Brexit, where law and politics deeply intertwine. At the

---

[86] See Bratislava Declaration (September 16, 2016).

[87] See Rome Declaration of the leaders of 27 Member States and of the European Council, the European Parliament and the European Commission (March 25, 2017).

[88] See European Commission White Paper, "The Future of Europe," (March 1, 2017).

[89] See *e.g.* European Parliament resolution of 16 February 2017 on possible evolutions of and adjustments to the current institutional set-up of the European Union, P8_TA(2017)0048.

[90] See *e.g.* Conseil des Ministres Franco-Allemand, Paris (July 13, 2017) (indicating plans for further integration in the field of defense and economic and monetary affairs).

same time, by combining the research of experts of UK public law and government, with those of scholars working on EU law, policy and institutions, the book attempts to shed light as comprehensively as possible on the manifold effects that Brexit creates—in the UK, and its internal constitutional settlement, as well as in the EU, and its institutional regime. Surely, more work will need to be done as Brexit moves along. Yet, so much is already on the table: This book therefore avoids speculations and focuses instead on the many and difficult political, legal and economic issues that the UK withdrawal from the EU has exposed.

The book is structured as follows. Part I considers the politics, process, and prospect of Brexit, sketching the transformations in the EU legal order that underpin Brexit, and considering the process of withdrawal and the options for future trade relations between the UK, the EU, and the world. Part II examines the implications of Brexit on the constitutional structure of the UK, considering how the withdrawal from the EU affects English nationalism, the prospect of a new Scottish secession referendum, as well as the status of Northern Ireland and relations with Ireland. Part III analyzes instead the implications of Brexit on the constitutional structure of the EU, focusing on three highly salient areas of EU policy-making: Europe's Area of Freedom Security and Justice (AFSJ), Economic and Monetary Union (EMU), and the internal market. Part IV, finally, looks beyond Brexit, and discusses the opportunities this offers to relaunch the EU integration project. Here, the book considers the implication of Brexit on Euroskepticism, on the balance of power between the EU Member States and the EU institutions, as well as on the practice of treaty change in the EU.

7. Brexit: Politics, Process, Prospects

Part I of the book includes the contributions by Kalypso Nicolaïdis, Paul Craig, and Giorgio Sacerdoti. This part analyzes three crucial dimensions of Brexit, considering how Brexit came about from an international relations perspective, how Brexit will be carried out from a legal viewpoint, and how post-Brexit the UK may remain connected to the EU and the world from an international trade perspective.

Kalypso Nicolaïdis paints a grand fresco of the history of international relations in Europe, suggesting that Brexit has to be understood in the complex tradeoff between independence and interdependence. As she argues, the EU constitutes the latest attempt in Europe to maintain a balance of power through the medium of supranational institutions. Culminating centuries of inter-state conflict, the EU institutionalized a system of peaceful coexistence between European states, while preserving national sovereignty—as ultimately revealed precisely by the decision of the UK to withdraw from the EU. According to Nicolaïdis, however, during the last twenty-five years the European order had undergone a number of important transformations, which have increasingly altered the balance between independence and interdependence, fostering greater calls to "take back control"—the political mantra of the Brexiteers. Drawing on Kant's notions of *ius gentium, ius cosmopoliticum*, and *ius civitatis*, Nicolaïdis explains that: First, the interstate system has transformed, with a number of Member States increasingly coming to dominate the EU, as revealed by the handling of the euro-crisis. Second, the polity has transformed, due to the redefinition of boundaries and immigration. And, third, the state itself has transformed, with European integration re-drawing the balance between the state and the market In this context, Brexit should be seen as an attempt to reassert control in a changing polity.

Paul Craig offers instead a holistic legal analysis of the treaty provision regulating withdrawal from the EU. He examines Article 50 TEU and maintains that the process of exit from the EU should be divided in three stages, each of which raises major substantive and procedural questions. Stage 1 is the triggering of Article 50 TEU. Stage 2 concerns the withdrawal negotiations. And stage 3 relates to the outcome of the negotiations. As Craig explains, each stage poses specific challenges for both the EU and the UK, and there are legal questions that have been—and will have to be—answered along the way. According to Craig, however, politics will heavily shape the law, with both the EU and the UK seeking to leverage specific legal argument in support of their preferred bargaining position. In particular, Craig identifies areas of tensions in stage 2 on the question whether negotiations on the withdrawal and the new partnership should be phased, as required by the EU, or conflated, as demanded by the UK. Moreover, he signals the possibility for future litigation in stage 3 on the questions whether the UK Parliament should be entitled to authorize the withdrawal agreement, or whether the UK may—tout court—be allowed to revoke its notification of withdrawal.

Giorgio Sacerdoti provides a thorough examination of the options available to the UK to trade with the EU and the rest of the world. His analysis departs from the understanding that the UK will not remain part of the EU single market or the EU customs union—as clearly indicated by UK Prime Minister May in January 2017 and never retracted since. Sacerdoti considers what could be the features of the new ambitious free trade agreement between the UK and the EU, and explains what would instead be the default rules of the World Trade Organization (WTO), which would kick in if the UK left the EU with no special trade deal. As Sacerdoti underlines, the international trade conditions set by WTO rules are significantly worse than those currently enjoyed by the UK as a member of the EU, and the negotiations of a free trade agreement between the UK and the EU is not doable in two years. Sacerdoti, instead, sees no problem in the UK inheriting the WTO schedule of the EU, and even suggests that the pre-WTO Global Agreement on Trade and Tariffs (GATT) may provide a custom-made solution to keep border-free trade between Northern Ireland and Ireland under the so-called "frontier traffic exception." Revealing the complex web of international trade norms, however, Sacerdoti also explains that Brexit will not only compel the UK to strike brand-new free trade deals with third countries, but may also force the EU to renegotiate trade agreements with partners, if they define the withdrawal of the UK as a fundamental change of circumstances justifying the repudiation of a treaty.

8. Brexit and Constitutional Change in Regional Perspective

Part II of the book collects the contributions by Stephen Tierney, Sionaidh Douglas-Scott, and John Doyle and Eileen Connolly. This Part of the book focuses on the implications that Brexit has on the internal UK constitutional settlement, on the status of devolution, as well as on the relations between UK and Ireland, specifically with reference to Northern Ireland.

Stephen Tierney examines Brexit and the English question, arguing that the vote to leave the EU ought to be understood partially as the result of the demotic process at play in England. As he explains, the UK is a highly asymmetric system, since England—one of the four nations composing the UK, together with Scotland, Wales and Northern Ireland—constitutes population-wise almost four-fifths of the entire UK. This situation has historically influenced devolution: While since the 1990s power has flown from London toward Edinburgh, Cardiff, and Belfast, due to its size England has never received an equivalent constitutional autonomy, and recognition, within the UK. As Tierney underlines, if England were to be given a separate Parliament and Government, this would almost render Westminster meaningless. Otherwise, proposals for regional devolution within England, with the transfer of powers to cities and provinces, have also failed. And the recent introduction within the standing order of the House of Common of the principle of English Votes for English Laws—a procedural tool that allows only Members of Parliament elected in English constituencies to vote on laws that only concern England, thus overcoming the well-known West Lothian question—is also an inadequate response to growing nationalist sentiments in England. In order to address this situation post-Brexit, therefore, Tierney concludes that the UK needs to reform its constitution, entrenching a coherent system of intergovernmental relations.

Sionaidh Douglas-Scott examines instead Brexit and the Scottish question, arguing that the UK secession from the EU may be the trigger for Scotland's secession from the UK. While Scottish voters had by majority rejected independence in a referendum in 2014, they voted overwhelmingly to remain in the EU during the Brexit referendum. At the same time, as Douglas-Scott explains, efforts by the Scottish government after June 2016 to obtain a special deal to remain within the EU single market have received only scant attention from the UK government. While the Scottish government had pointed at the Greenland-Denmark model, the letter of notification of Article 50 TEU by the UK government, have frustrated the Scottish hopes for a bespoke solution specifically catering Scottish interests. Moreover, as Douglas-Scott underlines, new tensions are likely to emerge between Holyrood and Westminster in the implementation of the UK government Great Repeal Bill, now formally known as the European Union (Withdrawal) Bill. Although pursuant to the Sewel Convention, Scotland should have a right to be consulted on any matter relating to its devolved powers, the UK government does not seem sensitive to the issue—not least because the UKSC in *Miller* classified constitutional conventions as nonenforceable legal norms. It is because of the unsuccessful exhaustion of all these alternative roads to protect Scotland's interest, that the Scottish executive decided to plan for a second independence referendum—and Douglas-Scott concludes that the 1707 Union between England and Scotland is at risk after Brexit.

John Doyle and Eileen Connolly look at Brexit and the Northern Ireland question, arguing that the withdrawal of the UK from the EU creates tremendous difficulties for the region. As they explain, the border between Northern Ireland and Ireland is the only physical frontier between the EU and the UK, and the introduction of a hard border would have huge impact: First, on free movement of goods, with implications for the economy; second, on free movement of people, with effect on the Common Travel Area, which has existed there since the 1920s; and, third, on the peace process, potentially threatening the endurance of the 1998 Good Friday Agreement, which put an end to over forty years of sectarian conflict. As they underlined, given the peculiar situation of Northern Ireland, specific solutions ought to be identified—and a number of options can be considered. In terms of the free movement of goods, Doyle and Connolly point to the Cyprus model, where goods produced in Northern Cyprus can enter into Cyprus without customs duties. In terms of the free movement of people, they suggest that, given the insular nature of Ireland, immigration controls could be moved into the Irish Sea—as they de facto already are, since people traveling from Northern

Ireland to Great Britain must show their ID. And in terms of the peace process, they recommend that the spirit if not the letter of the Good Friday Agreement be preserved, notably by avoiding any symbol of division (such as a hard border) which may catalyze opposition. As Doyle and Connolly conclude, however, both the UK and the EU seem fully cognizant of the sensitivity of the Northern Irish question, which raises some optimism on the possibility of finding a pragmatic solution for the region.

9. Brexit and Constitutional Change in European Perspective

Part III of the book contains the contributions of Michele Chang, Deirdre Curtin, and Catherine Barnard. These chapters examine the implications of Brexit on three crucial areas of EU policy-making—EMU, the AFSJ, and the internal market—and try to address the Brexit effect in two ways. On the one hand, the chapters consider whether and how EU integration in EMU, security and the internal market may advance without the UK. On the other hand, they discuss how the UK may remain connected to the EU in these specific policy fields after Brexit.

Michel Chang analyzes Brexit and EMU, an area of European integration where the involvement of the UK was at its lowest ebb. As is well-known, the UK enjoyed an opt-out from the euro, and traditionally remained on the side-lines of the project of integration in the field of monetary, fiscal, financial and economic policy. Nevertheless, as Chang explains, the UK was effectively influential in the shaping of EMU-related rules. The UK had strong interests in the market for financial services, and it successfully frustrated efforts by the European Central Bank to house in the Eurozone all clearing operations in euro. Moreover, the UK often acted as a shield for other non-Eurozone countries, *e.g.* by securing a double-majority requirement in the functioning of the EBA. Therefore, the withdrawal of the UK from the EU is likely to have an impact within the EMU, altering interstate alliances and changing the balance between euro-ins and euro-outs. While Brexit will not per se trigger further steps in the integration of the Eurozone, the lack of a veto player such the UK will reduce the need to act outside the perimeter of the EU in fiscal affairs—as was the case for the Fiscal Compact in 2012. Moreover, the shortfall in the EU budget resulting from the end of the UK financial contributions may change the stakes in fiscal negotiations, creating room for the establishment of a Eurozone fiscal capacity, as called for in several high-level EU institutional documents. According to Chang, instead, it is uncertain to what extent post-Brexit the EU may be able to push forward with the Capital Markets Union and whether the UK may stay connected to it.

Deirdre Curtin focuses instead on Brexit and the AFSJ, an area where the UK involvement was intermediate. As she emphasizes, in fact, the UK was always wary of full engagement in EU transnational policing and judicial cooperation: It enjoyed opt-out from the Schengen internal free-border zone, and just in 2014 it exercised a block-exit option from all AFSJ measures, only to re-join a selective number of them, including Europol and the European Arrest Warrant. Nevertheless, the UK was also a leader in the field of AFSJ: given its advanced intelligence capabilities it provided important support to the functioning of agencies like Europol, and its officers played key management roles in the EU. According to Curtin, therefore, Brexit creates the need to preserve some pragmatic forms of cooperation between the UK and the EU—a point that also seems to be shared by the UK security establishment. To this end, Curtin considers the example of Denmark as a possible model for the UK to follow. While Denmark rejected participation in Europol in a popular referendum, the Danish government obtained a deal from the EU institutions which allows it to remain associated to Europol with the status of a third country (despite the fact that it is a Member State of the EU). While the complex legal reality of AFSJ reveals how the EU remains a Europe of bits and pieces, at least in the field of internal security, Curtin critically underlines how all this tends to occur below the radar, raising potential issue of parliamentary accountability and democratic control.

Catherine Barnard finally considers Brexit and the EU internal market, an area where the involvement of the UK was at its maximum. Barnard emphasizes the role that the UK played in creating the EU internal market and critically examines the view that the four freedoms of the internal market—free movement of goods, services, capital, and people—are indivisible. While the "new settlement" between the UK and the EU of February 2016 had formally acknowledged the possibility of limiting one of the four freedoms, the decision of the UK to leave the EU has paradoxically contributed to entrench the view that the four freedoms are indivisible. This reduces the possibility for the UK to maintain access to the EU single market after Brexit—a fact acknowledged even by the UK government. According to Barnard, nevertheless, the European Economic Area model would be the best solution for the UK post-Brexit, as well as for the EU, and she suggests that this would be reflective of UK citizens' preferences—a view seemingly vindicated by the result of the June 2017 elections. At the same time, as she underlined, the withdrawal of the UK, a country which was largely favorable to the deepening of the internal market, may strengthen protectionist trends within the

EU. Moreover, Barnard emphasized that Brexit poses challenges for the UK internal market, which Westminster will need to address.

10. Beyond Brexit: Relaunching the EU?

Part IV of the book brings together the contributions of Marlene Wind, Uwe Puetter and Federico Fabbrini. The final part seeks to look beyond Brexit, considering the implications that the UK withdrawal from the EU has on the future of Europe itself, focusing on politics, inter-institutional relations, and constitutional reforms in the new Union of twenty-seven Member States.

Marlene Wind examines how Brexit affects Euroskepticism in the other EU Member States and argues that, in fact, the decision of the UK to leave the EU has weakened support for populist, anti-EU parties. By analyzing the electoral outcome in the Austrian presidential elections in December 2016, the Dutch parliamentary elections in March 2017 and the French presidential elections in April-May 2017, Wind shows how candidates and parties running on a pro-EU platform have systematically won elections since Brexit, defeating the doomsday scenario that Brexit would be followed by the exit of other EU Member States. As she emphasizes, the UK had historically developed a problematic relation to the EU, which makes its decision to leave the EU somehow exceptional. Nevertheless, Wind also underlines how concerns for national sovereignty and opposition to judicial review are not unique British characteristics: Rather, they are elements that can be found also in the constitutional tradition and politics of other European countries, particularly in Scandinavia. Wind therefore concludes that the likelihood of new exits from the EU depends on the terms of the deal that the UK will receive. If the UK is treated favorably, cherry-picking on EU benefits without paying the costs, this may prompt other EU Member States to follow suit.

Uwe Puetter focuses instead on the implications of Brexit on the EU inter-institutional balance, and inter-state relations, and argues that not much change is to be expected here. According to Puetter, the UK had over the recent years dramatically reduced its engagement with the EU institutions, and it had ended up punching below its weight. Despite being the third most populous EU Member State, and one of its economic powerhouse, the UK had isolated itself within the European Council—for example by being the only state (with Hungary) to vote against the appointment of Jean-Claude Juncker as Commission President in 2014. Moreover, the UK had lost influence in the European Parliament—mostly as a result of David Cameron's decision to take the Conservative party out of the European Peoples' Party (the largest political group in the European Parliament) into the marginal European Conservatives and Reformists group. While the withdrawal of the UK may open space for greater role and responsibility for countries like Italy and Spain, Puetter maintains that the German-French axis will likely remain dominant. Moreover, he suggests that the inter-institutional equilibrium within the EU will not change. During the last decade, the European Council has become central in the governance of the EU, along the logic of new intergovernmentalism. In this context, Brexit is unlikely to shift the balance back toward the continuum European Commission–European Parliament, although the former will negotiate the separation with the UK and the latter will have to approve the agreement setting out the arrangement for the UK withdrawal.

Federico Fabbrini considers how Brexit affects the EU treaties, and argues that withdrawal of the UK compels the EU institutions and the remaining Member States to engage in constitutional change at EU level. As he points out, once the UK leaves the EU, several provisions of the EU treaties and a number of quasi-constitutional EU norms—including the European Council decision on the composition of the European Parliament, and the rules on the financing of the EU—will need to be amended to adapt the EU to the reality of a Union at twenty-seven. The revision of these legal norms, however, may open a window of opportunity to discuss more far-reaching changes to the EU constitutional system. During the euro-crisis, and in the context of the celebrations for the 60th anniversary of the Rome Treaties, a number of roadmaps have been presented at the highest level by EU institutions and several national governments to reform the EU and fix its structural problems. Since these reform proposals mostly concern the functioning of the EU institutions and the financing of the EMU—precisely the two areas where legal changes will be needed after Brexit—this may create the space for a grand-bargain. Clearly, the track-record of treaty reforms in the EU is mixed, and Fabbrini underlines the many legal and political obstacles toward a new constitutional settlement in Europe. Nevertheless, he suggests that the current constitutional *status quo* is sub-optimal, and that the growing calls for a multispeed Europe signal a credible alternative: After Brexit, integration by a sub-group of states remains a distinctive possibility in case the efforts to reform the EU constitutional system were to falter due to idiosyncratic national reasons. Hence, Fabbrini concludes that while Brexit offers a chance to reform the EU at twenty-seven, Europe's future may lay in a federal union on a smaller scale.

***

As this book is going to press in August 2017, many new political issues and legal challenges continue to arise on the UK's withdrawal from the EU. Skeptics question whether Brexit will happen at all—while realists point to the clock ticking toward March 2019, the default date for withdrawal. Surely, the decision of the UK to leave the EU will remain at the heart of the debates for a long time to come. By outlining paths for further analysis, this book hopes to contribute some early, balanced thoughts on the causes, consequences, and possible cures for Brexit.

PART 1

BREXIT: POLITICS, PROCESS, AND PROSPECTS

2

The Political Mantra

Brexit, Control and the Transformation
of the European Order

Kalypso Nicolaïdis

1. Introduction: Equilibrium Transformed

'Taking Back Control'. It is hard to deny the power of the Brexiteers' mantra
in the run up to the June 2016 referendum, which set in motion Britain's exit
from the European Union. Obviously, the phrase meant different things to
different people depending on what control was about (our laws, our money,
our borders, our democracy), who it was taken back from (Brussels, Berlin,
London, Apple), and what it actually referred to (autonomy, independence,
freedom, sovereignty). But anyone can grasp its universal appeal. The question raised by this core tenet of the Brexit vote is as old as human social
life: how do different individuals or groups apprehend the trade-off between
cooperation and control? More than ever before, the modern era's growing
interdependence has exacerbated the tension. Western states' areas of responsibility have increased as their ability to control transnational interaction
decreased. Liberal economic policies, including free trade, further allowed for
the relinquishing of direct control over aspects of a state's economy, promis-
ing to abide by common rules in exchange for the benefits of freely moving
capital and even people. Even if larger states have less need of cooperation
than smaller ones, their governments are subject to the same pressures by
those (exporters, students, patients, idealists) who value cooperation over
control and those (import competing, migrant competing, identity sensitive)
who value control over cooperation.

One response to the Brexit mantra is to deny the trade-off altogether—call
it 'ideological crap', according to Tory grandee Chris Patten. If power is the
measure of control over outcomes, events or other actors, giving up control

The Political Mantra: Brexit, Control and the Transformation of the European Order. First edition.
Kalypso Nicolaïdis © Kalypso Nicolaïdis 2017. Published 2017 by Oxford University Press.

by conforming to shared EU rules, *actually* buys power or control in at least two ways. First, internally, through *reciprocal control*, that is the control which follows from co-shaping the actions of governments and other actors in other jurisdictions. Being able to tie the hands of others is a net increase in control to the extent that one's power can be translated into shared rules and to the extent the other side's actions impact us irrespectively. Secondly, externally, through greater *collective control* over extra-EU developments, or the 'power multiplier effect'. This is what Macron means when he describes the EU as 'the instrument of power' and 'the right level of sovereignty' enabling each country better to confront global challenges such as migration, terrorism, climate, or digitalization. In this light, in his words 'what is going to happen for Britain is not taking back control: it's servitude'. This was a core tenet of the argument to stay in: by ignoring such loss of reciprocal and collective control, popular decisions against EU membership fall prey to the delusion of what the Norwegians call 'distorted sovereignty'.

Nevertheless, the trade-off between control and cooperation remains, even if mitigated. And the challenge for a cooperative endeavour like the EU is to find the right balance between different national 'right balances'. We can assume that this is true for all exercises in transnational cooperation. The EU is simply a more extreme form of the tension: having engineered more interdependence through greater cooperation between its Member States than any other international organization, and yet home to the very same people whose forbears invented the idea of national sovereignty in the first place and who in their great majority remain wedded to the national as their preferred *locus* of collective control.

EU cooperation has led to different institutionalization of 'the right balance' depending on the issue at stake. But when it comes to an 'existential referendum' as with Brexit, each individual voter makes her own overall and subjective rough assessment. A basic understanding of the UK mainstream pro-leave position is that from the initial decision to join the 'common market' onwards, deeper cooperation has always been the 'price demanded' for continuing trade relations, rather than a goal in itself as it may have been for other Member States on the continent. Brexit then would be the obvious and inevitable consequence of demanding an ever-increasing price for something: eventually, you reach a price the Brits will no longer pay. The expanding costs in terms of 'sovereign control' simply outweigh the benefits of cooperation. Is this the key to Brexit?

This chapter does not pretend to *explain* the radical rupture that Brexit undoubtedly represents for European integration. Instead, I seek to situate Brexit in the *longue durée*, against a highly stylized account of the long-term transformation of the European order and the nexus between the EU, Brexit, and control. I believe that the 'Brexit moment' calls for systematically laying out what we could interpret as the building blocks, or primary material, upon which politics, political debate, and manipulation ultimately builds, eg the permissive context upon which we layer our explanatory theories. Obviously, this assessment depends on the theoretical lens one adopts to examine the integration process, what one thinks of the primacy granted to inter-governmentalism, whether one holds on to the international relations assumption of state-centricism, or whether one acknowledges existing limitations to materialist notions of power. We can also import into this exercise the insights of adjacent fields that become relevant to European integration with Brexit, namely theories of accommodation of secessionist demands in multinational democracies. Brexit, in other words, opens up a whole range of questions for political scientists, which in turn can help inform the kind of legal debates discussed in this volume.

The focus adopted here on the issue of 'control' is but one possible entry point into this vast agenda. But it is one which I believe is critical if we are concerned not only about Brexit per se but also about the future of Europe after Brexit. If we are, we need to ask: is Brexit primarily due to British exceptionalism and therefore Britain's problem, or is it the expression of a deeper *malaise* about 'control' across the EU, an echo of the French *Non* and Dutch *Nee* to the EU constitutional treaty a decade earlier? Even if we were to agree that the British public is an outlier on the EU, does it not matter to ask whether the EU system is more prone to accommodating differences and even 'exceptions' or weeding them out?

I argue that as scholars come to re-examine four decades of British membership in the EU and their culmination in withdrawal, they ought to pay special attention to developments that have sustained or conversely unsettled the balance between the legal and political constraints of EU cooperation and the technologies of control used by various actors in its political constellation. Our focus must move away from teleology and the implicit centralizing bias of functionalist theories to assess the ways in which the EU's sustainability has been predicated on the 'equilibrium' between cooperation and control imperatives, even if its instantiation has been changing over time.[1] In spite of its remarkable transformation, the EU must more than ever heed Weiler's post-Maastricht warning against unravelling its precious equilibrium.[2] What is at stake here is not merely who stays and who goes but the very essence

---

[1] Andrew Moravcsik and Kalypso Nicolaïdis, 'Keynote Article: Federal Ideals and Constitutional Realities in the Treaty of Amsterdam' (1998) 36 (Annual Review) *Journal of Common Market Studies* 13.

[2] J H H Weiler, 'The Transformation of Europe' (1992) 100(8) *Yale Law Journal* 2403.

of the EU. If a genuine principle of constitutional tolerance had found its expression in an EU constitutional discipline which is not rooted in a statist-type constitution, it would have meant that European peoples accept to be bound not by a majority of their own but a majority of others. It would have meant that the EU has managed to escape the false alternative between an association of sovereign states and turning into a federal state itself, deepening instead its credentials as a third way, a 'demoicracy in the making', a Union of peoples who govern together but not as one, and stay together by choice.

Brexit can be seen as a dramatic commentary on this transformative challenge which, in a most extreme interpretation lies with a kind of radi-cal agonistic bet: that the complex and deep social structure underpinning integration in Europe progressively created a space where conflict about the implications of 'togetherness' could take place not only through deliberation but also through contestation and even ultimately peaceful self-exclusion. Is this not the spirit of constitutional tolerance? If this is the case, I believe that the possibility of withdrawing from the Union to reassert control ought to be seen as an intrinsic part of the European project, not an aberration.

In this light, we need to draw lessons from what I call the Brexit paradox— that the possibility and manner of leaving (unilateral and unconditional) con-tradicts its rationale (eg the assumption that shackled countries need to 'take back control').[3] The Brexit paradox emerges from a tension between different expressions of "control": EU level bargaining over the *scope* of formal jurisdic-tional space versus how such bargains translate on the ground, or the *depth* of EU impact within each polity. The British state lies at one end of the spec-trum in its willingness and capacity to minimalize the formal loss of national control from jurisdictional cooperation; but it lies at the other end of the spectrum when it comes to the country's vulnerability to actual losses of con-trol once commitments have been made—a vulnerability that is political and subjective as much as linked to the UK's legal and economic material features.

In the rest of this chapter this argument unfolds in three phases, which cor-respond to the three legal orders of a federation of free states as identified by Kant (1795): (i) relations between states as governed by *ius gentium*, (ii) rela-tions between nationals and a foreign state as defined by *ius cosmopoliticum*, and (iii) relations between citizens and state as established by *ius civitatis*. In other words, the transformation of the European state system, the transfor-mation of European borders, and the transformation of European states or state-society relations. Each of these realms has evolved differently over time,

---

[3] Kalypso Nicolaïdis, *Exodus, Reckoning, Sacrifice: Three Meanings of Brexit* (Unbound Publishers and Penguin Random House, 2018).

is affected differently by EU membership, and affects the UK differently from other Member States. If exceptionalism resides with a country's specific way of combining common features, British exceptionalism must be sought in the paradoxical contrast between the first (where the UK maximizes control) and the other two (where the UK retains minimal control) dimensions of Europe's legal, political, and constitutional order.

2. *Ius Gentium*: The Transformation of the Inter-state System

If the 'law of nations' or *ius gentium* has been broadly understood as the 'reasoned compliance with standards of international conduct' since Antiquity, Britain has long played a central role in shaping its countless variations on the European continent.[4] If the EU is but the last iteration of the transformation of the European state system, Brexit represents but the last expression of the cycle of involvement and retreat between Britain and the continent. Arguably, however, the EU has offered a particularly British-friendly terrain for adjudicating between cooperation and control, which I discuss under the three rubrics of balance of power, constitutional order, and conflict of law. The Brexit paradox starts here.

2.1 The EU as Institutionalized Balance of Power

For the last 300 years, the meaning of 'control' when it came to Great Britain's involvement in the politics of the continent came under one main label: the balance of power. The idea gained currency among diplomats and scholars alike during the 17th century, with antecedents in Antiquity and Renaissance Italy, according to which the supreme object of international politics ought to be the maintenance of 'the' equilibrium between the most powerful actors in the system to ensure that none would be in a position to dominate others. As with Newtonian astronomy, states were seen to exert a pull on one another as a function of their respective masses and relative distances, so that the stability of the whole could be affected by changing mass, unless the distances were corrected, the alliances changed, the states regrouped.[5] The idea evolved from descriptive to normative, which not only led to alliances in order to resist the

---

[4] David J Bederman, *International Law in Antiquity* (Cambridge University Press 2004).
[5] Herbert Butterfield, *Dictionary of the History of Ideas* (University of Virginia Library 1973).

predominant power of the day but to a general assumption that this process itself would constantly need to be reinvented since it would inevitably generate new aggressors, who, demanding more and more security against the enemy, might slide imperceptibly into lust for 'universal dominion'. [6]

The idea was especially dear to Britain, loath to see its trade access dominated or cut off by some malevolent hegemon from the continent bent on extracting rents in the process. It made sense for the British, Danes, or Venetians to support France against the threat of 'universal dominion' from the Habsburgs, spreading from Austria to Spain, from Hungary to Italy, from the Netherlands to Germany. But it equally made sense to resist French hegemony later.

Crucially, its 17th and 18th century defenders claimed that the balance of power system was the only way to secure the existence of small states in a world at the mercy of force. Not only was distribution and dispersion of power important for stability but the system might in fact depend on these small states, capable of shifting their allegiance against the greatest current threat. Moreover, small states offered an intrinsic value against uniformity, bolstering a European civilization enriched by the variety of its national manifestations. Dominated in war, they became independent in peace and equal in diplomacy, sustaining an international system which in turn gave them their autonomy and freedom of action.

Equally crucially, defenders of the balance of power argued that such balancing could not occur in a vacuum, that a state system depended in fact on an underlying common sense of values and a preexisting community of tradition and custom.[7] The international order itself, and the balance within it, depended on the assumption that all the participants were akin to members of the same club to which loyalty was owed: the enlightened egotism of states—as opposed to self-righteous proselytism—meant that they should rise if 'their' international order were threatened.

The most successful instantiation of the this idea had been the Concert of Europe conceived in 1814 at the Congress of Vienna and founded by the 1815 Treaty of Hertslet, whereby the great powers in Europe laid the foundations of a European peace that would last for a century (although arguably the Concert itself formally ended in 1856 with the Crimean War). The new order was made possible when Britain announced its preparedness to relinquish military gains won in the course of the Napoleonic War in order 'to promote the general interest'.[8] This is the argument offered by French opinion-makers

---

    [6] ibid.   [7] ibid.

    [8] Cabinet Memorandum (26 December 1813), cited in Louise Richardson, 'The Concert of Europe and Security Management in the Nineteenth Century' in Helga Haftendorn, Robert O Keohane, and Celeste A Wallander (eds), *Imperfect Unions: Security Institutions over Time and Space* (Oxford University Press 1999) 48–79, at 48.

pleading with the British public to remain in the EU: 'Waterloo marked the beginning of an unprecedented era of peace, stability and development in Europe. Waterloo marked the end of the political cycle of the French Revolution and the beginning of the industrial revolution in Britain. For the next century, no major European war would erupt. After the Congress of Vienna, European monarchs took to meeting regularly to solve tensions and crises: a new system of collective security had emerged'.[9]

How did the Concert of Europe ensure peace-without-dominion? This was not a victor's peace as witnessed by France's rapid integration in the system. To use the language of contemporary international relations scholars, the leaders of the great powers created a loose institutional arrangement able to sustain cooperation between states and facilitate peaceful adaptation to changing relative power in the international system thanks to 'a set of habits and practices shaped towards the realization of common goals'.[10] Their relations were thus mediated by a complex set of norms included self-restraint, consultation in terms of crisis, no unilateral action, and affirmation of pacific intent, and initially at least bolstered by constant communication. They respected each other's prestige requirements and all came to consider maintenance of the concert as part of their 'national interest'. As a result and for four decades, the Concert 'served as an arena for the exercise of influence, constrained bargaining strategies, facilitated side payment, enabled signalling, enhanced predictability and specified obligations guiding state actions'.[11]

Sounds familiar? Of course, the new order did not end well in 1914. But to treat 20th century European integration as if it was uniquely a reaction against the 19th century European system, overlooks the thread that links Westphalia to Vienna and Vienna to Brussels, and the importance of power as the dominant currency of the historical search for peace in Europe. Has the EU done much more than cleverly institutionalize the balance of power on the continent initially between France, Italy, and Germany, eventually joined by the UK?

It can be argued that, by joining the EU in 1973, the UK entered a system of institutions that was to a great extent doing its bidding, designed to contain any potential hegemonic aspirations on the continent and to give small states disproportionate power in terms of representation (Commissioners, parliamentarians, representatives in Council meetings, and, of course, the rotating

---

[9] 'Editorial' *Le Monde* (18 June 2015).
[10] Hedley Bull, *The Anarchical Society: A Study of World Order in Politics* (Macmillan 1977) 74. On an institutionalist reading of the Concert see Richardson (n 8).
[11] See Richardson (n 8) 56.

presidency) and voting power.[12] In the process, trade access would be guaranteed through shared rules that had replaced even the remotest possibility of bilateral deals, arbitrary moves and blackmail between Britain and continental powers, thus granting the former what I earlier referred to as reciprocal control. And on the external front, Britain more often than not was able to harness the EU's collective trade power (or control) to its benefit.

This did not mean of course that the system failed to reflect asymmetries of power. But in short, Britain quickly became everyone's favourite balancer, of Germany on behalf of France, of France on behalf of the Germans, and of both on behalf of the so-called periphery. With France and Germany together encompassing 30 percent of the EU's population and almost half of its GDP, the UK's role in balancing their combined weight in the system was crucial from the view point of the many small and medium-sized Member States, from Denmark to the Baltics, from the Central European Visegrad Four to the Netherlands. After all, by 2016 the UK was equal to the twenty smaller states in the EU measured by GDP.

Things did change in the run up of the Brexit vote. While the system has continued formally to accommodate power imbalances between big and small states, it is no longer clear whether the 'institutionalised' part of the balance of power continues to mitigate the underlying power asymmetries between Member States or has instead come to magnify them. Britain has remained one of the core states around which others coalesce, but balancing has become a more arduous game. Particularly after the euro crisis, many states and not only Britain have felt that the EU's balance of power set-up is no longer in equilibrium. The choice seemingly offered by pre-Brexit Europe presents powerful echoes of the past: resist German preponderance from within, including through selective bandwagoning or resist and retreat outside its reach.[13] The later, however, might be illusionary.

2.2 The EU as a Differentiated Legal Order

But how constrained has Britain truly been as an EU member? In order to bring the question of control into focus substantively we would need to examine in detail the more fine-tuned features of inter-state law and politics in the EU. I can only provide some basic highlights from the relevant literature which is much too vast to summarize.

---

[12] Kalypso Nicolaïdis and Paul Magnette, 'Coping with the Lilliput Syndrome: Large vs. Small Member States in the European Convention' (2004) 13 *Politique Europeene* 69.

[13] As usually presented in the many dystopian novels published since the post-Maastricht year. See inter alia Andrew Roberts, *The Aachen Memorandum* (Weidenfeld & Nicolson 1995).

The first paradox of our story is that when the UK joined in 1973, the EU had already undergone its first mutation away from the traditional albeit highly cooperative inter-state system which the Treaty of Rome had codified. It had already been a decade since the European Court of Justice (ECJ, now the Court of Justice of the European Union (CJEU)) established in its early case law that *once* a state had voluntarily signed up to the Treaties, it would be subject to the CJEU interpretation of what these obligations entailed.[14] Such 'direct effect' of EU norms conferred rights on individuals, which the Member States' courts were bound to recognize and enforce, thus empowering (some) individuals and firms against their own state and shifting control not only upwards but downwards as well. To be sure, there were caveats or conditions established by the Court. Nevertheless, this move alone, which cannot be found in any other regime of inter-state law sets the EU apart in its approach to sovereignty.

Much has been written since then on the EU's emerging constitutional order, the autonomy of EU law, and the departure from classic international relations which these developments have entailed. EU legal theory has explored the need to revisit reigning legal paradigms beyond mere conceptual tweaking, through discussions of 'supranationality' or 'constitutional pluralism'.[15] Some have plausibly argued that EU law does not determine its own structure and is a result of the joint application of EU, national, and international law, thus making it far from a typical constitutional model—still to a great extent an international organization.[16] But at the same time, it can be argued that the EU's constitutional DNA whereby its powers are purposive and functional, leads to the pre-emption of essential choices through the normal course of politics within and between states.[17]

Why then could this early state of affairs be considered by the UK as falling under an acceptable equilibrium between the benefits of cooperation and the cost of national relinquishing of control, especially with the subsequent expansion of EU competences? One answer rests with the disaggregation of control into two separate dynamics, namely the realms of law and politics. Accordingly, while the CJEU's interpretation of the law's constraining effect made selective exit from these constraints harder, the political

---

[14] Case 26/62 *NV Algemene Transporten Expeditie Onderneming van Gend en Loos v Nederlandse Administratis der Belastingen* [1963] ECR 1, [1970] CMLR 1.

[15] Gráinne de Búrca and J H H Weiler (eds), *The Worlds of European Constitutionalism* (Cambridge University Press 2012).

[16] Pavlos Eleftheriadis, 'The Structure of European Union Law' (2010) 12 *Cambridge Yearbook of European Legal Studies* 121.

[17] Gareth Davies, 'Democracy and Legitimacy in the Shadow of Purposive Competence' (2015) 21(1) *European Law Journal* 2.

(or intergovernmental) side compensated for these developments through Member State veto capacity. The continued assertion of state 'voice' balanced the loss of legal exit capacity to sustain the EU constitutional equilibrium.[18]

Britain was of course a key agent in these developments, in particular in the crucial distinction between primary (eg Treaty) and secondary law which, albeit established clearly in the Treaties had been resisted by De Gaulle. In contrast, Margaret Thatcher so valued the benefits of cooperation in bring-ing about ('completing') the single market that she agreed to relinquishing control over secondary legislation by generalizing qualified majority voting (QMV) through the 1987 Single Act—without of course giving up control where it really mattered (eg Treaty change and in practice Council decisions). And while in the twenty-five intervening years since the Maastricht Treaty this equilibrium was stretched to its limits, three points can be highlighted in particular:

- First, and in spite of repeated attempts by euro-federalists to do away with the unanimity requirements for treaty reform, including during the 2002–2003 constitutional convention, these pressures were always resisted. The Member States remain collectively and individually masters of the treaty. One exception, however, is notable, namely the adoption of the 2012 Treaty on Stability, Coordination and Governance (otherwise known as the Fiscal Compact), in spite of British opposition.[19] While this Treaty was motivated by Germany's insistence on the introduction of a balanced budget rule in national constitutional arrangements for all Member States and not only EMU members, Britain did not like the idea of granting new powers to Brussels over national economic policy, unless compensated by assurances for the City of London. While the UK's veto was formally respected since the other states proceeded outside the confines of EU Treaties, new powers were nevertheless conferred on EU institutions through a veto override.

- Secondly, over the intervening period, the UK was able to retain more con-trol over its policy domain than any other Member State, save Denmark, through the systematic use of opt-outs, or what Adler-Nissen calls selected 'outsiderness', which allow states to draw a line in the sand, as it were, and establish an area where they are to remain sovereign.[20] While asymmetric federalism can be found in many other polities across the globe, it generally

---

[18] See inter alia Weiler (n 2).

[19] Paul Craig, 'The Stability, Coordination and Governance Treaty: Principle, Politics and Pragmatism' (2012) 37 *European Law Review* 231.

[20] Rebecca Adler-Nissen, 'Organized Duplicity? When States Opt Out of the European Union' in R Adler-Nissen and Thomas Gammeltoft-Hansen (eds), *Sovereignty Games* (Palgrave Macmillan 2008) 81–103.

does not concern the core elements of the shared polity. But as the EU's remit progressively expanded in areas of core state powers from economic governance to the area of justice and home affairs (JHA), the resort to 'variable geometry' allowed it to accommodate the different cooperation-control trade-offs of its Member States.[21] Given her experience in negotiating dozens of specific opt-ins and opt-outs in her prior responsibilities for JHA affairs, it is no surprise that Theresa May has envisaged Brexit in the same light.

- Thirdly then, and most crucially, the introduction of a formal exit clause in the Lisbon Treaty erected sovereign control as the Union's *sine qua non*, a move of crucial symbolic as well as material importance (even if only formalized a pre-existing right). For the essence of a Union is defined by the way one may leave it: that you can leave tells us something about the EU irrespective of who leaves or the circumstances of this leaving. This is the intuition that led to the drafting of Article 50 of the TEU during the 2002 European Convention, which meant that the EU would never cross the Rubicon to become a (federal) state as the United States did in 1861, when 'secession' was redefined as 'civil war'. Selective exit could now be turned into wholesale withdrawal unilaterally on the basis of a Member State's own constitutional rules.

These developments illustrate not only the continuing concern for control among EU states but also what could be termed the *paradoxes of control*.

For one, it is a basic fact of interdependence, especially of the deep kind practised in the EU, that carving out formal jurisdictional autonomy does not protect a state from the externalities produced by other states individually and by their cooperative endeavours collectively. In areas of variable geometry, what other Member States did together affected the UK anyway, before Brexit, and it will continue to do so after Brexit. The UK–EU deal negotiated by David Cameron with regard to Eurozone externalities on non-Member States was a case in point. This has led some analysts to argue that 'the management of opt-outs reflects a retreat from national sovereignty rather than an expression of it'.[22]

Secondly, in spite of their own country having opted out, members of the public can sometimes perceive other countries' evident loss of control over

---

[21] Dirk Leuffen, Berthold Rittberger, and Frank Schimmelfennig, *Differentiated Integration: Explaining Variation in the EU* (Palgrave 2013); Philipp Genschel and Markus Jachtenfuchs, 'More Integration, Less Federation: The European Integration of Core State Powers' (2016) *Journal of European Public Policy* DOI: 10.1080/13501763.2015.1055782.

[22] Rebecca Adler-Nissen, 'Opting Out of an Ever Closer Union: The Integration Doxa and the Management of Sovereignty' (2011) 34(5) *West European Politics* 1092.

their own affairs as a kind of 'loss of control by proxy'. The plight of the Greeks under the thumb of the Troika was often invoked during the Brexit campaign.

Thirdly, the real issue confronting control maximizers is to compare the domains where formal control over the rules applied within one's territory will be regained and those where EU rules will continue to apply for the sake of trade, but without a 'seat at the table' (*reciprocal control*)—turning the UK from rule-maker into rule-taker. Where EU standards continue to apply, the only question will be whether their enforcement by the ECJ will be 'indirect' instead of 'direct' in order to satisfy the theatre of sovereignty.

Finally, there is the value of *potential* rather than *actual* actions in assessing what 'control' really means, the kernel of the Brexit paradox. Brexit ought to demonstrate both to British and other EU citizens that this is a Union that you can leave under conditions of your own choosing—in the first instance. If this is the case, it is this very freedom to leave that ought to entice 'freedom loving' people to stay. This is the obvious contradiction in the pro-leave rhetoric: if the EU is a supranational Leviathan clipping Britain's sovereign wings, how can it be so easy to detach ourselves from it?

2.3 The EU as the Anointer of 'Home States'

When we turn to secondary legislation (directives and regulations), the picture is perhaps more complicated, but no less favourable to British concern for control. To be sure, as the scope of QMV increased along with the reach of cooperation, so did the potential for national interest over-ride. Member of the voting public in the UK understood that the other Member States could outvote the UK when discussing common standards, and that the CJEU could rule against it in any dispute arising. And indeed, CJEU jurisprudence has been one of the main targets of the leavers' discontent.

But much of the EU's legislative and judicial developments can be seen as attempts to maintain the equilibrium. For one, the CJEU has more often than not sided with the UK—as with its hugely significant rebuttal of French and ECB attempts to prohibit euro-clearing in the City of London.[23] Moreover, a number of Treaty revisions have sought to allow for greater 'national control' in EU law-making by empowering either national parliaments (subsidiarity protocol) or national courts (national identity clause), with various degree of success. Most importantly, it would be an understatement to note that, in spite of the loss of formal veto, the UK has retained throughout a vast amount of influence over the design of single market rules.[24]

---

[23] Judgment of 4 March 2015 in Case T-496/11 *United Kingdom of Great Britain and Northern Ireland v European Central Bank (ECB)* ECLI:EU:T:2015:133.

[24] See the contribution of Catherine Barnard in this volume.

Perhaps as important, however, is to consider the structure of state control that, once agreed, is set in place by single market rules. In a nutshell, the operating pattern of single market legislation has been to shift the control of economic agents operating transnationally from host to home country legislators and regulators. This is the familiar story of mutual recognition.[25]

In truth, mutual recognition in action in the EU was not supposed to entail a wholesale horizontal transfer of sovereignty, but was a kind of exercise in legal empathy on the part of the host state: the 'taking into account' of home rules—through principles known in the legal jargon as proportionality, balancing and the rule of reason. In my own work, I label this more complex version as 'managed mutual recognition', a management meant to mitigate the open-ended character of recognition.[26]

However 'managed', the principle of home country control has greatly benefited the UK in areas where it stands to gain as an exporter including to ensure the now infamous passporting rights for London-based banks operating across the EU. At the same time, in areas where it might have been reluctant to recognize other state standards (such as with the European arrest warrant which it has used extensively) it has generally availed itself of residual rights of host country control or safeguards: the best of all worlds!

3. *Ius Cosmopoliticum*: The Transformation of European Boundaries

Arguably, the most potent variation on 'taking back control' during the Brexit debates concerned the most basic meaning of sovereignty in the eyes of many citizens: national control over territorial borders, and in particular over the movement of people. There is no denying that the rights and obligations conferred by EU law have eroded such national control. But it can also be argued that this is the case to a great extent due to choices made in the UK itself.

---

[25] See Christine Janssens, *Mutual Recognition in the European Union* (Oxford University Press 2013); Kalypso Nicolaïdis, 'Kir Forever? The Journey of a Political Scientist in the Landscape of Recognition' in L Azoulai and M Maduro (eds), *The Past and Future of EU Law: The Classics of EU Law Revisited on the 50th Anniversary of the Rome Treaty* (Hart Publishing 2010).

[26] Kalypso Nicolaïdis, 'Trusting the Poles? Constructing Europe through Mutual Recognition' (2007) 14(5) *Journal of European Public Policy* 682; Kalypso Nicolaïdis and Gregory Shaffer, 'Transnational Mutual Recognition Regimes: Governance without Global Government' (2005–2006) 68 *Michigan Review of International Law* 267; Kalypso Nicolaïdis, 'Mutual Recognition of Regulatory Regimes: Some Lessons and Prospects Jean Monnet Paper Series No 7 (1997).

3.1 To Be or Not to Be a Cosmopolitan Federation

Kant's advocacy of *jus cosmopoliticum* as the glue that would sustain the aspiration to perpetual peace between independent states meant codifying these states' obligations to treat foreign nationals with respect, what we may think of as the basic obligations of hospitality. Much has been written to tease out Kant's idea of cosmopolitanism, but what seems clear is that for him, porous borders did not mean borderlessness, nor did hospitality amount to unqualified non-discrimination between nationals and non-nationals. Can we interpret the EU as an approximation of this Kantian ideal?

To be sure, for all the talk of the EU not being a state itself, when it comes to the control of national territorial borders, it seems to approximate something close to a state-like form: borderless inside, bordered outside. But while the ideal of free movement has become an EU mantra, this was not always the case, nor is it unqualified. In the abstract, free movement in the EU is cast as a humanist ideal defined as an exercise in individual freedom and a corresponding duty of non-discrimination vis-à-vis 'European citizens'. In practice and in law, free movement is an exercise in economic agency, a component of the free operation of (labour) markets. As discussed by Catherine Barnard in this volume, the indivisibility between the four freedoms has been constructed late in the day after decades of piecemeal and separate progress across these four realms in order to cement this part of the *acquis* and to turn the figure of the alien aspiring to become a settled migrant into the figure of the 'mobile Europeans' taking advantage of all the EU has to offer.

However, the problem of control arises because borders between countries actually correspond to an array of different kinds of boundaries between different kinds of realms, spatial but also functional. The lack of congruence between national, regulatory, jurisdictional, and political boundaries within the EU has always created a tension between free movement on the one hand, and the very real nature of these functional boundaries, on the other. Managing these borders is about providing criteria for determining who is and who is not entitled to participate within a particular scheme for producing such fundamental social goods as liberty, security, justice, and economic prosperity, and to reap the resulting benefits. Any appraisal of the EU will turn on how far it does or can retain those separations required for diversity or the sustainability of the welfare state, while removing those that involve unfair discrimination through a fine balance between inclusion and exclusion.[27] And because preferences regarding this balance vary significantly

---

[27] For a recent overview see Richard Bellamy, Joseph Lacey, and Kalypso Nicolaïdis, 'European Boundaries in Question?' (2017) *Journal of European Integration* http://www.tandfonline.com/doi/full/10.1080/07036337.2017.1333118 (last accessed 11 July 2017).

between Member States—as well of course as among stakeholders within Member States—the EU sets a high bar for openness, while recognizing that local conditions and state discretion will prevail. In spite of the Eurocrisis and the exodus of the young from South to North, only 3 per cent of Europeans avail themselves of the free movement rights.

3.2 Britain's Fatal Attraction

Is Britain an outlier against this backdrop? And if so, why? Sociologists, historians, and pollsters may have pondered extensively about the idiosyncratic 'island mentality' prevailing in vast swathes of the British population, but we have yet to be presented with conclusive evidence on the presumed mismatch between the UK and the continent. Whatever the case may be in terms of popular *sensitivity*, what concerns us here is Britain's *vulnerability* to EU constraints as a result of both contingent mismanagement and structural characteristics.

The point can be made by distinguishing between, on one hand, border control per se and, on the other hand, the right to reside, work, and access certain goods such as social welfare across Member States.

On the first count, eg border control per se, the most potent image of the EU's internal borderlessness is the ability of European citizens to cross-national borders freely as temporary travellers. And yet, in this case, the UK simply retained control of its borders by opting out of the 1985 Schengen Agreement. However, opt-out provisions may serve the theatre of sovereignty for local audiences, but they do not preclude the British and Danish governments from circumventing the legal obstacles to cooperation over border control.

The second dimension is of course at the heart of the Brexit decision. The Treaty of Rome focused on free movement of labour, that is, the right for workers to seek employment in other EU Member States, referred to ambiguously as 'free movement of people'. After much uncertainty over what this right entailed, a 2004 directive spelled out the extent and limits of this right, including the obligation either to work or have sufficient means of subsistence after a three-month stay, notwithstanding other rights linked to European citizenship.[28] When it came to the EU enlargement to Eastern Europe in the same year, most Member States availed themselves of a seven-year grace period

---

[28] Directive 2004/38/EC of the European Parliament and of the Council of 29 April 2004 on the right of citizens of the Union and their family members to move and reside freely within the territory of the Member States.

before extending these free movement rights to the new-comers. Ironically, in light of the concerns leading to Brexit, the UK under Tony Blair both championed enlargement and decided to forego the transition period. To be sure, this was taking into account the features of an economy characterized by labour shortages and heavily reliant on low-cost low-skill labour, rather than investment in productivity.

As a result, the fateful political choice was to locate 'territorial control' in the UK's labour market and its capacity to match high levels of both supply and demand, irrespective of other domestic considerations such as state capacity to adapt to increased demand for its services. Britain was especially vulnerable to the translation of EU legal constraints into popular domestic rejection, owing to a particular mix of national factors: (a) the openness and relative lack of regulation of its labour market, combined with the attractiveness of its 'anglo' environment; (b) its relatively low level of funding for public services compared, for instance, with its Scandinavian neighbour and a general lack of concern for regions subject to the steepest increase in 'migrant' numbers; (c) the absence of the kind of informal national job preference prevalent in other countries from apprentice schemes to the informal ring-fencing of professions including the infamous French *notaire* or Austrian tour guide; and (d) a general lack of state intrusiveness, from the lack of identity card to the ease of registration for the provision of public services, such as health or education. In other words, at least during the 2004–2016 period, the UK was more prone than any Member State to attract high levels of migrants from poorer Member States while privatizing the gains and socializing the costs that this entailed.

One could argue that EU law could not be blamed for this very British pattern. But we still must ask, given this very British pattern, whether EU law could have more flexibly allowed for taking into account the very differential impact of EU obligations on different Member States, especially Member States such as the UK, which take their legal commitments seriously. Arguably, the British government could have taken the initiative and made use of judicial safeguards to claim the right to restrict free movement under the 'public interest clause' in EU law—although such a move was rejected in the pre-referendum agreement over in-work benefits negotiated by then Prime Minister Cameron.[29] That this legal approach may have been receivable is underscored by recent judicial developments, with the CJEU leaning towards allowing greater leeway to Member States in determining access by

---

[29] Gareth Davies,'Brexit and the Free Movement of Workers: A Plea for National Legal Assertiveness' (2016) 41(6) *European Law Review* 925.

non-citizens to their welfare systems.[30] Even if the CJEU had not been on board, it is hard to see what could have stopped the UK from asserting control in this way—an option more palatable to many than asserting control by quitting the EU altogether.

When it comes to the movement of third-country nationals, the refugee saga of 2015–16 reveals all too tangibly how the removal of some borders invariably involves the creation of others. Having matured under the shadow of the Berlin wall and the Cold War, the EU never formulated an equivalent ideal of freedom to cross external boundaries as it had internally. With the prospect of enlargement post-1989, however, the open-endedness of its membership conjured up an entity that could not be defined once and for all by the kind of boundaries that we associate with sovereign states. If there was no ultimate territorial reach of the polity, then it was harder to imagine the kind of fixed and solid external boundaries which provide ontological security by excluding outsiders from entering. Like the limes of the Roman Empire, Member States whose borders correspond to an external boundary of the EU have been expected to deal with the lure, not of their own territory, but of the overall European space only protected by its weakest link. The British paradox in this realm is that, by not taking part in Schengen, it does not constitute a point of entry *for* other Member States, nor can it be an easy target for migrants entering *from* other Member States. Nevertheless, the UK is the most open EU Member State when it comes to non-EU migrants (short of refugees), owing above all to its migration policy vis-à-vis Commonwealth states. In other words, in the realm where it has the most control, it is not clear that it has chosen to exercise it for the purpose of closure.

To conclude, our European predicament today lies with free movement as both the best of things and the worst of things. The ideal of a Europe without borders has sustained the enthusiastic support of generations of students, pensioners, and tourists within Europe. But it has also become synonymous in many a citizen's mental maps with 'welfare tourism', face-to-face social dumping, and even invasion—feelings of insecurity on which populist campaigns thrive.[31]

Ironically, we are likely to observe in the next few years that the contestation of the ideal of a borderless Europe does not need to be as dramatic as wholesale withdrawal. Somehow, a European Union that has been built

---

[30] The latest judgment in a series of CJEU judgments on this issue rules that Member States may exclude Union citizens who go to that Member State to find work from certain non-contributory social security benefits. Judgment in Case C-67/14 *Jobcenter Berlin Neukolln v Alimanovic* EU:C:2015:597, [2015] WLR (D) 384.

[31] For a discussion of the term see Nicolaïdis, 'Trusting the Poles?' (n 23).

around the idea of 'space', space for free trade and free movement, needs to rediscover the value of 'place' and local belonging.[32] Conversely, Brexit will not necessarily bring about dramatically greater control over national boundaries as Britain may need to recover some of its lost power of attraction and reinvent itself as a cosmopolitan state, in or outside the EU.

4. *Ius civitatis*: The Transformation of the State

Arguably the most radical transformation spearheaded by European integration is not that of the overall state system but that of the units that compose it.[33] While Brexit was undoubtedly a vote for popular democratic control, here again the question arises: where and who is control supposed to be taken back from?

4.1 From Nation States to Member States

If we believe that the EU story has been about transforming rather than transcending the nation state, this transformation has in fact strengthened European Member States as attested by the spectacular growth of welfare states in the first three decades of European integration.[34]

Does this mean that there has been no significant trade-off between cooperation and national control? Not if we open the black box of the state itself. If we ask *who* has been in control within the state, there is little doubt that European integration has empowered national executives and administrations in charge of the integration process against their own legislatures and other agencies of domestic control. International cooperation always brings about domestic power shifts. The twist in the EU case is how deeply entrenched this shift has been, leading some analysts to assert that European integration has changed the very *nature* of the state itself, that while the EU is based on state-driven processes, they are driven 'by states that are fundamentally different from the traditional, egoistical bourgeois nineteenth-century nation states'.[35] To characterize the process of state transformation ushered in by European integration as moving from a Europe of traditional nation-states to one of 'member-states' is meant to express a fundamental change in the political

---

[32] David Goodhart, *The Road to Somewhere: The Populist Revolt and the Future of Politics* (C Hurst & Co 2017).

[33] Chris J Bickerton, *European Integration: From Nation-States to Member States* (Oxford University Press 2013) 4.

[34] A S Milward, G Brennan, and F Romero, *The European Rescue of the Nation-state* (2nd edn, Routledge 2000).

[35] Chris J Bickerton, *European Integration*, (n 32) 4.

structure of the state, with horizontal ties between national executives taking precedence over vertical ties between governments and their own societies.[36] Accordingly, the EU has set in motion a fundamental process of social and political change that may appear as an apolitical, essentially technical, matter of institutional reform, but which actually sidesteps domestic politics in favour of EU networks which become constitutive of statehood.

Britain clearly played a leading role in this story, under the leadership of both Margaret Thatcher and Tony Blair. If Thatcher's premiership was predicated on the partial dismantling of the Keynesian national corporatist state, this was made possible in great part by the adoption of a neo-liberal agenda in the rest of Europe in the wake of the 1987 Single Act.[37] Even if it is overly simplistic to state that the completion of the single market amounted to deregulation writ-large (after all, mutual recognition does not necessarily lead to a race to the bottom), European integration also induced widespread privatization of public services. And even if the most dramatic reforms took place in the UK, national failures to come to terms with the economic crisis of the 1970s and 1980s ensured that all Member States followed suit and mobilized EU policies to this effect. British and German interests converged in shifting money creation functions from national central banks to the private sector, resulting in both lower inflation and the dramatic financialization of the economy.

In effect, the story goes, European executives led by Britain were in part freed by the EU from societal control only to turn around and relinquish state control to global markets.

To the extent that citizens care about control in the form of public power, some would argue that it is less relevant for our societies to ask whether this public power is exercised domestically or through the EU, than to ask whether it is exercised at all in the face of corporate and private power.[38] Accordingly, the EU and European Member States have the same *raison d'être*, namely to protect citizens, physically and economically, while protecting their private sphere and individual freedoms. In other words, Hobbesian regalian powers are not a matter of level of competence in a system of multilevel governance but a matter of the effectiveness of the *puissance publique*, wherever it is exercised.[39] On this count, it is hard to deny that the EU has curbed some state power against markets while reinforcing it at the same time through enforcement of competition law.

---

[36] ibid 51.

[37] Mark Blyth,. *Austerity: The History of a Dangerous Idea* (Oxford University Press 2013).

[38] Thierry Chopin, 'Europe: la paix, le marché et après?' *Télos* (25 March 2017).

[39] This sentiment seems to be covered by Eurobarometer data, which, in June 2016, reported that 82% of citizens thought that Europe should do more to control terrorism, 75% to control tax

4.2 The Arrested Transformation of Transnational Democracy

However, the defence of public against private power was not where the core Brexit debate lay. Instead, the analysis of the emasculation of nation states into Member States is now part of the public sphere as the EU comes to be seen by swathes of the public in the UK and elsewhere as a danger to self-government, a pre-empter of national democracies, an instrument of integration by stealth.

Does this matter? Yes, if we believe in the transformation of democracy the better to manage democratic interdependence and hope that national and European democracy should not be a zero sum game.

Has this been the case? There are obviously many facets to this debate. In some countries, majorities believe that the trade-off between cooperation and popular control may be clear but is worth it. Alternately, the Greeks recognize their dramatic loss of democratic control but this cannot justify giving up the economic and psychological benefits they draw from keeping euros in their pocket. The Baltic states are macroeconomic rule-takers but these concerns are dwarfed by the need to be shielded from their overbearing Russian neighbour.

The most ardent defenders of the compatibility of the EU and democracy, however, will deny the trade-off itself. They will argue that the EU has helped to redistribute control to the people, empowering people as consumers, human rights advocates, or environmental activists, or defending them as victims of cartels, corporate power, and private property theft. They will point to the ways in which EU membership has enabled a better control of elite obfuscation, nepotism, and corruption by empowering civil society actors and monitory democracy at the national level. They will say that it has helped entrench democracy in Southern, Central, and Eastern Europe and further ashore. And they will note that it is governed by democratically elected and accountable governments and national parliamentarians who, thanks to the imperative of cooperation, are able to resist capture by special interests at the national level and better represent their median voters.[40]

In this latter perspective, Brexit is a product of British eccentricity. It speaks to the incapacity of remain campaigners to sell this version of the story to the electorate. And this in turn has to do with the British mindset, which we could call 'splendid democratic isolation', which harps back to

---

evasion, 71% to control external borders, and 66% in security and defence. See Eurobaromètre spécial du Parlement européen (juin 2016).

[40] Andrew Moravcsik, *The Choice for Europe: Social Purpose and State Power from Messina to Maastricht* (Routledge 2013).

the idiosyncrasies of the British political tradition and contemporary English nationalism.[41]

Alternatively, this is a story of EU disequilibrium, whereby cooperation has called for sacrifices of control beyond the threshold of public tolerance. Those who voted for Brexit in the name of democratic control belong to two broad categories of voters, demonstrators or simply citizens we can find across Europe: (a) protesting *against* Brussels *for* London, Budapest, or Athens; or (b) *against* London, Rome, or Paris *through* their no to Brussels.

In the first case, control is about recovering national sovereignty. The discourse about democracy is not about how much sovereignty is 'objectively transferred'. The UK government's 2017 white paper admits as much when it states that: 'Whilst Parliament has remained sovereign throughout our membership of the EU, it has not always felt like that'.[42] We cannot but conclude that Britain left the EU because of a 'feeling' about sovereignty. In this light, the EU's sin is its very *raison d'être*, to tame nationalism through agreed constraints as if not the slightest concession over control could be justified by the benefits of cooperation.

And yet is it not right to ask which of the existing EU constraints is necessary and which might not be, in the pursuit of the worthy goal of perpetual peace? What do you do when people feel they have lost something (eg their country) and want it back? Could they be on to something? Concerns about something called sovereignty must be taken seriously when they mean a yearning for a sense of place, for local autonomy, and collective control. International relations demonstrate daily the difficulties in disentangling self-determination and nationalism. But in the face of Brexit, the EU needs to resist the temptation to put all the onus of the vote on British exceptionalism, the British obsession with 'the sovereignty of Parliament', and century-old papal edicts. The resistance to being governed at a distance is a universal trope.

In the second case, control is about popular sovereignty. For this cohort, the true target of 'a people's Brexit' or Grexit or Frexit, is the insurgents' own national establishment, the system nurtured by their elites. Sovereignty will no longer be kept out of the hands of the people, a very long delayed corrective to England's 1688 glorious revolution and Europe's post 1789 not so glorious counter-revolution. But Euroscepticism is not simply the collateral

---

[41] See inter alia B Wellings, 'Losing the Peace: Euroscepticism and the Foundations of Contemporary English Nationalism' (2010) 16(3) *Nations and Nationalism* 488; E Vines, 'Reframing English Nationalism and Euroscepticism: From Populism to the British Political Tradition' (2014) 9(3) *British Politics* 255.

[42] HM Government, 'The United Kingdom's Exit from and New Partnership with the European Union' Cm 9417 (February 2017).

damage of the *malaise* of national democracy *tout court*. The EU has allowed the political class across Europe to escape domestic political constraints and hide behind EU law and decisions. For many, that national elected representatives meet in Brussels to pursue the greater good sounds more like co-optation than popular sovereignty writ large.

If national popular democracy as the constitutive bond is being replaced by transnational networks of cooperation, the ability to resist capture domestically is no match for the capture by global firms supranationally; and domestic accountability through national elections is annulled by the 'one size fits all' policies concocted in Brussels. The more the issues at stake are sensitive and entail redistributive choices, the less tolerance there is from the public in having the issues resolved outside their purview.

While we may be witnessing an anti-elite backlash worldwide, Europe's establishment is seen as top of the class, having managed to build the infamous Weberian iron cage of bureaucracy, but a cage even more remote than elsewhere, out of reach of the electoral cycles in its Euro-bubble: an iron cage in a bubble!

It is clear that these perceptions are real, whatever the extent of elite capture of the EU system. If this is the case, the challenge raised by Brexit is to reverse such capture and engage in a new 'transformation of democracy', which finds its resources in the process of European integration itself and its promise to eschew traditional forms of democracy at the EU level. It is this promise that I have tried to capture under the idea of *demoicracy*, that is a polity where the imperative self-government of the *demoi* is respected, *provided* these demoi are able and willing to conduct their affairs with utter regard for the interests of those with whom they share a deep interdependence.

In this perspective, the liberal account of European democracy needs to rely not only on the health and liberal credentials of its national democracies but on their radical openness to each other politically. More to the point, if the Brexit process is conducted in an authoritarian manner which ignores vast pluralities of disenfranchised citizens, this process which I have argued defines the essence of th EU, will itself be tainted as non-democratic. This is the ultimate aporia of Brexit, which now puts in British hands the democratic credentials of the EU as a whole.

By the same token, it is unclear whether Brexit is going to serve the people who feel they lack real control in an economy that does not work for them and whose problems run much deeper than the straightjacket of EU standards. As Marc Stears argues: 'Ultimately, Britain's crisis of control will not be addressed by Brexit. We urgently need change far removed from the mission to leave the European Union. We need most of all to change our economy so that people are really able to take control. That means working with communities, businesses, unions and public institutions to give people the tools they need to shape their lives for the better'.[43]

In the end, the profound problem in the EU today is not that of unaccountable governments in Brussels but that of discredited governments at home. The currency of power inside the EU is no longer between big and small countries or even creditor and debtors but in the divide between those who feel 'in control' and those who don't, which in turn threatens the kind of political mutual recognition that underpins the Community or Union paradigm. The euro crisis, the migration crisis, and, above all, Brexit have stretched the potential for sustainable EU transformation to its limits. The question of the democratic anchoring of the EU at national and local level has become both the deepest source of Europe's current *malaise* and the potential source of its most transformative promise yet. We can only engage with the promise if our political imagination enables us to recover the open-ended nature of European transformation.

5. Conclusion

There was of course nothing inevitable about Brexit—contingency reigns supreme with referenda. Indeed, as explored in the next part of this volume, the story looks utterly different seen from Scotland, Northern Ireland, or England. In this chapter, I did not set out to explain Brexit but instead to provide a conceptual bridge between the history of the UK in a transforming Europe and the specifics of the upcoming negotiations as analyzed by other contributors. I did so through a simple, in fact a simplistic, benchmark against which we may read the decision to join in and remain within a club such as the EU over time, that is the evolving balance between requisites of cooperation and the technologies of control. Normatively, I do believe that the EU's sustainability has been predicated on this 'equilibrium', but such a statement does not mean the same thing for different states and polities.

In this light, the pattern of arguments exchanged during the referendum campaign on the desirability of withdrawal is likely to endure after the deed. Remainers will continue to emphasize the theme developed in section 1 of this chapter, namely that given how much jurisdictional control Britain had managed to retain as an EU member, taking back control over border-crossers (section 2) and over 'our' laws (section 3) has entailed a disproportionate loss of cooperation benefits. Leavers will continue to believe and argue that where

---

[43] Mark Stears, 'Brexit is the Wrong Answer to Our Crisis of Control' *The Times* (28 March 2017).

control has been taken back, the loss of cooperation benefits, whatever they may be, is worth it, or, better still, that the trade-off is illusionary. The Brexit paradox will endure too, whereby the act of giving up membership of the club will have illustrated that much control had been retained all along and, yet, can never entirely be recovered.

3

The Process: Brexit and the Anatomy of Article 50

Paul Craig

The UK withdrawal process from the EU is framed by Article 50 TEU. There has been significant discussion of particular issues, such as revocability. There has not, however, been a more holistic examination of this Treaty provision, which analyses the stages of withdrawal from a UK and EU perspective. There are three stages in Article 50, which involve contestable issues of process and substance: triggering, negotiation, and outcome. Article 50 provides that:

1. Any Member State may decide to withdraw from the Union in accordance with its own constitutional requirements.
2. A Member State which decides to withdraw shall notify the European Council of its intention. In the light of the guidelines provided by the European Council, the Union shall negotiate and conclude an agreement with that State, setting out the arrangements for its withdrawal, taking account of the framework for its future relationship with the Union. That agreement shall be negotiated in accordance with Article 218(3) of the Treaty on the Functioning of the European Union. It shall be concluded on behalf of the Union by the Council, acting by a qualified majority, after obtaining the consent of the European Parliament.
3. The Treaties shall cease to apply to the State in question from the date of entry into force of the withdrawal agreement or, failing that, two years after the notification referred to in paragraph 2, unless the European Council, in agreement with the Member State concerned, unanimously decides to extend this period.
4. For the purposes of paragraphs 2 and 3, the member of the European Council or of the Council representing the withdrawing Member State shall not participate in the discussions of the European Council or Council or in decisions concerning it.

    A qualified majority shall be defined in accordance with Article 238(3)(b) of the Treaty on the Functioning of the European Union.
5. If a State which has withdrawn from the Union asks to rejoin, its request shall be subject to the procedure referred to in Article 49.

The Process: Brexit and the Anatomy of Article 50. First edition. Paul Craig © Paul Craig 2017. Published 2017 by Oxford University Press.

Stage 1 is the triggering stage in Article 50(1) TEU, whereby a Member State decides to withdraw in accord with its own constitutional requirements, and this includes the first sentence of Article 50(2), which is the notification of that intention to the European Council.

Stage 2 concerns negotiation and is contained in Article 50(2). The negotiations are conducted in the light of guidelines provided by the European Council. There is to be a withdrawal agreement negotiated in accordance with Article 218(3) TFEU. Article 50(2) also envisages another agreement concerning future relations between the state that has withdrawn and the EU.

Stage 3 concerns outcomes, and is dealt with in the last sentence of Article 50(2), and in Articles 50(3)–(4). Treaty rights and obligations apply to the state until the withdrawal agreement is concluded, or until two years from the date of notification, unless the European Council unanimously agrees to extend that period. Stage 3 may be affected by the possibility of revoking the notice of withdrawal prior to the end of two years; and by the possibility of a transition agreement.

1. Triggering Article 50

1.1 Process

Autumn 2016 was occupied with legal contestation as to the process for triggering Article 50, culminating in the decision in *Miller*.[1] The UK Supreme Court decided that the executive could not trigger withdrawal through the royal prerogative. Statutory approval was a constitutional condition precedent under UK law before the exit process could begin. There was a powerful dissent, most especially from Lord Reed. I believe that the majority was nonetheless correct, but the result was not simple or self-evident. This is not the place to rehearse these complex arguments; my detailed views can be found elsewhere.[2]

Suffice it to note that the *Miller* dispute was, as both the Divisional Court and the Supreme Court emphasized, about the UK constitutional process requirements to be satisfied before exit could begin. The courts were not adjudicating the substantive issue of whether it was desirable for the UK to exit the EU.

Suffice it to note also that this was a constitutional fight that never had to happen. Subject to limited exceptions, it takes two to litigate The salient

---

[1] *R (on the application of Miller) v Secretary of State for Exiting the European Union* [2017] UKSC 5.

[2] P Craig, '*Miller*, Structural Constitutional Review and the Limits of Prerogative Power' [2017] *Public Law* (forthcoming).

issue is why the government fought the action. It might be contended that the government believed that it should be able to trigger Article 50, through the prerogative. This argument is, however, relatively weak, since government lawyers would have told the prime minister that this was not an open and shut case, more especially because they did not wish to argue that Article 50 was revocable and thus could not easily rebut the claimant's argument that triggering of Article 50 would terminate rights derived from EU law. It might alternatively be argued that the prime minister was worried by backbench revolt if a Bill to authorize withdrawal were placed before Parliament, but this was unlikely for reasons explicated below.

The reality is that the prime minister could have secured her aims without litigation. Theresa May could have said in October 2016 that while she did not accept that she had, as a matter of law, to secure parliamentary authorization before triggering Article 50, she would nonetheless place the appropriate Bill before Parliament. The statute would have been duly enacted well before Christmas without litigation.

1.2 Substance

The European Union (Notification of Withdrawal) Act 2017 has 134 words, the operative section 1(1) stating that: 'The Prime Minister may notify, under Article 50(2) of the Treaty on European Union, the United Kingdom's intention to withdraw from the EU'. The Bill was placed before Parliament the day after the Supreme Court's decision. Truth to tell, it is highly likely that the government had a draft of such legislation in its top drawer considerably earlier. The notes accompanying the Bill were exiguous, forcefully exemplified by the statement that post-legislative scrutiny was not required, since 'the impact of the Bill will be both clear and limited'.[3] A greater mismatch between language and reality would be hard to find.

The government accepted that it would have to gain statutory approval, but rejected constraints on its negotiating position. Thus, it refused procedural constraints designed to impose reporting requirements during the negotiation process, and rejected also the amendment to the Bill in the House of Lords,[4] whereby the government would have been legally obliged to place a withdrawal agreement before Parliament prior to accepting or rejecting it.[5] It gave a political assurance that it would do this, while making clear that

[3] European Union (Notification of Withdrawal) Bill 2017, para 14.
[4] Hansard (7 March 2017) vol 779 col 1250.
[5] Hansard (13 March 2017) vol 623 col 38.

if Parliament rejected a withdrawal agreement, then the UK would exit the EU without an agreement and default to World Trade Organization rules.[6] In similar vein, it denied a substantive House of Lords' amendment to protect the rights of EU citizens living in the UK. The amendments failed in the House of Commons through a foreseeable concatenation of political circumstance: the great majority of Tories who voted to remain in the EU were unwilling to press amendments on the government; and the official Labour position was that it would not do anything to jeopardize ultimate enactment of the Bill, thereby reducing its political leverage in parliamentary debate to something approximating to zero.

The outcome of this saga may have been foreseeable, but it was not pre-ordained given our foundational constitutional axioms. Sovereignty resides with Parliament, and has done so for approximately 400 years. It does not reside with the executive. It is therefore constitutionally unarguable that Parliament could, at any time since 23 June 2016, have enacted a statute requiring the government to seek its approval before triggering Article 50. The statute would have trumped the prerogative, and Parliament could have imposed whatever procedural or substantive constraints that it felt were warranted. Parliament did not therefore need to await rescue by the courts.[7]

This begs the question as to why Parliament was quiescent in this respect, to which the answer is eclectic. Some MPs might genuinely have felt that the issue should, for reasons of principle, be left to the executive; others, particularly, hard Brexiteers, were committed functionally to the prerogative, since they were concerned at attempts to undo their victory in Parliament. The principal explanation was rather different. MPs were fearful of backlash from their constituents who had voted to leave, a fear reinforced by likely reaction from certain sections of the media. Much easier for MPs to remain largely silent on this, such that demands for Parliamentary voice rarely rose to whisper let alone clamour, and rely on the courts to give Parliament voice without the attendant political dangers of actively seeking it. Viewed from this perspective, the House of Commons' unwillingness to force amendments on the government was a continuation of this same theme.

---

[6] Prime Minister Theresa May sets out the Plan for Britain, including the 12 priorities that the UK government will use to negotiate Brexit (17 January 2017) 5 (Lancaster House Speech) https://www.gov.uk/government/speeches/the-governments-negotiating-objectives-for-exiting-the-eu-pm-speech; Hansard (7 February 2017) vol 621 col 272.

[7] I am fully mindful of the power wielded by the executive over the legislative process. It does not, however, alter the constitutional point made above. It is, moreover, doubtful in political terms whether the executive could have prevented serious consideration of such a Bill if MPs across the political divide had brought it to the House.

2. Negotiation of Withdrawal and Future Relations

2.1 Process

2.1.1 EU Level

Article 50(2) provides for negotiation of a withdrawal agreement, 'taking account of the framework for its future relationship with the Union'. There is a formal and informal dimension to this second stage of withdrawal.

The formal stage is set out in Article 50(2). The European Council provides the guidelines for negotiation, which frame discussions leading to the withdrawal agreement. It is the Commission, as affirmed by Article 218(3) TFEU, that conducts the detailed negotiation. The European Parliament has no formal role, but since it has a veto on the withdrawal agreement, its views will perforce be taken into account during the negotiation. It is the Council acting by qualified majority that concludes the agreement, after obtaining the consent of the European Parliament.

The informal dimension to the process is equally important. Foremost in this regard is the ordering of the negotiations, whether discussion of withdrawal and future trade relations should proceed in parallel, or whether there should be a phased ordering, such that discussion about the latter only commences when there has been sufficient progress on the former. The UK strongly favours parallel discussion, while the EU advocates phased ordering. The difference is readily explicable, since it affects the balance of power within the negotiations: parallelism would enable the UK to engage in trade-offs between the terms of withdrawal and future trade relations; the phased approach means that the EU can refuse to discuss trade relations until it has secured an acceptable withdrawal deal. The difference of view is apparent from the relevant documentation.

The UK's position was initially articulated in the Prime Minister's Lancaster House speech.[8] She emphasized the need for discussions concerning withdrawal and future trade to proceed in tandem when stating that: 'I want us to have reached an agreement about our future partnership by the time the 2-year Article 50 process has concluded'.[9] This sentiment was reinforced in the White Paper on Exit from the EU,[10] which stated that it was 'in no one's interests for there to be a cliff-edge for business or a threat to stability, as we

---

[8] Lancaster House Speech (n 6).   [9] ibid 10.
[10] The United Kingdom's Exit from and New Partnership with the European Union, Cm 9417 (2017).

change from our existing relationship to a new partnership with the EU'.[11] The point was reaffirmed in the Prime Minister's notification of withdrawal letter of 29 March 2017,[12] which stated that 'it is necessary to agree the terms of our future partnership alongside those our withdrawal from the European Union',[13] a sentiment that was thrice repeated in the letter.[14]

The response from President Tusk to the Prime Minister's letter was succinct in its rejection of parallelism. He outlined the fundamental principles that would inform the negotiations, which were: minimization of disruption caused by UK withdrawal; securing agreement on the rights of EU citizens living in the UK; ensuring that the UK honours its financial commitments; and avoiding a hard border between Northern Ireland and Ireland. He then continued in the following vein:[15]

These four issues are all part of the first phase of our negotiations. Once, and only once we have achieved sufficient progress on the withdrawal, can we discuss the framework for our future relationship. Starting parallel talks on all issues at the same time, as suggested by some in the UK, will not happen.

President Tusk reiterated this position before the European Council meeting in April 2017, stating that: 'before discussing our future, we must first sort out our past'.[16] The German Chancellor, Angela Merkel, reaffirmed this position,[17] as did the European Parliament.[18] The European Council formally endorsed the negotiation guidelines on 29 April 2017[19] and adopted the phased approach. The first phase is concerned with the withdrawal agreement, the 'disentanglement of the United Kingdom from the European Union'.[20] The second phase concerns future trade relations, which can only be finalized after the UK has left the EU; an overall understanding of the framework of this relationship may be agreed during the second phase, but 'preliminary and preparatory discussions to this end'[21] can only occur when the European

---

[11] ibid 12.2.

[12] Formal Notification of Withdrawal (29 March 2017) (Notification of Withdrawal) https://www.gov.uk/government/publications/prime-ministers-letter-to-donald-tusk-triggering-article-50.

[13] ibid 2.   [14] ibid 4, 5, 6.

[15] Remarks by President Donald Tusk on the next steps following the UK notification http://dsms.consilium.europa.eu/952/Actions/Newsletter.aspx?messageid=11790&customerid=16061&password=enc_3936444345424338_enc.

[16] Invitation letter by President Donald Tusk to the members of the European Council http://www.consilium.europa.eu/en/press/press-releases/2017/04/28-tusk-invitation-letter-euco-art50/.

[17] *BBC News* (27 April 2017) http://www.bbc.co.uk/news/world-europe-39730326.

[18] 'Red Lines on Brexit Negotiations' http://www.europarl.europa.eu/news/en/news-room/20170329IPR69054/red-lines-on-brexit-negotiations.

[19] European Council, Brussels (29 April 2017) EUCO XT 20004/17.   [20] ibid 4.

[21] ibid 5.

Council decides that sufficient progress has been made towards 'reaching a satisfactory agreement on the arrangements for an orderly withdrawal'.[22] The guidelines have, as will be seen below, been reaffirmed and rendered more specific in the Council's negotiating directives,[23] which were adopted based on Commission recommendations.[24]

2.1.2 UK Level

There are three important process issues at the UK level. The first concerns input by Parliament during the negotiations. The executive is under no legal obligation to keep Parliament informed during the negotiations. While the government has stated that it will 'continue to build a national consensus around our negotiating position by listening and talking to as many organisations, companies and institutions as possible',[25] it remains to be seen how far the executive chooses to inform Parliament during this period, and how far information is leaked. Parliament has established a select committee on Exiting the European Union.[26] Its brief is to consider the administration, expenditure and policy of the Department for Exiting the European Union, and it has published three reports thus far. There is in addition the House of Lords' Select Committee on the EU, which has undertaken studies on withdrawal,[27] and the House of Lords' Constitution Committee, which has analysed issues raised by what is now known as the European Union (Withdrawal) Bill.[28]

The second process issue concerns the role of the devolved areas in the negotiations. The Supreme Court decided that there was no legal obligation to secure the consent of the devolved legislatures before triggering Article 50.[29] Engagement of the devolved administrations is organized through the Joint Ministerial Committee (JMC),[30] and the JMC sub-committee on EU

---

[22] ibid.

[23] Council Decision (EU/Euratom) of 22 May 2017 authorising the opening of negotiations with the United Kingdom setting out the arrangements for its withdrawal from the European Union, Doc. XT21016/17.

[24] Recommendation for a Council Decision authorizing the Commission to open negotiations with the UK setting out the arrangements for its withdrawal from the EU, COM(2017) 218 final.

[25] White Paper (n 10) 1.6.

[26] http://www.parliament.uk/business/committees/committees-a-z/commons-select/exiting-the-european-union-committee/.

[27] http://www.parliament.uk/business/committees/committees-a-z/lords-select/eu-select-committee-/.

[28] http://www.parliament.uk/business/committees/committees-a-z/lords-select/constitution-committee/publications/.

[29] See *Miller* (n 1).

[30] Chaired in plenary by the prime minister and attended by the first ministers of Scotland and Wales and the first and deputy first ministers of Northern Ireland.

Negotiations (JMC (EN)).[31] The official government line is that the devolved administrations are fully engaged in Brexit preparations; that the deal will work for the whole UK; and that it will take into account the interests of the devolved regions.[32]

This does not, however, reflect political reality. There have been real tensions, because of differing views on hard and soft Brexit. The government opted for the former,[33] the devolved administrations for the latter. Thus Nicola Sturgeon, the Scottish First Minister, consistently maintained that Scotland's priority was to remain in the single market,[34] and this became Scottish government policy.[35] The same view was expressed by Wales.[36] The tensions were evident when the prime minister gave her Lancaster House speech, in which she opted for hard Brexit, two days before a JMC meeting, without having discussed Scotland's policy document released a month earlier. It prompted an angry response from Michael Russell, the Scottish Minister, who stated that Scotland 'must not be treated with contempt but as an equal partner in the negotiating process'; that 'Scotland overwhelmingly rejected a hard Brexit'; and that it was 'extremely disappointing that the Prime Minister chose to disregard the process and make a significant announcement about her position two days before the JMC even considered our paper'.[37] As Sionaidh Douglas-Scott noted, the reaction to JMC (EN) meetings by the devolved administrations has been one of 'frustration that their views were not being taken into account'.[38] The Westminster government's treatment of the devolved administrations was further in evidence in the withdrawal letter which, while acknowledging Northern Ireland as a special case, made no mention of special arrangements for Scotland and Wales.[39]

The third process issue concerns the government's approach if it does not like the way in which the negotiations are going. Much has been made of the prime minister's statement that 'no deal for Britain is better than a bad deal for Britain'.[40] This has been taken to mean that if the withdrawal agreement is

---

[31] Chaired by the Secretary of State for Exiting the European Union, with members from each of the UK devolved administrations.

[32] White Paper (n 10) 3.1.

[33] White Paper (n 10) 8.1–8.44; Notification of Withdrawal (n 12) 4.

[34] https://firstminister.gov.scot/fm-highlights-importance-of-single-market/; https://firstminister.gov.scot/joint-ministerial-committee-on-eu-referendum/; https://firstminister.gov.scot/3265-2/.

[35] Scottish Government, 'Scotland's Place in Europe' (December 2016) http://www.gov.scot/Resource/0051/00512073.pdf.

[36] Welsh Government, 'Securing Wales' Future: Transition from the European Union to a New Relationship with Europe' (January 2017) https://beta.gov.wales/sites/default/files/2017-02/31139%20Securing%20Wales%C2%B9%20Future_Version%202_WEB.pdf.

[37] https://news.gov.scot/news/jmc-meeting-on-brexit.

[38] S Douglas-Scott in this volume. [39] Notification of Withdrawal (n 12).

[40] Lancaster House Speech (n 6) 13.

not to the liking of the UK, it may simply walk away, with the consequence that it will default to WTO rules. The statement was made in the context of a trade deal that was not to the liking of the UK.[41] The UK documents are, however, predicated on parallelism. If this assumption were true, a decision to leave the negotiating table could be based on conclusions as to the desirability of the overall package on offer, withdrawal and trade agreement combined. Parallelism is, however, very unlikely to occur. Even if trade negotiations begin within the two-year period this will be a long process, such that the UK will not know whether the trade deal is worth taking when it needs to decide on acceptance of the withdrawal agreement.

The 'no deal' scenario has, moreover, been criticized by the select committee on Exiting the European Union. It was of the view that this would be bad for the UK and the EU, and it was critical because the government had not explained what terms would be demonstrably worse for the UK than 'no deal'. It was therefore incumbent on the Government to 'conduct a thorough assessment of the economic, legal and other implications of leaving the EU at the end of the Article 50 period with 'no deal' in place'.[42]

2.2 Substance

2.2.1 Withdrawal Agreement: Likely Content

There is no rigid, predefined divide between the two agreements contemplated by Article 50, save for the fact that the withdrawal agreement is essentially backward looking, while the trade agreement is essentially forward looking. The divide could nonetheless vary significantly, given the inherent ambiguity of Article 50(2), to the effect that the withdrawal agreement can take account of the framework for the state's future relationship with the EU. The reality is, however, that hard Brexit naturally inclines to a thin withdrawal agreement, with many issues left for resolution through the future trade agreement. The withdrawal agreement is therefore likely to cover the minimum for a divorce, money, people, and borders. These issues were identified in the European Council guidelines, and Council negotiating directives.[43]

Money matters and will feature prominently in the withdrawal negotiations. The financial settlement will cover liabilities, including contingent liabilities, concerning the Union budget; the termination of the UK's

---

[41] White Paper (n 10) 12.3.
[42] Select Committee on Exiting the European Union, 'The Government's Negotiating Objectives: The White Paper' (HC 1125, 2017) 293.
[43] European Council (n 19) 8]–21]; Council Decision (n 23) Annex 1.

membership in all EU institutions or bodies; the UK's participation in EU funds dealing with specific EU policies; and the cost of moving EU agencies currently located in the UK.[44] The Council negotiating directives mandate detailed supervision over payment of these liabilities,[45] the upper estimates being in the range of €60 billion or perhaps more. The ultimate bill will be determined as much by politics as by accountancy, since both sides will be playing to their respective political constituencies.

People matter too, pre-eminently so, and the withdrawal agreement will address the rights of EU citizens living in the UK, and UK citizens residing in the EU. Both sides regard this issue as important. It featured prominently in UK documentation.[46] President Tusk emphasized the need to think of people first, and to settle 'their status and situations after the withdrawal with reciprocal, enforceable and non-discriminatory guarantees',[47] and MEPs laid similar stress on this issue.[48] While there is, therefore, consensus on the need to resolve this issue the devil is, as always, in the detail. There are background political pressures, since hard Brexiteers, committed to control over immigration, will not readily accept a solution that accords large numbers of recent EU citizens the right to stay in the UK, with access to social/health care benefits. The European Council guidelines stressed, however, that guarantees for EU citizens in the UK 'must be effective, enforceable, non-discriminatory and comprehensive, including the right to acquire permanent residence after a continuous period of five years of legal residence'.[49] This has been further emphasized in the Council negotiating directives, which specified that the agreement must cover economic and non-economic migrants, and their family members. It set out a detailed list of rights that must be secured, including rights to residence and work; the right to take-up and pursue self-employment; rights to social welfare benefits; equality in relation to social and tax advantages; and the continued recognition of qualifications.[50]

Borders constitute the third topic in the withdrawal agreement, with the focus on the need to avoid a hard border between Northern Ireland and Ireland.[51] This was a constant feature in communications from the UK.[52] It was echoed by President Tusk, who spoke of the need to 'seek flexible and

---

[44] Council Decision (n 23) Annex 1, 24–26.   [45] ibid 30.
[46] Lancaster House Speech (n 6) 7; White Paper (n 10) 6.1–6.4; Notification of Withdrawal (n 12) 4.
[47] Remarks by President Donald Tusk (n 15).
[48] Red Lines on Brexit Negotiations (n 18).   [49] European Council (n 19) 8.
[50] Council Decision (n 23) Annex 1, 21–22.
[51] See the discussion by Doyle and Connolly in this volume.
[52] White Paper (n 10) 4.1–4.10; Notification of Withdrawal (n 12) 5.

creative solutions aiming at avoiding a hard border between Northern Ireland and Ireland',[53] and the European Parliament.[54]

There is, therefore, much to resolve concerning money, people, and borders. There are, in addition, further issues, such as cases pending before the CJEU at the date of withdrawal, and administrative issues pending before the Commission.[55] There is, moreover, the question of dispute resolution under the withdrawal agreement. The European Council guidelines state that the choice of this mechanism should be made 'bearing in mind the Union's interest to effectively protect its autonomy and its legal order, including the role of the Court of Justice of the European Union'.[56] This is reinforced by the Council Negotiating Directives, which state that the CJEU must have jurisdiction in relation to the terms of the withdrawal agreement that concern EU law, including citizens' rights and financial liabilities, and that an alternative adjudicative mechanism would only be acceptable for disputes on other matters if it offered equivalent guarantees of independence and impartiality.[57]

2.2.2 Future Relations: Likely Content

The agreement on future relations that is envisaged by Article 50(2) may well go beyond trade issues to encompass matters such as such security cooperation and the like.[58] The present discussion will focus on the trade dimension, which is central to these future relations. The conclusion of free trade agreements is a complex process at the best of times, and this is not the best of times. Even if a withdrawal agreement covering the preceding issues is secured within the two-year time frame, the European Council guidelines on trade are framed in terms of 'an overall understanding on the framework of the future relationship',[59] and the fact that the discussion during the second phase of the negotiations will be 'preliminary and preparatory'.[60] The Council will produce a more detailed negotiating mandate for the second phase if and when matters get to that stage.[61]

The UK government made the decision not to seek membership of the single market, since it required acceptance of free movement of people. The government also decided not to pursue a customs union deal, since it would unduly circumscribe the UK's ability to enter trading arrangements with

---

[53] Remarks by President Donald Tusk (n 15).
[54] Red Lines on Brexit Negotiations (n 18).
[55] Council Negotiating Directives (n 23) Annex 1, 34–38.
[56] European Council (n 19) 17.
[57] Council Decision (n 23) Annex 1, 42.
[58] See D Curtin in the present volume.   [59] European Council (n 19) 5.
[60] ibid.   [61] Council Decision (n 23) Annex 1, 19.

other parties. These choices have consequences, most notably that the future trade relationship to which Article 50 adverts is a clean slate. The UK government portrayed a far-reaching and comprehensive trade agreement as something that should follow readily from the commonality in regulation between the UK and the EU, coupled with enlightened economic self-interest of both parties. Thus, Theresa May, echoing earlier statements,[62] spoke of a bold and ambitious free trade agreement, while seeking to facilitate its passage by noting that the UK and EU have the same regulatory standards given the UK's membership of the EU.[63] This is a natural negotiating stance, but it does not capture reality.

The European Council guidelines emphasize the EU's interest in negotiating a future trade deal, subject to the qualifications that it cannot amount to participation in the single market; that it excludes participation in the single market on a sector-by-sector approach; and that a 'non-member of the Union, that does not live up to the same obligations as a member, cannot have the same rights and enjoy the same benefits as a member'.[64] The guidelines also state that any trade deal must ensure 'a level playing field, notably in terms of competition and state aid, and in this regard encompass safeguards against unfair competitive advantages through, inter alia, tax, social, environmental and regulatory measures and practices',[65] thereby responding to the UK's suggestion that it might become a low-tax haven if it did not obtain a trade agreement from the EU.

It is important to realize that free trade deals do not come in only one size. The core of a free trade agreement is the abolition of tariffs and quotas on goods. Beyond that the content is diverse in the extreme. It may be relatively simple, but normally is not, since FTAs cover issues such as technical barriers to trade, phytosanitary matters, rules of origin, investment, safeguards, cross-border trade, the environment, customs administration, and the like. The more ambitious trade agreements aim for liberalization in areas such as services and investment, cover intellectual property rights and competition, and include provisions on labour and environmental standards.[66] The US–Australia agreement is 264 pages long, and this is about par for the course, with intricate detail filling every page. This is dwarfed by the EU–Canada Comprehensive Economic and Trade Agreement, CETA, which took seven years to negotiate. It is in excess of 1,500 pages, and this is so even though its coverage of services is limited.[67]

---

[62] White Paper (n 10) 8.2.   [63] Notification of Withdrawal (n 12) 5.
[64] European Council (n 19) 1, 21.   [65] ibid.
[66] http://www.trade.gov/fta/; https://ustr.gov/trade-agreements/free-trade-agreements/australian-fta.
[67] http://ec.europa.eu/trade/policy/in-focus/ceta/.

The economic reality is that an FTA in a post-Brexit world with the EU would have to include services, since if it did not then its significance would be greatly diminished. This is reflected in the withdrawal letter, which was framed in terms of a bold and ambitious FTA that would include financial services and network industries.[68] The government's oft-repeated desire is that the FTA should be concluded within the two-year period.[69] This is unlikely to occur, given the complexity of the negotiations required to secure such a far-reaching deal. This is so even if discussion of the trade agreement takes place in parallel with the withdrawal agreement, which is unlikely to occur. It could take anywhere in the order of five to six years, before the terms of an ambitious FTA are secured. Such an agreement may, moreover, be a mixed agreement, the implications of which will be considered in stage three. There are many other complexities concerning UK–EU trade relationships in a post-Brexit world, which go beyond the scope of this chapter.[70] The UK cannot conclude FTAs with other countries while still in the EU.

3. Outcomes

3.1 Process

3.1.1 EU Level

The process for the conclusion of the withdrawal agreement is clear: a withdrawal agreement is concluded on behalf of the EU by the Council acting by qualified majority, after obtaining the consent of the European Parliament. Treaty rights and obligations apply until the agreement is concluded, or until two years from the date of notification, unless the European Council unanimously agrees to extend that period, and the withdrawing state also wishes to extend the time frame.

The process requirements for a trade agreement of the kind desired by the UK are more problematic, because if the subject matter of the agreement went beyond the EU's exclusive external competence it would be a mixed agreement under EU law.[71] It would then require ratification by the twenty-seven

---

[68] Notification of Withdrawal (n 12) 5.
[69] White Paper (n 10) 12.2–12.3; Notification of Withdrawal (n 12) 6.
[70] See G Sacerdoti in this volume.
[71] P Koutrakos and C Hillion, *Mixed Agreements Revisited: The EU and Its Member States in the World* (Hart Publishing 2010).

Member States, plus the regions of some states, as well as the EU.[72] However, the CJEU's expansive interpretation of the EU's common commercial policy and exclusive external competence renders this less likely.[73]

3.1.2 UK Level

It has been contended, in what is known as the *Three Knights'* Opinion,[74] that the enactment of the European Union (Notification of Withdrawal) Act 2017 does not suffice to entitle the executive to commit to a withdrawal agreement, or to leave the EU in the absence of an agreement, without securing statutory approval.[75] This decision, it is argued, can only be made when the consequences for the rights of British citizens and businesses are clear, which cannot be known two years in advance of withdrawal.[76] Parliamentary sovereignty and the principle of legality therefore require Parliament 'expressly to authorise withdrawal on the terms agreed with the European Union, or to authorise withdrawal if no acceptable terms can be agreed'.[77] The 2017 Act authorized the prime minister to notify the UK's intent to leave the EU, but did not remove rights, or change domestic law,[78] hence the need for a further statute.[79] It is argued, moreover, that Article 50 permits a Member State to revoke notification unilaterally if the Member State's constitutional requirements are not met.[80]

Mark Elliott[81] takes issue with the argument that only legislation enacted at the end of the negotiation process can authorize Brexit. He contends that this is inconsistent with the reasoning in *Miller*. Elliott argues that it was central to the *Miller* decision that notification could lead to the loss of rights associated with EU membership, there was a causal link between the two, and that it was for this reason that the Supreme Court decided that Parliament had to authorize the pulling of the trigger. The reasoning in the *Three Knights'* Opinion was, says Elliott, premised on the claim that no loss of rights was occasioned by triggering Article 50, because rights could not be removed except by legislation enacted when the terms of withdrawal were clear. Mark

---

[72] Opinion 2/15, *Conclusion of the Free Trade Agreement between the European Union and Singapore* (21 December 2016 Advocate General Sharpston).

[73] ibid (16 May 2017).

[74] 'In the Matter of Article 50 of the Treaty on European Union.' The title is explicable because three of the authors are renowned EU scholars, who are also knights; Sir David Edward, Sir Francis Jacobs, and Sir Jeremy Lever. There are two other authors, Helen Mountfield QC and Gerry Facena QC.

[75] ibid 2.i., 23, 35.   [76] ibid 2.ii, 20–21, 35.   [77] ibid 2.iii, 35.

[78] ibid 21.   [79] ibid 22, 36–62.   [80] ibid 2.vi, 2.vii.

[81] Mark Elliott, 'The *Three Knights'* Opinion on Brexit: A Response' https://publiclawforevery-one.com/2017/02/17/the-three-knights-opinion-on-brexit-a-response/.

Elliott contends that this is inconsistent with the premise in *Miller* that notification in itself could take away rights.

The judicial reaction to any such legal challenge remains to be seen, and it must be recognized that even if a court were to decide in accord with the *Three Knights'* Opinion the government could probably secure the requisite statutory approval without undue difficulty. There is, however, no inconsistency between the reasoning in *Miller* and that in the Opinion. The former stands for the proposition that parliamentary authorization should be required before triggering withdrawal, because of the impact that this could have on rights. It is unclear what rights would be impacted before negotiations start, but the normative premise is that Parliament might not wish to begin such a process because of the possible implications for rights. The reasoning in the Opinion stands for the proposition that statutory authorization should be required when the detailed impact on rights is known. The normative premise at this stage is that Parliament might believe that the detailed agreement placed before it should not be made because the effect on rights, combined with the other terms of the agreement, was unacceptable. To put the same point in a different way, statutory authorization at the first stage ensures parliamentary voice as a condition precedent to initiating withdrawal, since the impact on rights might be felt to be too far-reaching to warrant inception of withdrawal talks at all; statutory authorization at the second stage ensures such parliamentary voice as a condition precedent for concluding withdrawal, since it thereby enables Parliament to make a fully-informed assessment as to the desirability of the withdrawal agreement when the actual impact on rights is known. There is therefore no inconsistency between these two propositions.[82]

3.2 Substance: Revocability

There has been considerable discussion as to whether a withdrawal notice can be revoked prior to the end of the two-year period.[83] The issue can only

---

[82] It would in principle be open to Parliament to authorize notification through a statute that made it unequivocally clear that Parliament was content for a withdrawal agreement to be concluded that impacted on rights without knowing, when the legislation was enacted, the detail of the rights that would be affected. Such a statute might be undesirable, but if it had been expressly drafted in this way it would then obviate the need for subsequent legislation when the detail of the impact of the withdrawal agreement on rights became known. The European Union (Notification of Withdrawal) Act 2017 was not drafted in this manner. To the contrary, it merely provided the prime minister with discretion to trigger notification, which she then exercised.

[83] In favour of revocability: C Streeten, 'Putting the Toothpaste Back in the Tube: Can an Article 50 Notification Be Revoked?' *UK Constitutional Law Blog* (13 July 2016); A Dashwood, 'Invoking Article 50' *InFacts* (18 July 2016); House of Lords Select Committee on the Constitution, 'The

be finally determined by the CJEU. I favour revocability for the following reasons.

First, the decision to withdraw must be in accord with the constitutional requirements of the Member State. These may include parliamentary approval of the withdrawal agreement, or a referendum when such terms are known, assuming that these occur within the two-year time frame. If the notice to withdraw could not be revoked, then a state could be forced to leave the EU contrary to its constitutional requirements, since parliamentary approval, or the positive referendum vote, might not be forthcoming. This would be inconsistent with Article 50(1). A national constitutional court might, moreover, conclude that an interpretation of Article 50 that rendered national constitutional requirements otiose precluded ratification of the Lisbon Treaty.

Secondly, irrevocability could have far-reaching negative consequences for the Member State. Irrevocability would mean that nothing could be done to address a financial crisis caused by a withdrawal notice. It would also mean that if there were an election during the two-year period, a successful pro-remain party could do nothing to prevent withdrawal.

Thirdly, irrevocability could also have far-reaching negative consequences for the EU, for example where notice of withdrawal led to serious economic consequences across the Union. There would, moreover, be considerable gain to the EU if a Member State decided to remain in the EU when on the brink of departure, having realized the benefit of membership. This is based on the assumption that the state is acting bona fide and in accord with the principle of sincere cooperation.

Process of Withdrawing from the European Union' evidence of D Wyatt and D Edward (HL Paper 138, 2016); J-C Piris, 'Article 50 Is Not for Ever and the UK Could Change Its Mind' *Financial Times* (1 September 2016); A Sari, 'Biting the Bullet: Why the UK Is Free to Revoke Its Withdrawal Notification under Article 50 TEU' *UK Constitutional Law Blog* (17 October 2016); P Craig, 'Brexit: Foundational Constitutional and Interpretive Principles: II' *OxHRH Blog* (28 October 2016); T Tridimas, 'Article 50: An Endgame without an End?' (2016) *King's Law Journal* 297; A Sari, 'Reversing a Withdrawal Notification under Article 50 TEU: Can the Member States Change their Mind?' Exeter Law School Working Paper Series (19 November 2016); P Eeckhout and E Frantziou, 'Brexit and Article 50 TEU: A Constitutionalist Reading' UCL European Institute Working Paper (December 2016); *Three Knights'* Opinion (n 74). See also the Speech by President Donald Tusk at the European Policy Centre conference Speech 575/16 (13 October 2016); J-C Junker, 'Answer given by President Juncker on behalf of the Commission in response to European Parliamentary question p-008603/2016' (17 January 2017). Against revocability: N Barber, T Hickman, and J King, 'Pulling the Article 50 "Trigger": Parliament's Indispensable Role' *UK Constitutional Law Blog* (27 June 2016); J Rylatt, 'The Irrevocability of an Article 50 Notification: Lex Specialis and the Irrelevance of the Purported Customary Right to Unilaterally Revoke' *UK Constitutional Law Blog* (27 July 2016); S Smismans, 'About the Revocability of Withdrawal: Why the EU (Law) Interpretation of Article 50 Matters' *UK Constitutional Law Blog* (29 November 2016).

Fourthly, irrevocability does not comport with the drafting history of Article 50,[84] which was derived from Article I-60 of the Constitutional Treaty, and was headed 'Voluntary Withdrawal from the Union'. Lord Kerr, who was responsible for drafting that provision with Giuliano Amato, has stated that it was intended to provide a procedural framework for the pre-existing right of a Member State to leave the EU of its own free will, and that such a decision was revocable.[85]

Fifthly, the preceding arguments draw support from the Vienna Convention on the Law of Treaties (VCLT), Article 68 of which provides that: 'a notification or instrument provided for in article 65 or 67 may be revoked at any time before it takes effect'. Article 65 VCLT covers a withdrawal notice. There is disagreement as to whether this is also customary law. The present argument is not dependent on an affirmative answer to that point. The argument is that the architecture of Article 50 TEU is informed by VCLT principles; and that the VCLT shows that there is nothing illegitimate about revocability. Notification under Article 50 TEU only takes legal effect when the withdrawal agreement is concluded, or two years has elapsed.

Finally, it is argued that revocability would allow a state to revoke in the twenty-third month, make a new notice of withdrawal, and thus begin another two-year cycle. This argument is based on the implausible assumption that the state would get a better deal second time round. The other Member States would, however, regard such action as illegitimate, and refuse to shift from the pre-existing offer. The courts could, moreover, prevent such abuse. The CJEU could conclude that such behaviour was designed to circumvent the two-year time period; that it undermined the need for unanimity to extend that period; with the consequence that the state would only have one month before the two-year period expired. This argument could be reinforced by the principle of sincere cooperation in Article 4(3) TEU.

If the notice given under Article 50 were to be revocable there would be further inquiry as to whether it should be revocable unilaterally, by qualified majority or by unanimity. My own preference is for unilateral revocability, although a requirement of qualified majority, which is the test for EU assent to a withdrawal agreement, could be used if it were felt that this was required to protect the EU's interest.

The importance of this issue to the UK political process cannot, however, be doubted. If Article 50 were revocable then Parliament could in principle

---

[84] For analysis of the *travaux préparatoires* in the Constitutional Treaty see Eeckhout and Frantziou (n 83).

[85] BBC website (3 November 2016) http://www.bbc.co.uk/news/uk-scotland-scotland-politics-37852628.

decide to revoke the notification of withdrawal, and/or call a second referendum, but the interpretation of Article 50 as irrevocable means that Parliament has no leverage at this point, since once Article 50 is triggered there is no turning back.

3.3 Substance: Transition

While there has been considerable discussion concerning revocability, this is not so in relation to transitional agreements. In truth, the government has equivocated in this regard. It has contended that withdrawal and trade agreements can be concluded in two years.[86] It has also spoken of the need for 'implementation periods to adjust in a smooth and orderly way to new arrangements'.[87] While the political reality is that a transitional agreement may be needed, its legality is uncertain.[88] The European Council spoke of a transition agreement to the extent to which it was necessary and legally possible.[89] It might assume three different forms.

3.3.1 *Transition and Change*

A transitional agreement might be directed to the future, providing a bridge between the status quo and the future agreement, the details of which may not be concluded within two years. This is the assumption in the Council negotiating directives.[90] It might be conceived as part of the withdrawal agreement, or as independent thereof. There are, however, difficulties in both respects.

There are substantive issues as to how far transitional provisions concerning future trade could be appended to the withdrawal agreement. Article 50(2) states that the withdrawal agreement can take account of the state's future relationship with the EU, which undoubtedly contains interpretive leeway, but if transitional provisions are to be of practical use they will have to be detailed.

This leads to a procedural difficulty, which is that detailed transitional provisions smoothing future trade relations might not fall within the EU's exclusive competence. They would require ratification by all Member States, following the logic of mixed agreements, and hence could not readily be part of a withdrawal agreement, although the CJEU's expansive interpretation

---

[86] Notification of Withdrawal (n 12) 6.   [87] ibid 4.

[88] See also Pavlos Eleftheriadis, '"Parallel Sources": How to Construct the Transitional Brexit Arrangement' https://www.law.ox.ac.uk/business-law-blog/blog/2017/02/how-make-transitional-brexit-arrangement.

[89] European Council (n 19) 6.

[90] Council Negotiating Directives (n 23) Annex 1, 19.

of exclusive external competence renders this less likely.[91] If ratification in all Member States as well as the EU were required this could lead to considerable delay, hence undermining the rationale for transitional provisions. This problem would persist even if the transitional agreement were a separate agreement.

3.3.2 Transition and Continuity

The concept of transition might alternatively connote continuation of some EU treaty provisions, pending conclusion of a future agreement. If there is no meaningful discussion of future trade relations within the two-year period the concept of transition could not connote a bridge between the old and the new, since by definition the content of the new order would not be known. The existing EU rules provide a framework that would obviate the dangers of the cliff-edge. There will be political challenges in securing acceptance of any deal in the UK and the EU. Such a transitional agreement might be part of the withdrawal agreement, or independent thereof, but there are legal difficulties.

There are substantive issues as to compatibility with the EU legal order. International agreements are regularly scrutinized in this regard.[92] It would therefore have to be decided whether continuation of some EU provisions was compatible with the EU Treaty, and its underlying principles, which would be determined by the CJEU. The CJEU would, moreover, have jurisdiction over the transitional provisions. Denial of its interpretive authority over Treaty provisions during a transitional period would be regarded as infringing the autonomy of the EU legal order.[93] As the European Council guidelines noted, prolongation of the EU acquis 'would require existing Union regulatory, budgetary, supervisory, judiciary and enforcement instruments and structures to apply'.[94]

There are, moreover, procedural problems if the transitional provisions are appended to the withdrawal agreement. Article 50(3) provides that the

---

[91] Opinion 2/15 (n 73).

[92] Opinion 1/00, *Proposed Agreement between the European Community and non-Member States on the establishment of a European Common Aviation Area* [2000] ECR I-3498, 12–13; Opinion 1/91, *Draft agreement between the Community, on the one hand, and the countries of the European Free Trade Association, on the other, relating to the creation of the European Economic Area*, EU:C:1991:490, 61–65; Opinion 1/92, *Draft agreement between the Community, on the one hand, and the countries of the European Free Trade Association, on the other, relating to the creation of the European Economic Area*, EU:C:1992:189, 32, 41; Opinion 2/13, *Draft international agreement—Accession of the European Union to the European Convention for the Protection of Human Rights and Fundamental Freedoms*, EU:C:2014:2454, 201.

[93] Opinion 2/13 (n 92) 205. [94] European Council (n 19) 6.

Treaties cease to apply to the Member State from the date when the withdrawal agreement enters into force. This creates a Catch 22. The agreement must be legally in force for the transitional provisions to apply. However, when the agreement enters into force Article 50 stipulates that the Treaties cease to apply. There is no provision allowing some of the Treaty articles to continue pending completion of a trade agreement at an unspecified future date.

It is, moreover, questionable whether a withdrawal agreement could perpetuate some provisions of membership beyond two years, given that the voting rules for the withdrawal agreement only require a qualified majority, whereas unanimity is the criterion for extension of the time to secure a withdrawal agreement over and beyond two years. A withdrawal agreement concluded by qualified majority that did not terminate all the withdrawing state's rights and obligations on the date when the agreement took effect could be regarded as circumventing the unanimity requirement in Article 50(3) for an extension beyond the two-year period.

3.3.3 *Transition, Change and Continuity*

The third possibility is that a transitional agreement is in part continuation of the past, in part a window to the future. This is likely, given that the first option is predicated on the assumption that the future trade relationship has been worked out to some degree. There may, however, be scant by way of agreement on future trade relations within the two-year period, or the terms may be exiguous in the extreme, such that the transition would perforce be directed in part towards continuation with the EU status quo, and in part to smoothing the path towards whatever might have been concluded on trade relations. The legal concerns associated with transition and change, and those associated with transition and continuity, would both be relevant. It may well be that the best way to secure transition pending conclusion of an FTA with the EU would be for the UK to join EFTA and the EEA for a period of time.

4. Conclusion

The Brexit negotiations will be an acute mix of the political and the legal. It remains to be seen whether a deal is secured. The trajectories are more complex than commonly imagined.

The conclusion could be no withdrawal agreement, and no trade agreement. The consequence would be a plethora of unresolved issues concerning matters such as the UK's financial liabilities, the rights of EU citizens in the UK, and UK citizens in the EU. The UK would default to WTO trade rules, and a future EU trade relationship would be more difficult if the talks on withdrawal were acrimonious and unresolved.

The conclusion could be a withdrawal agreement dealing with the issues adumbrated above, but scant progress on future trade relations. Much would then turn on whether a transitional agreement on trade could be concluded. If it could not, then the WTO would become applicable on trade matters pending conclusion of a trade deal between the UK and the EU.

The third possibility is that a withdrawal agreement and a comprehensive trade agreement can be secured within the two-year period. The likelihood of this transpiring is, however, remote, given the phased approach to the Brexit negotiations, coupled with the fact that a comprehensive trade agreement will require lengthy discussion.

4

The Prospects: The UK Trade Regime with the EU and the World

Options and Constraints Post-Brexit

Giorgio Sacerdoti

1. Introduction

The UK government has indicated that it intends to maintain after Brexit the existing 'deeply integrated trade and economic relationship between the UK and the EU', while at the same time not seeking to remain part of the EU single market, or to establish a customs union with the EU. The EU Guidelines for Brexit negotiations under Article 50 of the TEU, on the other hand, have made clear that, as to substance, a non-member of the Union cannot enjoy the same benefits as a member, nor participate in the single market based on a sector-by-sector approach. As to timing, the position of the EU is that while work on an agreement on trade relations can be initiated pending the Article 50 TEU negotiations it can be finalized only 'once the UK is no longer a Member of the EU'. As a consequence, establishing a trade regime 'as frictionless as possible' as aimed at by the UK appears problematic.

Against this uncertain outlook, this chapter highlights what type of post-Brexit trade agreement might be envisaged between the EU and the UK, considering the rules of the WTO notably as to free trade agreements (FTAs). The frontier traffic exception in GATT could be a basis for avoiding, as both parties desire, re-establishing a hard border between the Republic of Ireland and Northern Ireland. As to future UK trade relations with third countries, the chapter looks first at those with the many countries with which the EU has bilateral agreements in place to which the UK is part as member of the EU. Based on several legal and political reasons the conclusion is that the UK could not maintain its membership in them, even if it so wished, except for agreeing some kind of transitory regime with the non-EU partners.

The Prospects: The UK Trade Regime with the EU and the World: Options and Constraints Post-Brexit. First edition. Giorgio Sacerdoti © Giorgio Sacerdoti 2017. Published 2017 by Oxford University Press.

As to the future trade relations between the UK and other WTO members, this contribution considers that the UK will retain its status as a full 'original' member of the WTO and that its schedule of concessions (mainly customs duties) will be initially that of the EU in place at the date of Brexit. A delicate issue will be represented, however, by the apportionment between the EU and the UK of EU tariff-rate quotas for some agricultural products, which will imply negotiations by both the EU and the UK with third countries that currently benefit from them. Finally, the UK will be freely able after Brexit to negotiate FTAs with any WTO member, notably with the US. For as long as the EU–UK post-Brexit trade regime is not defined it will, however, be difficult for the UK to finalize any such deal, both for legal reasons and because the terms of the UK–EU agreement will impact the conditions of competition on the UK market for goods and services originating from other WTO members. This will make it difficult for them to establish beforehand the exact commercial benefits of a FTA with the UK.

2. UK–EU Post-Brexit Possible Trade Regime

2.1 UK Objectives versus the EU's Guidelines for Brexit Negotiations

The Brexit White Paper of 2 February 2017 has clarified the aims that the UK government pursues as to the trade (and other) relationship it wishes to establish with the EU at 27 following its withdrawal from the EU. This has been further clarified by the official letter of 29 March 2017, by which the UK has notified the European Council of its decision to leave the EU, in conformity with Article 50 of the TEU. Within a few days, the European Council's guidelines to the Commission for negotiating with the UK, as provided in Article 50, have been issued, thus allowing a clearer picture of the flexibilities and also limits that the UK will encounter in trying to accomplish its objectives.

In her speech of 17 January 2017, the UK Prime Minister had set twelve principles that will guide the UK government 'in fulfilling the democratic will of the people of the UK'. The objects of Principle 8 'Ensuring free trade with Europe' are spelled out as follows: 'We will forge a new strategic partnership with the EU, including a wide reaching, bold and ambitious free trade agreement and will seek a mutually beneficial new customs agreement with the EU'.[1]

---

[1] To realize the importance of this objective let's not forget that 45% of UK exports are towards the rest of the EU. By contrast, the share of exports to the UK on the total varies for major EU

The objects of Principle 9 'Securing new trade agreements with other countries' are: 'We will forge ambitious free trade relationships across the world'.

Since it takes two to tango, the nature of the relationship to be established with the EU depends of course on the EU response and objectives and on the outcome of a complex negotiation that includes several other issues. The European Council has made clear that the EU has three paramount objectives in the Article 50 negotiations: ensuring the rights of EU citizens presently residing in the UK and those of UK citizens living in the EU; settling the financial obligations of the UK; and ensuring that no hard border will be re-established between the Republic of Ireland and Northern Ireland. Procedurally, the Council Decision authorizing the Commission to open negotiations with the UK foresees that negotiations on the framework for the future relationship should be identified in a second phase of the negotiations under Article 50, once the Brexit negotiations have advanced substantially.

The EU Guidelines do not make it easy for the UK to pursue its trade objectives to have an open flow of goods while being out of the EU single market or the customs union, although 'The European Council welcomes and shares the United Kingdom's desire to establish a close partnership between the Union and the United Kingdom after its departure'.[2] The Guidelines acknowledge that the 'British government has indicated that it will not seek to remain in the single market, but would like to pursue an ambitious free trade agreement with the European Union. Based on the Union's interests, the European Council stands ready to initiate work towards such an agreement, to be finalised and concluded once the United Kingdom is no longer a Member State'.[3] Following the 8 June 2017 elections, the UK government has not changed its position not to seek to remain a member of the single market, nor to aim at establishing a full customs union with the EU.

The EU Guidelines 'reiterate' in non-ambiguous terms in Core Principle 1 that: 'any agreement with the United Kingdom will have to be based on a balance of rights and obligations, and ensure a level-playing field. Preserving the integrity of the Single Market excludes participation based on a sector-by-sector approach. A non-member of the Union, that does not live up to the same obligations as a member, cannot have the same rights and enjoy the same benefits as a member'.[4] The European Parliament on 5 April 2017 approved these negotiating objectives for the pending talks. Thus, both the European Parliament and European Council objectives state that the UK will

---

countries between 14% (Ireland) and less than 6% for Italy, with Germany around 8%. 16% of UK exports (goods and services) are directed to the US and less than 4% to China (2014, UK White Book, Table 9.2).

[2] European Council Guidelines, para 18.   [3] ibid para 19.   [4] ibid para 1.

not have similar or better benefits as a third country as it had as a Member State of the EU.

2.2 What Features for 'An Ambitious and Comprehensive Free Trade Agreement and a New Customs Agreement' Aimed by the UK Government?

It is therefore difficult at the moment to highlight what type of relations will be established post-Brexit. While the UK has not specified the legal features of the new trade framework it seeks with the EU, stressing rather its aims to maintain the existing 'deeply integrated trade and economic relationship between the UK and the EU', it has made clear that it does not intend to remain part of the single market. This would entail accepting the four basic freedoms of the single market: free movement of goods, services, capital, and people as the EEA countries (Norway, Iceland, and Liechtenstein have accepted), the UK objecting especially to the last one. The UK has also ruled out becoming part of a customs union with the EU, as is the case for Turkey, because such a scheme would curtail the UK's ability freely to establish its trade relations with the world within the existing World Trade Organization (WTO) system and oblige the UK to accept fully the EU customs regime.[5]

In her letter triggering the Article 50 process, the UK Prime Minister has written that: 'The UK wants to agree with the European Union a deep and special partnership that takes in both economic and security cooperation ... If however, we leave the European Union without an agreement the default position is that we would have to trade on World Trade Organization terms'. As to the future relationship with EU, the White Paper under Principle 8 explains: 'The Government will prioritize securing the freest and most frictionless trade possible in goods and services between the UK and the EU. We will not be seeking membership of the Single Market, but will pursue instead a new strategic partnership with the EU, including an ambitious and comprehensive Free Trade Agreement and a new customs agreement'.

As to the positive features of the new agreement, the White Paper is vague, and probably it could not be otherwise: 'This should include a new customs

---

[5] See generally Jennifer Hillman and Gary Horlick (eds), 'Legal Aspects of Brexit—Implications of the United Kingdom's Decision to Withdraw from the European Union' (2017) http://iielaw.org. For a fresh evaluation of the UK options after the 8 June 2017 elections, which have reinvigorated the supporters of a 'soft Brexit' see Michael Emerson, 'What's next after Theresa May's spectacular own goal?' CEPS Paper (12 June 2017) www.ceps.eu/publications. The EU-Turkey custom union does not cover agriculture however.

agreement with the EU, which will help to support our aim of trade with the EU that is as frictionless as possible … That agreement may take in elements of current Single Market arrangements in certain areas as it makes no sense to start again from scratch when the UK and the remaining Member States have adhered to the same rules for so many years. Such an arrangement would be on a fully reciprocal basis and in our mutual interests'.[6]

As mentioned above, the EU is, however, not willing to allow the UK to cherry pick those parts of the single market regime, such as 'financial passporting', which best suits the UK interests, rejecting other elements. The EU Guidelines specify that: 'Any free trade agreement should be balanced, ambitious and wide-ranging. It cannot, however, amount to participation in the Single Market or parts thereof, as this would undermine its integrity and proper functioning. It must ensure a level playing field, notably in terms of competition and state aid, and in this regard encompass safeguards against unfair competitive advantages through, inter alia, tax, social, environmental and regulatory measures and practices'.[7]

Some more detailed indications as to the UK's aims are found in the specific sub-section of the UK White Paper 'A mutually beneficial new customs arrangement', where, on the one hand, the benefits of the 'deep model' represented by the current EU Customs Union are highlighted, and, on the other, it is stressed that the UK does not want a system whereby due to a common external tariff Member States are prevented from entering FTAs with third countries.

It is not clear, however, how the UK can maintain the advantages of the internal free movement of goods and services, including the uniform regulations which 'underpin the provision and high standards of goods and services', while rejecting all existing models of association with the EU. The single market is based on common regulation and standards (effected through unification, harmonization, or mutual recognition of equivalence), and single supervision by EU regulatory authorities to make the abolition of internal barriers both possible and effective. By being out of the single market, the UK would either face barriers to its non-conforming exports or have to accept those standards with little to say on their adoption and updating, as is the case for the EEA members and Switzerland.

The White Paper restates that: 'In leaving the EU, the UK will seek a new customs arrangement with the EU, which enables us to make the most of the opportunities from trade with others and for trade between the UK

---

[6] White Paper, para 8.3.   [7] EU Guidelines, para 20.

and the EU to continue to be as frictionless as possible'. In its the 'Future Partnership Paper' of 15 August 2017 on 'Future Custom Arrangements' the UK Government has envisaged two alternatives: either a 'highly streamlined custom arrangement', which implies subjecting reciprocal trade to custom processes however simplified, or an 'unprecedented' 'new custom partnership with the EU, alligning our approach to the customs border in a way that removes the need for a UK-EU custom border' whithout the UK becoming however part of a customs union with the EU.[8]

It is thus easier to say what this envisaged 'Cross-Channel Trade and Investment Partnership' will not resemble, than what it will look like, once existing models associating Norway, Turkey,[9] or even Switzerland to the EU have been ruled out.[10]

What comes therefore into play is in both cases a form of 'stronger' or 'typical' FTA. According to Article XXIV of GATT, under this scheme internal barriers must be eliminated 'on substantially all the trade between the constituent territories' but only 'in products originating in such territories'.[11] This precludes the possibility of entering trade agreements applicable only to selected sectors, even if the EU were to accept such pick-and-choose arrangements.[12] More liberalization can of course be agreed and the agreement may also cover other matters, such as mutual recognition of certifications, regulatory cooperation in the enactment of new standards, enhanced protection for intellectual property, investments, and dispute settling.[13] This is the model of the CETA, the 'Comprehensive Economic and Trade Agreement' between the EU and Canada of 2016, which is proposed by some as a model for future UK–EU relations.[14] The fact that 99 per cent of the tariffs will be abolished between the EU and Canada in due time

---

[8] White Paper, para 8.45. Future Customs Arrangements paper, paras 27 ff. How the UK may attain its various pro-trade and pro-business objectives under either scheme appears problematic, see Jacques Pelkmans, 'The Brexit Customs Vision—Frictions and Fictions', 22 August 2017, www.ceps.eu.

[9] See Michael Emerson, 'After the UK's Brexit White Paper: What's the next move towards a CFTA?' CEPS Policy Insights No 2017/07 (February 2017) www.ceps.eu.

[10] Switzerland has been able somehow unilaterally to control the freedom of access of EU workers to its market and retains the freedom to conclude free trade agreements (FTAs) with third countries as a member of EFTA while having established an association 'à la carte' with the EU through a network of 120 specific agreements. Moreover, both Norway and Switzerland contribute to the EU budget, specifically to the 'cohesion funds'.

[11] GATT, Article XXIV.8(b).

[12] For an analysis of the various models of trade agreements see Friends of Europe, 'How to (Br) exit: A Guide for Decisions-makers: The Key to an Agreement between the EU and the UK' (March 2017) www.politico.eu.

[13] Preferential trade in services is allowed under liberalization agreements among some WTO members only by GATS Article V.

[14] See Emerson (n 9).

does not make, however, CETA an instrument comparable to a customs union or participation in the single market in ensuring a 'frictionless' trade regime.[15] For instance, the imposition of anti-dumping duties is not automatically excluded within a FTA.

It must thus be clear that any 'customs arrangement' with the EU, short of a customs union, will entail new barriers as to the reciprocal flow of goods, even if no tariffs were established between the EU and the UK. Customs controls will be unavoidable owing to the cessation of common rules as to the standards of products and rules of origin. Products imported from third countries into the UK could not—as is currently the case—be transferred further into the EU without control and possibly imposition of EU import duties. To sum up, such an FTA will be a second best as compared with the current regime and business will face an unavoidable uncertainty for some time to come as to freedom of trade between the UK and the EU after Brexit.[16]

2.3 What UK–EU Trade Relations If No Agreement Is Reached? Reciprocal Trading under WTO Rules

As the official letter of 29 March 2017 spells out: 'If however, we leave the European Union without an agreement the default position is that we would have to trade on World Trade Organization terms'. The WTO regime that would govern in this case the UK–EU trade relations would be the same as the one that will be generally applicable between the UK and the rest of the world post-Brexit.

As between the UK and the EU, the WTO multilateral rules are currently inapplicable since the EU Member States are part of the customs union governed by EU law. In respect of the EU, the future UK situation would be similar to that of a newly admitted member of the WTO which has no trade agreement in place with the EU. The EU customs tariff, according to the list of commitments ('schedule') of the EU filed with the WTO would apply to UK exports to the EU, a tariff which is estimated to be 4 per cent *ad valorem* on average, but presents high peaks on selected 'sensitive' products.[17] This is

---

[15] See Elaine Fahey, 'CETA and Global Governance Law: What Kind of Model Agreement Is It Really in Law' European Papers (9 February 2017) www.europeanpapers.eu.

[16] Customs checks will be the first and most obvious hurdle, see 'Brexit and the Borders: The Custom Crunch' *Economist*, (8 April 2017) 26. See also there 'Descending Mount Brexit' at 25: 'Mrs May now calls for a "deep and special partnership" with the EU. That implies a trade relationship that extends beyond goods to the services Britain likes to export, particularly the financial sort, and a means to ensuring its standards and rules do not deviate from Europe's. The deeper the trade deal, therefore, the more Britain must play by the EU's rulebook and, perhaps, accept the de facto supervision of its courts'.

[17] See 'From Farm to Pharma' *Economist* (8 April 2017) 64: 'Half of Ireland's exports go to Britain and some would face tariffs of almost 60% in the event of a cliff-edge Brexit, in which trade reverts to the WTO rules'.

the Most-Favoured-Nation (MFN) tariff applicable to exports into the EU from any member of the WTO with which the EU has no comprehensive trade agreement, as is the case currently in respect of Japan, Australia, or the USA.

The UK would not benefit from any special advantage, such as tariff-rate quotas, currently granted by the EU either, assuming that the UK would be an exporter of products covered, since these quotas, essentially covering agricultural products, are addressed to specific beneficiary countries. All other WTO disciplines, such as the WTO agreements on Anti-Dumping, on Technical Barriers to trade (TBT) and the one on Sanitary and Phytosanitary Measures (SPS), would apply reciprocally between the UK and the EU. The EU would be able to levy anti-dumping and anti-subsidy duties against UK exports sold at less than their 'normal' value, applying the rules and procedures of its Antidumping Regulation. The UK could do the same once it has established an anti-dumping authority able to perform anti-dumping investigations in compliance with WTO rules.

Matters are more complicated regarding imports into the UK, since currently the UK has no separate customs tariff or regime. Based on the principles of the EU (Withdrawal) Bill introduced by the UK government in Parliament on 13 July 2017 ('the [Great] Repeal Bill'), EU directly applicable regulations presently in force (such as the Common Customs Tariff and the Union Customs Code[18]) will become part of the domestic law of the UK after withdrawal, subject to the necessary adaptations since reference to EU law, EU authorities, and the Court of Justice of the European Union (CJEU) will become inapposite and will have to be replaced as appropriate.

In the absence of a FTA, the trade regime between the UK and the EU would hardly represent that 'freest and most frictionless trade possible in goods and services' that the UK government intends to prioritize in the negotiations, or that 'close partnership between the Union and the United Kingdom after its departure' that the European Council welcomes in its Guidelines.[19]

---

[18] The Union Customs Code (UCC) was adopted on 9 October 2013 as Regulation (EU) No 952/2013 of the European Parliament and of the Council. It entered into force on 30 October 2013, although most of its substantive provisions apply from 1 May 2016.

[19] Some of the dispute settlement clauses (mostly weak and sometime squarely ineffective) of existing FTAs of similar agreements of the EU have been annexed to the White Book as possible models for dispute settlement clauses of a future trade agreement between the UK and the EU. Let us not forget, however, that these procedures are all purely intergovernmental, of an administrative or arbitral nature. They invariably deny access to their procedures to private parties, such as importers and exporters who are mostly affected by breaches, differently from the EU judicial protection system by the Member States' judges and the CJEU.

2.4 A Special Solution for the Irish Question: Keeping Free Trade between the Republic of Ireland and Northern Ireland under the 'Frontier Traffic' Exception of Article XXIV.3 GATT

One of the objectives set by the UK government in its White Paper is that: 'When the UK leaves the EU we aim to have as seamless and friction-less a border as possible between Northern Ireland and Ireland, so that we can continue to see the trade and everyday movements we have seen up to now'.[20] Also, the EU has emphasized that one of its core objectives is, for evident political reasons, which all the EU Member States share with the Republic of Ireland, is avoiding a hard border between the latter and Northern Ireland.[21]

A little explored provision of GATT makes this possible as to trade relations also in respect of other WTO members. Article XXIV.3 states that the GATT 'shall not be construed to prevent: (a) Advantages accorded by any contracting party to adjacent countries in order to facilitate frontier traffic'. In practice, this means that any such facilitation would not be subject to MFN obligations, so that if reciprocal trade between the two territories were to be exempted from customs control and other restrictions of trade, other WTO members could not complain that their goods would be subject instead to customs duties when exported to the same territories.

There is no definition of 'frontier traffic' in the GATT, so that it can be assumed that a regime covering an area as large as the whole of Ireland could be admissible, although extending well beyond a traditional concept of local commerce adjacent to a border. A bigger issue would be how to avoid circumvention, that is both further shipment of goods benefiting from this regime for final destination beyond the chosen area, such as in the rest of the UK, and, on the other hand, further shipment of Northern Ireland goods from the Republic of Ireland to the continental part of the EU.[22]

---

[20] See White Paper, para 4.4.

[21] See John Bruton, 'Reflections on Brexit and Its Implications for Ireland' CEPS Paper (2 May 2017) www.ceps.eu/publications/. John Bruton is a former Prime Minister of Ireland. The UK government has elaborated on the issue in its Position Paper of 16 August 2017 'Northern Ireland and Ireland'.

[22] See also John Doyle and Eileen Connolly in this volume, who point to the even more liberal model in place in Cyprus, which rests on the Protocol of Accession and the so-called 'Green Line Regulation' (EU Council Reg. n. 866/2004): Goods produced in Northern Cyprus are considered of EU origin; they can enter the Republic of Cyprus without customs duties and automatically circulate within the whole of the EU single market. Another issue is how to ensure free movement of agri-food products should the UK no longer apply the EU's high phyto-sanitary standards.

3. The UK and Trade with Countries Associated with the EU

3.1 What Destiny for the UK Participation in EU Agreements with Third Countries Post-Brexit?

As is well known, besides the EEA, the agreements with Switzerland and the customs union with Turkey, the EU has negotiated a number of trade agreements with most countries all over the world based on Articles 37 of the TEU and Articles 216 and 217 of the TFEU.[23] These basically bilateral agreements[24] are difficult to systematize owing to their variety in scope and content, although the EU has tried to frame them according to different models. Some are closely linked with the EU opening to progressive enlargement and the objective to establish a European Neighbourhood Policy under Article 8 of the TEU to stabilize and reinforce the rule of law countries falling within this policy.[25] Other agreements are predominantly trade only, such as the FTAs with Korea, Mexico, and various countries in South and Central America.[26]

After the entry into force in 2009 of the Lisbon Treaty, by which the EU has acquired exclusive competence, as part of an expanded common commercial policy including the commercial aspects of intellectual property and direct foreign investments (Article 207 TFEU), the 'new generation' FTAs also include an investment chapter, as is the case of the FTA with Viet Nam (2016), CETA (2016), and that negotiated with Singapore.

There are also other international agreements entered into by the EU and its Member States which concern economic relations, notably the US–EU

---

[23] www.ec.europa.eu/neighbourhoodenlargement/instruments/overview.

[24] There are cases of agreements between the EU and several other parties when the latter are part of an economic union, as is the case of the Economic Partnership Agreement between the EU and the CARIFORUM States of the Caribbean of 2008 (or the proposed agreement with the MERCOSUR countries). These agreements are, however, framed as bilateral agreements between the EU and its Member States on the one side and the other entity and its members on the other side.

[25] Besides pre-accession agreements, we can recall the stabilization and association agreement with countries in the Balkans, the Euro-Mediterranean association agreements with countries on the eastern and southern shore of the Mediterranean, the Partnership and Cooperation Agreements with countries that were part of the Soviet Union, and the three Deep and Comprehensive Free Trade Agreements concluded with Ukraine, Moldova, and Georgia. Most of them provide, directly or indirectly, for technical and financial assistance by the EU to the partner country.

[26] The possibility for the UK 'to take over' these existing EU agreements, that we exclude for the reasons stated in the text, has been mentioned also in respect of autonomous (unilateral) preferential regimes adopted by the EU, and thus currently including the UK, such as the Generalized System of Preferences and the elimination of tariffs and quotas on imports from least developed countries under the 'Everything but Arms' initiative of 2001.

Air Transport Agreement of 2007 (Open Sky Treaty), but which are outside of the realm of the WTO.[27]

Another relevant distinction is that between agreements which are within the exclusive competence of the EU and 'mixed agreements', whose purview extends to matters which are shared between the EU and its Member State states. While the first type are negotiated and concluded only by the EU, but 'are binding on the institutions of the Union and on its Member States' under Article 216(2) of the TFEU, mixed agreements are concluded by the EU and its Member States and require the ratification also of all Member States according to their constitutional provisions (which may entail, in some of them, also the approval of sub-national entities) to enter into force.

This distinction is often not clear at the outset and the matter has been the object of a number of disputes before the CJEU between Member States and the Commission.[28] Once a mixed agreement has been concluded, distinguishing between provisions which fall within the competence of the EU and those which pertain to the competence of the Member States is difficult. It is also a fruitless exercise because the agreement is indivisible and the EU and its Member States are just 'one party', as these agreements almost invariably define them jointly.

It seems that the UK does not count much on the maintenance of these agreements. The UK government White Paper advocates an independent trade policy for the UK also through trade deals: 'Our approach to trade policy will include a variety of levers including: bilateral FTAs and dialogues with third countries, participation in multilateral and plurilateral negotiations, market access and dispute resolution through the WTO, trade remedies, import and export controls, unilateral liberalisation, trade preferences and trade for development. Without the need to reflect the positions of the EU27, an independent trade policy gives us the opportunity to strike deals better suited to the UK and to make quicker progress with new partners, as well as those where EU negotiations have stalled'.[29]

---

[27] To note, as a possible precedent for the UK, that Iceland and Norway subsequently joined the agreement through a distinct agreement in 2011, becoming parties 'as though they were party to the EU'.

[28] See TFEU, Article 218(11), which empowers Member States, the European Parliament, the Council, or the Commission to obtain the opinion of the CJEU as to whether an agreement envisaged is compatible with the Treaties, with the effect that if the opinion of the CJEU is adverse, the agreement envisaged may not enter into force unless it is amended. In its Opinion No 2/15 of 16 May 2017 the CJEU has considered that the proposed EU–Singapore FTA is a mixed agreement, in view of the provisions on portfolio investment and investment dispute settlement which exceed the EU's exclusive competence. The Court has considered on the other hand that all other trade chapters are within the exclusive competence of the EU.

[29] White Paper, para 9.6-7.

The exit of the UK from agreements in force will in any case be an issue also for the EU since the territorial application of any such agreement will be reduced, requiring at a minimum a notice to the other party. The dropping out of the UK may in some cases impact the scope of their application from an economic and trade point of view, affecting the balance of mutual benefits and possibly leading to a request of renegotiation by the non-EU party.

As to the participation of the UK to these agreements after Brexit, even if the UK might be interested in maintaining its participation in some of them, the answer cannot but be generally negative, both for reasons of substance and legal requirements. The EU Guidelines have taken the same position, although they show some temporal flexibility on the part of the EU.[30] This conclusion is legally inevitable for agreements entered into only by the EU within its exclusive competence which bind also the Member States as a consequence of them being Member States of the Union.[31] After Brexit, the UK would cease to be bound by them, while the EU would be incapable of performing the agreement in respect of the territory of the UK.

Even as to mixed agreements, the participation of Member States is inextricably connected with them being Member States of the EU, bound as such by its provisions and obliged to assist in the performance of the EU obligations in accordance with the principle of sincere cooperation of Article 4(3) of the TEU. These agreements provide, moreover, for their application to the territory of the EU and that would automatically rule out their application to the UK. Finally, in respect of all the treaties which have a strong political objective of tying the non-EU party to the EU economy, principles, policies, such as those falling within the EU Neighbourhood Policy, a further participation of the UK would run contrary to their object and purpose.

3.2 State Succession Principles and Fundamental Change of Circumstances as an Obstacle to EU Treaties Remaining in Force in the UK

An additional formal argument is decisive: all these agreements are bilateral, between the EU on one side and the other contracting country on the other.

---

[30] See Guidelines para 13: 'Following the withdrawal, the United Kingdom will no longer be covered by agreements concluded by the Union or by Member States acting on its behalf or by the Union and its Member States acting jointly. The Union will continue to have its rights and obligations in relation to international agreements. In this respect, the European Council expects the United Kingdom to honour its share of all international commitments contracted in the context of its EU membership. In such instances, a constructive dialogue with the United Kingdom on a possible common approach towards third country partners, international organisations and conventions concerned should be engaged'.

[31] TFEU, Article 216.2.

They are bilateral not multilateral treaties. They normally define who the (two) parties are, and to which territory they apply.[32] For the EU, it is the territory where the relevant EU treaties are applicable. Moreover, they provide for bilateral joint or mixed organs, such as Commissions or Committees, and bilateral mechanisms of dispute settlement.[33] The participation of the UK as an additional separate Member State would turn them into trilateral, that is multilateral agreements,[34] a change that would be incompatible with the operating of such treaties.

This conclusion finds support in international treaty law, specifically in the UN Vienna Convention on Succession of States in respect of Treaties of 1978. Although it is in force (since 1996) only between a few countries (including six Member States of the EU), we can assume that it reflects customary law.[35] Mutatis mutandis, the UK might be considered as a state which separates itself form a larger state, considering the EU as a state since its Member States have devolved to it part of their sovereign prerogatives.[36] Separation,

---

[32] See eg Article 1 (Definitions) of the EU–US Air Transport Agreement of 2007: '6. "Party" means either the United States or the European Community and its Member States; 9. Territory means ... for the European Community and its Member States, the land areas (mainland and islands), internal waters and territorial sea in which the Treaty establishing the European Community is applied and under the conditions laid down in that Treaty and any successor instrument'. Article 1.2 of the EU (and its Member States) FTA with Korea (2011) provides at Article 1.2 (General Definitions): 'Throughout this Agreement, references to: the Parties mean, on the one hand, the European Union or its Member States or the European Union and its Member States within their respective areas of competence as derived from the Treaty on European Union and the Treaty on the Functioning of the European Union (hereinafter referred to as the "EU Party"), and on the other hand, Korea'.

[33] See eg Article 15.1 of the EU–Korea FTA, which establishes a Trade Committee 'comprising representatives of the EU party and representatives of Korea'. As to territorial application the FTA provides at Article 15.15: 'This Agreement shall apply, on the one hand, to the territories in which the Treaty on European Union and the Treaty on the Functioning of the European Union are applied and under the conditions laid down in those Treaties, and, on the other hand, to the Territory of Korea'.

[34] I recall that under the Vienna Convention on the Law of Treaties (1969), which reflects customary international law, the regime of multilateral treaties is different in several respects from that of bilateral treaties, notably as to Amendments (Part IV of the VCLT, Article 40) and Extinction (Part V, Articles 55, 58).

[35] On this Convention see generally Andrea Zimmermann, 'State Succession in Treaties' Max Planck Enc. Public Int'l Law http://opil.ouplaw.com.

[36] This approach is supported by the well-known constant jurisprudence of the CJEU as to the innovative nature of the European Communities, since the seminal decisions *Van Gend and Loos* Case 26/62, and *Costa v ENEL*, Case 6/64. This configuration is especially warranted as to agreements in the sphere of the common commercial policy, where the EU has exclusive competence (cf the participation of the EU as an original member to the WTO under Article XI.1 of the Agreement establishing the WTO). In its Opinion No 2/15 of 16 May 2017, at para 248, the CJEU recalls that it is 'undisputed ... that the European Union can succeed the Member States in their international commitments when the Member States have transferred to it, by one of its founding Treaties, their competences relating to those commitments and its exercises those competences'. Brexit involves a similar process in the opposite direction, with the UK succeeding *pro parte* to the EU.

dissolution, and dismembering of states, as well as transfer of territories are all covered under the heading of 'state succession', but it is not easy to select the applicable regime in the peculiar case of Brexit.

There are two different, even opposite regimes, in such a case. According to the one of Article 15 of the Convention, EU treaties would cease to be applicable to the UK.[37] According to the regime of Article 34 instead, EU treaties would remain in operation also for the UK.

Applying the first paragraph of Article 15, which is referred to as the 'mobility of borders as to treaty application' or 'the moving frontiers' principle, EU treaties shall cease to apply to the territory of the UK since the UK will replace the EU as the territorial sovereign also in the matters previously pertaining to the EU competence.

According to Article 34 on 'Succession of States in cases of separation of parts of a State', EU treaties would remain in force also for the UK except if (a) the states concerned otherwise agree; or (b) it appears from the treaty or is otherwise established that the application of the treaty in respect of the successor state would be incompatible with the object and purpose of the treaty or would radically change the conditions for its operation.

The application of this provision would imply not only the continuity of the applications of the EU treaties in the EU 27[38] but also in and by the UK. This result appears, however, to be prevented by the caveat of the last sentence, when such application by the successor state to a part of the territory where a treaty was applicable 'would be incompatible with the object and purpose of the treaty or would radically change the conditions for its operation'.

This conclusion is warranted in the light of the structure, object, and purpose of FTAs. These EU agreements are essentially bilateral and are premised, as to the EU party, on the exercise by the EU of its prerogatives under the EU Treaties according to their rules, which are applicable only in the

---

[37] According to Article 15 ('Succession in respect of part of territory'): 'When part of the territory of a State, or when any territory for the international relations of which a State is responsible, not being part of the territory of that State, becomes part of the territory of another State: (a) treaties of the predecessor State cease to be in force in respect of the territory to which the succession of States relates from the date of the succession of States; and (b) treaties of the successor State are in force in respect of the territory to which the succession of States relates from the date of the succession of States, unless it appears from the treaty or is otherwise stablished that the application of the treaty to that territory would be incompatible with the object and purpose of the treaty or would radically change the conditions for its operation'. The Article 15 approach has been followed since the German Democratic Republic acceded to the Federal Republic of Germany in 1990, the territory of the European Communities being thereby extended, a process contrary to the one resulting from Brexit; see also R Mullerson, 'The Continuity and Succession of States by Reference to the Former USSR and Yugoslavia' (1993) 42 *International & Comparative Law Quarterly* 473.

[38] This would result also from Article 35, which affirms in principle the continuity of application in the predecessor State (here the EU) if it continues to exist after separation of part of its territory.

EU territory. As a result, it is rather the regime of Article 15 of the UN Convention that appears more in conformity with the peculiarities of these treaties.[39] The issue is not moot but could be relevant in relation to certain multilateral treaties not of the FTA model, such as some environmental treaties, the Energy Charter Treaty, or the Government Procurement Agreement, a 'plurilateral' agreement which is not part of the WTO 'single undertaking'. Nothing would prevent these treaties remaining in force for the UK in accordance with the rule of Article 34.

In addition to the Convention on State Succession, Article 62 of the Vienna Convention on the Law of Treaties of 1969 (VCLT) on 'Fundamental Change of Circumstances', the well-known *rebus sic stantibus* clause, may also come into play.[40]

This exceptional ground for terminating a treaty[41] could be invoked both by the EU and the other party, but not by the UK that would not be a party ('anymore') of the treaty. Giving for granted that Brexit may involve in some instances 'a fundamental change of circumstances', for sure 'unforeseen by the parties', invoking Article 62 VCLT by either party would require showing that the UK market being part of the EU single market was (a) 'an essential basis of the consent' to the treaty by the party invoking Article 62, and (b) that a strong imbalance of rights and obligations would ensue due to the exit of the UK from the EU, such as to 'radically to transform the extent of obligations still to be performed under the treaty' by the party invoking Article 62. This is unlikely but not impossible.[42] In any case, it might be an argument for renegotiation from the side of the non-EU party.

---

[39] 'State concerned' would include not only the EU and the other party to the treaty but also the UK. Maintaining the substance of a specific EU FTA might be considered by the UK not to be in its interest on a bilateral basis, so that Article 15 (but not Article 34) of the UN Convention of 1978 would provide an (additional) basis for considering such a treaty not in force anymore for the UK upon Brexit.

[40] See the text of Article 62(1): 'A fundamental change of circumstances which has occurred with regard to those existing at the time of the conclusion of a treaty, and which was not foreseen by the parties, may not be invoked as a ground for terminating or withdrawing from the treaty unless: (a) the existence of those circumstances constituted an essential basis of the consent of the parties to be bound by the treaty; and (b) the effect of the change is radically to transform the extent of obligations still to be performed under the treaty'.

[41] The ICJ has stated in the *Gabcikovo-Nagymaros Project (Hungary v Slovakia)* judgment of 25 September 1987, that: 'the stability of treaty relations requires that the plea of fundamental change of circumstances be applied only in exceptional circumstances'.

[42] In order to anticipate instances of such a move, one would need to know the economic balance underlying the conclusions of the relevant treaty. It has been mentioned that a substantive consideration for Peru concluding the FTA with the EU was the large consumption of its quinoa, mainly by UK consumers. If this is so, Peru might be able to claim if not termination at least renegotiation of the FTA. One could envisage that without the UK the Open Sky Treaty between the US and the EU might show substantial imbalances, the US losing its rights in respect of UK airports. See also the Irish Independent, 21 August 2017: 'Singapore may renegotiate EU trade deal after Brexit removes British markets', www.independent.ie/business/brexit.

In fact an agreement between 'the parties concerned' to resolve any issue, as stated in Article 34 of the 1978 Convention will be the most likely development. This could take the form of a provisional agreement for a transitory period.[43] The UK might be interested to go on applying a given EU FTA, say with Korea, on a bilateral basis with the other party, thus going on reciprocally to enjoy the previous liberalization regime applicable while a new FTA is being negotiated.[44]

4. The UK Position in the WTO after Brexit: Operating as an 'Independent' WTO Member

4.1 The UK as an Original Member of the WTO May Go on Keeping the EU Schedules

First of all, the EU will have to notify the WTO that one of its members, the UK, is not 'represented' any more by the EU, since that member and its territory have ceased to be part of the EU. Such notification seems not to be problematic at the WTO.[45]

Discussions are ongoing among trade law experts whether the EU's WTO tariff schedule can be automatically assumed as its own by the UK, possibly through a simple notification to the WTO, once the UK will cease to be a EU Member State, just declaring or notifying to the WTO that this tariff goes on being the one of the UK as an 'independent' member.[46]

---

[43] This is what is advocated by G van der Loo and S Blockmans, 'The Impact of Brexit on the EU's International Agreements' CEPS (21 July 2016) www.ceps.eu/publications/impact-brexit-eu.

[44] It has been pointed out that the EU–Korea FTA also liberalizes many services, such as financial services and telecommunications, providing to the parties a much more advantageous access to selected service sectors of the other party than under the GATS; see UK Trade Policy Observatory, 'The WTO: A Safety Net for a Post-Brexit UK Trade Policy?' Briefing Paper 1 (July 2016) https://blogs.sussex.ac.uk/uktpo/.

[45] The breaking up of Czechoslovakia into the Czech Republic and Slovakia was the object of a simple notification by them to the GATT Secretariat in 1993. No other contracting party raised objections or asked for any renegotiation. The 'transformation' of the European Communities into the European Union was also the object of a simple communication in 2009.

[46] Some 'technical' changes will be most probably requires, such as converting in British pounds the EU tariffs expressed currently in euros. Determining the 'official' EU schedules for each product at the WTO is not a simple matter. EU schedules had to be amended and renegotiated after each expansion of the EU, by which new EU Member States adopted the EU common tariff, thereby causing losses or resulting in advantages to other WTO members. Currently, the EU tariffs 'certified' by the WTO at the end of this process (as recently as only December 2016) are still those following the enlargement of the EU from 15 to 25 members in 2004. See '12 Years On, EU's Certified WTO Goods Commitments Now Up to Date to 2014' https://tradeblog.worldpress.com/2017/02/04/ (last accessed 10 April 2017).

I do not see why this should not be so. The UK, which was an original contracting party of the GATT in 1947, is also an original member of the WTO by virtue of both the WTO Agreement and EU law. The WTO Agreement, comprising the agreement establishing the WTO and the various multilateral and plurilateral agreements annexed to it have been concluded and ratified as 'mixed agreements', that is also by all the individual members of the EU.

There is thus no issue of state succession, nor any need of admission of the UK as a spin-off part of an existing member of an international organization. The UK was, is, and remains a member of the WTO so that the EU schedule, which is currently also the UK's schedule, remains its schedule.

The UK Government White Paper takes substantially this position:

As part of leaving the EU the UK will need to establish our own schedules covering trade in goods and services at the WTO, providing clarity for UK business about their access to overseas markets around the world and also providing a clear basis for negotiating new trade agreements, not just with the EU, but with old friends and new allies from outside Europe too … Our aim is to establish our schedules in a way that replicates as far as possible our current position as an EU Member State, thus creating a mutually beneficial, simple and inclusive outcome, so that the interests of the UK and other WTO members are protected.

If, at least initially, the UK will adopt the current schedules applicable to it as a Member State of the EU, other members of the WTO could not object to having the EU (EU 28) split between the EU 27 and the UK since, in principle, this would not negatively affect the original, previous balance of benefits and obligations.[47] Establishing a new WTO schedule would entail instead a painstaking process of negotiations, which does not necessarily lead to replicating the EU schedule, especially if the UK would aim at obtaining more concessions from other Members than those reflected in the schedule currently in force (and vice versa).[48]

---

[47] As submitted by L Bartels, 'Understanding the UK's Position in the WTO after Brexit' pts I and II (26 September 2016) www.ictsd.org/opinion and paper (23 December 2016) 'The UK's Status in the WTO after Brexit'.

[48] The constraints of the process of renegotiating schedules under Article XXVIII GATT (Modification of Schedules) has been highlighted in the recent WTO Panel Report of 28 March 2017 in *European Union: Measures Affecting Tariff Concessions on Certain Poultry Meat Products* (DS492), adopted without appeal on 19 April 2017, concerning China's objections to a modification by the European Union of tariff concessions (TRQs) on certain poultry products pursuant to negotiations held under Article XXVIII concerning in particular the granting of TRQs by the EU.

Although some WTO members might be tempted to ask for renegotiation,[49] this position is unsupported by WTO law.[50]

Also, the argument that other members will be prejudiced because their exporters will lose the benefits of shipping their goods freely from and to the UK to and from the rest of the EU is a *non sequitur*.[51] The territorial extension of a WTO member can change and is not a relevant element of a concession. In any case, it is not clear how other WTO members would be able effectively to challenge the UK retaining the EU schedule, except through bringing a case against the UK within the WTO dispute settlement system: a cumbersome and lengthy process leading to an uncertain outcome, while in the meantime the UK would be entitled to maintain its announced unchanged tariff regime.[52]

In the future it is to be assumed that the UK will want to adjust or modify its schedules and the WTO grants the necessary flexibility also outside multilateral negotiating rounds. In any case, this cannot be done unilaterally since schedules and other commitments are part of multilateral obligations of each member. Articles XXVIII of GATT and XXI of GATS on Modification of Schedules provide the framework for such negotiations, allowing them to be conducted only with those other members who 'have a principal supplying interest'.

4.2 Apportioning the EU Tariff-rate Quotas (TRQ) between the UK and the EU

The most complicated issue is according to most observers that of the TRQ and similar restrictions, as far as allowed, that have been granted by the EU as a

---

[49] The reason therefor is possibly the one exposed by Jim Bacchus, the first US member of the WTO Appellate Body, in his Commentary 'Making Room for Britain at the WTO' in *The Wall Street Journal* of 7 February 2017. According to him, the legal argument that the UK could simply cut and paste its current obligations from the EU list 'is more likely to persuade other legal scholars than canny trade negotiators seeking greater access to the UK market'.

[50] If the status of the UK as an original member of the WTO would not to be applicable to the GPA, then the principles of state succession of Article 34 of the 1978 Convention would result in the UK going on participating in it as a successor of the EU. For a contrary (unconvincing) view see UK Trade Policy Observatory (n 44).

[51] This issue does not affect concessions under GATS, which are in the form of allowing service providers of other WTO members to access in the various forms envisaged the market of another member, since the EU GATS schedules are mostly limited to individual EU Member States and vary from one to the other. A specific UK GATS schedule can thus already be identified; see Bartels (n 47) 12.

[52] According to Jim Bacchus (n 49), should the UK instead refuse to renegotiate, 'other members may retaliate by refusing to continue their current trade commitments to the UK, which have been made in exchange for the commitments made by the EU as a whole as listed in the EU schedule'. Since the same schedule will remain in place for the EU 27, this undermines such a position by another member. In such a case, however, it would be for the UK to start dispute settlement proceedings to challenge such refusal to recognize the validity of the UK schedule.

whole to third countries and would need to be apportioned between the EU 27 and the UK (except in the unlikely event that the UK would liberalize its agricultural imports, allowing them without limits at the tariff rate currently limited to the quota). In this respect, even if the EU and the UK would find an agreement inter se, they would not be able to oblige third parties to accept their decision. It is to be expected that negotiations under Article XXVIII would follow both with the EU and with the UK.[53]

The EU has many tariff-rate quotas on imports of agricultural products, which includes a specific quantitative amount to be imported at a given tariff, while beyond the quota the rate is much higher. A similar problem of apportioning exists as to the cap on expenditure on trade-distorting agricultural subsidies that the EU negotiated in the Uruguay Round, the so-called 'blue box'. In both cases, one could envisage that the EU 27 will want to reduce its commitments to take into account the loss of the UK market for exporters from outside the EU 28, while the UK may want to accept as few TRQs as possible. The matter is further complicated by the fact that WTO members who benefit from a given TRQ may have a different interest towards the EU 27 or the UK markets, depending upon their established trade flows and commercial relations.[54]

As to trade in services, most commitments of the EU under the GATS are limited to individual EU Member State countries (since the regime for non-EU nationals providing services is in great part still governed by national, not European, legislation) making the transition somehow simpler.[55]

---

[53] See *European Union: Measures Affecting Tariff Concessions on Certain Poultry Meat Product* (n 48).

[54] To give an example and an idea of what can be expected, the EU has a tariff quota for high quality, hormone-free beef, commonly named the 'Hilton quota'. It was introduced initially pursuant to a 2009 Memorandum of Understanding (MOU) with the USA to compensate the US for the EU not having implemented the outcome in 1998 of the *Hormones* dispute and maintaining the prohibition of imports of hormone-treated beef. (The US recently submitted that the EU is not respecting the MOU, threatening additional duties on selected EU exports to the US as a countermeasure.) The EU's current official commitment is 37,800 tons charged 20% import duty. Outside the quota, the duty is much higher: €2,700–€4,700 per ton. Since it is unlikely that the UK will renounce the quota (or admit hormone-treated beef) applying the 20% tariff to all imports, the quota would have to be renegotiated by both the EU and the UK with the major exporters of the product to the EU and the UK (such as the US, Argentina, and Uruguay), which may have different interests of accessing these two markets. For a detailed analysis see Peter Ungphakorn, 'The Hilton Beef Quota: A Taste of What Post-Brexit UK Faces in the WTO', https://tradebetablog.wordpress.com/2016/08/10/hilton-beef-quota (last accessed 25 November 2016).

[55] Thus, while rules on establishment and freedom of services for banks and insurance—including non-EU based—have been harmonized across the EU, this is not so for the services and establishment of non-EU lawyers. The EU and the US have recently (as at the end of 2016) concluded an agreement on the mutual recognition of qualifications for insurance companies, which is not yet in force. Post-Brexit, the UK will have to negotiate its own agreement.

Liberalization of services under the GATS is modest; FTAs covering also services are therefore crucial in order to obtain reciprocal access for service with relevant markets.

4.3 The UK Negotiating and Concluding New FTAs

This is clearly fundamental for the UK post-Brexit in order to replace the EU existing network from which it will be cut off. The UK has signalled its intent to 'strike free trade agreements with countries around the world', to use the expression of Objective 12 of the White Book 'Securing new trade deals with other countries', notably with the US and members of the Commonwealth. Transitory agreements with the countries currently linked to the EU by FTA and similar agreements are essential, since until the Article 50 agreement has not been finalized the UK will not be able to formally negotiate and conclude international treaties with non-EU countries.

The UK will have full capacity and ability to frame such agreements by negotiation with the other parties, since the WTO gives almost complete freedom to members as to their content and structure, provided they respect the principles of Article XXIV of GATT and Article V of GATS: elimination of duties and other restrictive regulations in respect of substantially all trade in goods between the partners (customs unions) or in respect of products originating from them (FTAs); no increase of the incidence of the members duties in respect of third parties; elimination of duties in a reasonable period not exceeding ten years if a staged decrease of duties is provided for. The UK will have many models from which to take inspiration.[56] The quantity and variety of such existing agreements (bilateral and regional), including those currently binding the EU and therefore the UK (such as the FTA with Korea), or negotiated by the EU but not fully in force (CETA) and others which have been extensively negotiated (such as the TTIP) or even concluded (TTP), but that will not result in binding treaties under the current US Administration, is well known.[57] They offer many solutions also as to 'WTO+' clauses in sectors covered or not covered by the WTO agreements. If the UK would 'break away from the EU' and adopt positions more similar to those of the US on sensitive issues such as financial services regulatory cooperation, standard

---

[56] The policy options available to the UK and the unavoidable constraints that negotiating trade agreements based on reciprocity of mutual concessions are highlighted by S Dhingra, G Ottaviano, and T Sampson, 'A Hitch-hiker's Guide to Post-Brexit Trade Negotiations: Option and Principles' (2017) 33 *Oxford Review of Economic Policy* 22.

[57] For some reflections see James Bacchus, 'Balanced Approach Needed to UK–US Trade Agreement' www.gtlaw.com (March 2017).

setting, and the precautionary principle (thus allowing hormone-treated meat or opening its market to GMO products at large), as has been advocated by some US commentators, it might be able to strike a better deal for its exports to the US, but at the cost of putting its access to the EU market at risk.[58]

5. Conclusion

It will be an uphill challenge for the UK to succeed in negotiating a trade agreement with the EU that is capable of ensuring reciprocal trade flows freedom as unimpeded as is currently the case under the single market, without accepting a customs union with the EU either. Any UK–EU FTA will offer a second-best solution, the price that the UK will have to pay to be able to negotiate trade relations across the world freely. The principles of the WTO, of which the UK is and will remain an original member, allows the UK to maintain the current customs regime of the EU as its own without having to renegotiate with third countries, except in respect of EU tariff-rate quotas in place for certain agricultural products. Trade agreements with other WTO countries, including with those which have such agreements with the EU, from which the UK will be cut off, may be negotiated by the UK based on its future trade policy choices in accordance with WTO rules, but only once the Brexit negotiations with the EU have been concluded.

---

[58] See Inside US Trade, 'Brexit Could Lead UK to Avoid Snags in Trade Talks with the US' (21 April 2017) www.InsideTrade.com. See also The Times 26 and 27 July 2017, 'Chlorination Chicken' and 'Cabinet is split as Gove vows to ban US chicken.'

PART 2

BREXIT AND CONSTITUTIONAL CHANGE IN REGIONAL PERSPECTIVE

5

Brexit and the English Question

Stephen Tierney

1. Introduction

The result of the Brexit referendum took many by surprise. In particular, the clear support within England itself for leaving the European Union and the fact that many of the most economically marginalized citizens were motivated to vote Leave in such large numbers was a shock to the political establishment. The result is, however, also symptomatic of a growing disillusionment with England's position not only within Europe but within the UK itself. Looked at in broader context, the Brexit vote can be seen as something of a backlash not only against the encroachment on UK national sovereignty from the outside, but also in reaction to the way in which powers have steadily been devolved to Scotland, Wales, and Northern Ireland, with England and its poorer regions appearing side-lined.

This chapter will address how the Brexit referendum took place at a time of political awakening in England, with the constitutional position of England at last being addressed after decades of neglect. We will explore how it is that a sense of marginalization has led to a strengthening of English nationalism. It would be too crude to argue that the lop-sidedness of devolution as it has developed over the past two decades is the true cause of the Brexit vote, but it would also be unwise to underestimate the degree of dissatisfaction within England over devolution and the opportunity the Brexit referendum offered to provide England, at last, with a distinctive constitutional voice: opinion polls regularly show that those most inclined towards Brexit in England also tend to be those most dissatisfied with devolution.[1]

---

[1] Charlie Jeffery and others, 'Taking England Seriously: The New English Politics' The Future of England Survey (2014) http://www.centreonconstitutionalchange.ac.uk/sites/default/files/news/Taking%20England%20Seriously_The%20New%20English%20Politics.pdf.

Brexit and the English Question. First edition. Stephen Tierney © Stephen Tierney 2017. Published 2017 by Oxford University Press.

It is no surprise that, even before Brexit, the unsatisfactory neglect of England's constitutional position was coming into focus. As the House of Lords Constitution Committee put it in a major report on the Union and Devolution: 'The governance of England is becoming a key concern for those considering the territorial constitution'.[2] In recent years we have seen the introduction of a special law-making procedure (English Votes for English Laws) and the passage of legislation that could lead to radical new forms of local and regional government in England. England's position is changing, and this will be explored as we focus upon how the UK is building a new constitution at the same time as it prepares for Brexit.

The chapter will also reflect upon how the UK appears to be moving in a federal direction. This was always going to be very difficult to achieve until the constitutional position of England was clarified. Much will depend upon what kind of EU exit arrangements are arrived at, and how the constitutional imbalance between England and the rest of the UK can be corrected.[3] The Brexit process is likely to test the UK's territorial constitution to the limit, and the chapter will address whether the UK's political institutions are ready to face the challenge of Brexit at a time when the territorial constitution is itself in flux. Having addressed England's constitutional position the chapter will ask whether a coherent system of intergovernmental relations can be consolidated in the heat of the Brexit negotiations which is itself robust enough to build sufficient consensus around the Brexit process and in so doing save the UK state.

2. Outlining the English Question

It is curious that when nationalism is discussed in the UK context England is rarely considered. The Brexit decision must be looked at in terms of the UK's demotic composition. The UK is a multi-nation state composed of three nations– Scotland, England and Wales, and Northern Ireland which contains two groups with separate national identities which straddle between an internal territorial identity and an affinity to a broader national identity— Britishness and Irishness respectively. Accounts of nationalism in the United

---

[2] House of Lords Select Committee on the Constitution, 'The Union and Devolution' 10th Report of Session 2015–16, HL Paper 149, para 353.

[3] The issue of England, as will be discussed, cannot of course be separated from issues also affecting Scotland and Northern Ireland, for which see contributions by Sionaidh Douglas-Scott and Eileen Connelly and John Doyle in this volume.

Kingdom tend to focus upon Scotland, Wales, and the fraught situation in Northern Ireland. There is less attention on England as a sub-state nation.

There are obvious reasons for this. Until devolution in the late 1990s there was little reflection within England upon Englishness as distinct from Britishness; in fact, the two identities tended to be treated by the English as synonymous. Devolution itself has, however, coincided with a transformation in English self-identity. The past two decades have seen a rise in English national identity as distinct from Britishness. This has coincided with disaffection over devolution: a disillusionment not only with the constitutional imbalance that has resulted, but the perception that the constitutional advantages acquired by the devolved territories has also lead to economic advantages, in particular the allocation of disproportionate shares of state resources to Edinburgh, Cardiff, and Belfast.[4] This has coincided with a weakening of affinity with the EU, a sentiment that has grown particularly strong within the Conservative Party which itself enjoys the bulk of its electoral success in England. English support for Brexit in the end determined the issue in the 2016 referendum, with majorities in Scotland and Northern Ireland voting to remain, a result that serves both to demonstrate the rise of English nationalism and to deepen existing national cleavages within the UK.

The referendum itself is highly significant. This exercise in popular mobilization, and the different result in England from that in Scotland and Northern Ireland, has put pressure on the UK's internal unions. However, before we consider the direct impact of the Brexit referendum upon the territorial constitution, we will turn to the story of devolution and how it has led to the emergence of the English question which, in revitalizing English national identity, puts more and more pressure on the territorial constitution itself at this potentially the most defining moment of its existence.

3. Constitutional Change ... But Not for You

Since the Scottish independence referendum in 2014 there have been efforts to address England's position within the British Union, and recognition that there is an 'English question'.[5] This is in fact the story of two decades of devolution, culminating in the attempt by Scottish nationalists to leave the UK that has led to the constitutional challenge presented by England itself.

---

[4] House of Lords Select Committee on the Constitution, 'The Union and Devolution' (n 2) para 354.
[5] ibid.

The House of Lords Constitution Committee undertook an inquiry into the Union and Devolution in 2015. In the course of its report, it referred to the 'English question' as follows:

Attention should be paid... to England's governance and place in the Union. England predominates in the UK both economically and demographically. Its representatives have an overwhelming majority in the House of Commons. It could be argued that devolution is a way for the other nations in the UK to distinguish themselves from England. The 'English Question' encompasses a number of questions about England's governance. How, within the Union, should England be governed? Is there a way to allow England a separate voice within the UK without undermining the Union? Should power be devolved or decentralised, and if so how?[6]

England's constitutional position is the big anomaly as we turn to consider constitutional change in the UK over the past two decades. Devolution in the UK can be described as a system of double asymmetry. Unlike other multi-level territorial states, the UK is unusual.[7] Devolution to Scotland, Wales, and Northern Ireland is itself heavily asymmetrical but what also stands out is that England, the largest nation in the UK has no measure of sub-state government, being governed by the UK institutions.

There are of course good reasons for this, the most obvious being size. England represents some 85 per cent of the UK population. Were English government to be devolved it would rival and potentially swamp UK government. Indeed, if a devolved English government were created with similar powers to those that have been devolved to the Scottish institutions, UK government would be hollowed of most of its functions. An English Parliament would so rival the UK Parliament that the relevance of the latter could well be called into question.

Because of this, England's constitutional position has gone unchanged while elsewhere the constitution has been rapidly developing, and not only in relation to devolution. Since 1998 we have seen the passage of the Human Rights Act 1998, the abolition of the Judicial Committee of the House of Lords and its replacement by the Supreme Court of the United Kingdom,[8] reform of the composition of the House of Lords,[9] the introduction of fixed parliamentary sessions for the House of Commons,[10] the extension of Parliament's power over treaty-making,[11] and an Act setting out clearly Parliament's supremacy over EU law.[12]

---

[6] ibid para 352.
[7] Stephen Tierney, "Federalism in a Unitary State: A Paradox Too Far?" (2009) *Regional and Federal Studies* 237.
[8] Constitutional Reform Act 2005.   [9] House of Lords Act 1999.
[10] Fixed-term Parliaments Act 2011.
[11] Constitutional Reform and Governance Act 2010, pt 2.
[12] European Union Act 2011.

However, of all of these, devolution has been the most dramatic change to the constitution. Its trajectory has also been one of expansion: increased powers, deeper institutional entrenchment, and seemingly, further detachment of the devolved territories from the UK. An already strong set of powers for the Scottish Parliament, set out in the Scotland Act 1998, has been increased in the Scotland Acts 2012 and 2016. The Scottish Parliament has always had full primary law-making powers, and the range of competences over which it had devolved power was more extensive than that enjoyed by the Welsh Assembly. The initial devolution package for Wales was on reflection fairly modest. Although the new National Assembly for Wales acquired competence over a significant range of policy areas, most of these powers continued to be shared with the UK Parliament, and its capacity to make law was carefully circumscribed to ensure Westminster's consent. The result was a situation of great complexity. It also led Welsh nationalists to agitate constantly for a model of devolution closer to that enjoyed by Scotland. The Government of Wales Act 2010 and the Wales Act 2017 have gone a considerable way to achieving this. By contrast, the Northern Ireland arrangements are entirely *sui generis*, reflecting that the primary purpose of devolution for Northern Ireland was to end conflict; devolved government was one of the means by which to do so. As such, the institutional arrangements were fashioned very much with conflict resolution in mind. The Northern Ireland Assembly received power over an extensive range of competences, more similar to Scottish than Welsh devolution. Its real mark of distinction, however, is a complex series of power-sharing arrangements between the two main political communities, based upon a d'Hondt model of government, and cross-border engagement with the Republic of Ireland.

The steady dissipation of the power of Westminster across the UK continued in the period leading to the 2014 Scottish independence referendum. The Government of Wales Act 2010 and the Scotland Act 2012 were the latest stages in this, the latter, inter alia, giving further tax powers to the Scottish Parliament in the hope of seeing off the kind of radical nationalism that would, nonetheless, in the end lead to the 2014 referendum. The Northern Ireland arrangements always intended further devolution on certain key issues, and that has been the direction of travel, culminating in the devolution of corporation tax.[13]

Another feature of devolution is the implicit recognition of nationhood that comes with it. It is notable that each of the three settlements in 1998 involved a referendum and that these were held exclusively in the devolved

---

[13] Corporation Tax (Northern Ireland) Act 2015.

territory itself.[14] In this way, the UK finds itself part of a widening international trend. The use of referendums is growing around the world for major constitutional decisions.[15] One observation we can make as we address this proliferation in direct democracy is that constitutional referendums are not merely instrumental mechanisms by which decisions are made. They can also be nation-building or nation-affirming devices. The people come together as one collectivity to make a decision. That gives the decision a certain legitimacy in its foundation through popular authorship. However, it can also have a reflexive impact on the authors themselves, helping to build a strong demotic bond with their fellow citizens with whom they make the decision. It is not clear to what extent it is due to devolution itself or to the referendums that brought it about, but it is certain that Scottish and Welsh national identity has grown since the initial devolution referendums in 1979.[16] The fact that 48 per cent voted for Scottish independence in 2014 speaks to the continuation of this trend.

The Northern Ireland referendum served a slightly different purpose. It was not nation-building in that identities of Irish nationalists and of British unionists were already well entrenched. But it did serve a purpose beyond merely deciding on the agreement. It involved the citizens of both communities coming together, not as one national people, but as one collective set of authors—a public—to endorse the agreement. In addition, the 1998 referendums in Scotland and Northern Ireland were preceded by long conversations about the constitutional future, culminating in the Scottish Constitutional Convention process and the Belfast Agreement itself. These were processes that involved a specifically 'territorial conversation', where it was apparent to citizens that their interlocutors were not in fact fellow citizens from right across the UK, but more narrowly, only those of the sub-state territory in question.

When we reflect that England did not receive any constitutional devolution in this period it is important to note that it also missed out on the national conversation that came with the creation of devolution. Looking at the referendums across the territories of the UK, and the identity-building functions they seemed to have, it is surely significant that England has never had such a national 'demotic moment'. English citizens have looked on

[14] Although it is also notable that mutually dependent referendums were held in Northern Ireland and the Republic of Ireland in relation to the Belfast Agreement.
[15] S Tierney, *Constitutional Referendums: The Theory and Practice of Republican Deliberation* (OUP 2012).
[16] A Park and others (eds), 'British Social Attitudes: the 30th Report', NatCen Social Research (2013) www.bsa-30.natcen.ac.uk.

while all of this has taken place. Part of the sense of English marginalization, I would submit, is caused not only by the lack of devolution but also by this lack of any national moment; of any constitutional event in which the English people were able to come together as such to speak as 'the English', the way their fellow citizens elsewhere were able to confront and present their sub-state national identity.

Despite not having any direct say in the devolution agreements for each of the devolved territories, except through Parliament itself, the creation of the devolved administrations did not lead to any serious resentment in England, and in many ways devolution was largely ignored until very recently. In practical terms, England was in many ways unaffected in that Westminster continued to exercise competence for England over all of the issues devolved elsewhere. However, over time devolution has come to have several consequences for England and there now appears to be a growing sense of resentment and/or a declining sense of Britishness and a growing sense of Englishness within England.

The first issue is that of special treatment. Carefully tailored and bespoke systems were being established for the three devolved territories while England itself went, in constitutional terms at least, unrecognized. There was some sense of the incongruity of devolution's double asymmetry in the early days of devolution. However, this merely led to a proposal for regional government in England for which there was no appetite. This was an initiative of the Blair Labour Government to promote elected regional assemblies. The experiment was tried but killed off by the rejection of the proposed North East Assembly in 2004 in a referendum in which few participated and even fewer were in favour.[17] This was an attempt to compensate in England for the lack of devolution. It collapsed owing to the widespread unpopularity of the initiative, and what emerged was a sense that England did not want regional government but instead a recognition of England itself as a country.

A second issue is a sense of unequal benefit. There has been a growing view that the devolved territories gain from devolution in a very disproportionate way, at England's expense. This applies particularly in relation to the funding for devolution. In fact, the funding model—the Barnett formula—predates devolution. The Barnett formula is a mechanism used by the Treasury to adjust automatically the amounts of public expenditure allocated to Northern Ireland, Scotland and Wales to reflect changes in spending levels allocated to public services in England, England and Wales, or Great

---

[17] House of Lords Select Committee on the Constitution, 'The Union and Devolution' (n 2) para 380.

Britain, as appropriate. The formula applies only to expenditure on issues for which the devolved administrations are responsible. The Barnett system provides that any increase or reduction in expenditure in England will automatically lead to a proportionate increase or reduction in resources for the devolved governments in Scotland, Wales, and Northern Ireland. The way it works in practice, per capita public expenditure is year on year markedly lower in England than the other regions. Despite predictions that devolution would lead to a significant evening out of spending, this has not happened. For example, the change in Scottish identifiable expenditure as a percentage of English expenditure from 2001/02 to 2012/13 only went down from 121.3 per cent to 119.0 per cent.[18] The consequence is a net dividend for the devolved territories, particularly Scotland, which has over time been used, for example by the UK Independence Party, to stoke resentment in England.

A third issue is the consequence of the second spoke of the double asymmetry of devolution. The central institutions of government were relatively unchanged. The number of MPs which the devolved territories returned to Westminster diminished to some extent by virtue of the devolution statutes.[19] But the so-called West Lothian question remained an issue. The West Lothian question refers to whether Westminster MPs from Northern Ireland, Scotland and Wales should be able to vote on matters that affect only England, while MPs from England are unable to vote on matters that have been devolved to the devolved legislatures. The issue was first raised by Tam Dalyell, the Labour MP for the Scottish constituency of West Lothian, when he questioned the coherence of asymmetrical devolution when it was first proposed in the late 1970s.

This has become a more stark issue as more and more competences are devolved, and as government majorities diminish, giving MPs from devolved territories a potentially determining say on important issues. As the House of Lords Constitution Committee observed: 'Where votes are close, this situation can create—and has on a small number of occasions created—a situation where proposed laws affecting England alone are passed (or rejected) against the wishes of a majority of MPs for English constituencies'.[20]

---

[18] HM Treasury, 'Public Expenditure Statistical Analyses 2014' Chapter 9, Table 9.2 https://www.gov.uk/government/statistics/public-expenditure-statistical-analyses-2014.

[19] See eg Scotland Act 1998, s 86, which led to a reduction of Scottish MPs from 72 to 59.

[20] House of Lords Select Committee on the Constitution, 'The Union and Devolution' (n 2) para 363.

4. Scottish Independence Referendum: England Awakens

A catalyst for a particularly dramatic change in attitudes was the 2014 referendum on Scottish independence. This brought into sharp focus the extent of devolution: it had provided Scottish nationalists with a platform with which to stage a referendum and the institutional infrastructure with which to make separate statehood a feasible project. This in itself served as a reminder to the rest of the UK of just how dislocated Scotland had become. There was also resentment that Scotland was taking a unilateral decision in which England had no part, and a sense of a loss of reciprocity; the UK had surrendered wide powers to Scotland but the response was not contentment but separatism. This could be seen as a lack of gratitude: Scotland had benefited from devolution and from the Barnett formula, but almost half of its voters still put national self-interest above any sense of comity with the UK and were prepared to vote for independence.

Matters came to a head in the few days before the referendum vote. As the polls tightened, on 16 September, a mere two days ahead of the vote, UK leaders of the Conservative, Labour, and Liberal Democrat parties issued 'the vow',[21] undertaking that in the event of a majority No vote they would produce agreed proposals on additional powers for the Scottish Parliament. The vow also set out a short timeframe within which these powers would be agreed. The result was that the day after the referendum, the Prime Minister announced that Lord Smith of Kelvin, a non-political figure, had agreed to oversee the process to take forward this commitment to grant further devolution to the Scottish Parliament.[22] The terms of reference of the Smith Commission were:

"To convene cross-party talks and facilitate an inclusive engagement process across Scotland to produce, by 30 November 2014, Heads of Agreement with recommendations for further devolution of powers to the Scottish Parliament. This ... will result in the publication of draft clauses by 25 January. The recommendations will deliver more financial, welfare and taxation powers, strengthening the Scottish Parliament within the United Kingdom.[23]

These developments led within two years to the passage of the Scotland Act 2016, containing extensive new powers for the Scottish Parliament. The

---

[21] http://www.dailyrecord.co.uk/news/politics/david-cameron-ed-miliband-nick-4265992.
[22] https://www.gov.uk/government/news/scottish-independence-referendum-statement-by-the-prime-minister.
[23] https://www.smith-commission.scot/about/.

2016 Act has realigned significantly the balance of competences set out in the Scotland Acts of 1998 and 2012 (the 1998 Act and the 2012 Act). The Scottish Parliament is assuming a range of new powers in policy areas such as taxation, welfare, employability, transport, energy efficiency, fuel poverty, and onshore oil and gas extraction. These proposals have required significant amendments in particular to Schedules 4 and 5 of the 1998 Act. It is the provisions on taxation that have attracted the most attention since Scotland will acquire far more fiscal responsibility.[24] In particular, the Scottish Parliament has been given extensive powers in relation to income tax raised in Scotland which is important in symbolic as well as practical terms. This builds upon the more modest tax powers that were included in the 2012 Act, a number of which had, by 2016, not yet been implemented.

To many in England it seemed that Scottish nationalists, whose debates had so unsettled the union, were now being rewarded with a potentially open-ended list of further devolved powers, all tied to no change in the Barnett formula, which would continue to apply to those areas over which Scotland did not have its own tax-raising powers. It is no surprise therefore that, in light of the 2014 referendum, it was apparent to Prime Minister David Cameron that English voters were deeply unsettled and increasingly resentful not only of the referendum itself but of the promises made at the end of the campaign. Accordingly, the very morning of the referendum result he announced: 'We have heard the voice of Scotland - and now the millions of voices of England must also be heard'. And the focus for the Prime Minister was the greater imbalance in Parliament that would attend the devolution of extensive new powers to the Scottish Parliament: 'The question of English votes for English laws - the so-called West Lothian question -requires a decisive answer'.[25]

Therefore, although the process towards the Scotland Act 2016 was a rapid one following the 2014 referendum, a parallel process has now produced change for England in two areas: to parliamentary legislative procedure— English Votes for English Laws (EVEL) -, and to local government, in a way that could also lay the basis for the ad hoc devolution of extensive spending power to cities in England. For the Constitution Committee these reflect: 'two major facets of the English Question: the representation of England as a

[24] House of Lords Constitution Committee, 'Proposals for the Devolution of Further Powers to Scotland' (18 March 2015) para 95 http://www.publications.parliament.uk/pa/ld201415/ldselect/ldconst/145/14502.htm.

[25] http://www.bbc.co.uk/news/uk-politics-29271765, quoted in: 'The "English question" Answered: Scottish MPs to be Barred from Voting on English Laws' *Daily Telegraph* (19 September 2014).

whole, and devolution or decentralisation to regional or local levels within England'.[26] We will consider both issues, starting with the latter.

5. Local and Regional Government

There has been and continues to be no enthusiasm for regional government for England. We have noted how proposals for English regional government stalled under the Blair government.[27] In this regard it may be that local government is the only way to devolve some powers in England, given this scepticism about regional government. In recognition of this the Government started to promote 'devolution deals' in 2010. As the Constitution Committee observed: " 'Devolution deals" are the most recent focus of the "localism" agenda promoted by the UK Government... in place of the previous Labour Governments' regional approach. These "deals" allow for the devolution of a bespoke set of powers and the reorganisation of local government in a county, city or region; they usually include the creation of a combined authority with a directly-elected mayor'.[28]

The first 'devolution deal' was announced in November 2014, creating a Greater Manchester Combined Authority. By the middle of 2015, there were also deals for Sheffield and Cornwall. In late 2015, further deals were announced for the North East, Tees Valley, the West Midlands, and Liverpool. The Budget in March 2016 announced four more deals covering East Anglia, Greater Lincolnshire, and the West of England.[29] The Cities and Local Government Devolution Act 2016 brings forward radical proposals to make these reforms to local government more extensive and general in England. It takes forward the Government's plans for more powers for cities and regions, creating the opportunity for a 'combined authority' and directly elected mayor to be created for the areas which seek these powers. It empowers the Secretary of State to make significant changes to local authority structures, create directly-elected mayors, and transfer functions from other public bodies to new combined authorities. The range of competences over which the Government might seek to devolve powers is potentially extensive judging by a speech given by the Chancellor of the Exchequer George Osborne on 14

[26] House of Lords Select Committee on the Constitution, 'The Union and Devolution' (n 2) para 359.

[27] Regional Development Agencies Act 1998.

[28] House of Lords Select Committee on the Constitution, 'The Union and Devolution' (n 2) para 388.

[29] ibid para 389.

May 2015 in which he said the Bill would 'pave the way for ... cities ... to take greater control and responsibility over all the key things that make a city work, from transport and housing to skills, and key public services like health and social care'.[30]

However, there is scepticism of how the system, which began before the statute and will continue on a statutory basis, will work. One criticism is that the development is not particularly democratic. As the Political Studies Association has put it: 'the whole debate on English devolution has been an elite-to-elite one. Whilst making occasional reference to how [English votes for English laws], City Deals and the Northern Powerhouse agenda would help [in] improving democracy, in practice so far the government has paid very little attention to what the people really want from devolution in England (or if they have any appetite for it at all)'.[31] The House of Lords Constitution Committee also criticized the extent of central government power. In its report on the Bill it noted the wide-ranging powers granted to the Secretary of State, who may make significant changes through secondary legislation. It also compared this unfavourably with 'the devolution processes for Scotland, Wales and Northern Ireland in 1997–98, where the statutes clearly identified the recipients of devolved authority, the matters devolved, and the limitations upon those powers'. In its report on the Union, it also said that: 'Given how much of England's economy is based in areas that will be covered by these deals, the broad ministerial powers are particularly concerning'.[32]

Another issue was the lack of public engagement. The House of Lords Constitution Committee was hard-hitting on this. 'The lack of public and community engagement around the "devolution deals" is a weakness in the current policy for the governance of England. There should be a requirement for informing and engaging local citizens and civil society in areas bidding for and negotiating 'devolution deals'.[33] In addition, the Committee emphasized:

Local politicians seeking 'devolution deals' should lead this engagement ... If public concerns about the governance of England are properly to be addressed, the UK Government, and individuals engaged in political activity at all levels, need to engage with the public on these issues and to understand their concerns. There needs to be a greater effort to understand what people and communities want from devolution or decentralisation. This requires far greater public engagement, both in

---

[30] Rt Hon George Osborne, 'Chancellor on Building a Northern Powerhouse' Speech at Victoria Warehouse, Manchester (14 May 2015) https://www.gov.uk/government/speeches/chancellor-on-building-a-northern-powerhouse.

[31] House of Lords Select Committee on the Constitution, 'The Union and Devolution' (n 2) para 356.

[32] ibid para 393.   [33] ibid para 588.

general across England and in those areas seeking or agreeing greater powers, with real discussions about what those powers should be and by whom they should be exercised.[34]

Leaving aside any democratic deficit it is also immediately noticeable that there is a considerable distance between these proposals and the levels of devolution enjoyed by Scotland, Wales, and Northern Ireland. Indeed, before the election the House of Commons Political and Constitutional Reform Committee was sceptical of these plans, which they felt did not promise 'the genuine transfer of power from the centre to localities which many are seeking'.[35] Therefore, the Committee recommended a 'Convention for England, held over the term of the next Parliament, with broad popular representation from the public and civil society'. This could 'examine the relationship between England and the United Kingdom and develop a process for further agreed devolution from the centre to regions and localities'.[36] No such process has taken place and it is also the case that a recent Future of England Survey noted that there was 'very significant support for the constitutional recognition of England as a whole as a political unit' but markedly less for regional government.[37]

6. English Votes for English Laws

While it is not at all clear that regional government is popular in England, English votes for English laws (EVEL) is. The 2014 Future of England Survey report concluded that there was very low support for the status quo and for regionalism and no clear preference for strengthening local government, but it did identify 'very significant support' for proposals that would recognize England as a nation, with English votes for English laws emerging as the preferred option.[38] At the same time as it was pushing ahead with reforms to English local government it is therefore no surprise that the House of Commons also adjusted its own legislative procedures to take recognition of devolution.[39]

---

[34] ibid paras 423–4.
[35] House of Commons Political and Constitutional Reform Committee. 'The Future of Devolution after the Scottish Referendum', 11th Report of Session 2014–15 (23 March 2015) HC para 75.
[36] ibid para 79.   [37] See Jeffery and others (n 1).
[38] House of Lords Select Committee on the Constitution, 'The Union and Devolution' (n 2) para 361.
[39] HC Deb vol 600 col 1159 (22 October 2015).

The 2014 referendum illuminated starkly the fact that the constitutional position of England had not changed despite the dramatic developments since 1998. England continued to be governed from Westminster with no realignment of how Parliament operated to take account of the West Lothian question. The Prime Minister's statement after the Scottish referendum was a clear pointer to the need for change. In his view, new powers for Scotland would require to be mirrored by a concomitant recalibration of the influence of Scottish MPs at Westminster.

The House of Lords Constitution Committee took evidence on this issue. It found that, although the West Lothian question was not a top priority for citizens, opinion polls since the late 1990s have shown 'strong support for removing the right of Scottish MPs to vote on English-only matters'.[40] The Committee also heard that the principle is popular in both England and Scotland, 'with surveys showing at least 64% support in England (and less than 15% opposition) and around 50% support in Scotland'.[41] One risk pointed out by John Curtice is that the general election in May 2015 had the potential to change this consensus. The election of fifty-six MPs from the Scottish National Party (SNP) out of fifty-nine Scottish constituencies, had the potential to change the future narrative of EVEL in Scotland: 'what originally appeared an embarrassment for Labour is now, perhaps, at risk of being portrayed as an attempt to silence 'Scotland's party', viz. the SNP'.[42]

Various proposals were put forward in the past ten years to deal with this issue, most notably the recommendations of the McKay Commission, which were in the end not implemented.[43] However, after the 2014 referendum it seemed clear that action would be taken. 'English Votes for English Laws' was a manifesto commitment of the Conservative Party ahead of the 2015 General Election. In July Chris Grayling, Leader of the House of Commons announced a government proposal to change House of Commons standing orders to give MPs representing English constituencies an effective veto over new bills affecting only England. The new procedures broadly reflect those proposed by the McKay Commission, but with an express 'veto' for English (or English and Welsh) MPs over legislation affecting only their territories in

---

[40] House of Lords Select Committee on the Constitution, 'The Union and Devolution' (n 2) para 366.

[41] ibid para 497.   [42] ibid para 498.

[43] 'Report of the Commission on the Consequences of Devolution for the House of Commons' (McKay Commission) (March 2013) http://webarchive.nationalarchives.gov.uk/20130403030652/http:/tmc.independent.gov.uk/.

areas that are the responsibility of devolved legislatures elsewhere. The key aspects of the new system are that the Speaker must determine if a bill or parts of it relate only to England, or England and Wales; if so an England-only committee stage will consider those bills that have been determined to be 'England-only in their entirety'. The Committee membership reflects the number of MPs each party has in England. If there are England only or England and Wales only provisions in any bill, then a grand committee com-posed of all English (and Welsh) MPs would be required to approve the bill for it to pass. This model was put in place by changes to the standing orders of the House of Commons passed on 22 October 2015.[44]

The system given effect in 2015 does not, as some proposed, exclude MPs from constituencies outside England (or England and Wales) from debates and votes on matters that have been devolved. Instead it is a compromise solution, offering a double veto whereby the whole House of Commons can still reject matters agreed by English (and Welsh) MPs, but which also gives the latter their own veto over devolved matters affecting England (or England and Wales) that have been voted upon by the whole House.

The House of Lords Constitution Committee was asked to review the procedures after only one year and found that while there were no major problems with the system it was too early to tell if was working well.[45] It recommended that if the EVEL arrangements are maintained they should be subject to an extended trial and reviewed by a Joint Committee examining both the technical and the constitutional aspects of EVEL. In its report on the Union and Devolution it also took the opportunity to offer important insights into the relationship between the new procedures and, respectively, 'the English question' in the territorial constitution, and the structure and trajectory of devolution and the union.

One option of which it was highly sceptical was an English Parliament. In particular, the House of Lords underlined the issue of stability:

The creation of an English Parliament is an apparently simple solution, which would address the desire for a single, separate voice for England. However, it throws up problems of potential instability at least as great as those it attempts to solve. The overwhelming size of England and thus the political and economic power of an English Government compared with the Scottish and Welsh Governments and

---

[44] HC Deb vol 765 col 1159 (22 October 2015).
[45] House of Lords Select Committee on the Constitution, 'English Votes for English Laws' 6th Report of Session 2016–17, HL Paper 61. See also M Elliott and S Tierney, 'House of Lords Constitution Committee Reports on "English Votes for English Laws"' UK Constitutional Law Blog (2 November 2016) https://ukconstitutionallaw.org/.

Northern Irish Executive would not bring real symmetry to the system and could risk instability and resentment.[46]

It heard evidence to the effect that 'England would dominate a UK federation if it were a single unit'.[47] Another witness said:

If you had an English First Minister with the powers of the Scottish First Minister, that English First Minister would have a bigger budget and would be more powerful and important than the United Kingdom Prime Minister. That is a recipe for collapsing the Union rather than strengthening the Union.[48]

The Committee concluded:

'Given the relative size of England within the UK, the creation of an English Parliament would introduce a destabilising asymmetry of power to the Union. Meanwhile, creating a new legislature and administration covering 84% of the population that the UK institutions currently serve would not bring decision-making significantly closer to the people and communities of England. An English Parliament is not a viable option for the future of the governance of England.[49]

7. The English Question after the Brexit Referendum

EVEL is of course designed to address only one aspect of the English Question. But even taking into account that the new arrangements only concern the issue of parliamentary representation, the House of Lords Constitution Committee identifies a key weakness in the model. While giving English MPs an effective veto, EVEL is still arguably an incomplete answer to the West Lothian question, since it provides only a veto and not the capacity for distinctive English policy formation: 'the capacity of English MPs to pursue a distinct legislative agenda for England in respect of matters that are devolved elsewhere does not equate to the broader capacity of devolved legislatures to pursue a distinct agenda on matters that are devolved to them'.[50]

The Committee is therefore highly sceptical of any notion that EVEL adequately deals with the general dissatisfaction felt in relation to England's

---

[46] House of Lords Select Committee on the Constitution, 'The Union and Devolution' (n 2) para 507.

[47] ibid para 508.

[48] Professor Adam Tomkins, John Millar Professor of Public Law, University of Glasgow.

[49] House of Lords Select Committee on the Constitution, 'The Union and Devolution' (n 2) para 376.

[50] House of Lords Constitution Committee, 'English Votes for English Laws', 6th Report of Session 2016–17, HL Paper 61, para 90.

place in the constitution. In the report on the Union and Devolution the Committee stated: 'the English Question remains one of the central unresolved issues facing decision-makers grappling with the UK's territorial constitution'. In its EVEL report, the Committee confirms that this remains its view and concludes that the proposed Joint Committee 'should try to establish whether the introduction of EVEL has by then affected public perceptions in England of a "democratic deficit"'.[51]

As we approach Brexit, we do so with a territorial constitution that is in flux. The Scotland Act 2016 is just beginning to take effect and the Wales Act 2017 is yet to do so. The two dimensions of the English question are still to be fully addressed: the representation of England within the Union, and the devolution or decentralization of power within England.

This is a time when the Union is under strain, given differing views on Brexit within the four national territories of the UK. There is a risk that constitutional changes such as EVEL will in fact unsettle the Union further. One consequence of ad hoc changes to the territorial constitution has been unintended consequences. A possible risk with EVEL is that an attempt to provide more balance to a lop-sided system may in fact have the perverse effect of further unsettling the Union. As the Constitution Committee observes: 'Parliament is a unifying body at the centre of the political union, where all citizens, regardless of where they live, have the same say in the laws and policies that govern them. Using the same institution to provide a separate and distinct role for England could risk undermining Parliament's position as a UK, rather than English, institution'.[52]

Greater threats to the Union apply now in light of Brexit and the likely extension to the UK government of extensive delegated powers through a Great Repeal Bill.[53] This will give extraordinary power to the UK government to give effect to Brexit. This comes in the wake of a referendum on Brexit which produced different results across the UK. It has led to a sense that Brexit is in fact a predominantly English initiative. This is potentially damaging for the Union if it is not seen to be a pan-British project. Accordingly, it is imperative that there are efforts to coordinate the transposition of powers in a way that respects the Union. Ironically, the move is unsettling nationalists in Scotland and Northern Ireland, increasing demands for referendums on independence and the reunification of Ireland respectively.[54]

---

[51] ibid Summary of Conclusions and Recommendations, para 47.   [52] ibid.

[53] European Union (Withdrawal) Bill 2017. See also M Elliott and S Tierney, 'The "Great Repeal Bill" and Delegated Powers', UK Constitutional Law Blog (7 March 2017) https://ukconstitutionallaw.org/.

[54] Again, see chapters by Douglas-Scott and Eileen Connelly and Doyle in this volume.

However, the Brexit referendum was very much an English constitutional moment as well as a British constitutional moment. It is the only time since 1975 that the English people have had the chance to vote in a referendum about a matter of fundamental, existential constitutional importance. This seems to have been missed by those who view the referendum as an unfortunate event, or by the courts which in the *Miller* case seemed to take no account of its significance as a mass popular event.

We are in a moment of great instability. The rise of sub-state nationalism in Scotland and Wales has gradually been diminishing a sense of British nationalism. Inevitably this is now being felt in England too. The consequence could well be the complete destabilization of the state. What the European Union (Withdrawal) Bill reminds us of, as does the move to EVEL, is that there needs to be much more joined up thinking about the territorial constitution. The only feasible way forward is a coherent system of inter-governmental relations. This will be needed to ensure that policy proposals to retain or repeal particular EU policies, to share EU competences across the UK, and to ensure the operation of a coherence common market are agreed across the UK.

Intergovernmental relations have been redesigned since the Scottish independence referendum in 2014. The Joint Ministerial Committee met on 24 October 2016 and as a sign of how seriously matters were being taken, the participants included the prime minister, senior UK cabinet ministers and the first ministers of the three devolved territories. Afterwards,[55] in a Communiqué, the heads of government agreed to take forward multilateral engagement. A new Joint Ministerial Committee on EU Negotiations (JMC (EN)) has been established, committed to working together collaboratively in EU negotiations, and to regular meetings.

The Government's White Paper published before the European Union (Withdrawal) Bill addressed intergovernmental relations:

[w]e will begin intensive discussions with the devolved administrations to identify where common frameworks need to be retained in the future, what these should be, and where common frameworks covering the UK are not necessary. Whilst these discussions are taking place with devolved administrations we will seek to minimise any changes to these frameworks. We will work closely with the devolved administrations to deliver an approach that works for the whole and each part of the UK.[56]

The European Union (Withdrawal) Bill will accord UK ministers with extraordinary powers. In particular, they will have extensive powers to make

[55] Joint Ministerial Committee Communiqué (24 October 2016) https://www.gov.uk/government/publications/joint-ministerial-committee-communique-24-october-2016.
[56] UK Government, 'The Great Repeal Bill: White Paper' (30 March 2017) para 4.4.

delegated legislation with which to amend or repeal vast areas of incorporated EU law. Inevitably many of the laws which will be changed are in areas which are devolved or which overlap between devolved and reserved matters. This is even more inevitable given the Scotland Act 2016 and the Wales Act 2017, which extend competences to the devolved legislatures and which include many more areas of shared competence.

However, how will Brexit overlap with devolution? The European Union (Withdrawal) Bill (clauses 10 and 11) leaves the UK Government with firm control over the distribution of powers returning from Brussels. One issue the White Paper does refer to, however, is the need for a coherent UK single market.[57] This is a pressing concern. It is vital for the future of England's relations with the devolved territories and hence for the Union as a whole, that the approach to Brexit is consensual and that planning for the incredibly intricate process of extricating the UK from the EU is properly coordinated.

To this end, intergovernmental relations is set to be perhaps the most significant constitutional issue as Brexit takes place. The new Joint Ministerial Committee on EU Negotiations (JMC (EN)) will be crucial to the ongoing development of the English question. Coordination of policy is crucial to ensure that Brexit works coherently across the UK. As the House of Lords Constitution Committee puts it:

[If] the 'Great Repeal Bill' will leave to ministers in the devolved administrations the ability to prepare amendments to those elements of EU law that will, following Brexit, fall within their competence. ….. it is essential that the devolved institutions work closely with the UK Government to ensure that EU law does not 'fall between the cracks' of their respective jurisdictions and that decisions on the repeal or adoption of domesticated EU law are taken in a way that has regard to the coherence of the Union.[58]

The Law Society of Scotland gave evidence to the House of Lords Constitution Committee. It suggested that where circumstances require the UK government to make subordinate legislation to deal with EU legal issues that fall within the competence of the devolved institutions, '[a]t the least discussions should take place at the Joint Ministerial Council and agreement reached on the terms of such UK delegated legislation. Following on such a Ministerial agreement this legislation should be laid in each of the devolved legislatures

---

[57] ibid paras 4.2 and 4.4.
[58] House of Lords, Constitution Committee, 'The "Great Repeal Bill" and Delegated Powers', 9th Report of Session 2016–2017, HL Paper 123, paras 121–2.

for information only'.[59] The need for consensus at the political and constitutional levels, if not at the strictly legal level, is a clear imperative. Interestingly, however, the more that powers overlap and that joint decisions need to be made, the more we might imagine that the UK will be of clear relevance to citizens in the devolved areas, and the more that devolution might come to be seen in England as a normalized part of the constitutional architecture of the UK.

To conclude, England's position in the constitution is changing. We see this in the potential for a radical redesign of local and regional government. It is also the case that EVEL has worked well so far, but that may be as much by luck as by design. What is clear is that England as a political force has awakened. However, this happens at a time when Brexit is putting new strains on the UK union since it is a decision that is widely perceived in the rest of the UK as having been driven by England and English politics. But it is also the case that Brexit may offer opportunities for the mettle of devolution and of the intergovernmental mechanisms which are designed to manage it to be tested. It is incumbent upon political leaders in London to emphasize throughout the UK that the Union is a multinational one, and to make a success of Brexit in a way that can sustain a strong Union needs this to be properly recognized. To this end, what will be needed is a constitutional recognition that devolution requires government of the British union by consensus. The constitutional rights of the devolved territories must be recognized in England, but at the same time England's dominant position, which has in recent times not been properly respected, must also be recognized. An asymmetrical devolved UK can work but it can only work through realism and mutual respect.

---

[59] Written evidence from the Law Society of Scotland (LEG0046). On 27 October 2016, Secretary of State for Scotland, David Mundell, gave a strong commitment to close intergovernmental relations on the issue of legal change during Brexit in evidence to the Scottish Parliament's Culture, Tourism, Europe, and External Relations Committee.

6

Brexit and the Scottish Question

Sionaidh Douglas-Scott

1. Introduction: A Chronicle of Two (or Three?) Referendums

The EU Referendum Act 2015 made provision for a referendum on whether the UK should remain a member of the EU, a commitment included in the 2015 Conservative Party manifesto. On 23 June 2016, 62 per cent of those voting in Scotland voted to remain in the EU, whereas in the UK overall, 51.9 per cent of those voting voted to leave. Overall, Scotland tends to be less Eurosceptic than most of England[1] and the Scottish government has expressed opposition to the prospect of leaving the EU. For example, the Scottish government's 2014 *Agenda for EU Reform* paper disagreed with the proposed renegotiation of Britain's EU membership, did not support the subsequent referendum, and argued that EU reform could be delivered without major treaty change.[2] In December 2016, six months after the EU Referendum result, the Scottish government published its proposals for a differentiated solution for Scotland, in its Paper, *Scotland's Place in Europe*,[3] making a case that even in the event of a 'hard Brexit' in the rest of the UK, Scotland could retain its single market membership. Such a differentiated solution seems, however, to have been rejected by the UK government and, in March 2017, the Scottish Parliament voted formally to request from the UK government

---

[1] Although we should not forget London, and some other English cities, that buck England's Eurosceptic trend; see eg T Oliver, 'Londoners Are Not Little Englanders' (2014) *British Policy and Politics Blog*.

[2] Scottish Government, *Scotland's Agenda for EU Reform* http://www.gov.scot/Publications/2014/08/5067/0.

[3] Scottish Government, *Scotland's Place in Europe* (December 2016) www.gov.scot/Resource/0051/00512073.pdf.

Brexit and the Scottish Question. First edition. Sionaidh Douglas-Scott © Sionaidh Douglas-Scott 2017. Published 2017 by Oxford University Press.

the powers to stage a fresh independence vote at around the time Britain leaves the EU.[4]

Scotland's role in Brexit has to be seen in the broader context of its relations with the United Kingdom union. On 18 September 2014, in an historic referendum, the Scottish people voted by 55 per cent to 45 per cent to remain in the UK.[5] During the independence referendum campaign, the pro-UK, 'Better Together' side notably raised the issue of EU membership. They suggested that the only way Scotland's EU membership would be assured would be by remaining in the UK, and that an independent Scotland's application for EU membership could take years, with no guarantee of success.[6] Thus, in voting against independence, many Scots might have thought they were securing EU membership. This has proved not to be the case. Furthermore, a vote to remain in the UK was also presented as ensuring greater devolution when, immediately before the vote,[7] the leaders of the three largest unionist parties (Conservative, Labour, Liberal Democrat) gave a 'vow' to the Scottish electorate[8] that, in the event of a 'No' vote, there would be further devolution of power to Scotland. Shortly thereafter, the Smith Commission produced a report[9] recommending a number of areas where power should be devolved. Legislation was introduced to the UK Parliament, which included greater taxing powers for Scotland, as well as provisions supposedly rendering the Scottish Parliament 'permanent' and placing the Sewel Convention on a legislative basis,[10] and the Scotland Act 2016 became law shortly before the 2016 Scottish Parliament election. However, the issue of 'repatriation' of powers following Britain's EU withdrawal now raises the possible threat of retrenchment of the devolution settlement, which is discussed further below.

Brexit and its convulsions may reinvigorate the cause of Scottish independence. The SNP manifesto for the 2016 Holyrood elections stated that another independence referendum should take place if there were a 'material change in circumstances' from the vote in 2014—such as Scotland being removed

[4] 'Scottish Parliament backs referendum call' *BBC News* (28 March 2017).

[5] This followed the election of an SNP government in 2011, with an overall parliamentary majority, with a manifesto commitment to hold a referendum on independence.

[6] See further on this S Douglas-Scott, 'Scotland, Secession and the EU' in A McHarg, T Mullen, and N Walker (eds), *The Scottish Independence Referendum: Constitutional and Political Implications* (OUP 2016).

[7] When a *You Gov* poll suggested that Scots might actually vote for independence; see 'Scottish Independence: Poll Shows Yes Side in the Lead' *The Guardian* (7 September 2014).

[8] Published on the front page of the *Daily Record* (Scotland's highest circulating newspaper).

[9] The Smith Commission, *Report of the Smith Commission for Further Devolution of Powers to the Scottish Parliament* (27 November 2014).

[10] Scotland Act 2016, s 2.

from the EU against its wishes. The SNP regard this as a mandate since they were re-elected in 2016.[11] From the time of the EU referendum, while the UK government has been following a UK-wide approach to Brexit which has found little room for the concerns of the devolved nations, Scotland has been accentuating its specific political and legal identity, and First Minister, Nicola Sturgeon, has described the prospect of the country's removal from the EU as 'democratically unacceptable'.[12]

This chapter considers the question of Scotland and Brexit, both from the perspective of Scotland's relations with the EU and from the standpoint of British constitutional law and the impact of Brexit on the union of Scotland and England. The impact of Brexit raises the stakes for Anglo–Scottish relations and the continuance of the (UK) union generally. In voting to leave one union (the EU), the British people may well find that they are bringing about the end of another, older union (the UK).

2. The EU Referendum

This set the Brexit train in motion. However, the 2015 EU Referendum Act imposed no obligation on the UK government to implement its results—it was a consultative referendum, and indeed, there are no constitutional provisions in the UK requiring the results of a referendum to be implemented. This contrasts with eg Ireland, where the Irish constitution states circumstances in which a binding referendum must be held.

Further, the 2015 Act set no condition of a 'quadruple lock' threshold, requiring each constituent part or nation of the UK (England, Scotland, Wales, and Northern Ireland) to vote to leave before the UK can withdraw from the EU. The EU Referendum Act 2015 takes a unitary, UK-wide approach to the vote. This contrasts with the situation in some federal countries. In Australia, for example, referendums to approve changes to the constitution must achieve a majority of voters as a whole, and a majority in a majority of states.[13] While the UK Referendum Act was progressing through the House of Commons, the SNP tabled an amendment to require such a double-majority threshold, but were unsuccessful. In the words of Alex Salmond, 'nations within a multi-national state should be recognised as more than regions, counties or areas

---

[11] Albeit as a minority government, with support from the Green Party.
[12] 'Brexit: Scotland Leaving EU is "Democratically Unacceptable", says Nicola Sturgeon' *The Independent* (24 June 2016).
[13] Constitution of Australia, s 128.

and should not be counted by population; they are national entities in their own right, and that confers a relationship of respect'.[14]

The UK government was under no binding obligation to leave the EU as a result of the Referendum, but nonetheless, in March 2017, Theresa May delivered a letter to Brussels formally setting in motion the process for triggering Article 50 of the TEU and the UK's withdrawal from the EU. Shortly thereafter, the UK government published a White Paper[15] on the 'Great Repeal Bill', the means by which it intends to repeal the European Communities Act (ECA) 1972 and disentangle EU law from domestic law.

Thus, a first point to note is that it is extremely easy to bring about a major change in the British constitution (namely exit from the EU)—even if that change can be demonstrated to have major and unfortunate consequences for a particular nation of the UK, ie Scotland. Further, as will be elaborated in this chapter, unlike in some federal, and even non-federal states, it seems that as British constitutional law now stands, Scotland has no *legal* means of contesting an EU exit against the will of the Scottish government and a majority of its voters.

3. Scotland and Europe

An important aspect of Scotland's EU membership involves access to the single market. The EU is the main destination for Scotland's international exports, 'accounting for around 46 per cent of Scotland's international exports in 2013, value c. £12.9 billion'.[16] According to a 2016 report by the Fraser of Allander Institute, Brexit will have a significant negative impact on the Scottish economy, resulting in a GDP down by 2–5 per cent, and employment down by 1–3 per cent, than if the UK remained in the EU.[17] Furthermore, EU Common Agricultural Policy (CAP) and regional funding tends to benefit Scotland (and Wales and Northern Ireland) more than it does England. For example, in 2014–2020, Scotland's projected CAP funding is €4.3 billion.[18]

---

[14] Alex Salmond, HC Debate 16 June 2015, col 192.
[15] Department for Exiting the European Union, *Legislating for the United Kingdom's Withdrawal from the European Union*, Cm 9446 (March 2017).
[16] House of Commons Briefing 7213, 'Exiting the EU: Impact in Key UK Policy Areas', (4 June 2015).
[17] Fraser of Allander Institute, 'Long-term Economic Implications of Brexit: A Report for the Scottish Parliament' (October 2016) https://www.sbs.strath.ac.uk/economics/fraser/20161006/Long-term-Economic-Implications-of- Brexit.pdf.
[18] House of Commons Briefing 7213 (4 June 2015).

Indeed, in recent years, the EU has provided a congenial setting for sub-states and regions.[19] All UK nations have their own government representation in Brussels and regional ministers may attend EU Council meetings (at the discretion of the UK government).[20] Devolved governments have an important role in implementing and applying EU law, which applies in the field of many devolved competences, and, because EU law has permitted differentiated implementations of EU laws such as directives, distinctive approaches to EU agricultural and environmental law have been adopted in the different nations of the UK.[21]

Therefore it is not surprising that, in its December 2016 paper, *Scotland's Place in Europe*, the Scottish government argued for continued single market membership. It stated as its priority, first, continued UK participation in the single market. However, if that could not be maintained for the UK, the paper proposed that Scotland continue to participate in the single market through the EEA, necessitating separate arrangements for Scotland. This paper was produced before the UK government's February White Paper[22] on Brexit, and compares well with it—being much more substantive and detailed in nature, throwing into contrast the UK government's own rather sparse publication.

Notwithstanding these Scottish aspirations, in her Lancaster House speech[23] in January 2017, Theresa May clearly stated that the UK would leave both the single market and the customs union. Therefore, she necessarily rejected at least the first limb of the Scottish government's suggestions for future EU/UK relations. Further, no mention at all is made in the UK government's March letter triggering Article 50 of the TEU[24] of any particular arrangements for Scotland (although Northern Ireland is singled out as a special case) and it seems that the UK government has rejected the Scottish government's proposals.[25] This leaves very little space for Scotland to protect

---

[19] The EU's relationship with regional governments has evolved, partly in response to claims of Belgian regions and German Länder; see eg C Panara and A De Becker (eds), *The Role of the Regions in EU Governance* (Springer 2010).

[20] See TFEU, Article 16.

[21] See eg J Hunt, 'Devolution and Differentiation: Regional Variation in EU Law (2010) 30 *Legal Studies* 421.

[22] Department for Exiting the European Union: *The United Kingdom's Exit from and New Partnership with the European Union*, Cm 9417 (2 February 2017).

[23] 'The Government's Negotiating Objectives for Exiting the EU' PM speech (17 January 2017 https://www.gov.uk/government/speeches/the-governments-negotiating-objectives-for-exiting-the-eu-pm-speech.

[24] Prime Minister's letter to Donald Tusk triggering Article 50 (29 March 2017) https://www.gov.uk/government/uploads/system/uploads/attachment_data/file/604079/Prime_Ministers_letter_to_European_Council_President_Donald_Tusk.pdf.

[25] 'Article 50 a Leap in the Dark—Sturgeon' *BBC News* (29 March 2017).

its interests in the context of the withdrawal process, where it is the UK that will do the negotiating.

4. A 'UK Approach'

It is notable that one of the first actions taken by Theresa May when she became Prime Minister in July 2016 was to visit First Minister Nicola Sturgeon at Bute House in Edinburgh, where May said she would trigger Article 50 only if there were a 'UK approach and objectives for negotiations'.[26] This statement implied cooperation between the devolved administrations and the UK government. May also said that she would consider proposals from the Scottish government on Brexit.

Although foreign policy, which includes relations with the EU, is reserved to the UK government,[27] nonetheless, it is too simplistic to state that devolved administrations have no interest in EU matters, given that a large part of EU law relates to devolved competences. Additionally, many areas of EU law fall across the boundaries of devolved and reserved competences.[28] There also exists an intra-UK government machinery, which deploys principles (through a Memorandum of Understanding) by which the governments of the UK work together, and there is a specific Concordat on EU policy issues.[29] This Concordat provides that the UK government will involve the devolved administrations 'as directly and fully as possible in decision making on EU matters', through discussions by way of an institutional forum—the EU formation of the Joint Ministerial Committee, JMC(E). By October 2016, an EU Negotiations configuration (JMC (EN)) had been established, chaired by David Davis, with the aim of discussing the 'UK approach' to Brexit promised by the Prime Minister.[30] However, since then, the reaction to JMC (EN) meetings from the devolved nations has largely reflected frustration that their views were not being taken into account.

---

[26] See 'Brexit: PM is "Willing to Listen to Options" on Scotland', *BBC News* (15 July 2016).

[27] Foreign policy is a reserved matter under Scotland Act 1998, Schedule 5.

[28] For example, issues relating to the free movement of persons and immigration, which is reserved, may impact on health policy, which is devolved.

[29] Cabinet Office, *Memorandum of Understanding and Supplementary Agreements* (October 2013) https://www.gov.uk/government/uploads/system/uploads/attachment_data/file/316157/MoU_between_the_UK_and_the_Devolved_Administrations.pdf.

[30] See further Cabinet Office, Joint Ministerial Committee communiqué (24 October 2016) https://www.gov.uk/government/publications/joint-ministerial-committee-communique-24-october-2016).

All in all, there are reasons to be anxious about Scotland's place in the Brexit negotiations. The Article 50 letter stresses that: 'we will negotiate as one United Kingdom, taking due account of the specific interests of every nation and region of the UK as we do so'. However, it is unclear, to say the least, that the UK government gave any meaningful consideration to *Scotland's Place in Europe*, dismissing its proposals as 'not workable'.[31] Nor were the contents of the Article 50 notification discussed or shared with the Scottish government prior to its publication.[32] Overall, the Prime Minister's approach to Brexit, insisting on a UK approach, appears to be that of a unitary state. However, the archetype of 'unitary' state has been undermined by two decades of devolution in the UK.[33]

5. Would a Differentiated Solution Be Possible for Scotland?

To date, no guarantee has been given by the UK government to negotiate with the EU for a differentiated solution on Scotland's behalf. But would such a distinct arrangement for Scotland in any case be workable?

5.1 'Reverse Greenland'

For a while, immediately after the 2016 Referendum, the 'reverse Greenland' option was floated as a possibility for Scotland. In 1985, Greenland, which is part of Denmark, withdrew from the (then) EEC, although Denmark remained.[34] As the EEC treaties at that time contained no provision for the withdrawal either of a Member State or a part thereof, the necessary arrangements had to be negotiated.[35] The basis for Greenland's withdrawal was former Article 236 EEC (now Article 48 TEU). Following withdrawal, Greenland became associated with the EU as an Overseas Country and Territory through the Greenland Treaty.

---

[31] 'Article 50 a Leap in the Dark—Sturgeon' (n 25).   [32] ibid.

[33] See eg R Hazell and R Rawlings, *Devolution, Law Making and the Constitution* (Imprint Academic 2005); J Mitchell, *Devolution in the UK* (Manchester University Press 2009); V Bogdanor, *The New British Constitution* (Hart Publishing 2009).

[34] This took a considerable time—3 years. See further on the Greenland case eg F Weiss, 'Greenland's Withdrawal from the European Communities' (1985) *European Law Review* 173; also, M Nash, 'Could Britain Leave the European Union? The Greenland Option' (1996) 46 *New Law Journal* 6752.

[35] See on this eg *Status of Greenland: Commission Opinion* COM (83) 66 final (2 February 1983) 12.

Therefore, it was suggested that the EU treaties might be similarly amended, enabling Scotland to remain a member of the EU, even if England/'rUK' were to leave. However, there are obstacles to this. The main issue to be negotiated at the time of Greenland's departure concerned fishing rights, whereas there are multiple issues of contention in the case of Brexit. Furthermore, the part of Denmark that remains within the EU contains its central government, in Copenhagen. However, if 'rUK' were to withdraw and Scotland remain in the EU, the UK's central government would be located in England.

However, the Greenland case at least provides a precedent. It is possible for only part of a state to secede from the EU. Article 29 of the Vienna Convention on the Law of Treaties provides: 'Unless a different intention appears from the treaty or is otherwise established, a treaty is binding upon each party in respect of its entire territory'.[36] This implies it would be possible for a new amendment treaty to redefine which parts of UK territory fall within the scope of EU law. Indeed, when the Federal Republic of Germany enlarged in 1990, (then) EEC Member States accepted that the treaties could apply to its expanded territory without even being specifically amended, thus avoiding the lengthy and risky amendment procedure.

There are also further examples, not of partial secession, but of ways in which diverse parts of a state may have different relationships with the EU. One such example is the Isle of Man and Channel Islands. These are not part of the UK or EU, but possessions of the British crown. Nonetheless, Protocol 3 of the Accession Treaty of the UK to the (then) EEC permits trade for their goods without non-EU tariffs. However, they are excluded from the provisions governing free movement of people.[37] Another example is that of Gibraltar, which is a British overseas territory with its own constitution and self-government, except for defence and foreign affairs for which the British government is responsible. Although part of the EU, Gibraltar is outside the customs union and VAT area, exempted from the CAP, and does not form part of Schengen. Gibraltar has no option of cancelling its EU membership separately from the UK, but has stated that it wishes to remain in the EU, notwithstanding the Brexit vote. Yet while the Northern Irish border was mentioned in the letter triggering the UK's withdrawal under Article 50 of the TEU, Gibraltar was not. On 1 April 2017, a draft document on the EU's Brexit strategy said no agreement on the EU's future relationship with the UK

---

[36] See further eg O Dörr and K Schmalenbach (eds), *The Vienna Convention on the Law of Treaties: A Commentary* (Springer 2012).

[37] Their relationship with the EU generally is set out under TFEU, Article 355(5)(c), and Protocol 3 of the Act of Accession, annexed to the Treaty of Accession 1972.

would apply to Gibraltar without the consent of Spain, giving it a potential veto.[38]

The present situation of Gibraltar causes concern, but, overall, this survey of partial state membership of the EU illustrates that such complex and differentiated relationships are possible and have been acknowledged by the EU itself.

5.2 Scotland's place in Europe: single market membership for Scotland?

It is time to turn to the solution proposed in the Scottish Government Paper, *Scotland's Place in Europe*. This paper contemplates continued single market membership for Scotland, even in the absence of single market membership for 'rUK'. The Scottish paper recognizes that this would require some legal engineering. Indeed, it would require at least three major legal changes.

First, there would have to be a change to EFTA and EEA rules to allow in a sub-state such as Scotland (whether as full or associate member or member 'through' the UK). Scotland, although a nation in its own right, lacks the external legal competence to enter into treaties on its own behalf—unlike some other sub-state entities, for example, the Belgian regions.[39] In traditional international law, the 'state' is a formal category, with legal personality, in a way that the region, or sub-state, usually is not.[40] It would also be necessary for Scotland to acquire legal personality in its own right.

Secondly, Scotland's application for EEA membership would depend on 'UK sponsoring', as the UK government would have to negotiate this as part of a UK withdrawal treaty. The Scottish Government Paper gives the example of the Faroe Islands, which explored the EEA option under Danish sponsorship. However, this has not yet been achieved. In any case, it is not clear that the political will exists for this purpose in the UK government. The Scottish paper, however, also argues from analogy that, whatever solutions might be

---

[38] 'Brexit: Gibraltar Angered by Spain's EU "veto" ', *BBC News* (1 April 2017).

[39] See eg D Criekemans (ed), *Regional Substate Diplomacy Today* (Martinus Nijhoff 2010).

[40] See eg Montevideo Convention on Rights and Duties of States 1933, Article 1. As with the EU (Article 49 TEU), under UN Charter Article 4, only 'States' can be admitted to UN membership. However, the PCIJ analysis in the *Western Sahara* case is a good example of the clash between the classical concept of statehood and other cultural concepts of control over territory (ICJ Reports (1975) 10); see also R Portman, *Legal Personality in International Law* (CUP 2013); M Koskeniemmi, 'The Future of Statehood' (1991) 32 *Harvard Journal of International Law* 397; H Michelmann and P Soldatos (eds), *Federalism and International Relations: the Role of Subnational Units* (OUP 1990); C Schreuer, 'The Waning of the Sovereign State: Towards a New Paradigm for International-Law?' (1993) 4 *European Journal of International Law* 447.

found for the Irish border (promised by the UK government) should also be applied to relations between Scotland and 'rUK'.

Thirdly, there would need to be a wider-ranging devolution of powers to Scotland to enable it to comply with single market rules ranging from employment and social policy to product and professional standards, health and safety, consumer protection, and migration. For example, powers over immigration might need to be devolved. Such a transfer of power could not be achieved by the 'Great Repeal Bill' but would require separate UK primary legislation, devolving powers to Scotland, and providing it with legal personality and the ability to conclude international agreements in its own right, as well as subsequent Scottish legislation on EU single market matters. So far, there is little evidence that the UK government is contemplating this. For example, although the notion of 'regional visas' could also be explored for other parts of the UK,[41] devolution of immigration is something Theresa May seems to have ruled out.[42]

More generally, there are issues with a differentiated settlement for Scotland that require, in the words of the Scottish government, some legal 'engineering'. *Scotland's Place in Europe* suggests that Scotland would remain in a customs union with 'rUK', so that the internal border between Scotland and rUK would not be a customs border, thus avoiding the potential problems facing the island of Ireland. However, it would still be necessary to distinguish Scottish exports to the EU from 'rUK' exports, which would need to pay EU tariffs. The situation would be more complicated still with non-tariff barriers, as the situation of 'rUK' goods which are non-compliant with EU standards reveals. These could be sold in Scotland under what the paper terms 'parallel marketability'[43] but not to other EEA countries. However, there would be a need for some system to ensure these goods were not then exported to the EU, thus circumventing EU rules.

In any case, no mention is made in the Article 50 letter of any particular arrangements for Scotland, which leaves one wondering where Scotland's proposals stand. Presumably this means the UK government has rejected the Scottish government's proposals. This leaves very little space for Scotland to protect its interests in the context of the withdrawal process, where it is the UK that will do the negotiating—a feature that will certainly have consequences, as discussed further below.

---

[41] Price Waterhouse Cooper, *Regional Visas – A Unique Immigration Solution*, (October 2016) prepared for the City of London Corporation.

[42] 'Theresa May rules out Scots deal on immigration despite warnings', *The Herald* (5 February 2017).

[43] *Scotland's Place in Europe* (n 3) para 152.

6. EU Withdrawal Bill ['Great Repeal Bill']

In March 2017, the UK government also produced a White Paper on the 'Great Repeal Bill'.[44] In July 2017, this Bill was published and renamed the EU (Withdrawal) Bill (EU(W)B),[45] although many in the media continue to refer to it as 'Great Repeal' or 'Repeal' Bill. This Bill has three main tasks. First, it is intended to remove the European Communities Act 1972 (ECA) from the statute book following completion of Brexit negotiations—hence the 'repeal' terminology. However, secondly, the Bill will also conserve, for it will convert EU law (as it stands at the moment of exit) into UK law. Otherwise, given the many EU provisions currently applicable in the UK, there would be a risk of huge gaps in national law on exit day. Thirdly, the Bill will make provision for ex-EU legislation to be amended or repealed by secondary legislation.

However, the EU(W)B is liable to provoke devolved administrations in Edinburgh, Cardiff and Belfast, at a time when the union of the United Kingdom is already fragile. As stated, an aim of the Bill is to convert EU law into national law. However, a good part of EU law relates to competences that have been devolved—for Scotland this includes agriculture, fishing within Scottish waters, and environmental law.[46] If the EU(W)B translates such matters into UK law this would amount to legislation on devolved areas—a contentious issue that would require the formal legislative consent of the Scottish Parliament.

The issue of the EU(W)B thus raises several specific issues for Scotland that will be dealt with in turn, namely: the issue of repatriation of competences from Brussels (and their financing); the question of whether further powers should be devolved to Scotland in the event of a differentiated Brexit deal; the necessity of legislative consent (invoking the Sewel Convention) in this context; and the utilization of secondary legislation to effectuate power transfers post Brexit to the detriment of Scotland.

---

[44] *Legislating for the United Kingdom's Withdrawal from the European Union* Cm 9446 (March 2017).

[45] EU (Withdrawal) Bill (HC Bill 05). Explanatory notes to the Bill, prepared by the Department for Exiting the European Union, are published separately as Bill 5—EN.

[46] According to the EU's Committee of the Regions, around 70% of EU legislation must be implemented by local or regional authorities; Committee of the Regions, *A New Treaty: A New Role for Regional and Local Authorities* (Brussels 2009). However, in a paper produced for the Scottish Parliament, Professor Alan Page suggested that many existing EU competences are currently reserved to the UK Parliament. See A Page, 'The Implications of EU Withdrawal for the Devolution Settlement' (2016).

Unfortunately, given its considerable implications for devolution, the 'Great Repeal Bill' White Paper devoted very little space to it—just six short paragraphs. The EU(W)B itself, together with its Explanatory notes, adds little that would please the devolved nations. Indeed, the White Paper's dominant theme was the need to ensure stability and consistency across the UK, rather than any meaningful focus on the devolution settlement. This approach appears to have been carried over into the Bill itself.

6.1 Repatriation of competences

The Brexit process is intended to remove the limits and checks that EU law places on national legislation, ensuring that competences will be returned or 'repatriated'[47] to the UK. However, there is a question mark over how these powers will be repatriated and whether this will impact on devolved powers. The UK government's view is that, even in the case of devolved powers such as agriculture and the environment, the 'repatriation' process will first 'return' them to Westminster and then decisions will be made as to where they should go from there: 'as the powers to make these rules are repatriated to the UK from the EU, we have an opportunity to determine the level best placed to make new laws and policies on these issues'.[48] This is the approach taken in the EU(W)B. Clause 11 of the EU(W)B amends devolution legislation, so modification of retained EU law will fall outside devolved competence. Section 29 of the Scotland Act 1998 is to be amended to this effect. Thus, clause 11 freezes devolved competence on the day the UK exits the EU and repatriated powers will flow, at first instance, back to London.

The view of the Scottish government, in contrast, is that competences that are not reserved are not being 'repatriated', because they are already located within the devolved sphere, although regulated by constraints on their use.[49] Devolved policy fields should automatically revert to Scotland unless explicit legislation is adopted to change this.[50] *Scotland's Place in Europe* signalled that Scotland would resist attempts to reserve repatriated competences such as agriculture, fisheries, education, health, justice, and environmental protection.[51]

---

[47] The word used in the 'Great Repeal Bill' White Paper at 4.3.

[48] *The United Kingdom's Exit From, and New Partnership With, the European Union* White Paper Cm 9417 (February 2017) para 3.5.

[49] *Scotland's Place in Europe* (n 3) 4.

[50] Interestingly, this view was shared by the Supreme Court in *R (Miller) v Secretary of State for Exiting the European Union* [2017] UKSC 5, para 130: 'The removal of EU constraints on withdrawal from the EU Treaties will alter the competence of devolved institutions unless new legislative constraints are introduced. In the absence of such new restraints, withdrawal from the EU will enhance devolved competence'.

[51] *Scotland's Place in Europe* (n 3) 2, 4, 40.

On the day the EU(W)B was given its first reading, 13 July 2017, the First Ministers of Scotland and Wales issued a joint statement, describing the Bill as: '[a] naked power-grab, an attack on the founding principles of devolution and could destabilise our economies'.[52]

Increasing the power of the UK government would also undermine the vow made before the 2014 independence referendum and the recommendations of the Smith Commission—which were for considerably more devolution, not less.

The UK government has indicated that no 'decisions'[53] currently taken by devolved institutions will be removed, and this was reiterated in the Prime Minister's letter triggering Article 50. However, it might be argued that 'decisions' (as opposed to implementation) on eg agriculture are currently taken by European institutions, and not by devolved institutions. Although the 'Great Repeal Bill' White Paper envisages that 'the outcome of the withdrawal process will be a significant increase in the decision making power of each devolved administration',[54] it also states: 'As powers are repatriated from the EU, it will be important to ensure that stability and certainty is not compromised, and that the effective functioning of the UK single market is maintained'.[55] The later Factsheet on Devolution, published by the Department for Exiting the EU on the day the EU(W)B was published states that: 'As powers are repatriated from the EU, our guiding principle is that no new barriers to living and doing business within our own union are created when we leave the EU. We will therefore need to examine these powers carefully to determine the level best placed to take decisions on these issues'.[56]

Indeed, the Great Repeal Bill White Paper stated that it will 'replicate the current frameworks provided by EU rules through UK legislation'.[57] This is reiterated in the 'Devolution Factsheet' published with the Bill. This has been described as a 'holding pattern'[58] which would continue until it is decided whether a UK-wide framework is appropriate. According to the 'Devolution Factsheet', there 'will be a transitional arrangement to provide certainty after exit and allow intensive discussion and consultation with devolved authorities on where lasting common frameworks are or are not needed', although it does not clarify what format these discussions will take, nor whether it is

---

[52] See Joint Statement of First Minister of Scotland Nicola Sturgeon and First Minister of Wales Carwyn Jones on EU (Withdrawal Bill) 13/07/2017 https://news.gov.scot/news/eu-withdrawal-bill.
[53] 'The Government's Negotiating Objectives for Exiting The EU' PM Speech (17 January 2017).
[54] *Legislating for the United Kingdom's Withdrawal from the European Union* (n 15) 8, 28.
[55] ibid 27.   [56] Department for Exiting the EU, 'Factsheet 5 Devolution'.
[57] ibid 27 para 4.4.
[58] According to Alun Cairns, Welsh Secretary see 'Brexit "Holding Pattern" for EU Laws in Great Repeal Bill' *BBC News* (30 March 2017).

the UK government that will take the final decision. It does, however, state that: 'Where it is determined that a common approach is not required, the Bill provides a power to lift the limit on devolved competence in that area'.[59] Clause 11 of the EU(W)B states that it will be possible, by Order-in-Council, to specify that the prohibition on modifying retained EU law does not apply regarding certain matters.

However, it is unclear what the UK government means by 'frameworks'. Such 'frameworks' could take the form of Westminster statutes, or new transversal regulations to secure the UK single market, or simply intensified intergovernmental cooperation. However, given present dissatisfaction with the JMC as an institution for securing intergovernmental cooperation, it seems unlikely that frameworks based on UK legislation and JMC cooperation would satisfy the Scottish government.

In any event, any adjustments to the devolution settlement would require the consent of the Scottish Parliament and use of a legislative consent motion (LCM) (Sewel) and are discussed below.

6.2 UK internal market

To date, EU law has set constraints so that its Member States have to legislate in compliance with the EU internal market. However, once the UK exits the EU, these EU structures and legal constraints will no longer exist. Yet, in the absence of EU common principles, barriers to trade within the UK may materialize. As mentioned, both the Great Repeal Bill White Paper and the Factsheets published with the EU(W)B argue for national 'common frameworks'. Furthermore, policy harmonization might also be needed to comply with WTO rules and any trade deal the UK might sign with the EU or other parties.

The problem is that UK devolution took place within the structures of the larger EU internal market, so it was not necessary to provide a detailed framework for a UK internal market. Prior to the UK's accession to the (then) EEC, the 1973 Kilbrandon Report on the constitution was able to state that 'the UK is a unitary state in economic terms ... It has, for example, a single currency and a banking system responsible to a single central bank. Its people enjoy a right of freedom of movement of trade, labour and capital and of settlement and establishment anywhere within the UK'.[60]

---

[59] Factsheet 5,
[60] *Royal Commission on the Constitution 1969–1973*, vol 1 Report (HMSO 1973) (Cmnd 5460) para 57.

Now the position is somewhat different, and the UK is no longer a unitary state (at least from the perspective of the devolved nations) and instead more 'multi-layered'.[61] Federal and other non-unitary states have had to make provision to ensure policy harmonization or prevent barriers to trade. For example, the US has its commerce clause, which states that the United States Congress shall have power 'to regulate Commerce with foreign Nations, and among the several States, and with the Indian Tribes'.[62] Article 73(1)(5) of the German constitution states that: 'The Federation shall have exclusive legislative power with respect to: ... the unity of the customs and trading area, treaties regarding commerce and navigation, the free movement of goods, and the exchange of goods and payments with foreign countries, including customs and border protection'. According to Anderson, 'there is always a judgment about the relative priority—and even legitimacy—to be assigned to the objective of an integrated internal market versus other objectives'.[63]

It is difficult to determine what the UK government has in mind—whether it plans to set up some new intra-governmental machinery or to legislate to put in place UK-wide free movement principles which courts could enforce. However, whatever the mechanism, the UK government will need to act with attention to the devolutionary settlement and the Sewel Convention.

6.3 Finances

However, even if former EU competences flow to devolved levels, their financing will not automatically do so. Post-Brexit, the UK's contributions to the EU will revert to the UK Treasury, and therefore some mechanism will be needed to distribute it across the UK. Scotland, unlike Wales and Northern Ireland, is a net contributor to the EU. However, Scotland does benefit more than England from funding in three main spending areas of agricultural policy, structural funds, and research.[64]

What will happen to this funding post-Brexit? There are three possible models for future funding. First, it could be needs-based, resulting in different levels of funding in different parts of the UK, essentially following the present EU model for agriculture and structural funds. However, agreeing

---

[61] See eg N Bamforth and P Leyland (eds), *Public Law in a Multi-Layered Constitution* (Hart Publishing 2003).

[62] United States Constitution (Article I, Section 8, Clause 3).

[63] G Anderson (ed), *Internal Markets and Multi-level Governance: The Experience of the European Union, Australia, Canada, Switzerland and the United States* (OUP 2012) 1.

[64] A Greer, *The European Referendum, Agriculture, Food and Rural Policy Issues* (Royal Society of Edinburgh 2016); SPERI Political Economy Research Brief No 24, *UK Regions and European Structural and Investment Funds* (University of Sheffield 2016).

the definition and measurement of need could be difficult given the differ-ing conditions across the UK. Secondly, funding could be distributed on a population basis, which would allocate funding on an equal per capita basis, to the detriment of Scotland in agriculture, where its funding exceeds its share of population. Finally, present spending levels could be incorporated into the Barnett Formula. In such a system, Scotland would keep its existing levels of spending but adjustments in future years would be based on changes in English spending in those fields. This would expose Scotland to changes made in English expenditure levels, for example a decision to reduce regional development spending or agricultural support.

6.4 Secondary Legislation

The prospect of a 'Great Repeal Bill' caused further alarm in Scotland when a report authored by Professor Alan Page[65] suggested that many laws affect-ing devolved issues could be unilaterally scrapped by Westminster as a con-sequence of Brexit, because secondary legislation could be used to unpick former EU laws. However, because brought about by secondary legislation, such changes would not require the consent—or even the knowledge—of the Scottish Parliament.

Clearly, secondary legislation will be used in the Brexit process. The UK White Paper explained that the 'Great Repeal Bill' will provide a power to correct the UK statute book using secondary legislation, and Clauses 7–9 of the EU(W)B itself provide that power. Clause 10 and Schedule 2 confer powers on devolved administrations for similar purposes, although subject to exceptions. Westminster simply will not have enough time to issue primary legislation to manage the manifold repeals or amendments of EU law neces-sary, so much of this will fall to the executive, using powers delegated to it by the EU(W)B. The problem is that Parliament has a minimal role in secondary legislation. Indeed, it is clear that the EU(W)B will include a 'Henry VIII' clause, namely a provision that enables *primary* legislation to be amended or repealed by secondary legislation, hardly a means for Parliament to 'take back control', given that they permit ministers to override existing legislation.

However, the situation is more critical for Scotland. As Page writes: 'The situation could thus arise in which the UK legislated extensively in areas devolved to Scotland without seeking the consent of the Scottish Parliament as there would be no requirement of its consent in relation to subordinate legislation altering the effects of EU law in the devolved areas'.[66]

---

[65] See Page (n 45).   [66] ibid 6.

There is thus a sizeable potential gap in the architecture of the Scottish Parliament's control over UK law-making in devolved areas. In October 2016, the Secretary of State for Scotland, David Mundell, gave evidence to the Scottish Parliament's Culture, Tourism, Europe, and External Relations Committee. When asked about the possibility of former EU laws falling within Scotland's devolved competence being repealed by secondary legislation in the UK Parliament, he gave the undertaking that 'no laws will be changed of the type that you refer to without consultation with this Parliament'.[67] It remains to be seen whether the UK government will hold good to this undertaking—unfortunately, the EU(W)B, and particularly the extraordinarily broad clause 7, lacks clarity here.

7. Legislative Consent

Under section 28(7) of the Scotland Act 1998, the UK Parliament, as a sovereign legislature, retains the power to make or unmake any law for Scotland whatever. However, under the 'Sewel convention', legislative consent of the Scottish Parliament would be needed when Westminster legislation touches on devolved matters. This requires a LCM. Indeed, the UK government's Devolution Guidance Note 10 states that a Bill requiring Scottish parliamentary consent under the Sewel Convention is one which 'contains provisions applying to Scotland and which are for devolved purposes, *or* which alter the legislative competence of the Parliament or the executive competence of the Scottish Ministers'.[68]

As the term suggests, the 'Sewel Convention', as a constitutional convention, takes the form of a political as opposed to a legally binding undertaking. However, as part of the post-independence referendum 'vow' on entrenching Holyrood's powers, section 2 of the Scotland Act 2016 inserted a new subsection (8) into section 28 of the Scotland Act 1998, giving statutory recognition to the Convention in the following form: 'But it is recognised that the Parliament of the United Kingdom will not normally legislate with regard to devolved matters without the consent of the Scottish Parliament'. To many, this looked to be a legal right for Holyrood to refuse consent to changes to its powers and renders its status as a 'mere' convention somewhat less clear.

---

[67] Official Report, Culture, Tourism, European, and External Relations Committee (27 October 2016) 12http://www.parliament.scot/parliamentarybusiness/report.aspx?r=10584&mode=pdf.

[68] Cabinet Office, 'Devolution Guidance Note 10: Post-Devolution Primary Legislation Affecting Scotland' (23 August 2011) para 4 (emphasis added).

Nonetheless, in the *Miller* case,[69] the Supreme Court unanimously held that constitutional conventions are political in nature, and not enforceable by the courts.[70] As much of the famously uncodified British constitution rests on such conventions, this means that a great deal of it is legally unenforceable. The Court held that judges can recognize the operation of convention in the context of deciding a legal question[71] but they cannot give legal rulings on its operation or scope.

Indeed, the Supreme Court in *Miller* went further. It considered the provisions in the Scotland Act 2016 that supposedly put the Sewel Convention on a statutory basis. However, the Supreme Court found that embodying the Convention in law does not in fact turn it into law but rather 'entrench it as a convention'. According to the Court, this had the consequence that while Sewel 'has an important role in facilitating harmonious relationships' between Westminster and devolved administrations, it was not for courts to 'police' its operation.[72]

Yet for the Supreme Court to hold that the Sewel Convention has no legal force is disputable. For a start, there exist precedents in which courts *have* ruled on operation of conventions (eg the *Evans* case[73]). Further, surely giving statutory recognition to Sewel in the 2016 Scotland Act amounts to more than a merely symbolic effect? Indeed, the notion of an 'entrenched convention' is bewildering if it adds nothing to the ability to enforce it, and certainly provocative in the context of the current fragile state of UK–Scottish constitutional affairs.

The status of Sewel is highly salient because, unlike in the context of the *Miller* litigation, which concerned who could lawfully trigger Article 50 of the TEU, it is likely that the EU(W)B will require the legislative consent of the Scottish Parliament. This is because it will enact into UK law parts of the EU *acquis* that are currently devolved (eg agriculture or environment) and may also modify the powers of devolved legislatures, which are currently unable to legislate contrary to EU law. The UK Government Scottish Secretary, David Mundell, suggested that legislative consent would be needed for the Great Repeal Bill, but there was no mention of this in the UK government White Paper on the 'Great Repeal Bill'. More recently, however, David Davis confirmed that legislative consent motions would be sought on the Repeal

---

[69] *R (Miller) v Secretary of State for Exiting the European Union* [2017] UKSC 5.

[70] To be clear, the Court did not hold that legislative consent of the devolved nations would not be required at all, as some reports of the case suggested; rather, that they could not be enforced legally.

[71] As in *Attorney-General v Jonathan Cape Ltd* [1976] QB 752.

[72] See *Miller* (n 49) para 151.   [73] *R (Evans) v Attorney-General* [2015] UKSC 21.

Bill[74] and the UK government's Explanatory Notes on the EU(W)B clearly state that it will seek legislative consent on the Bill.[75]

At the very least, it may be argued that the express inclusion of the Sewel Convention in the Scotland Act 2016 makes it impossible to ignore politically. To be sure, the provision is that Westminster will not 'normally' invade devolved competences without their consent, and much has been made of this. But if 'normally' simply means the UK government's stipulated interpretation of the term, then the provision is pointless. LCMs only make sense if they go beyond trifling and commonplace issues. If the UK government ignores Sewel, then devolution loses its point.

So clearly, there are very considerable implications for devolution. What would happen if Westminster ignored constitutional practice and enacted the 'EU Withdrawal Bill' without the consent of the Scottish Parliament? There exist precedents in which the Welsh Assembly has refused consent to UK legislation, but in which the UK government pressed on regardless, and the Welsh Assembly also enacted its own legislation. The Welsh legislation was challenged in the UK Supreme Court (being a non-sovereign legislature this is possible) and, in the 2014 case, *In re Agricultural Sector (Wales) Bill*, the Welsh legislation was upheld.[76] A direct challenge to an 'EU Withdrawal Act' would be unlikely to succeed due to the doctrine of parliamentary sovereignty, as such an Act would of course be primary legislation. Article IX of the Bill of Rights Act operates to prevent proceedings in Parliament from being questioned in the courts. In *Pickin v British Railways Board*[77] it was held that an Act of Parliament must be accepted as conclusively valid by the courts, even if there is some evidence that it was brought about by deception.

7.1 Continuation Bills?

However, suppose the Scottish Parliament legislated its own 'Great Continuation Act', affirming the continuation in Scottish law of all areas previously a matter of EU law that fell within its devolved competence? What constitutional objection could there be to the Scottish Parliament legislating within its own devolved competences? Indeed, the Welsh Assembly debated a motion on the question of a Welsh Continuation Bill shortly after the 'Great Repeal Bill' White Paper was published.[78]

---

[74] 'Brexit: Devolved institutions' consent sought on Repeal Bill' *BBC News* (28 June 2017).
[75] EU (Withdrawal) Bill Explanatory Notes, para 69.
[76] *Reference by the Attorney General for England and Wales* [2014] UKSC 43.
[77] *Pickin v British Railways Board* [1974] AC 765.
[78] National Assembly for Wales: Plenary (4 April 2017) Motion NND 6289.

Such a Bill might have several purposes. First, Scotland could resolve to act in compliance with EU law in any future legislation it adopted within the scope of devolved competences.[79] There might be a question of why Scotland might wish to shadow EU law and so curtail its legislative competence—however, as Scotland has to date had to act within the confines of EU law, this would not mean a massive change of circumstances.

But there might be reasons why Scotland would wish to continue to comply with EU law within devolved competences—the desire for future EU membership of a possible independent Scotland might be one example. Scotland also might wish to continue to attract high-calibre students from the EU to foster migration and free movement and eschew any raising of fee income in this way. Other areas of EU law might in any case prove attractive on their own account. For example, the EU Charter might be continued to apply to matters within devolved scope. This might be perceived as attractive in terms of adherence to a more progressive, up to date Bill of Rights than the European Convention on Human Rights (ECHR).

Secondly, a Continuation Bill could target the UK government's intention to introduce UK-wide frameworks, setting out possible procedures for Scottish Parliament or government participation in UK-wide frameworks. A Scottish Bill could, for example, provide that the Scottish Parliament/Government must be consulted and give its consent where any UK-wide frameworks (including legislation or more informal provisions) are introduced that are deemed necessary for the realization of a UK single market, where those frameworks have any impact on a devolved competence.

Thirdly, a Continuation Bill could address the impact of delegated legislation. It could give detail on procedures that could be required in devolved Parliaments where delegated legislation impacts on devolved matters, thus dealing with the risks highlighted in the Page report.

Subsequent UK legislation could, of course, as a consequence of Westminster sovereignty, override such Continuations Acts. However, if this were the case, it would further debilitate the UK's fragile territorial constitution and risk constitutional crisis.

---

[79] It might seem strange if the law of a treaty that no longer bound the UK was still observed under the devolution settlement. But there are precedents for voluntary compliance with treaties by non-contracting parties. For example, the EU in Article 6 of the TEU declares that: 'The Union shall respect fundamental rights, as guaranteed by the European Convention for the Protection of Human Rights and Fundamental Freedoms'.

8. A Contested Constitution

The Article 50 withdrawal letter delivered in March 2017 stressed that: 'we will negotiate as one United Kingdom, taking due account of the specific interests of every nation and region of the UK as we do so'. However, it is unclear that the UK government is taking due account of the devolved nations' interests. No mention at all is made in the Article 50 letter of any particular arrangements for Scotland, nor of the Scottish government's proposals in *Scotland's Place in Europe*. How then could Scotland protect its interests in the context of the withdrawal process, where it is the UK that will do the negotiating, if the UK government has no plan to argue on Scotland's behalf? As already discussed, the JMC (EN) has proved deeply frustrating to devolved ministers.

This lack of any formal voice for Scotland in the withdrawal negotiations reveals not only the frustrations of the Brexit process, but also of devolution more generally. It also reveals radically different views of the nature of the British constitution.

From the perspective of the UK government, the British constitution is unitary in nature, possessing certain key elements: foreign affairs are reserved to the UK government, and this includes EU membership. This view approaches the devolved nations as lacking legal rights in this area, at most to be consulted as matter of courtesy.

But there exists a contrasting view of the constitution, held by many in devolved nations and some in England. This alternative approach views the UK as a union founded on treaties (Treaty of Union 1706, Good Friday Agreement) and reliant on ongoing consent. This alternative interpretation of the British constitution also recognizes that the UK has been transformed by external developments and memberships (such as of the EU and Council of Europe) and recalibrated internally by devolution arrangements since 1998 (but also by the Human Rights Act, and a desire for a more principled constitutional development than parliamentary sovereignty allows). As well as enshrining the Sewel Convention in law, the Scotland Act 2016 declared the permanence of the Scottish Parliament, a provision which, if it is to have any meaning, flies in the face of orthodox constitutional law's assertion of parliamentary sovereignty. We also see a concept of the decentralized and fragmented state at work in Northern Ireland, where the Good Friday Agreement sets out complex provisions regarding cross-community consent, self-determination, and also a role for the Republic of Ireland (and the EU).

However, in spite of Lady Hale's comment that 'The United Kingdom has indeed become a federal state with a Constitution regulating the relationships between the federal centre and the component parts',[80] the UK is neither federal nor unitary. The UK is not federal in the sense of having legally guaranteed powers granted to the devolved authorities.[81] Various alternative descriptions have been applied to the UK—'union state', 'state of unions', 'quasi federal'.[82] Yet, given the somewhat ad hoc way in which devolution has developed to date, there has been no attempt to address Britain's constitutional status in a more principled way. Brexit brings these issues into sharp focus, without however suggesting any solution, other than the imposition of a resolute parliamentary sovereignty. There is little evidence that Brexit will provide a 'constitutional moment' in which a common solution will be found to these constitutional conundrums. It is unlikely that a federal UK or written constitution will emerge, however much new constitutional arrangements are needed to deal with Brexit. Advocates of Scottish independence, or a united Ireland, have little enthusiasm for an arrangement that would entrench them in the UK, even if it provided authoritative procedures protecting different national communities within the state. And those satisfied with Brexit are unlikely to desire a written constitution or federal option, given that a desire for strong parliamentary sovereignty motivated their Euroscepticism in the first place. Such distinct political identities militate against a comprehensive approach that could enable the British constitution to deal with issues of disputed authority and challenges of Brexit.

At present, intergovernmental relations between the UK government and Scotland seem at a low point.[83] Part of the problem is that, although the UK has decentralized to a certain extent, it has almost no legal, and little constitutional, machinery for determining conflicts between the centre and devolved governments. The JMC is not a decision-making body and has proved unequal to the task of providing an effective UK intergovernmental machinery.[84] What then is the point of devolution? Why take the trouble

---

[80] Lady Hale, 'The Supreme Court in the UK Constitution' Legal Wales Lecture (12 October 2012).

[81] See eg W Riker, *Federalism: Origin, Operation, Significance* (Little, Brown 1964); D Elazar, *Exploring Federalism* (University of Alabama Press 1987).

[82] See eg S Rokkan and D Unwin, 'Introduction: Centres and Peripheries in Western Europe' in S Rokkan and D Unwin (eds), *The Politics of Territorial Identity* (Sage 1982); M Keating, 'Reforging the Union: Devolution and Constitutional Change in the United Kingdom' (1998) 28 *Publius: The Journal of Federalism* 217; Mitchell, *Devolution in the UK* (n 33).

[83] See eg 'Theresa May and Nicola Sturgeon Meet Ahead of Article 50' *BBC News* (27 March 2017).

[84] N McEwen and W Swenden, 'Between Autonomy and Interdependence: The Challenges of Shared Rule after the Scottish Referendum (2015) 86 *Political Quarterly* 192; House of Lords, Select Committee on the Constitution, *Intergovernmental Relations in the United Kingdom* (HL Paper 146, 11th Report of Session 2014–2015) ch 2.

to establish devolved institutions, yet give them so little power in the UK constitutional order?

The push for Scottish independence was not inevitable in the Brexit context. Indeed, the active pursuit of other options: the formation of the Standing Council on Europe to advise the Scottish government, the creation of a Scottish Brexit Minister Michael Russell, and the *Scotland's Place in Europe* options paper, published before any UK government White Paper, illustrate this. Likewise, what appears to be a shift from a demand to continue Scotland's EU membership to a less ambitions focus on maintaining single market membership indicate a willingness to take pragmatic steps, and compromise if necessary.

Which view of the British constitution will prevail, and will the British constitution, and indeed the union, survive the Brexit process? In *On Fantasy Island*, Conor Gearty writes that: 'the problem when political fantasy collides with legal facts is that fantasy can never win'. Perhaps many aspirations for Brexit will be revealed as political fantasy when confronted with the legal challenges of withdrawal under Article 50 and the complexities of the 'Great Repeal Bill' (or Bills)?

However, what are the 'legal facts' here? The British constitution, let alone its constitutional law, does not provide determinate answers to many of the questions posed by Brexit. We might argue this is unsurprising, that Brexit is an extraordinary event, constitutionally unforeseeable, introducing a potential new revolution into UK law and society. Yet the British constitution has long been vaunted for its adaptability and its ability to cope with new circumstances (the loss of empire, major world wars, and so on) and for its flexibility and enduring nature. However, the challenges of Brexit reveal the constitution's 21st century weaknesses. An event as momentous as a British withdrawal from the EU requires clear and principled constitutional law as a guide But we do not have that. As the late Lord Bingham put it, commenting on the UK's lack of a codified constitution: 'constitutionally speaking, we now find ourselves in a trackless desert without map or compass'.[85] How Scotland will face this challenge remains to be seen.

---

[85] Tom Bingham, *Lives in the Law* (OUP 2011) ch 6.

7

Brexit and the Northern Ireland Question

John Doyle and Eileen Connolly

1. Introduction

Northern Ireland, although it voted as a region to remain in the European Union by a 10 per cent margin in the UK wide 'Brexit' referendum in June 2016, faces the inevitability of leaving the EU and also the problem of having the UK's only land border with the EU. This will create difficulties for trade and mobility on the local level and at the inter-state level, but more importantly, it also raises serious concerns for the future stability of the Northern Ireland 'peace process'. The 1998 Good Friday Agreement, on which the peace process is based, that put an end to thirty years of armed conflict, was signed in the context of EU membership and the increasing degree of openness and cooperation with the rest of the island of Ireland that the EU framework provided.[1] The proposed withdrawal of the UK from the EU creates a set of conditions for Northern Ireland that will weaken the capacity of the political system to maintain peace and build economic development. The result of the referendum vote alone indicated that the internal political divisions in Northern Ireland are being reinforced by the changed relationship of the UK to the EU. In the referendum campaign the two major Irish nationalist parties, Sinn Féin and the Social Democratic and Labour Party (SDLP), along with the leadership of the Ulster Unionist Party (UUP) and the moderate pro-union Alliance Party supported the 'remain' position, while the largest unionist party the Democratic Unionist Party (DUP) supported Brexit. As a result, the overwhelming majority of Irish nationalists voted to remain in the EU, while Ulster unionists voted 60:40 to leave. During the Brexit negotiations these divisions will become more pronounced, as a key

---

[1] For background on the conflict and the peace process see Brendan O'Leary, *The Politics of Antagonism: Understanding Northern Ireland* (2nd edn, Athlone Press 1996); John Doyle, 'Governance and Citizenship in Contested States: the Northern Ireland Peace Agreement as Internationalised Governance' (1999) 10 *Irish Studies in International Affairs* 201.

Brexit and the Northern Ireland Question. First edition. John Doyle & Eileen Connolly © John Doyle & Eileen Connolly 2017. Published 2017 by Oxford University Press.

part of this discussion will include the location of the EU/UK border and the right of Northern Ireland, as part of a future United Ireland, to automatic membership of the EU.[2]

Ireland has historically shared a common travel area with the UK, and abandoning this will be both politically and socially disruptive. A benefit of the common travel area, especially following the peace process, has been close trading and business links with the Republic of Ireland, Northern Ireland's largest 'export' market. The loss of the economic benefits of EU membership, including open borders, is likely to have a more severe impact on Northern Ireland than on the rest of the UK as its economy is still in a weak post-conflict condition, with the public sector representing approximately 60 per cent of GDP. The small scale of the private sector in Northern Ireland and the continued importance of agriculture for the economy are the economic legacy of conflict and Northern Ireland's future stability also rests on improving economic development and employment. Avoiding a hard land border would help mitigate, at least in the short term, the negative economic impact of Brexit on Northern Ireland.

The question of the location of the border between the EU and the UK is the single most significant question not only for the development of Northern Ireland's economy but also for its future political stability. That a 'hard' border will be necessary is beyond doubt, as the withdrawal of the UK from membership of the single market will mean that the EU will insist on a hard customs border[3] and the UK government's focus on controlling migration, will also require a hard border. A hard land border will impact negatively on the economy but it will also threaten the existence of the Good Friday Agreement and exacerbate existing political conflicts. The alternative of a negotiated sea border (between the islands of Ireland and Britain), that defined Northern Ireland as a special case, and places it outside the core UK territory, would be strongly resisted by Unionists. For nationalists, the imposition of a hard land border on the island of Ireland would be equally unacceptable. The issue of the location of the future border between the UK

---

[2] See formal Government of Ireland press release on Brexit strategy (2 May 2017), referencing as priorities, the land-border, the Common travel area with the UK, and the peace process (para 2) http://www.taoiseach.gov.ie/eng/News/Government_Press_Releases/Government_Statement_on_Brexit_Preparations.html; see also European Council statement on Article 50 negotiation guidelines (29 April 2017), which also include references to these three issues. http://www.consilium.europa.eu/en/press/press-releases/2017/04/29-euco-brexit-guidelines/.

[3] EU Chief Negotiator with the United Kingdom, Michel Barnier, in a speech to the Irish *Oireachtas* (parliament) on 11 May 2017 said that: 'Customs controls are part of EU border management. They protect the single market. They protect our food safety and our standards' https://static.rasset.ie/documents/news/michel-barnier-address-to-the-oireachtas.pdf.

and the EU was a key issue for unionists[4] during the referendum campaign and the division on the location of the 'border' has the capacity to increase internal political tensions and to undermine the Good Friday Agreement, which is premised on an open land border. The increased pressures on the relatively fragile polity of Northern Ireland, as a result of Brexit, will inevitably deepen political divisions and weaken its capacity to maintain a power-sharing executive.

This chapter analyses the political impact of alternative outcomes of the Brexit negotiations on Northern Ireland, through a discussion of four inter-related issues—political divisions in Northern Ireland; the single market; the common travel area; and the Good Friday Agreement. It first discusses the Brexit referendum, and the observable polarization in the voting patterns of the Irish nationalist and unionist communities on EU membership and all-island integration. It places this polarization in the context of a significant change in the balance of communal politics in Northern Ireland following the Good Friday Agreement. Secondly, it explores the impact of the disruption of leaving the single market for Northern Ireland. It considers possible solutions, including the adoption of a flexible arrangement, based on the Cyprus accession model, allowing Northern Ireland produced goods to be exported via the Republic of Ireland as EU goods. Following this, it analyses the potential impacts of ending the policy of open borders and the Common Travel Area, which has existed between Ireland and the UK since Irish independence in 1922. It details the negative impacts of a 'hard border' land border and the alternative of a sea-border between the island of Ireland and Britain as the de facto point of security and migration control. The final section outlines the direct impacts of Brexit on the Good Friday Agreement. It analyses the way in which the peace process, and the structures that it put in place, were underpinned by an assumption of a EU framework and the political challenges that the UK withdrawal from the EU present to the future of the agreement.

2. The Referendum

The 'remain' vote in the referendum in Northern Ireland was 56 per cent, but this average conceals major differences between the two main political

---

[4] For the most comprehensive post referendum survey see John Garry, 'The EU Referendum Vote in Northern Ireland: Implications for Our Understanding of Citizens' Political Views and Behaviour' Northern Ireland Assembly Knowledge Exchange Seminar Series, 2016–2017 (Northern Ireland Assembly 2016).

traditions, reflecting views on the 'national question'.[5] A survey of 4,000 adults in Northern Ireland by the 'Northern Ireland Assembly Election Study'[6] found that 85 per cent of those 'brought up' as Catholics voted to remain in the EU, of those 'brought up' as Protestants only 40 per cent supported this position. When the same question was put to respondents who were asked to self-define as Irish nationalist, as unionist, or as neither, the impact of an individual's political views on whether or not they voted to remain became more pronounced. The result for self-defined Irish nationalists was slightly higher than for 'Catholics', as 88 per cent voted to remain in the EU, but for self-defined unionists, 66 per cent voted to leave compared to 60 per cent of 'Protestants', and 70 per cent of those who chose to identify as 'neither' voted to stay in the EU.[7] This voting behaviour reflects the positions of the Northern Ireland political parties.[8] The two major Irish nationalist parties, Sinn Féin and the Social Democratic and Labour Party (SDLP), called for a vote to remain in the EU, as did the two smaller pro-union parties, the Ulster Unionist Party (UUP) and the centrist Alliance Party. The major unionist party the Democratic Unionist Party (DUP) and the small and more conservative, Traditional Unionist Voice, campaigned to leave. The political parties campaigning for remain polled just over 58 per cent in the May 2016 Northern Ireland Assembly elections and this was reflected in the 56 per cent that voted to remain in the referendum. However, the results of the Brexit vote include a significant bloc of unionist voters who did not follow their parties' leads. While the more moderate unionist UUP called for a vote to remain—58 per cent of their voters voted for Brexit and 25 per cent of DUP

---

[5] Political divisions in Northern Ireland, while rooted in the colonial settlement and largely reflecting traditional religious communities of Catholic and Protestant, are focused on the key political question of whether Northern Ireland should remain part of the UK or join the rest of Ireland in an all-island state. The partition of Ireland in 1922, and the creation of 'Northern Ireland' reflected the largest land mass in which the UK could command a secure majority in favour of UK membership, but it contained a minority of Irish nationalists making up one third of the population, who were systematically discriminated against in employment, public services, and even voting rights over the following 50 years. The armed conflict, which erupted in 1969, was eventually brought to an end with the 1998 'Good Friday Agreement', which set up a devolved Assembly and Executive based on a power-sharing or consociational model, along with structured North-South (all-island) cooperation and integration, and a programme of equality measures, policing reform and demilitarization. Voting patterns continue to reflect the fundamental political division, with Irish nationalists now making up 40% of voters and a majority of those under 25 years of age.

[6] John Garry, 'The EU Referendum Vote in Northern Ireland: Implications for Our Understanding of Citizens' Political Views and Behaviour' Northern Ireland Assembly Knowledge Exchange Seminar Series, 2016–2017 (Northern Ireland Assembly 2016).

[7] John Garry, 'The EU Referendum Vote in Northern Ireland ' (n 4).

[8] All of the significant political parties in Northern Ireland are local and none of the mainstream UK parties has any significant electoral support in Northern Ireland.

supporters meanwhile voted to remain, despite their party being the leading voice in the local Brexit campaign.

During the referendum campaign in Northern Ireland, the issues that dominated the debate were different from those that engaged the rest of the UK. In spite of the media dominance of BBC, ITV, and Sky TV news bulletins, the campaign was largely fought on the specific impacts of Brexit on Northern Ireland.[9] Immigration was not a major issue of debate, and the public discourse was dominated by the impact of Brexit on the peace process; the economic impact of withdrawal from the single market; the feasibility of continuing a common travel area; and the implications for social policy and the protection of human rights. Sinn Féin, which aligns with the European United Left/Nordic Green Left (GUE/NGL) bloc in the European Parliament, had in the past opposed EU membership, but over a period of time has shifted their position to one that they describe as 'critical engagement'.[10] This was defined as being 'against the kind of Europe' exemplified 'in recent years in the appalling treatment of the Greek people; or of a fortress Europe which turns its back on refugees'. Sinn Fein argued that the 'possibility that a part of our nation could end up outside the European Union while the other part stays in is not a situation that will benefit the Irish people'.[11] During the campaign, Sinn Féin focused on the threat of restricted mobility across the border; the negative economic impact; the loss of civil rights; and the undermining of the peace process. The late Martin McGuiness, then Northern Ireland Deputy First Minister, stated that Brexit would be 'bad for Ireland, bad for business and trade, bad for our farmers and bad for human rights and workers' rights'.[12] The SDLP focused on its long-term commitment to European integration, stressing the economic benefits of EU membership, including direct EU transfers to the region and the impact of the EU in encouraging Foreign Direct Investment in Northern Ireland.[13] The Ulster Unionist Party leader Mike Nesbitt was clearly pro-EU, but the party as a whole ran a low-key campaign, reflecting the divisions within the party on this issue. As the only large party campaigning for Brexit, the DUP's campaign reflected its long-standing opposition to European integration. It was

[9] Gerard McCann and Paul Hainsworth, 'Brexit and Northern Ireland: The 2016 Referendum on the United Kingdom's Membership of the European Union' (2017) 3292) *Irish Political Studies* 327.

[10] Statement from Party President Gerry Adams TD (9 June 2016). http://www.sinnfein.ie/contents/40268.

[11] Adams, statement 9 June 2016.

[12] Martin McGuinness (3 June 2016) https://www.rte.ie/news/2016/0603/793106-brexit-campaign/.

[13] Colum Eastwood SDLP Party Leader (7 March 2016) http://www.sdlp.ie/news/2016/eastwood-addresses-ni-affairs-committee-on-eu-referendum/.

also the party in Northern Ireland that engaged with the UK-wide Brexit debates on sovereignty and UK 'independence' and from this position it focused on rejecting the argument of those who wanted to remain in the EU that the negative economic impact on Northern Ireland would be greater that for the rest of the UK if Brexit proceeded.[14]

Given the close cultural ties between Northern Ireland and Scotland, the linking of Scottish independence, to the desire of the majority of Scots to remain in the EU, inevitably impacted on the election debates in Northern Ireland. In Scotland there was a strong vote to remain, at 62 per cent[15], and as this vote followed the narrow defeat for Scottish nationalists in the referendum on independence in 2014, it gave the question of independence for Scotland a wider political significance. The implications of this for the integrity of the UK was recognized by Mike Nesbitt (UPP) who characterized Brexit as an 'existential threat to the United Kingdom should there be an overall vote for Brexit but with Scotland voting to remain'.[16] Scottish nationalists project a solution to their problems with Brexit, through independence and rejoining the EU. If the result of Brexit was to increase the demand for independence in Scotland in the medium term, this would undermine the current construction of Unionist identity, which has culturally defined itself as closer to Scotland than to England.

Independently of debates about Scotland, the question of the reunification of Ireland has surfaced as a solution to the problems that arise from placing Northern Ireland outside the EU. It is not surprising that during the campaign Sinn Féin identified Irish unity as the route through which Northern Ireland could remain in the EU arguing that in the event of a UK referendum result for leaving the EU, with a Northern Ireland majority for remaining, 'there would then be a democratic imperative for a border poll to provide Irish citizens with the right to vote for an end to partition and to retain a role in the EU'.[17] In the aftermath of the Brexit result, the Irish government diplomatic effort with other EU Member States, in addition to prioritizing the issues of the peace process, an open land-border and the Common Travel Area with the UK, also devoted considerable time to seeking a formal decision that in the event of a future vote for Irish unity, Northern Ireland would be deemed to be automatically within the EU without the need for a Treaty agreement or a vote of other Member States, relying heavily on the German

---

[14] For example, party adverts and statements by party Leader Arlene Foster *Belfast Telegraph* (17 June 2016).

[15] See contribution by Sionaidh Douglas-Scott in this volume.

[16] http://uup.org/news/4128#.WNuq_BIrK-o.

[17] Gerry Adams, *Irish Independent* (18 June 2016).

precedent. The Irish government was successful in this effort, with agreement reached at the same European Council of 29 April 2017, which agreed the Article 50 negotiation guidelines.[18]

The divisions within Northern Ireland on the Brexit referendum mirror the core political divisions in Northern Ireland and the process of British withdrawal from the EU has the potential to destabilize the idea of incremental progress embodied in the Good Friday Agreement. The potential also exists for increased instability to be deepened by the worsening economic situation of Northern Ireland in a post-Brexit world.

3. Northern Ireland and the Single Market

The economy in Northern Ireland since its foundation has been comparatively weak. Economic underdevelopment, combined with a history of employment discrimination against Irish nationalists, resulted in the large-scale emigration of people from the nationalist community, which lasted up to the end of the 1980s. This weakness was characterized by Rob Rowthorn and Naomi Wayne as a 'workhouse economy', where most of the population was either involved in policing the 'other' or in providing services, primarily to their own community.[19] The dominance of security factors and the impact of the conflict itself has meant that the public sector still continues to be a very significant part of the economy—providing approximately 60 per cent of Gross Value Added.[20] Levels of poverty are among the highest of all UK regions.[21] Agriculture and fisheries, supported by EU policies and subsidies, continue to play a comparatively important role in the economy, given the weak state of the industrial sectors. EU funding, including subsidies from the Common Agricultural Policy and the designated Peace Funds, from 2007 to 2013 was equivalent to approximately 8.4 per cent of Northern Ireland's GDP.[22] Brexit will inevitably mean a significant loss to an already weak economy.

---

[18] *The Irish Times* (29 April 2017).

[19] Bob Rowthorn and Naomi Wayne, *Northern Ireland: The Political Economy of Conflict* (Polity Press 1988).

[20] Nevin Economic Research Institute, *Quarterly Economic Observer* (Spring 2017) 9–11 http://www.nerinstitute.net/download/pdf/qeo_spring_2017_final_version.pdf.

[21] Feargal McGuinness, *Poverty in the UK: Statistics* House of Commons Library Briefing Paper, No 7096 (2 May 2017).

[22] L Budd, 'The Consequences for the Northern Ireland Economy from a United Kingdom Exit from the European Union' Briefing note: Committee for Enterprise, Trade, and Investment (Open University March 2015).

Brexit will also disrupt both Northern Ireland's high levels of integration with the economy of the Republic of Ireland, and the Northern Ireland economy's reliance on EU markets. In the ten years up to 2014, exports to the EU have remained at approximately 60 per cent of all Northern Ireland's exports, whereas for the UK as a whole this EU/non-EU export balance has converged to approximately 50:50. Between 2004 and 2014, in all but one year, Northern Ireland has exported more to the EU than it has imported from it, in contrast to the UK where this balance is reversed.[23] Northern Ireland is now more reliant on the EU as an export market than the UK as a whole and the region is therefore much more exposed to the withdrawal of the UK, both from the EU and from the single market.[24] The Republic of Ireland, as might be expected, is by far the largest single destination within the EU market, accounting for 21 per cent of all exports and 37 per cent of EU exports from Northern Ireland, illustrating the importance of integration on the island.[25] One analysis very conservatively estimates that the impact of a UK exit from the single market would be a 3 per cent reduction in Northern Ireland's GDP, compared to an estimated 2 per cent reduction in UK GDP, a significant drop for a fragile economy.

When the UK leaves the single market and the EU Customs Union, it will necessitate the creation of a hard border. According to Peter Sutherland, a former Director General of the World Trade Organization, as the customs union requires a common external tariff to be maintained by all EU countries, this tariff will apply to the UK following its withdrawal, therefore goods 'will have to be checked at borders' and this 'will require a hard border between north and south in Ireland'.[26] If the UK was also outside of EU environmental and labour protection standards, as well as outside the single market, this would be an additional reason for the EU to insist on a closed border. In these circumstances, given the importance of cross-border trade for the underdeveloped private sector, it would be in Northern Ireland's interests to seek a special deal. This approach was effectively confirmed by Michel Barnier, in his speech to the Irish *Oireachtas*.[27] The Scottish government has also raised the issue of a special deal for Scotland in the single market[28] but

---

[23] Aidan Stennett, 'The EU Referendum and Potential Implications for Northern Ireland' Northern Ireland Assembly, Research and Information Service, NIAR 32-16 Research Paper (2016) 7–9 http://www.niassembly.gov.uk/globalassets/documents/raise/publications/2016/eti/2116.pdf.

[24] See contribution by Catherine Barnard in this volume.

[25] UK Parliament, Northern Ireland Affairs Committee, *Northern Ireland and the EU Referendum* (2016) http://www.publications.parliament.uk/pa/cm201617/cmselect/cmniaf/48/4804.htm#footnote-104.

[26] *The Irish Times* (2 September 2016).   [27] See Barnier (n 3).

[28] Scottish Government, *Scotland's Place in Europe* Edinburgh (2016).

the UK government has expressed its absolute resistance to a special deal for Scotland, even if the EU were willing to allow it. This is reflected in the fact that Scotland was not mentioned in Prime Minster May's Article 50 TEU letter, while the relationship with the Republic of Ireland and the Northern Ireland peace process was explicitly highlighted. This indicates that the UK may be more flexible on a special deal for Northern Ireland. The EU has also expressed concerns about the impact of Brexit on Northern Ireland and in its negotiation guidelines explicitly state that nothing in the final agreement with the UK should 'undermine the objectives and commitments set out in the Good Friday Agreement' and that negotiations should 'in particular aim to avoid the creation of a hard border on the island of Ireland', while respecting the union's legal order.

A number of factors make agreement of a separate deal on Northern Ireland that would allow it to remain within the single market possible. In the first place, the Irish Sea is an obvious place to control trade access between the UK and the EU, without the negative consequences of closing the Irish land-border. The geographical context would also make any agreement between the UK and the EU likely to be judged as compatible with the 'frontier traffic exception' of Article XXIV.3 of GATT.[29] Secondly, EU special status for Northern Ireland could be presented as a response to the peace process, the particular circumstances of Northern Ireland and the UK's international commitments under the Good Friday Agreement. Thirdly, there is the question of scale: the small size of Northern Ireland and, in particular, its private sector can allow it to be situated amongst the wide range of other flexible territorial arrangements, which the EU has already agreed, from Greenland to the Channel Islands to the French Overseas Territories.[30] Fourthly, there is the precedent of Cyprus, which although not identical, also arises from the existence of disputed sovereignty in the context of an ongoing search for a settlement.[31]

There are a number of technical ways in which Northern Ireland could remain, or largely remain, within the single market after Brexit. The maximalist position as advocated by Sinn Féin wants Northern Ireland to remain inside the EU as a special region.[32] This was also the view of the

---

[29] See contribution by Giorgio Sacerdoti in this volume.

[30] D Kochenov (ed), *On Bits of Europe Everywhere. Overseas Possessions of the EU Member States in the Legal-Political Context of European Law* (Kluwer Law International 2013).

[31] Nikos Skoutaris, *From Britain and Ireland to Cyprus: Accommodating 'Divided Islands' in the EU Political and Legal Order* (European University Institute, Academy of European Law AEL 2016/02, 2016) http://cadmus.eui.eu/bitstream/handle/1814/42484/AEL_2016_02.pdf?sequence=1.

[32] Sinn Fein, *The Case for the North to Achieve Special Designated Status within the EU* (Sinn Fein 2016).

Irish parliamentary committee on European Affairs.[33] It has been referred to as a 'reverse Greenland', following the EU acceptance that Greenland could leave the Union while the rest of Denmark remained inside the EU.[34] This approach would mostly fully safeguard Northern Ireland's position, but it seems unlikely the UK will agree to this, although initially the UK did not explicitly rule it out. A second option would be for Northern Ireland to join the European Economic Area (EEA). This would exclude Northern Ireland from schemes such as the Common Agricultural Policy and Research Funding, but would allow access to the single market.[35] It is likely that the UK would also object to this approach, as it would separate Northern Ireland from the rest of the UK in a way that makes its international status ambiguous.

A model for an alternative solution exists in the accession agreement that allowed the Republic of Cyprus to join the EU, and which could be used either in conjunction with EEA membership or instead of it. The accession agreement not only recognized the Government of the Republic of Cyprus as the sovereign power for the island as a whole, it also very pragmatically, allows goods produced in Northern Cyprus to enter EU markets as 'EU goods', once they are certified as being produced in Northern Cyprus by the Turkish Cypriot Chamber of Commerce.[36] This organization was chosen and accepted by the Government of the Republic of Cyprus to avoid any implied recognition of the Turkish Republic of Northern Cyprus, a position which would have been vetoed by Greece. Goods originating in Northern Cyprus are deemed to have originated in Cyprus/EU and are not subject to customs duties.[37] This 'Green Line Regulation' deals in a flexible way with the de facto Cyprus border, including the provision that, goods which are allowed to cross the line should not be subject to export formalities.[38] A similar arrangement could empower the Northern Ireland executive to identify goods as originating in Northern Ireland (and not simply travelling through Northern Ireland from the UK or a third country). As part of a Brexit deal, the EU could allow certified goods from Northern Ireland to enter the EU market via the

---

[33] Joint Oireachtas Committee on European Union Affairs, *Report on the implications of Brexit for Ireland* Irish Parliament (June 2016).

[34] Adam Ramsey, 'A Reverse Greenland: the EU Should Let Scotland Stay' https://www.opendemocracy.net/uk/adam-ramsay/reverse-greenland-letting-scotland-stay.

[35] Brian Doherty and others, *Northern Ireland and Brexit: the European Economic Area Option* European Policy Centre (7 April 2017) http://www.epc.eu/documents/uploads/pub_7576_northernirelandandbrexit.pdf.

[36] Protocol 10 to the Act of Accession, Article 2,.

[37] Commission Decision 2004/604/EC of 7 July 2004 on the authorisation of the Turkish Cypriot Chamber of Commerce according to Article 4(5) of Council Regulation (EC) No 866/2004, [2004] OJ L 272/12.

[38] Council Regulation (EC) No 866/2004, Article 5, [2004] OJ L 161/1.

Republic of Ireland and to be treated as EU goods. At the same time, the UK could allow such goods enter the UK market as 'domestic goods', and this would allow the UK to present this arrangement as a symmetrical one, meeting the needs of both nationalists and unionists, and therefore acceptable to the unionist parties and to pro-Ulster Unionist conservatives. Such an agreement would require considerable political will to achieve, but given the small scale of the Northern Ireland economy, and the benefits of avoiding a closed Irish border, it is within the sphere of what could be envisaged. Such an arrangement still requires a hard border with border checks; but it opens the question of where that border will be.[39]

4. The common travel area and open borders

Currently no hard border exists on the island of Ireland pursuant to the Common Travel Area between Ireland and the UK. The UK and Ireland have operated a common travel area since Irish independence, preceding the States' entry into the EEC in 1973, by fifty years. Article 2, Protocol No 20 to the EU Treaties, explicitly recognizes the Common Travel Area. In practice, this means that citizens of either state, moving from one state to another, have not only a right of entry without requiring a visa, but also have the right to work, access to health and welfare services, and even to vote. While its historic origins were a result of the limited UK recognition of Irish sovereignty in 1922, the common travel area became normalized and any restrictions on the free movement of people between the two countries would be both practically disruptive and politically sensitive. Even though there is no legal requirement to show a passport when travelling between Ireland and the UK, this provision only applies to people born in Ireland or the UK and who are citizens of one of the states, therefore in theory individuals can be asked to prove their citizenship when crossing between the two states. Airlines operating between the islands of Ireland and Britain require passengers to have a photo ID, most insist on a passport, and the UK also officially advises UK citizens to carry a passport when travelling to Ireland, even though it is not strictly required.[40] In practice, therefore, a passport is carried by most people when moving from the island of Ireland (including Northern Ireland) to Britain. However, a passport is not required to travel between the two jurisdictions on the island of Ireland, and since the creation of the single market in 1992

---

[39] James Anderson, *The Irish Times* (22 March 2017).
[40] https://www.gov.uk/foreign-travel-advice/ireland/entry-requirements.

and the implementation of the peace process, there has been no visible border between the two parts of the island. When the UK leaves the EU, it will inevitably impact on this agreement, opening up the possibility of restrictions on the freedom of movement across the Irish land border. While Prime Minister Theresa May's letter to the EU on the triggering of Article 50 TEU says the UK wants 'to avoid a return to a hard border ... and ... to be able to maintain a Common Travel Area' between the UK and Ireland. The UK government did not suggest any way in which this could be achieved and as this is only one of many objectives of the UK government it may lose out to other priorities, during negotiations.

Sealing the 499 km Irish land border will be difficult, as was demonstrated by the experience of the Northern Ireland conflict. During the conflict, as a security measure the British Army closed more than 200 of the smaller roads crossing the border, by a mixture of destroying bridges, creating physical barriers, and cratering roads. There were also major security installations on the official crossing points, which existed even after the creation of the single market in 1992, and were only gradually removed in the aftermath of the 1998 Good Friday Agreement. However, even with a presence of over 30,000 troops at the height of the conflict, the border was never 'sealed' from a security point of view—and it never successfully prevented the IRA from moving members and equipment across it.[41] However, road closures and border checks were very disruptive for business, including agriculture, as many farmers had land on both sides of the border. Frequent delays at crossing points, together with the negative experience of a heavy British Army security presence, discouraged cross-border traffic and trade.

The UK's insistence on the absolute control of migration as a non-negotiable issue means stricter monitoring at ports and airports to implement this policy, and therefore it will not be possible to leave open this potential route from continental Europe to Britain via Ireland.[42] Even if the border were not initially closed to the free movement of people, the use of the route by illegal migrants would inevitably lead to demands for physical controls. This has been clear to political actors in Northern Ireland from the moment the referendum was called. Managing both migration and the flow of goods across the Irish Sea from three airports and two ports is a simpler operation than policing a nearly 500 km land border. However, for a majority of unionists, having a de facto security and migration 'border'

---

[41] See resource on Irish Border form Queen Mary University, London. http://www.irishborderlands.com/living/roadclosures/index.html.

[42] See Anderson, *The Irish Times* (22 March 2017).

between Northern Ireland and Britain is ideologically difficult to accept. The issue of the location of a post-Brexit border including the suggestion that pragmatically this border might be in the Irish Sea—as the much easier border to secure—leaving Northern Ireland inside the UK, but outside the de facto migration and security border, was a subject of contentious debate. [43] For example, the Ulster Unionist Party manifesto for the Northern Ireland Assembly elections in May 2016, conceded that 'bitter experience makes clear it is not possible to fully secure the border' but that 'there will need to be a hard border' and that as 'it will not be on the actual border, it is likely to be at Great Britain's ports and airports—Cairnryan, Gatwick, Heathrow'—a prospect that was not welcome to them.[44] Having the control of migration take place across the Irish Sea is the more practical option. The three small airports and two small ferry ports already have a security infrastructure in place that can be enhanced, and freight checks can happen at a small number of specialist facilities, rather than requiring a mix of fixed and mobile customs checks covering approximately 300 roads. Most crucially it would still be possible, as at present, to drive across the border on the Dublin–Belfast motorway at 120 kph, and there would be no physical infrastructure on the border (with a required security presence) to act as a target for armed groups opposed to the peace process.

This solution has practical and political difficulties. The practical problem that would need EU–UK agreement would be acceptance of the continuing de-facto freedom of movement of EU citizens into Northern Ireland. This is politically achievable. Under the Good Friday Agreement, the right of the people of Northern Ireland 'to hold both British and Irish citizenship is accepted by both Governments and would not be affected by any future change in the status of Northern Ireland'.[45] Therefore there is no practical barrier to any Irish or UK citizen in Northern Ireland having the legal right to enter the EU or the UK, as everyone is legally entitled to both passports. For other persons, in order to get to the Irish land border, a person must have already entered either the UK or the Republic of Ireland. The Irish government could agree measures to monitor illegal immigrants coming into Ireland to meet UK concerns, and this may not be a major problem, given the exiting tight migration controls put in place by the Irish government. The more significant challenge would be around EU citizens who have a right to travel to Ireland, or non-EU

---

[43] ibid.

[44] UUP Manifesto for 2016 NI Assembly Election (Belfast UUP 2016). See also post-Brexit call from SDLP leader Colum Eastwood for any border controls imposed post-Brexit to be imposed between the islands of Ireland and Great Britain http://www.londonderrysentinel.co.uk/news/eastwood-impose-border-with-britain-not-on-island-1-7448357.

[45] Good Friday Agreement, Constitutional Issues para 1(vi).

citizens who might have been granted a visa to come to Ireland, but who do not possess a UK visa. Such individuals could enter Northern Ireland, a part of the UK, thus circumventing UK immigration rules. This is the de facto situation currently, but in practice illegal immigration to Northern Ireland via Ireland is not a significant problem and, as a result, migration hardly featured as part of the Brexit debate in Northern Ireland. The UK would still be able to exercise control at ports and airports and prevent any attempts by either EU or non-EU citizens to enter Britain via Northern Ireland, as is the case in the pre-Brexit world. The major challenge of not having a land border, however, is the political issue of the symbolic significance of the location of the 'border' for Northern Ireland's unionists (and some English conservatives). An Irish Sea border would place Northern Ireland outside the UK border control area and create a sense for Ulster unionists that their link with the UK had been weakened.

5. Brexit and the Peace Process

It is the issue of the existence of a hard border, and all that it implies in both economic and political spheres, irrespective of where it is located, that is central to the impact of Brexit on the Northern Ireland peace process. The 1998 Good Friday Agreement reflected a bi-national polity, imbedded in its system of consociational power-sharing; in the special position accorded to the Irish government; in the requirement for 50:50 nationalist/unionist recruitment to the new police service; and in the legal commitment from the UK government to legislate for Irish unity should concurrent voting majorities exist in Ireland, North and South. The Good Friday Agreement is rarely referred to as a peace settlement, and never by nationalists or the Irish government. It is an agreement, that is part of a wider peace process.[46] The 1998 Agreement was designed to consolidate the IRA ceasefires, and contained an integrated programme for regional government, North–South (on the island of Ireland) cooperation and increasing integration, and a programme of demilitarization, human rights, and equality. Many issues could not be agreed at that time of signing, but have, over time, been substantially achieved. This included major issues such as the transformation of policing; the destruction of IRA

---

[46] See speech by Pat Doherty, then Sinn Féin MP, at an Irish Unity conference in London (20 February 2010) http://cain.ulst.ac.uk/issues/politics/docs/sf/pd200210.htm; James W McAuley, 'Fantasy Politics? Restructuring Unionism after the Good Friday Agreement Éire-Ireland' (Spring/Summer 2004) 39(1–2) *Earrach/Samhradh* 189.

weaponry; and the withdrawal of the British army from security operations.[47] As part of this process, setting up the political institutions took time and it was 2007 before local governance was consolidated after a number of failed starts. Some issues have still not progressed, including the question of how to deal with 'the past'. This demonstrates that the Good Friday Agreement did not establish an end point but began a process.

The ceasefires and the destruction of IRA weapons were premised on a peaceful, but evolving process, which had no predetermined outcome. As part of the referendum endorsing the God Friday Agreement, in the Republic of Ireland, the Irish Constitution was amended to change the wording on Irish unity from a declaration of territorial claim to a wording which both guarantees the entitlement to Irish citizenship for everyone born on the island of Ireland (including within Northern Ireland) and also to assert the 'firm will of the Irish nation, in harmony and friendship, to unite all the people who share the territory of the island of Ireland', while accepting that a united Ireland can only come about by the consent of the people in both jurisdictions.[48] The Irish government, or the Irish nationalist community, were not asked to abandon their political objective of Irish unity; they simply agreed to pursue it by exclusively peaceful means. While accepting that the majority of the population in Northern Ireland at that time wanted to maintain Northern Ireland's membership of the UK, the 1998 Agreement affirms that:

if, in the future, the people of the island of Ireland exercise their right of self-determination ... [on the basis of separate and concurrent majorities North and South] ... to bring about a united Ireland, it will be a binding obligation on both Governments to introduce and support in their respective Parliaments legislation to give effect to that wish;[49]

This fluidity, and for nationalists a sense of progress, is essential to the success of the peace process.[50] This position has been opposed from a range of political perspectives; those with a vested interest in supporting the union with Britain including pro-agreement unionists[51] and academic analysts such as Murray and Tonge have argued that it is a settlement in which nationalists

---

[47] See John Doyle (ed), *Policing the Narrow Ground: Lessons from the Transformation of Policing in Northern Ireland* (Royal Irish Academy 2010).

[48] Constitution of Ireland, Articles 2 and 3.

[49] The Northern Ireland Peace Agreement, 'The Agreement reached in the multi-party negotiations 10 April 1998' (The Good Friday Agreement), Constitutional Issues para 1(iv).

[50] Jennifer Todd, 'Nationalism, Republicanism and the Good Friday Agreement' in Jennifer Todd and Joe Ruane (eds), *After the Good Friday Agreement* (UCD Press 1999).

[51] Paul Bew, *The Irish Times* (15 May 1998).

have accepted Northern Ireland's place in the UK.[52] Similarly, opponents of the peace process, who see it as abandoning the objective of a united Ireland have characterized the agreement as a static acceptance of the status quo.[53] Irish nationalists, who support the agreement, recognize that the fluidity of the Agreement on the ultimate end point is central to its success. It has allowed both unionists and nationalists to work within its framework, and this was also facilitated by the integration of the Irish state and the UK within the EU, including the open borders and cross-border cooperation that is part of that wider EU integration process. Nationalists argue that increased functional cooperation through cross-border institutions will create a political dynamic towards unity—a point also feared by unionists.[54]

Since the signing of the agreement in 1998, the internal political dynamics of Northern Ireland have shifted in a way that has reinforced the saliency of integration on the Island of Ireland. The 2017 elections to the Northern Ireland Assembly resulted, for the first time since partition, in a representative assembly in Northern Ireland which does not contain a majority of members who could be described unequivocally as Unionists, that is those committed in every circumstance to Northern Ireland remaining in the United Kingdom. In that election, only 45 per cent of the population voted for traditional unionist parties; 40 per cent voted for parties committed to Irish unity, with just under 15 per cent voting for smaller parties and independents, many of them defining themselves as 'cross-community', or campaigning on other issues such as 'anti-economic austerity', the environment etc. This is an historic event that reverses the experience of the first fifty years of Northern Ireland, during which time the percentage of the population of Northern Ireland that was Irish nationalist had remained static at one-third. This change began in the late 1980s with a major reduction in nationalist migration, partly as a response to new anti-discrimination legislation. Conversely, from this period Unionist migration increased as the public sphere in Northern Ireland shifted to create a space for Nationalist identities in addition to Unionist identities. The fact that less than 50 per cent of the population voted for parties for whom opposition to Irish unity is a core policy is a significant symbolic and practical change, all the more so as it reflects ongoing demographic change.[55]

---

[52] Gerard Murray, and Jonathan Tonge, *Sinn Fein and the SDLP: From Alienation to Participation* (O'Brien Press 2005).

[53] Anthony McIntyre, 'Modern Republicanism and the Belfast Agreement' in Rick Wilford (ed), *Aspects of the Belfast Agreement* (Oxford University Press 2001); Ed Moloney, *A Secret History of the IRA* (Penguin 2003).

[54] See eg Robert McCartney, Northern Ireland Assembly (22 November 1982).

[55] Northern Ireland Executive, *Statistical: Labour Force Survey Religion Report 2015* (2017).

This change of political dynamics has been visible from the early stages of the peace process, at which time unionist politicians expressed their fears that reform based on 'parity of esteem' between nationalism and unionism, allied with North–South links, would weaken support for unionism among elements of their own community.[56] Drawing on ideas of European Union functionalism, unionist politicians have argued that North–South bodies would inevitably develop deep and wide roots and that the people involved in them would 'go native' and lose their allegiance to unionism.[57] In this context, Unionist political elites have been openly critical of leading employers and business organizations from their own community, seeing them as less than wholehearted in their support for the positions adopted by mainstream unionism and willing, at least partly, to shift their allegiance or their political practice for the economic benefits of a Dublin–Belfast economic corridor, all-Ireland or cross-border EU funding arrangements and the promotion of tourism and investment on an all-Ireland basis.[58] Individuals from a unionist background, who were engaged in business, trade, or cross-border engagement, were amongst those active in campaigning within Northern Ireland for the UK to remain in the EU.[59] This emphasizes the link that the 'remain' campaign identified between maintaining peace, improving the economic condition of Northern Ireland and continued membership of the EU. The consequences for attitudes to Irish unity are long-term rather than immediate, but those in the unionist community who are strongly committed to EU membership face both a practical and ideological challenge. Irish unity was historically portrayed, by some unionists, as a move from a large, cosmopolitan, and internationally focused state to a smaller and more inward looking Irish state. This has now reversed, and it is Ireland which is linked to Europe and cosmopolitanism, and the UK seems inward-looking and parochial. If Scotland votes for independence at any time in the future, that clash of images will be all the stronger.[60]

Brexit will have important implications for the functioning of the Good Friday Agreement as it is underpinned by an assumption of EU membership. The agreement sets up a North South Ministerial Council (modelled in some

[56] See eg Cedric Wilson, NI Forum (13 June 1997) vol 34, p 41.

[57] See eg Bob McCartney, NI Forum (29 November 1996) vol 20, pp 2–5.

[58] See eg St Clair McAlister (DUP), NI Forum (20 February 1998), vol 62, p 32; John Hunter (UUP), NI Forum (24 October 1997) vol 48, p 10, claims that: 'The sort of stooges that represent the business community tend to be of the pan-Nationalist front'.

[59] Gerard McCann and Paul Hainsworth, 'Brexit and Northern Ireland: The 2016 Referendum on the United Kingdom's Membership of the European Union' (2017) 32(2) *Irish Political Studies* 327, 333.

[60] See contribution by Sionaidh Douglas-Scott in this volume.

respects on the EU Council of Ministers) and, in order to prevent unionists from boycotting such meetings (or to stop nationalists boycotting a Northern Ireland Assembly), the agreement states that:

It is understood that the North/South Ministerial Council and the Northern Ireland Assembly are mutually inter-dependent, and that one cannot successfully function without the other.[61]

This institution interdependence is strongly written in to those aspects of the agreement that deal with the North/South Ministerial Council. Pursuant to the agreement, in fact, the North/South Council

Will identify and agree at least 6 matters for cooperation and implementation in each of the following categories:
  (i) Matters where existing bodies will be the appropriate mechanisms for cooper-
       ation in each separate jurisdiction;
  (ii) Matters where the co-operation will take place through agreed implementa-
       tion bodies on a cross-border or all-island level.[62]

It was assumed that such bodies would operate in an EU context where regulations on issues such as water quality, animal health, trade etc were framed by EU policy and that these policy areas would be the 'matters' around which cooperation would take place. It is not impossible for such bodies to exist between an EU Member State and an EU non-Member State, but their ability to make decisions will be much more limited and therefore one of the neo-functionalist assumptions of the peace agreement is potentially undermined. The agreement also refers to the Special Peace Programme from the European Union and also explicitly refers to views from the North–South Council being represented 'at relevant EU meetings'.[63]

The European Convention on Human Rights (ECHR), although not an EU body, is an integral part of the framework of the Good Friday Agreement. The agreement explicitly limits the devolved Assembly's powers with the ECHR—saying any legislation passed by the Assembly would be 'null and void' if found to be in breach of the ECHR.[64] Concerns have been expressed that, post-Brexit, the European Court of Human Rights and the ECHR will come under further attack, from those in the British Conservative Party opposed to any supra-national authority. The lack of commitment on the part of a UK government to the ECHR would weaken, or even render inoperative, this provision of the agreement.

---

[61] Strand 2, para 13.   [62] GFA, Strand 2 para 9 (emphasis added).
[63] GFA, Strand 2.   [64] GFA, para 26, Strand One (1998).

The agreement between the two governments also clarifies who is entitled to vote in a future Irish unity referendum.

The British and Irish Governments declare that it is their joint understanding that the term 'the people of Northern Ireland' in paragraph (vi) of Article 1 of this Agreement means, for the purposes of giving effect to this provision, all persons born in Northern Ireland and having, at the time of their birth, at least one parent who is a British citizen, an Irish citizen or is otherwise entitled to reside in Northern Ireland without any restriction on their period of residence.[65]

Following Brexit there may be restrictions on EU citizens, including Irish citizens, right to reside in Northern Ireland; in these circumstances the meaning, as understood at the time of signing of this clause, will have been retrospectively altered. The UK government will now be able to restrict those 'entitled to reside in Northern Ireland' in a way that was not envisaged in 1998. This could weaken the rights of Irish citizens, potentially even influencing the result of a future referendum. Irish citizens, as EU citizens, currently living in Northern Ireland, have full voting and citizenship rights that they have enjoyed under the common travel area, including the right to vote in a referendum. This right may be limited post-Brexit. At the same time, any UK citizen would continue to have the right to vote in a referendum on the future of Ireland, even if they had lived in Britain for many years.

While Brexit will weaken the text of the Good Friday Agreement, it is the reimposition of a hard land border that has the potential to set up a negative dynamic that will undermine the progress that has been achieved since 1998. Former British Secretary of State for Northern Ireland, Peter Mandelson, has noted that:

the re-imposition of a formalised border would be a radical departure from the established strategy of the administrations in Dublin, London and Belfast. Anything in my view that strengthened a sense of separatism between Northern and Southern Ireland – physically, economically, psychologically – has the potential to upset the progress that has been made and serve as a potential source of renewed sectarianism that would always bear the risk of triggering further violence in Ireland, particularly in the North.[66]

Brexit will be most visibly and immediately seen in the disruption to the movement of people and trade across the border. It will reinstate the idea of an insular Northern Ireland that requires a secure border to ensure its territorial

---

[65] GFA, Agreement between British and Irish Governments—final para.
[66] Peter Mandelson, 'EU Exit Risks Peace Process and Return to Violence' *Belfast Newsletter* (15 March 2016).

integrity. From a Unionist perspective, this will strengthen demands to abandon the reform process embedded in the Good Friday Agreement and in particular its North–South dimension. From a Nationalist perspective, a hard border will provide practical and symbolic targets for attack by IRA dissidents opposed to the peace process. These groups are currently marginal to the Irish nationalist community in the North but physically closing the border will greatly increase their capacity to attract support. If customs posts and security installations are built on the border they will become part of a narrative, from opponents of the peace process, that it has 'failed' and will be a strong mobilization tool for those seeking to collapse the peace process in its entirety.

6. Conclusion

Brexit represents a serious threat to the Northern Ireland peace process, in its disruption of the process of all-island cooperation and integration, which underpins the 1998 Good Friday Agreement. A 'hard' Irish land border will be economically disruptive and a powerful symbol that the peace process is in crisis. Installations on the border will be an inevitable target for armed groups opposed to the peace process, leading to a cycle of increased fortification on the border in response to attacks. The Northern Ireland economy is more dependent on the EU than any other region of the UK and it is particularly reliant on access to the market of the Republic of Ireland. The disruption to normal mobility on the island of Ireland, including cross-border trade and the routine commuting of individuals, from a hard EU external land border would be seriously damaging. This could be ameliorated if a special status agreement for Northern Ireland, in de facto terms, moved that physical border to the Irish Sea, allowing free movement of goods and people within the island of Ireland and giving Northern Ireland origin goods access to the single market. Such special status has the precedent of Cyprus to build on.

Other implications of Brexit are unclear and depend on a number of factors, including the short-term impacts on the peace process and the outcome of a future Scottish independence referendum. If Northern Ireland is taken out of the single market and if there is a hard EU frontier on the Irish Border, then Irish nationalists will be strengthened in their view that Irish unity is the only practical means to restore the region's links to Europe, to grow its economy and to consolidate the peace process.[67] In those circumstances,

[67] Irish reunification is the 'biggest and best idea around' and must now be considered in light of 'Brexit', according to SDLP leader Colum Eastwood, *Irish Independent* (20 July 2016) http://www.independent.ie/business/brexit/irish-reunification-is-best-idea-around-post-brexit-sdlp-leader-says-34899305.html.

the demographic growth of the Irish nationalist community is likely to be reflected in a growing demand for a referendum on unity. The majority of Ulster unionists will continue to oppose Irish unity in such circumstances. This is a reassertion of a traditional unionist position, as many of those campaigning for Brexit also opposed the reform agenda of the Good Friday Agreement and the gradual integration with the South of Ireland. From this perspective, Brexit can be seen as a means of reinforcing Northern Ireland's separation from the Republic of Ireland and many unionists would pay the price of the collapse of power-sharing institutions to achieve this. However, it is unclear what unaligned voters or pragmatic 'pro-union' voters would do if faced with a choice between remaining in a diminished UK, with a faltering economy, and isolated from Europe. Whatever the longer-term implications, Brexit will create an immediate crisis for the peace process. If the negotiations result in a 'hard' land border, it will undermine the basis of the peace process so completely that it is difficult to see it surviving in its current form.

PART 3

BREXIT AND CONSTITUTIONAL CHANGE IN EUROPEAN PERSPECTIVE

8

Brexit and the EU Economic & Monetary Union

From EMU Outsider to Instigator

*Michele Chang**

1. Introduction

Since joining the European Community in 1973, the UK has participated as an "awkward partner."[1] This status as a relative outsider was cemented by the Maastricht Treaty that included an opt-out from joining Economic and Monetary Union (EMU). The UK's departure from the EU would not have the same impact on EMU as the exit of a euro area country.[2] Nevertheless, Brexit could affect EMU in the following ways: changing economic conditions that create incentives for further integration; altering the alliances within the EU, both between the euro-ins and outs, as well as within the euro area; and shifting political resources to deal with the consequences of Brexit. The focus of the chapter will be on the effect that Brexit could have on EMU, not how the UK itself might be affected.

Section 2 briefly outlines the UK's participation in the main pillars of EMU (monetary, financial, fiscal, and economic integration). Section 3 analyzes the potential impact of Brexit on each of these pillars, recalling how integration in these pillars historically has occurred and how Brexit may

* I would like to thank Federico Fabbrini, Michael Breen, Stephanie Bergbauer, David Cleeton, David Howarth, Erik Jones, Miguel Otero-Iglesias, and the participants of the conference, "The Law and Politics of Brexit," at Dublin City University on April 20–21, 2017 for their helpful comments. All errors remain my own.

[1] Stephen George, *An Awkward Partner: Britain in the European Community* (3rd edn, Oxford University Press 1998).

[2] Moreover, no legal mechanism exists for a euro area exit.

Brexit and EU Economic & Monetary Union: From EMU Outsider to Instigator. First edition. Michele Chang © Michele Chang 2017. Published 2017 by Oxford University Press.

change such dynamics. This includes Brexit's effect on potential reforms that were identified in the 2015 Five Presidents' report on "Completing Europe's Economic and Monetary Union"[3] and the Commission's 2017 "White Paper on the Future of Europe,"[4] as well as reforms suggested by prominent politicians and analysts. It is important to note that Brexit does not pose the only challenge to EMU in the near future; elections and domestic political developments in euro area countries would play a greater role, particularly those involving Euroskepticism.[5] Section 4 considers whether Brexit will act as a force for euro area integration or disintegration.

2. EMU and the UK

The UK government officially joined the European Monetary System in 1979 but declined participation in the Exchange Rate Mechanism (ERM), a system of fixed exchange rates between the currencies of the European Community. The pound joined the ERM in October 1990, only to have it ejected from the system during the 1992–1993 currency crisis; on "Black Wednesday" (September 13, 1992), the pound and the Italian lira left the ERM and the UK's traditional Eurosceptic stance hardened. The UK (and Denmark) obtained an opt-out from the Maastricht Treaty's plans for monetary union. Besides the UK and Denmark, there are seven others EU Member States (so-called pre-ins)[6] that are expected to join the euro area once they achieve the Maastricht Treaty convergence criteria on inflation levels, interest rates, debt and deficits, and exchange rate stability. Nevertheless, both the opt-out countries and the pre-ins have various responsibilities and have participated in activities in the four pillars of EMU (monetary, financial, fiscal, and economic). Each of these pillars will be considered in turn, focusing on the UK's involvement.

---

[3] Jean-Claude Juncker in close cooperation with Donald Tusk, Jeroen Dijsselbloem, Mario Draghi, and Martin Schulz, "Completing Europe's Economic and Monetary Union" Brussels (June 22, 2015) https://ec.europa.eu/commission/sites/beta-political/files/5-presidents-report_en.pdf (last accessed March 15, 2017).

[4] European Commission, "White Paper on the Future of Europe: Reflections and Scenarios for the EU27 by 2025" Brussels (March 1, 2017) https://ec.europa.eu/commission/sites/beta-political/files/white_paper_on_the_future_of_europe_en.pdf (last accessed March 15, 2017).

[5] See Marlene Wind's contribution in this volume, "Brexit and Euroskepticism."

[6] Sweden, Bulgaria, Croatia, the Czech Republic, Hungary, Poland, and Romania.

2.1 Monetary integration

The monetary pillar entails three main elements: the use of the euro as the national currency, the setting of monetary policy by the European Central Bank (ECB), and the participation in the euro area bailout fund, the European Stability Mechanism (ESM). The UK has retained the pound sterling as its currency, and the Bank of England continues to set monetary policy. Nevertheless, the Bank of England participates in the European System of Central Banks (ESCB, composed of the ECB and all EU national central banks) but is not part of the Eurosystem; the central bank governors of the latter and the six members of the executive board comprise the Governing Council of the ECB, its main decision-making body. While euro-outs retain independence for setting monetary policy, they do participate in the committees[7] and working groups that advise the General Council.

In summary, the opt-out largely fulfilled the objective of separating EMU from UK interests. British participation in the monetary pillar was limited to the inclusion of the Bank of England in the ESCB.

2.2 Financial integration

Participation in EMU's financial pillar is more complicated, as financial integration is an integral part of the EU's single market. Indeed, the legislation governing areas such as capital requirements applied to all EU Member States, and the UK was a key player in such negotiations.[8] EU financial regulations were created through the Lamfalussy Process, in which national supervisors and regulators would meet to decide on common regulations and ensure their smooth implementation. After the global financial crisis, EU financial governance was reformed through the creation of the European System of Financial Supervision. This included a new institution for EU financial surveillance, the European Systemic Risk Board, as well as an upgrading of the Lamfalussy Process's so-called "level 3" committees of national supervisors to supervisory authorities: the European Banking Authority (EBA, in

---

[7] These committees are: the Accounting and Monetary Income Committee, the Banking Supervision Committee, the Banknote Committee, the Committee on Cost Methodology, the Eurosystem/ESCB Communications Committee, the Eurosystem IT Steering Committee, the International Relations Committee, the Legal Committee, the Market Operations Committee, the Monetary Policy Committee, the Payment and Settlement Systems Committee, the Statistics Committee, the Budget Committee, and the Human Resources Conference. European Central Bank, *The European Central Bank, the Eurosystem, the European System of Central Banks* (ECB 2008) 19.

[8] Lucia Quaglia, "The Politics of Financial Services Regulation and Supervision Reform in the European Union" (2007) 46(2) *Journal of Common Market Studies* 269–90.

London), the European Securities and Markets Authorities (ESMA, in Paris), and the European Insurance and Occupational Pensions Authority (EIOPA, in Frankfurt).

Financial integration shifted from an issue concerning the single market to the euro area with the widespread belief in the doom loop between banks and their sovereigns.[9] In order to break the "vicious circle,"[10] weak banks that could require public assistance thereby made it more likely for a sovereign to default, further weakening the banks that held a major portion of sovereign debt, which worsened the sovereign's credibility. One way out of this doom loop was banking union, particularly an integrated banking supervisor. This led to the creation of the euro area's Banking Union, which refers to the Single Supervisory Mechanism (SSM) housed at the ECB, the Single Resolution Mechanism (SRM), and the Single Rulebook. Euro-ins are automatically part of the SSM and the SRM, while euro-outs can join Banking Union under a system of "closer cooperation" between the SSM and national supervisory authorities. The Single Rulebook[11] is considered a pillar of Banking Union but predates agreement on the establishment of single financial supervision that marked the beginning of Banking Union in 2012, as the term "Single Rulebook" was coined already in 2009.[12] The legislation associated with the Single Rulebook concerns all EU Member States as an internal market issue.

The shift towards strengthening euro area governance of financial markets potentially threatened the role of the UK in European finance. The UK is the most important financial center for euro-denominated transactions, boasting a daily turnover in excess of €927 billion.[13] Its four clearing houses benefited from the consolidation of operators since the euro's introduction.[14] The ECB attempted to shift the settlement of euro-denominated transactions to the

---

[9] Jean Pisani-Ferry, "The Euro Crisis and the New Impossible Trinity" (2012) 1 *Bruegel Policy Contribution*; David Schäfer, "A Banking Union of Ideas? The Impact of Ordoliberalism and the Vicious Circle on the EU Banking Union" (2016) 54(4) *Journal of Common Market Studies* 961–80.

[10] Euro Area, "Euro Area Summit Statement" (June 29, 2012).

[11] Capital Requirements Directive (CRD IV, Directive 2013/36/EU), Capital Requirements Regulation (CRR, Regulation (EU) No 575/2013), Deposit Guarantee Schemes Directive (DGS, Directive 2014/49/EU), and the Bank Recovery and Resolution Directive (BRRD, Directive 2014/59/EU).

[12] European Banking Authority, "The Single Rulebook" http://www.eba.europa.eu/regulation-and-policy/single-rulebook (last accessed March 15, 2017).

[13] Uurintuya Batsaikhan, "Brexit and the UK's Euro-denominated Market: The Role of Clearing Houses" *Bruegel blog post* (June 7, 2016) http://bruegel.org/2016/06/brexit-and-the-uks-euro-denominated-market-the-role-of-clearing-houses/ (last accessed March 15, 2017).

[14] Marcel Magnus, Alienor Anne Claire Duvillet-Margerit, and Benoît Mesnard, "Brexit: The United Kingdom and EU Financial Services" (2016) *Briefing for the European Parliament*.

euro area in its 2011 policy framework.[15] The UK countered that this went beyond the ECB's competence and violated single market provisions on the free movement of capital, services, and establishment by discriminating on the basis of location and sought an annulment. On March 4, 2015, the Court of Justice of the European Union (CJEU) supported the UK position,[16] and the ECB arranged a swap line with the Bank of England in case of liquidity shortages.[17]

The UK defended the interests of euro-outs as financial integration continued apace. The British government pressed for a double-majority voting system in the EBA, as its extant majority system would have effectively allowed the euro area to govern the technical standards that would have been applied to all EU banks.[18] Article 3.6 of the 2014 revised voting procedure therefore requires that decisions be adopted after a simple majority of euro-ins and a simple majority of euro-outs.[19] Chancellor of the Exchequer George Osborne considered EBA voting as a significant test case that had wider application for the role of the UK in a two-speed Europe.[20]

Shortly after the inauguration of Banking Union came plans for the loftily-named Capital Markets Union (CMU). The EU 28 hosts seventeen major national stock exchanges with a market capitalization of listed companies of €10.6 trillion at the end of 2015.[21] When CMU was launched in 2015, stock market capitalization as a percentage of GDP varied substantially (see Figure 8.1), with the UK as the second-highest cap-to-GDP ratio. According to the Commission, the lack of venture capital markets of a similar depth to that in the US cost the EU economy €90 billion over the previous five years.[22]

---

[15] ECB, "Eurosystem Oversight Policy Framework" (July 2011) https://www.ecb.europa.eu/pub/pdf/other/eurosystemoversightpolicyframework2011en.pdf (last accessed February 27, 2017).

[16] ECJ, Case T-496/11 *United Kingdom of Great Britain and Northern Ireland v. European Central Bank*, ECLI:EU:T:2015:133.

[17] Jim Brunsden, "ECB Steps Up Warning on UK Clearing after Brexit" *Financial Times* (January 22, 2017).

[18] Alex Barker, "Britain Threatens to Block Banking Union" *Financial Times* (November 8, 2012).

[19] European Banking Authority, "Decision adopting the Rules of Procedure of the European Banking Authority Board of Supervisors" https://www.eba.europa.eu/documents/10180/15718/EBA+DC+001+(Rules+of+Procedure+EBA-BoS+Rev3)_final.pdf/b5bb9d8e-050e-4b0b-95ff-cf86e2547b2c (last accessed April 20, 2017).

[20] Alex Barker, Peter Spiegel, and George Parker, "UK Close to Clinching Bank Union Safeguards" *Financial Times* (December 12, 2012).

[21] Jan Schildback and Martin Waibel, "European Exchange Landscape: Too Fragmented" *Deutsche Bank Research Talking Point* (May 2, 2016) https://www.dbresearch.de/servlet/reweb2.ReWEB?document=PROD0000000000401796&rwnode=DBR_INTERNET_EN-PROD$NAVIGATION&rwobj=ReDisplay.Start.class&rwsite=DBR_INTERNET_EN-PROD (last accessed March 1, 2017).

[22] European Commission, "Capital Markets Union: Factsheet" (Brussels, September 30, 2015).

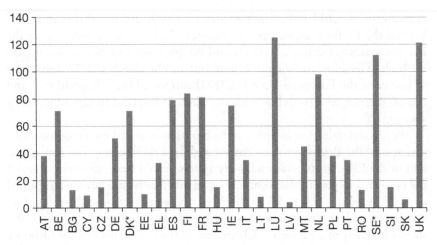

Figure 8.1 Stock market capitalization (as % of GDP) in 2013 in each EU28 country (*2012)

Source: data from European Commission, "Capital Markets Union: Factsheet," (September 30, 2015) <https://ec.europa.eu/commission/publications/capital-markets-union-factsheet_en> (last accessed August 19, 2017) © European Union 2016.

A report from the House of Lords supported CMU as "a project for the whole EU, and not just the Eurozone, and the UK stands to benefit through its role as a financial markets hub."[23]

Despite the similar monikers, plans for CMU differ substantially; while Banking Union aimed to stabilize financial markets through centralized supervision, CMU is about creating new financing opportunities. The financial fragmentation that accompanied the sovereign debt crisis led to vastly different funding conditions across borders and inhibited the return of economic growth, particularly to peripheral economies that had to pay higher interest rates than similar firms in core economies like Germany, Austria, or the Netherlands. Promoting the development of European capital markets could open new avenues of funding for firms and encourage investment and growth.

When the Juncker Commission began in 2014, Jonathan Hill was appointed the Commissioner for the new Directorate General of Financial Services and Markets (DG FISMA). On the one hand, Hill's appointment was in line with the objective of reinvigorating capital markets, given the

---

[23] House of Lords European Union Committee, "Whatever It Takes: The Five Presidents' Report on Completing Economic and Monetary Union" 13th Report of Session 2015-16 (May 12, 2016).

crucial role played by British capital markets. It also contained symbolic significance to have a British Commissioner at the helm to remind people of the important benefits that EU membership conferred on the City of London. On the other hand, plans to hold a referendum on the UK withdrawal from the EU also made it impossible for CMU to propose anything too ambitious: with the future of the UK's membership uncertain, Commissioner Hill could not embark on bold new commitments that would implicate the UK. When the 2015 Five Presidents' report had advocated a single capital markets supervisor for the EU,[24] for example, this prompted protests from the UK.[25]

On September 30, 2015, a Commission action plan outlined measures to achieve a "well-functioning and integrated Capital Markets Union ... by 2019."[26] Some of the associated proposals included boosting the moribund market for securitization, creating new prospectus rules to lower costs for companies trying to access capital markets (especially small companies), supporting long-term infrastructure investment through Solvency II,[27] and strengthening venture capital markets. The Five Presidents' proposal on supervision, however, had been dropped from the action plan.

In summary, the UK had fully participated in financial market integration until the sovereign debt crisis shifted it from an issue for the single market to the euro area, thanks to the doom loop between banks and sovereigns threatening the integrity of the euro area. Therefore, the UK remains outside of banking union (specifically supervision and resolution) but participates in other areas of financial integration like the Single Rulebook and CMU.

2.3 Fiscal Policy Cooperation

Fiscal policy cooperation began with the Maastricht Treaty convergence criteria to enter EMU on deficits (3% of GDP) and debt (60% of GDP). Article 125 of the TFEU, the no-bailout clause, prevented fiscal transfers across Member States, and the fiscal criteria were supposed to render bailouts

---

[24] Juncker *et al.*, "Completing Europe's Economic and Monetary Union" (n. 3) 12.

[25] Nicolas Véron, "Europe's Capital Markets Union and the New Single Market Challenge" *Bruegel blog post* (September 30, 2015) http://bruegel.org/2015/09/europes-capital-markets-union-and-the-new-single-market-challenge/ (last accessed March 20, 2017).

[26] European Commission, "Action Plan on Building a Capital Markets Union" Communication to the European Parliament, the Council, the European Economic and Social Committee and the Committee of Regions (September 30, 2015) http://eur-lex.europa.eu/legal-content/EN/TXT/?uri=CELEX%3A52015DC0468 (last accessed March 17, 2017).

[27] European Commission, "Capital Markets Union—Accelerating Reform" Communication to the European Parliament, the Council, the European Economic and Social Committee, and the Committee of Regions (September 14, 2016) http://ec.europa.eu/finance/capital-markets-union/docs/20160914-com-2016-601_en.pdf (last accessed March 19, 2017).

unnecessary. These convergence criteria were codified in the Stability and Growth Pact (SGP) rules on deficits and debt levels. The SGP established a preventive arm warning states that approached the deficit limits and a corrective arm triggering the Excessive Deficit Procedure (EDP), which eventually could impose fines on the euro area Member State in violation of the SGP. Euro-outs could be found in violation of the SGP and be placed under the EDP, but they would not be fined. The UK most recently was under the EDP in 2015. All Member States are required to submit to regular reporting of their fiscal situation to the European Commission, with euro area countries submitting a "Stability Programme" and euro-outs a "Convergence Programme". The independent Office for Budget Responsibility (established in 2010) prepared the UK's forecasts for its Convergence Programme.

Although the SGP's rules were relaxed in 2005, the euro crisis prompted the tightening of the SGP as part of the six-pack and the two-pack. The UK's opt-out exempts it from the two-pack regulations that tighten fiscal surveillance, the six-pack's new sanctions for noncompliance with fiscal rules, and the directive requiring Member States to set domestic numerical rules for achieving fiscal targets.[28] These fiscal reforms were reinforced (and in some cases duplicated) by measures in the 2012 Treaty on Stability, Coordination and Governance (TSCG). Having been urged on by Draghi's call for a "fiscal compact,"[29] the EU's attempt to enact the necessary treaty changes was blocked by the UK. Member States therefore opted to use an intergovernmental treaty to circumvent the unanimity required by treaty changes.[30] All EU countries except the UK and the Czech Republic signed the TSCG. While UK Chancellor of the Exchequer Osborne accepted the "remorseless logic"[31] that a single currency imposed on further fiscal integration, the UK once again opted out. To support fiscal consolidation across the euro area, the Five Presidents' report proposed the creation of a European Fiscal Board,[32]

[28] UK Government, "Review of the Balance of Competences between the United Kingdom and the European Union: Economic, and Monetary Policy" (December 2014) https://www.gov.uk/government/uploads/system/uploads/attachment_data/file/388847/2903003_BoC_EMP_acc.pdf (last accessed April 6, 2017).

[29] Mario Draghi, "Hearing before the Plenary of the European Parliament on the Occasion of the Adoption of the Resolution on the ECB's 2010 Annual Report" (December 1, 2011) https://www.ecb.europa.eu/press/key/date/2011/html/sp111201.en.html (last accessed March 15, 2017). See also Jonathan Yiangou, Micheal O'Keeffe, and Gabriel Glöckler, "'Tough Love': How the ECB's Monetary Financing Prohibition Pushes Deeper Euro Area Integration" (2013) 35(3) *Journal of European Integration* 223–37.

[30] Federico Fabbrini, *Economic Governance in Europe* (Oxford University Press 2016).

[31] Chris Giles and George Parker, "Osborne Urges Eurozone to 'Get a Grip'" *Financial Times* (July 20, 2011).

[32] Juncker *et al.*, "Completing Europe's Economic and Monetary Union" (n. 3) 14.

which was set up in October 2016. The European Fiscal Board operates in strictly an advisory capacity, and its members come from both the Eurozone and euro-outs.

The sovereign debt crisis also prompted the creation of bailout funds. The UK's participation in bailouts was not straightforward, despite its opt-out. The EU responded to the first Greek crisis in 2010 with a comprehensive package that included the European Financial Stability Facility (EFSF, €440 bn), as well as the European Financial Stability Mechanism (EFSM, €60 bn). The latter used the EU budget as collateral to borrow money on financial markets, thereby implicating the UK. At the December 2010 European Council summit, Prime Minister David Cameron agreed to the treaty change that would be needed to create the European Stability Mechanism (ESM), the permanent euro area bailout fund established in 2012. In return, the EFSM would no longer be used for euro area bailouts.[33] The UK (like other euro-outs) does not participate in the ESM. Cameron's deal regarding a new settlement for the UK within the EU also excluded the use of funds provided by euro-outs for euro area crisis management.[34] Nevertheless, the UK did participate in the Irish bailout through bilateral loans.

In summary, the UK's participation in fiscal policy cooperation is limited to budgetary surveillance and the submission of a Convergence Programme to the European Commission. It has opted out of all fiscal policy cooperation agreements, including those outside of the framework of EU law. It voluntarily contributed to the Irish bailout and negotiated the separation of EU-backed funds for future euro area bailouts.

2.4 Economic policy cooperation

Economic policy cooperation is less institutionalized than the other pillars of EMU in that it is limited to coordination, with few powers delegated to the EU. The main instruments of economic policy cooperation are the Broad Economic Policy Guidelines (BEPG), Europe 2020, and the Macroeconomic Imbalances Procedure (MIP) that was established as part of the six-pack. The BEPG and Europe 2020 are procedures governed by soft law, in which the Commission makes recommendations for the Member States, along with

---

[33] Matthew Holehouse, "EU Demands Britain Joins Greek Rescue Fund" *The Telegraph* (July 13, 2015).

[34] Fabian Amtembrink, Anastasia Karatzia, and Rene Repasi, "Renegotiation by the United Kingdom on its Constitutional Relationship with the European Union: Economic Governance" In-depth analysis prepared for the European Parliament's Committee on Constitutional Affairs, (September 2016).

country-specific recommendations (CSR). The European Semester was introduced in 2010 so that the reporting of economic policy coordination (National Reform Programmes) and fiscal policy coordination (the aforementioned Stability and Convergence Programmes) were coordinated under a common timeline that would enable Member States to take into account the CSRs in national budgetary proceedings. Multilateral surveillance applies to all EU Member States, with the exception of the adoption of sections of the BEPG relating to the euro area (Article 121(1) TFEU).

The MIP aims to identify economic imbalances such as asset bubbles, financial crises, or competitiveness imbalances before they become excessive. A scoreboard of eleven indicators was developed to screen for potential imbalances, which are published in the Alert Mechanism Report (AMR). Countries deemed at risk of imbalances are subject to an in-depth review (IDR) to confirm suspected imbalances, with follow-up measures included in the CSR. Should such imbalances be confirmed, the Member State enters the Excessive Imbalances Procedure (EIP), which can eventually lead to fines for euro area countries (in contrast to the soft law used for the BEPG and Europe 2020). The UK underwent an IDR every year from 2012–2016. None of these imbalances was ever found "excessive," and its 2016 IDR yielded "no imbalances."[35]

In summary, the UK participates in EU economic policy coordination organized under the European Semester. Its status as a euro-out exempts it from the fines associated with the EIP, and the other aspects of economic policy coordination pose few constraints on national governments.

3. Brexit and EMU

Although the UK opted out of the single currency, the UK's presence in the EU still affected its development. It will continue to affect economic conditions in the foreseeable future; depending on how hard of a Brexit ensues (referring to the existence or nonexistence of transitional arrangements for access to EU markets), the loss of economic growth and output in both the UK and the EU could be substantial. Moreover, Brexit could alter alliances within the EU. First, the UK was an ally to other countries that voluntarily remained outside of the euro area. Brexit affects that balance considerably and removes the largest economy from that group. Second, the UK tended to pursue market-friendly policies that suited the interests of like-minded countries

---

[35] Commission, "Alert Mechanism Report 2017" (November 16, 2016) 5.

both in and out of the euro area.[36] Brexit could transform this dynamic. Finally, dealing with Brexit could shift political resources as countries deal with the ramifications of Brexit and the loss of British markets and financial support.

This section considers the impact of Brexit on each of the aforementioned pillars and the likelihood of either further integration or disintegration, depending on: changing economic conditions that recast incentives for euro area integration; altering alliances within the euro area and between the euro-ins and euro-outs; and shifting political resources due to the consequences of Brexit. Both the impact of Brexit on the *status quo*, as well as the possibility for future reforms will be analyzed. The latter will be drawn both from priorities stated by the euro area in the Five Presidents' report[37] and Commission White Paper,[38] as well as reforms suggested by prominent politicians and analysts. Numerous actors have noted the opportunity that Brexit poses for further European integration, with one of the main dissenters no longer in the game. Indeed, some have even considered further integration to be a necessity, both due to the need for a united Europe to successfully negotiate Brexit and for the long-run sustainability of EMU.[39]

3.1 Monetary Integration

What explains progress in monetary integration, and how would Brexit influence these factors? Some of the leading theories include: liberal intergovernmentalism, which emphasizes the role of large Member States, especially Germany; neofunctionalism, which gives a critical role to supranational institutions; constructivism, which looks at shared ideas; and domestic politics and institutions.[40]

A consensus emerged on the need to reinforce the "timber-framed"[41] governance structure of EMU after the euro crisis rocked its foundations, and much has been done to reinforce over the last decade. What remains for the monetary pillar? Two of the most contentious reforms, debt restructuring and the introduction of Eurobonds, would require a Treaty change[42] and are

---

[36] See also Catherine Barnard's contribution in this volume, "Brexit and the EU Internal Market."

[37] Juncker *et al.*, "Completing Europe's Economic and Monetary Union" (n. 3).

[38] European Commission, "White Paper on the Future of Europe: Reflections and Scenarios for the EU27 by 2025" (n. 4).

[39] See also Federico Fabbrini's contribution in this volume, "Brexit and EU Treaty Reform."

[40] Michele Chang, *Economic and Monetary Union* (Palgrave Macmillan 2016).

[41] Wolfgang Schäuble, "Banking Union Must Be Built on Firm Foundations" *Financial Times* (May 12, 2013).

[42] Federico Fabbrini, "Reforming Economic and Monetary Union: Legislation and Treaty Change" *Spotlight Europe* #2017/01.

unlikely to be pursued after Brexit negotiations have concluded; it lacks the support of large Member States like Germany, and no consensus exists on their utility. Other euro area reforms appear more viable. Institutional innovations suggested by the Five Presidents' report included a full-time Eurogroup presidency, a euro area finance ministry, and single representation of the euro area.[43] Finally, monetary union could expand to include more euro-outs in the coming years.

Brexit would add additional challenges to achieving these ends. First, Brexit will lead to changing economic conditions through exchange rate fluctuations. The uncertainty generated by Brexit has led to a weaker pound. If a soft Brexit were to emerge, the exchange rate would likely stabilize. In the case of a hard Brexit, the exchange rate volatility that would ensue could affect the incentives for euro-outs to join. In the past, exchange rate volatility has served as an impetus for more cooperation in Europe; both the Snake and the European Monetary System were created in part as a response to the instability of the European currencies against the dollar.[44] Indeed, the 1992–1993 ERM crisis convinced many European leaders that monetary union was the better option, given the difficulty in maintaining a fixed exchange rate in a world of mobile capital.[45] Could a similar calculation be made by the euro-outs to get closer to EMU? Or for the euro-ins to strengthen cooperation? Currently, only Denmark is part of the ERM II, in which membership is required for two years without devaluation before adopting the euro. During the global financial crisis, there was some acknowledgement that the existence of the euro had prevented it from becoming a currency crisis as well, and Denmark briefly considered euro membership.[46] The euro-outs have declined to join EMU for political reasons as well as economic,[47] and the exchange rate volatility would have to be sustained and severe for them to abandon their political reservations and adopt the euro. The 2016 Eurobarometer poll showed 52 percent of respondents across the seven pre-ins are against euro adoption, an increase from 49 percent in 2015.[48]

Second, Brexit could alter alliances between remaining EU Member States, both inside and outside of the euro area. For those remaining euro-outs,

---

[43] Juncker *et al.*, "Completing Europe's Economic and Monetary Union" (n. 3).

[44] Peter Ludlow, *The Making of the European Monetary System* (Butterworths Scientific 1982).

[45] Paul De Grauwe, "What Have We Learnt about Monetary Integration since the Maastricht Treaty?" (2006) 44(4) *Journal of Common Market Studies* 711–30.

[46] Marcus Walker, "Denmark Pushes for Vote to Adopt Euro" *Wall Street Journal* (November 5, 2008).

[47] See Chang, *Economic and Monetary Union* (n. 40).

[48] Flash Eurobarometer 440, "Report: Introduction of the Euro in the Member States that Have Not Yet Adopted the Common Currency" (April) doi:10.2765/12914.

the division with the euro area could harden. The euro-ins already can out-vote euro-outs under the qualified majority voting rules introduced by the Lisbon Treaty, and Brexit has intensified interest in multispeed integration. In February 2017, the Benelux countries declared that, in their vision of the future of Europe, "different paths of integration and enhanced cooperation could provide for effective responses to challenges that affect member states in different ways."[49] Among the Commission White Paper scenarios,[50] a mul-tispeed Europe emerged quickly as the favored option of Germany, France, Italy, and Spain. While French President Francois Hollande deemed the idea of a multispeed Europe "necessary", others viewed it as "dangerous"[51] in that it could exacerbate the existing divisions between EU Member States over issues like the euro, Schengen, and migration and create a second-class EU citizenship. Bulgaria and Romania, for example, expressed concern that Brexit would lead to their marginalization;[52] euro-outs were difficult to marginal-ize when the UK figured among their ranks, but Brexit would reduce euro-outs to a group of small- and medium-sized countries. If multispeed Europe emerges as the preferred integration path, some euro-outs likely would recon-sider euro area membership. Most have accepted the need for the euro area to intensify integration to be viable in the long term, which would exacerbate the notions of a "core" and a "periphery" in the EU.

Institutionally, the Eurogroup would gain importance. Although the Economic and Financial Affairs Council (Ecofin) retains formal decision-making authority, the subset of finance ministers of the euro area known as the Eurogroup has become a key institution in EU governance. The Eurogroup began as an informal group in which members could discuss matters of common interest. The sovereign debt crisis solidified its power and influence; the European Stability Mechanism's Board of Governors, its highest decision-making body, consists of the Eurogroup members. Critical decisions on EMU are made by the Eurogroup, not Ecofin,[53] and a multi-speed Europe would intensify this pattern. Remaining outside of the euro

[49] Charles Michel, "Benelux Vision on the Future of Europe" (February 3, 2017) http://premier.fgov.be/en/benelux-vision-future-europe (last accessed March 12, 2017).

[50] European Commission, "White Paper on the Future of Europe: Reflections and Scenarios for the EU27 by 2025" (n. 4).

[51] Alex Barker, Paul McClean, and Stefan Wagstyl, "Will EU Core States Leave Partners Behind after Brexit?" *Financial Times* (March 7, 2017).

[52] Almut Möller and Tim Oliver (eds.), *The United Kingdom and the European Union: What Would a "Brexit" Mean for the EU and Other States around the World?* DGAPanalyse Deutsche Gesellschaft fuer Auswaertige Politik e.V, 2014).

[53] Article 136(2) states that "only members of the Council representing Member States whose currency is the euro shall take part in the vote" for matters involving the proper functioning of EMU.

area would therefore entail costs in terms of engagement and influence in the EU, although some euro-outs might accept this price.

Even within the euro area, Brexit could provoke shifting alliances.[54] The euro crisis contributed to rising intergovernmentalism in EU governance[55] that left Germany as the euro area's "reluctant hegemon."[56] Brexit would solidify German leadership within the euro area and the EU, as "other EU member states have already directed their attention increasingly towards Berlin, with this in part a result of Britain's growing isolation."[57]

3.2 Financial Integration

Brexit's impact on the euro area will be more direct in that the UK participated in EU financial cooperation as part of the single market. The withdrawal of the UK will have major changes on the EU's financial system. Its banking sector's asset size is between a third and a half of that of the euro area, its bank balance sheets are three times the euro area's GDP, and it is much more international. About 10 percent of all euro area and 15 percent of noneuro area bank branches or subsidiaries are in the UK, and five of those subsidiaries are supervised by the SSM.[58]

The European Commission contends that work on CMU will continue and that the basic building blocks will still be in place by 2019. According to Commission Vice President for Financial Services Valdis Dombrovskis, "The prospect of Europe's largest financial centre leaving the single market makes our task more challenging, but all the more important."[59] Concrete plans beyond 2019, however, appear to be modest. In the Commission's White Paper,[60] CMU is only mentioned twice. Under the "Carrying on" scenario, the Commission envisions that "further steps are taken to strengthen financial supervision … and to develop capital markets to finance the real economy."[61]

---

[54] See also Uwe Puetter's contribution to this volume, "Brexit and EU Institutional Balance of Power."

[55] Christopher J. Bickerton, Dermot Hodson, and Uwe Puetter (eds.), *The New Intergovernmentalism: States and Supranational Actors in the Post-Maastricht Era* (Oxford University Press 2015).

[56] William Paterson, "The Reluctant Hegemon? Germany Moves Center Stage in the European Union" (2011) 49 *Journal of Common Market Studies* (Annual Review) 57–75.

[57] Tim Oliver, "European and International Views of Brexit" (2016) 23(9) *Journal of European Public Policy* 1323.

[58] Ignazio Angeloni, "Banking Union and the United Kingdom in the Single Market" Speech to the Barclays Annual Bank Capital Conference (March 9, 2016).

[59] Fiona Maxwell, "EU's Capital Markets Disunion" *Politico* (February 22, 2017).

[60] European Commission, "White Paper on the Future of Europe: Reflections and Scenarios for the EU27 by 2025" (n. 4).

[61] ibid 16.

This seems to exclude expanding the supranational reach of European institutions across capital markets. Only the more ambitious "doing more together" scenario advocates "fully integrated capital markets."[62]

Previous research on the political economy of European financial regulation indicates the importance of large Member State interests[63] and the domestic politics behind them,[64] converging ideas,[65] and the institutional features of national banking sectors.[66] These will be affected by the aforementioned factors that Brexit will alter and thus impact the development of financial sector integration in the future. For example, Brexit will reconfigure the extant alliances present in European financial integration. France, Italy, and Spain's "market-shaping" coalition seeking "financial stability and consumer protection, as well as the protection of national industry" conflicted with the UK, the Netherlands, and Nordic countries' "market-making" coalition, prizing "competition and market efficiency."[67] Brexit deprives the latter of its largest and most influential member and largest beneficiary of Capital Markets Union, as the UK, Luxembourg, Sweden, Ireland, and the Netherlands were the strongest advocates of CMU; Germany, France, Italy, and Austria viewed CMU more cautiously, and the Central and Eastern European states were unlikely to benefit substantially based on the presence (or lack) of a large, nonbank-based financial sector.[68] Questions have been raised if this will affect EU support for the completion of CMU,[69] but Commissioner Dombrovskis insisted that Brexit makes CMU "more urgent."[70]

Brexit provides the opportunity to reconsider CMU's next steps. Brexit will lead to a "regulatory splintering" once EU capital markets cease to be subject

---

[62] ibid 24.

[63] Shawn Donnelly, "Power Politics and the Undersupply of Financial Stability in Europe" (2014) 21(4) *Review of International Political Economy* 985–1005.

[64] Alexandra Hennessey, "Redesigning Financial Supervision in the European Union (2009–2013)" (2013) 21(2) *Journal of European Public Policy* 151–68; Scott James, "The Domestic Politics of Financial Regulation: Informal Ratification Games and the EU Capital Requirement Negotiations" (2016) 21(2) *New Political Economy* 187–203.

[65] Schäfer, "A Banking Union of Ideas?" (n. 0).

[66] David Howarth and Lucia Quaglia, *The Political Economy of European Banking Union* (Oxford University Press 2016).

[67] Lucia Quaglia, *Governing Financial Services in the European Union: Banking, Securities and Post-Trading* (Routledge 2010) 8.

[68] Lucia Quaglia, David Howarth, and Moritz Liebe, "The Political Economy of European Capital Markets Union" (2016) 54(S1) *Journal of Common Market Studies* 185–203.

[69] Philipp Ständer, "What Will Happen with the Capital Markets Union After Brexit?" (2016) Jacques Delors Institute Policy Paper No.191.

[70] Jim Brunsden, "Brexit Makes EU Capital Markets Union More Urgent, Says Commissioner" *Financial Times* (September 14, 2016).

to the UK's Prudential Regulation Authority.[71] Moreover, Brexit has revived the question of euro-denominated transactions being cleared in London. The aforementioned ECJ ruling[72] and ECB swap agreement will no longer apply after the UK exits.[73] In May 2017, the Commission announced the EU's intention to move clearing activities to the EU as part of its plans for the reform of the European Market Infrastructure Regulation (EMIR): "CCPs that play a key systemic role for EU financial markets are subject to the safeguards provided by the EU legal framework, including, where necessary, enhanced supervision at EU level and/or location requirements."[74]

How can the UK's relationship with the EU be preserved, at least in financial services? This will be a major topic for Brexit negotiations. British firms would lose passporting rights, referring the ability of firms to provide financial services across the EU. To retain them, UK banks would need subsidiaries in the EU, as the only nonEU countries given passporting rights are in the European Economic Area. Banks moving from the UK to the EU would have to comply with EU regulations and the SSM framework.[75] For those without EU subsidiaries, another option is equivalence, in which both sides agree that rules and legislation are similar. Equivalence arrangements, however, suffer from their "piecemeal" approach, as the rights are narrowly defined in specific articles and can be quickly withdrawn.[76] Bank of England Governor Mark Carney has called for a system of "mutual recognition and cooperation" of UK and EU financial rules.[77]

A window of opportunity could arise allowing for a reassessment of the roles of the ESAs more generally[78] and for furthering CMU to include supervision. For example, the ESAs will already be affected through the relocation of the EBA from London to the Continent. The EBA's double majority voting

---

[71] Reza Moghadam, "How a Post-Brexit Redesign Can Save the Capital Markets Union" *Financial Times* (February 13, 2016).

[72] ECJ, Case T-496/11 *United Kingdom of Great Britain and Northern Ireland v. European Central Bank* (n. 16).

[73] Batsaikhan, "Brexit and the UK's Euro-denominated Market" (n. 13).

[74] Commission, "Commission Proposes Simpler and More Efficient Derivatives Rules", Press release (May 4, 2017) http://europa.eu/rapid/press-release_IP-17-1150_en.htm (last accessed May 7, 2017).

[75] ECB, "Relocating to the Euro Area" https://www.bankingsupervision.europa.eu/banking/relocating/html/index.en.html (last accessed May 7, 2017).

[76] Alienor Anne Claire Duvillet-Margerit, Marcel Magnus, Benoît Mesnard, and Aspasia Xirou, "Third Country Equivalence in EU Banking Legislation" European Parliament Briefing (March 7, 2017) 1 http://www.europarl.europa.eu/RegData/etudes/BRIE/2016/587369/IPOL_BRI(2016)587369_EN.pdf (last accessed April 21, 2017).

[77] Mark Carney, "The High Road to a Responsible, Open Financial System" Speech to Thomson Reuters, Canary Wharf (April 7, 2017).

[78] Ständer, "What Will Happen with the Capital Markets Union After Brexit?" (n. 69).

system likely will be reconsidered due to Brexit. In addition, Schoenmaker and Véron have proposed the expansion of ESMA's powers, noting that: "It is in the interest of the United Kingdom to have a well-regulated, well-supervised EU-27 financial system as its neighbour."[79]

Finally, there is the possibility that Brexit and its aftermath will discourage further integration, including CMU. This is not only possible; some would argue that it is preferable, given the "broadly varying financial practices and structures" in the EU, and priority should be given to euro area integration.[80] Moreover, "the absence of strong spillovers and availability of domestic options to unilaterally contain financial stability"[81] had prevented shifting financial regulation to the EU in the past and could continue to do so after Brexit. With its strongest advocate leaving the EU, the remaining proponents are relatively small and would have difficulty winning over more ambivalent Member States.

3.3 Fiscal Integration

The flurry of euro area fiscal reforms since 2010 have exacerbated the complexity of the rules concerning fiscal policy cooperation. To that end, the Commission advocated the "streamlining and reinforcement of the European Semester."[82] In the longer term, the Five Presidents' report suggested that the euro area could acquire a fiscal stabilization function, as "all mature Monetary Unions have put in place a common macroeconomic stabilisation function to better deal with shocks."[83] Brexit could facilitate the creation of a euro area fiscal capacity. Post-Brexit, the EU will be poorer; this would be a consequence of declining trade and investment with the UK as well as the loss of Britain's contributions to the EU budget. Brexit would lead to a "permanent funding gap" for the EU budget that could amount to €10 billion per year.[84] Conflict

[79] Dirk Schoenmaker and Nicolas Véron (2017). "Brexit Should Drive Integration of EU Capital Markets" *Bruegel blog post* (February 24, 2017) http://bruegel.org/2017/02/brexit-should-drive-integration-of-eu-capital-markets/ (last accessed (February 27, 2017).

[80] Anton Brender, Florence Pisani, and Daniel Gros, "Building a Capital Markets Union … Or Designing a Financial System for the Euro Area?" (2015) *CEPS Commentaries* (June 2, 2015).

[81] Lucia Quaglia and Aneta Spendzharova, "The Conundrum of Solving 'Too Big to Fail' in the European Union: Supranationalization at Different Speeds" (2017) *Journal of Common Market Studies* DOI 10.1111/jcms.12531.

[82] Jean-Claude Juncker, "A Deeper and Fairer Economic and Monetary Union: Two Years On" Speech on the State of the Union to the European Parliament (September 14, 2016) 7 https://ec.europa.eu/commission/sites/beta-political/files/2-years-on-emu_en_0.pdf (last accessed April 7, 2017).

[83] Juncker *et al.*, "Completing Europe's Economic and Monetary Union" (n. 3).

[84] Jörg Haas and Eulalia Rubio, "Brexit and the EU Budget: Threat or Opportunity?" (2016) Jacques Delors Institute Policy Paper No.183.

between net contributors to the EU budget and net beneficiaries would ensue, as the former (including Denmark, Germany, the Netherlands, and Sweden) would be under pressure to increase their national contributions. Moreover, EU programs would face the threat of major cuts. Brexit therefore presents a "window of opportunity" for reform of the multiannual financial framework and even the creation of a separate euro area budget.[85] The latter is a longstanding idea that was raised in the 1970 Werner Report,[86] the European Community's original blueprint for EMU, but was not included in the 1989 Delors Report[87] that set the conditions for EMU under the Maastricht Treaty. The idea of a euro area budget enjoys renewed interest, which would logically be accompanied by a euro area finance ministry.

Nevertheless, disagreement remains over building a euro area fiscal capacity. Germany, in particular, has opted to pursue stronger fiscal rules to strengthen euro area fiscal governance, with no indications of a shift in attitude towards reforms that could lead to fiscal transfers or risk sharing across the euro area.[88] Instead, the German government has supported intergovernmental measures rather than risk-sharing ones. For example, German Finance Minister Wolfgang Schäuble advocated upgrading the ESM to a European Monetary Fund that would take over the monitoring of euro area budgets from the Commission,[89] which is quite different from a euro area finance ministry that could engage in countercyclical spending. German reluctance to approve reforms that would have cross-border budgetary implications have also prevented the creation of euro area deposit insurance, something that is essential for the completion of banking union and, according to Guntram Wolff, is a "prerequisite for a euro-area fiscal capacity."[90] While Brexit presents the greater possibility for such reforms, substantial political obstacles remain; Germany's reform proposals continue to involve stronger rules rather than shared risk.

[85] See also Federico Fabbrini's contribution in this volume, "Brexit and EU Treaty Reform."

[86] Pierre Werner (chair), "Report to the Council and the Commission on the Realisation by Stages of Economic and Monetary Union in the European Community" Luxembourg (October 8, 1970).

[87] Reference was made instead to "binding rules for budgetary policies" with no euro area budget for cyclical adjustment; see Jacques Delors (chair), "Report on Economic and Monetary Union in the European Community" (1989) 16.

[88] Matthias Matthijs, "Powerful Rules Governing the Euro: The Perverse Logic of German Ideas" (2016) 23(3) *Journal of European Public Policy* 375–91.

[89] Albrecht Meier, "Berlin Continues Quest for 'European Monetary Fund'" *Der Tagesspiegel* (March 8, 2017).

[90] Guntram Wolff, "What Are the Prerequisites for a Euro-Area Fiscal Capacity?" *Bruegel Policy Contribution* (September 9, 2016).

3.4 Economic Policy Coordination

The Five Presidents' report suggested a euro area system of Competitiveness Authorities in which Member States assigned independent entities to assess issues like the evolution of wages vis-à-vis other euro area countries and major trading partners.[91] These national bodies would meet annually to coordinate actions. In addition, the report proposed strengthening the Macroeconomic Imbalances Procedure in a way that would encourage structural reforms by making more use of the corrective arm.

Structural reforms may be necessary, as Brexit will likely lead to worsening economic conditions for both the UK and the EU: "There is a consensus, even including the proponents of 'leave', that there would be a short-term negative shock to the EU economy from Brexit."[92] Eight euro area countries figure among the UK's top import and export destinations[93] and will be affected strongly by Brexit. Nevertheless, it is not clear that EU economic policy coordination would be able to improve the situation. Indeed, one study found "strong and robust evidence that neither [the SGP] nor the Lisbon Strategy have had a significant beneficial impact on. .... economic performance."[94]

Moreover, the soft law nature of economic policy cooperation has always made compliance with recommendations uneven at best, as consequences for noncompliance were limited.[95] A recent study indicated that in 2016 the situation had worsened, with the proportion of country-specific recommendations that were followed dropping from 7 percent in 2014 to 2 percent in 2016; the excessive imbalances procedure seems to have made little difference.[96] While many agree on the need for reform, the nature of the reforms have been contested. In contrast to shifting views of the relationship between the single currency and financial supervision discussed above, other areas

---

[91] Juncker *et al.*, "Completing Europe's Economic and Monetary Union" (n. 3) 8.

[92] Iain Begg and Fabian Mushoevel, "The Economic Impact of Brexit: Jobs, Growth and the Public Finances" (2016) https://www.lse.ac.uk/europeanInstitute/LSE-Commission/Hearing-11---The-impact-of-Brexit-on-jobs-and-economic-growth-sumary.pdf (last accessed March 12, 2017).

[93] Germany, France, Netherlands, Ireland, Belgium, and Luxembourg, Spain, and Italy. See "Statistical Bulletin: UK Trade: January 2016" Office for National Statistics https://www.ons.gov.uk/economy/nationalaccounts/balanceofpayments/bulletins/uktrade/january2016 (last accessed March 12, 2017).

[94] Demosthenes Ioannou and Livio Stracca, "Have the Euro Area and EU Governance Worked? Just the Facts" (2014) 34 *European Journal of Political Economy* 1.

[95] See Chang, *Economic and Monetary Union* (n. 40).

[96] Philipp Ständer, "Numbers of the Week" *EU Economy Brief* 12/2017.

have been prone to "ideational stickiness and inertia, and despite some policy experimentation, overarching policy frameworks and their rationales have not been overhauled."[97] Brexit is unlikely to change these dynamics.

4. Conclusion

Monnet's prediction that Europe will be forged in crisis has been recalled frequently over the last decade, and Brexit presents a major challenge for European integration. Nevertheless, the UK's nonparticipation in EMU means that Brexit will have more of an indirect effect, particularly on monetary and financial integration. The divide between the euro-ins and euro-outs will become larger, which could give the needed impetus to a Eurozone enlargement. In terms of further integration within the monetary pillar, however, Brexit would strengthen the already-dominant position of Germany. In the financial pillar, the exit of the UK will affect further integration decisively by changing the EU financial landscape and altering alliances between the remaining Member States. While the pursuit of CMU would continue under its currently narrow remit, further supranationalism in supervision and regulation is questionable due to opposition to risk sharing by Germany and others. The loss of the EU's foremost advocate (and beneficiary) of financial market liberalization offers a window of opportunity to reconsider existing structures but likely would lead to only incremental changes, absent another crisis or the emergence of German leadership in this direction. It impact on fiscal integration is less certain, with the budgetary pressures on the post-Brexit multiannual financial framework presenting new challenges that require reforms that could lead eventually to a euro area budget. Nevertheless, German opposition to risk sharing could again stymie reforms in this direction. Finally, Brexit's impact on economic policy will likely reinforce existing tendencies.

Will Brexit promote integration or disintegration in EMU? The euro crisis already prompted substantial reforms in euro area governance and the recognition that further integration is needed. Brexit's impact on economic conditions, existing alliances, and political resources ensure that the euro area integration will continue, at least in some areas. It may even expand in euro area membership. In this way, the EU's biggest euro-out would have (inadvertently) instigated further euro area cooperation.

---

[97] Andrew Baker, "Varieties of Economic Crisis, Varieties of Ideational Change: How and Why Financial Regulation and Macroeconomic Policy Differ" (2015) 20(3) *New Political Economy* 342.

9

Brexit and the EU Area of Freedom, Security, and Justice

Bespoke Bits and Pieces

*Deirdre Curtin**

1. Introduction

The history of European integration has for many decades been one of unity but at the same time of differentiation. *The Many Faces of Differentiation* was the title of a book published after the Treaty of Amsterdam in 1997,[1] consisting of an elaborate account of a whole panoply of existing flexible and differentiated arrangements in the EU among different Member States. Differentiation at that time took many legal forms, ranging from primary to secondary EU law and soft law instruments, and from external agreements with third states to 'internal' agreements between the Member States themselves. Twenty years later, one would assume that the vista is very different. But is it? Differentiation is today a defining feature of the European Union polity, warts and all. The follow-up book, by largely the same editors, bears the title: *Between Flexibility and Disintegration. The Trajectory of Differentiation in EU Law*.[2] Among legal scholars, differentiation and flexibility were not originally perceived as a threat to European integration but rather as a tool to promote further integration by allowing a group of Member States to forge ahead with

* I would like to thank Nathalie McNabb for excellent research assistance and Janneke van Casteren for help with editing.

[1] B De Witte, D Hanf, and E Vos (eds), *The Many Faces of Differentiation* (Intersentia 2001).
[2] B De Witte, A Ott, and E Vos (eds), *Between Flexibility and Disintegration: The Trajectory of Differentiation in EU Law* (Edward Elgar Publishing 2017) 2.

Brexit and the EU Area of Freedom, Security and Justice: Bespoke Bits and Pieces. First edition. Deirdre Curtin © Deirdre Curtin 2017. Published 2017 by Oxford University Press.

closer cooperation, while leaving the door open for the remaining Member States to join later (for example the Schengen and Prüm Conventions).

The vista of disintegration has, however, always been there; as long ago as the Treaty of Maastricht in 1993 I labelled it a 'Europe of Bits and Pieces'.[3] Is differentiation a 'negation of the idea of European integration'?[4] Allowing opt-outs can also be seen as a pragmatic way of integrating states.[5] The term disintegration inevitably takes on a different connotation in the light of the political realities of Brexit. The issue is not so much anymore whether the many 'faces' of flexibility have over the years contributed to the fragility of the EU legal and political orders. As the EU has moved into areas that were previously exclusive to the nation state, such as criminal law and border control, a preference by some for 'outsiderness' over full membership has progressively come to the fore. For example, during the Lisbon Treaty negotiations the UK, Poland, and the Czech Republic secured exemptions from the Charter of Fundamental Rights. Another example is the (very recent) Danish opt-out of the European Police Office (Europol) following a referendum on this specific issue. Political sociologists have challenged the claim that opt-outs lead to the marginalization of certain Member States and contribute to European disintegration.[6] This is particularly true for the existing British and Danish opt-outs from borders, asylum, migration, and justice policies. The counterintuitive argument is in fact made that opt-outs and other differentiation processes may actually reinforce the integration process. The coping strategies used by British and Danish officials reveal that the EU is partially created through the 'stigmatization of transgressive states'.[7]

But what is the situation when those 'transgressive states' opt out (by referendum) in part (Europol–Denmark) and fully (the EU–the UK)? The object of this chapter is to explore the existing opt-outs specifically in the field of the EU Area of Freedom, Security, and Justice (AFSJ) in an attempt to elaborate some paths of flexible integration or involvement for the future for the UK in particular as a fully-fledged outsider post-Brexit. Can a full outsider opt back in in specific regards? By what mechanisms may that take place? Are there areas likely to fall under the political and legal radars?

In exploring these issues, the chapter is structured as follows: section 2 considers the peculiar status of the UK in the AFSJ before Brexit and underlines

---

[3] D Curtin, 'The Constitutional Structure of the Union: A Europe of Bits and Pieces' (1993) 30(1) *Common Market Law Review* 17.
[4] G Verhofstadt, *The United States of Europe* (Federal Trust 2006) 214.
[5] R Adler-Nissen, *Opting Out of the European Union: Diplomacy, Sovereignty and European Integration* (Cambridge University Press 2014) 2.
[6] ibid 3.   [7] ibid.

how the UK government has specifically expressed its wish and intention to remain connected to several AFSJ measures after Brexit. Section 3 considers participation in Europol and the peculiar nature of the Danish 'precedent' as an assumed 'third country'. Section 4 examines information exchange and Prüm and section 5 looks at the European Arrest Warrant (EAW) and joint investigation teams. In conclusion, section 6 asks the question of whether Brexit finds in AFSJ a road back to the future and provides a few concluding reflections on the perspectives of further integration in this field by the EU 27.

2. The UK: Inside EU, Outside-Inside AFSJ

The UK has never been a full participant in the policy areas of the AFSJ. During the Treaty of Amsterdam negotiations in 1996, the UK acquired the right to 'opt out' of various EU initiatives in the field of police and judicial cooperation.[8] It never joined the Schengen Convention and maintained the right to 'opt out' from the Schengen border control system, which enabled the UK to continue exercising controls at its borders.[9] The Treaty of Lisbon in 2009 merged police and judicial cooperation in criminal matters into the main structure of the EU, making initiatives in this policy domain subject to qualified majority voting and the supranational institutions of the EU. The UK negotiated a block opt-out,[10] giving it the option to 'opt out' of pre-Lisbon police and criminal justice measures (around 100 measures) or whether to remain bound by them.[11] The UK exercised this block opt-out in 2014 but rejoined thirty-five measures, including participation in EU agencies such as Europol and Eurojust, later that year.[12]

---

[8] Jörg Monar, 'The "Area of Freedom, Security and Justice": "Schengen" Europe, Opt-Outs, Opt-Ins and Associates' in K Dyson and A Sepos (eds), *Which Europe? The Politics of Differentiated Integration* (Palgrave Macmillan 2010); Ian Bond and others, 'Europe after Brexit: Unleashed or Undone?' (2016) https://www.cer.org.uk/sites/default/files/pb_euafterBrexit_15april16.pdf.

[9] See Monar (n 8) 276.

[10] Protocol No 21 on the position of the United Kingdom and Ireland in respect of the Area of Freedom, Security and Justice [2010] OJ C-83/201; House of Lords, 'Brexit: Future UK-EU Security and Police Cooperation' (2016) paras 17–19 http://www.publications.parliament.uk/pa/ld201617/ldselect/ldeucom/77/77.pdf.

[11] Protocol No 36 on Transitional Provisions concerning acts adopted on the Basis of Titles V and VI of the Treaty on European Union prior to the entry into force of the Treaty of Lisbon [2008] OJ 115/322, Article 10; Research Section for European Affairs (German Bundestag), 'Consequences of Brexit for the Realm of Justice and Home Affairs: Scope for Future EU Cooperation with the United Kingdom' (2016) 11 http://www.statewatch.org/news/2016/oct/uk-brexit-german-bundstag-report.pdf.

[12] Sergio Carrera, Elspeth Guild, and Ngo Chun Luk, 'What Does Brexit Mean for the EU's Area of Freedom, Security, and Justice?' (Centre for European Policy Studies 2016) para 3 https://www.

The scrutiny that took place in the House of Lords in the assessment of whether to rejoin the thirty-five measures in 2014 has been described as a 'mini-Brexit' by Baroness Prashar, a member of the European Union Committee of the House of Lords.[13] She highlighted that the measures were 'thoroughly assessed', 'judged to be in the national interest, and deemed "vital"'.[14] Since the Treaty of Lisbon, the UK has opted to join a further thirty or more police and criminal justice measures, including the Passenger Name Record (PNR) Directive and the Prüm decisions.[15] The measures opted into have been 'the subject of a positive decision and assessment' and it is unlikely that those assessments will have 'changed in the few intervening years'.[16]

As the UK exits the EU, however, the measures on cooperation in police and criminal justice matters will in principle no longer apply and the measures previously deemed 'vital' will no longer fall within the UK's jurisdiction. The UK will therefore leave EU agencies such as Europol unless an agreement can be reached on the terms of future cooperation. One of the top four over-arching objectives of the Brexit negotiations is after all 'to keep our justice and security arrangements at least as strong as they are'.[17] This is in the UK's own interest, as is acknowledged by UK law enforcement agencies. The EU tools and capabilities they would like to see retained or adequately replaced include Europol, Eurojust, the second generation Schengen Information System (SIS II), the EAW, the European Criminal Records Information System (ECRIS), the Prüm decisions, and PNR.[18] The UK's future relationship with Europol was identified as 'a critical priority'.[19] From a general perspective, membership of agencies is not strictly limited to EU Member States alone. The management boards of some agencies allow for the participation of industry groups and for observers from non-EU Member States.[20] But there are even more specific (Scandinavian) precedents for 'third countries' remaining within AFSJ agencies. In particular, the peculiar saga how Denmark was legally enabled to remain part of Europol in spite of the fact that a national referendum specifically decided it would not may provide some indications how elites can

---

ceps.eu/publications/what-does-brexit-mean-eu's-area-freedom-security-and-justice (last accessed 25 January 2017).

[13] House of Lords, 'Brexit: UK-EU Security (EUC Report)' (2017) https://hansard.parliament.uk/lords/2017-02-07/debates/CEFE6A09-6ACD-44BA-8500-5104771A65DB/BrexitUK-EUSecurity(EUCReport).

[14] ibid.   [15] ibid.   [16] ibid.

[17] David Davis, HC Deb 10 October 2016 col 55.

[18] See further House of Lords, 'Brexit: Future UK-EU Security and Police Cooperation' (n 10).

[19] ibid para 68.

[20] Berthold Rittberger and Arndt Wonka, 'EU Agencies' in Jeremy Richardson and Sonia Mazey (eds), *European Union: Power and Policy-making* (4th edn, Routledge 2015) 235.

construct legal and pragmatic ways out of clear political dilemmas. Where there is a will it seems there may well be a way, in particular in areas that are more under the political radar than others (eg police cooperation and information sharing).

3. Differentiated Participation in Europol

3.1 Europol and a Norwegian Hitch

Europol dates back to the 1992 Maastricht Treaty, where it was given a limited mandate to combat drug trafficking.[21] The first Europol Convention gave Europol a mandate to tackle all forms of serious international crime,[22] was drafted in 1995, and entered into force in 1999 following ratification by all EU Member States.[23] Europol was therefore considered an intergovernmental organization established by international law. Despite its substantial experience in law enforcement cooperation, Europol was only formally recognized as an EU agency in 2010[24] by virtue of Council Decision 2009/371/JHA.[25] Europol was recently reformed further in Regulation 2016/794, which entered into force on 1 May 2017, thereby replacing the Council Decision of 2009.[26]

The UK has been a member of Europol since its creation in 1998 and included the 2009 Council Decision as one of the thirty-five measures that it rejoined following its block opt-out.[27] In November 2016, the UK announced that it will opt in to the new Europol Regulation.[28] The government highlighted the timing of this opt-in in the context of Brexit by stating that, whilst the UK is leaving the EU, 'the reality of cross-border crime

---

[21] David Brown, *The European Union, Counter Terrorism and Police Co-operation, 1992–2007* (Manchester University Press 2010) 122.

[22] ibid.

[23] Christian Kaunert, 'Europol and EU Counterterrorism: International Security Actorness in the External Dimension' (2010) 33 *Studies in Conflict & Terrorism* 652, 654.

[24] Alexandra De Moor and Gert Vermeulen, 'The Europol Council Decision: A New Legal Basis for Europol' (2010) 1 *New Journal of European Criminal Law* 178, 179.

[25] Council Decision 2009/371/JHA establishing the European Police Office (Europol) OJ L 121/37.

[26] Regulation (EU) 2016/794 of the European Parliament and of the Council of 11 May 2016 on the European Union Agency for Law Enforcement Cooperation (Europol) and replacing and repealing Council Decisions 2009/371/JHA, 2009/934/JHA, 2009/935/JHA, 2009/936/JHA and 2009/968/JHA [2016] L 135/51, Article 77(1).

[27] House of Lords, 'Brexit: Future UK-EU Security and Police Cooperation' (n 10) 43.

[28] Home Office, 'Parliament Notified of Europol Opt-in Intention' (2016) https://www.gov.uk/government/news/parliament-notified-of-europol-opt-in-intention (last accessed 3 March 2017).

remains'. The UK considers Europol to be a 'valuable service to the UK and opting in would enable us to maintain our current access to the agency, until we leave the EU'.[29] The National Crime Agency (NCA) has listed a UK opt-in to the new Europol regulation as an 'immediate priority' and has classified membership of Europol or an alternative arrangement as their most important priority among all the AFSJ measures that the UK would be expected to leave upon exiting the EU.[30] Whilst some EU agencies allow for non-EU Member States to enjoy a level of participation in the workings of the agency, which may be used as a precedent for future UK relations with Europol, these non-EU states do not always enjoy voting rights.[31] For example, the new Europol Regulation states that the management board is to be composed of 'one representative from each Member State and one representative of the Commission'. Each representative has a voting right.[32] The management board can invite non-voting observers to its meetings.[33] Given that Europol merely allows EU Member States and the Commission to be represented in the management board, the UK must negotiate an agreement with Europol to remain connected and retain some form of influence. Europol may establish and maintain cooperative relations with third countries,[34] but the Council must publish a list of third states with which Europol may conclude such agreements.[35]

Before any agreement can be concluded with the UK on its future cooperation with Europol, the Council must therefore first add the UK to the list of countries that Europol may conclude agreements with. Europol furthermore recognizes two types of agreements with third parties, namely strategic and technical agreements. Strategic agreements are 'limited to the exchange of general intelligence whereas operational agreements allow for the exchange of data'.[36] For example, Norway signed a strategic agreement with Europol in 2001, thereby removing obstacles for the exchange of data. Norway's position is limited in comparison with full membership. Norwegian police cannot search Europol's database directly and must go through Europol's operational centre to check for compliance with Europol rules before being granted access to the analysis forums.[37] According to Adler-Nissen, Norway 'has failed to

---

[29] ibid.

[30] House of Lords, 'Brexit: Future UK-EU Security and Police Cooperation' (n 10) 51.

[31] Miroslava Scholten, *The Political Accountability of EU and US Independent Regulatory Agencies* (Koninklijke Brill 2014) 92.

[32] Regulation (EU) No 2016/794, Article 10(1).   [33] ibid, Article 14(4).

[34] Council Decision 2009/371/JHA, Article 24.   [35] ibid, Article 26(1).

[36] Europol, 'Partners & Agreements' https://www.europol.europa.eu/partners-agreements (last accessed 27 January 2017).

[37] Saskia Hufnagel, ' "Third Party" Status in EU Policing and Security: Comparing the Position of Norway with the UK before and after the "Brexit" ' (2016) 3 *Nordisk politiforskning* 165, 175

secure agreements with the EU on matters such as the transfer of sentenced prisoners and has yet to reach an agreement on common rules on documents in legal proceedings and evidence gathering'.[38] Hufnagel furthermore highlights that Norway's agreement with Europol is conditioned on it being closely associated with law enforcement cooperation in the EU 'through its association with the Schengen cooperation mechanisms' and as it is a member of the European Economic Area.[39] This is a crucial difference with the UK, which has never been part of Schengen as such. A UK agreement with Europol will therefore be much more problematic if the UK moves toward a hard Brexit, with no participation in Schengen nor in the single market.[40] Of course, it will always be an option—unlikely though it is—that the UK as a non-EU Member State joins the Schengen area in the future—a status that would then be shared with Iceland, Switzerland, Norway, and Liechtenstein. There are, however, no non-Schengen states outside the EU with which the EU engages in anything comparable to its cooperation with Member States or Schengen states. There has of course never been an existing Member State that has exited before, so a further bespoke arrangement in specific regards cannot be ruled out—provided that there is no hard Brexit. In such circumstances, it would be difficult to envisage or justify a cherry-picking bespoke arrangement in AFSJ.

3.2 Europol and a Danish Twist

The possibility of a UK cooperation agreement with Europol being conditioned on continued cooperation in other EU policy areas such as the single market is not entirely unrealistic, particularly in view of recent discussions on Denmark's future relationship with Europol. In a referendum that took place in December 2015, the Danish electorate rejected a proposal to transform the Danish opt-out system into an opt-in on EU matters on Justice and Home Affairs. The Danish public also voted to opt out of the new Europol Regulation and Denmark is no longer considered to be a member of Europol as from 1 May 2017. To ensure future cooperation between Denmark and Europol, on 17 February 2017 the Council added

---

https://www.idunn.no/nordisk_politiforskning/2016/02/third_party_status_in_eupolicing_and_security_-_comparin.

[38] Rebecca Adler-Nissen, 'Through the EU's Front and Back Doors: The Selective Danish and Norwegian Approaches in the Area of Freedom, Security and Justice' in Caroline Howard Grøn, Peter Nedergaard, and Anders Wivel (eds), *The Nordic Countries and the European Union: Still the Other European Community?* (Routledge 2015) 195.

[39] See Hufnagel (n 37) 175.   [40] ibid 176.

Denmark to the list of 'third States' with which Europol may conclude agreements.[41]

As Denmark is the first EU Member State to negotiate an agreement with Europol with the status as third party, the negotiations may very well set a precedent for the UK's negotiations. The Commission has considered it 'vital to provide for cooperation between Europol and Denmark on key matters', particularly given that it is 'one of the key contributors to the Europol database'.[42] In a meeting of the European Parliament Committee on Civil Liberties, Justice, and Home Affairs the Commission set out its position in the negotiations, namely that the arrangements to be concluded will be 'Denmark-specific and will not in any way equal full membership of Europol'.[43] The Commission furthermore stated that the arrangement would be conditioned on Denmark's continued membership of the EU and the Schengen area, Denmark's full implementation of the Directive on cooperation in police matters, Danish acceptance of the jurisdiction of the European Court of Justice (CJEU), and its acceptance of the competence of the European Data Protection Supervisor.[44]

Danish representatives have emphasized that, while the government fully respects the result of the Danish referendum, the negative result is not to be considered as a rejection of the work carried out by Europol.[45] The Danish government fully supports continued close cooperation between law enforcement authorities and considers internal security of the Union to be a shared responsibility for all Member States.[46] The Agreement[47] on Operational and Strategic Cooperation between Denmark and Europol entered into force on 30 April 2017 after being approved by a Council Implementing Decision.[48] The agreement emphasizes the 'urgent problems arising from international crime' and the wish to ensure cooperation between Europol and Denmark. Article 8 of the agreement allows a representative to be invited to the Europol Management Board and its subgroups as an observer but does not grant it the right to vote. The agreement explicitly recognizes the jurisdiction of the

[41] Council Implementing Decision 2017/290 of 17 February 2017 amending Decision 2009/935/JHA as regards the list of third States and organisations with which Europol shall conclude agreements [2017] OJ L 42/17.

[42] 'LIBE Committee: Meeting 24/01/2017' (2017) http://www.europarl.europa.eu/news/en/news-room/20170118IPR58664/committee-on-civil-liberties-justice-and-home-affairs-meeting-24012017-(am).

[43] ibid.   [44] ibid.   [45] ibid.   [46] ibid.

[47] 'Agreement on Operational and Strategic Cooperation between the Kingdom of Denmark and the European Police Office' (2017) https://www.europol.europa.eu/publications-documents/agreement-operational-and-strategic-cooperation-between-kingdom-of-denmark-and-europol.

[48] http://data.consilium.europa.eu/doc/document/ST-7281-2017-INIT/en/pdf.

CJEU in any decision of the European Data Protection Supervisor,[49] as well as on the validity or interpretation of the agreement.[50] The agreement is furthermore conditioned on an obligation for Denmark to remain bound by the Schengen *acquis*, whereby a breach will result in the termination of the Europol cooperation agreement.[51] This condition was, however, strongly disputed by the Danish People's Party (Dansk Folkeparti) as the party had been adamant on reintroducing border controls and exiting Schengen.[52] Prior to the referendum, the Danish People's Party had promised voters that a 'no' vote would still ensure full membership of Europol, yet an exit from Schengen. The new agreement certainly does not meet this promise.[53]

In debates in the Danish Parliament (Folketinget), the Ministry of Justice representative Søren Pape Poulsen highlighted that, whilst the electorate had voted to leave Europol, cooperation in the field of cross-border crime and terrorism must continue. He expressed concern for the possibility of Denmark losing access to information collected by Europol and its databases such as the Europol Information System (EIS).[54] This concern was equally shared by Zenia Stampe of the Social Liberty Party (Radikale Venstre). She highlighted doubts on the perceived benefit of reintroducing border controls considering that authorities would be unable to search for foreign records on individuals stopped at the border as Denmark would no longer have access to this information via Europol.[55] The concern that Denmark may lose access to Europol information can be considered well founded, given that the agreement excludes any provision on this matter. Following the agreement, Denmark will lose the possibility to search directly in Europol databases following the principle of interoperability. Denmark will, however, have the possibility to assign up to eight Danish-speaking staff to handle Danish requests,[56] and to input and retrieve data from Danish authorities in the Europol processing systems.[57] What this will mean in practice remains to be seen but it cannot

---

[49] Article 18. [50] Article 20. [51] Article 27(1).

[52] Karoline Garulund Nøhr, 'Vælgerbedrag? Her Er Dansk Folkepartis Europol-Garantier' (*Politiken*, 2016) Vælgerbedrag? Her er Dansk Folkepartis Europol-garantier (last accessed 24 March 2017).

[53] Nadja Schou Lauridsen and Catharina Sørensen, 'Europol-Udkast Afsører Nye Detaljer Om Dansk Særaftale' (*TænkeTanken* 2017) 1 http://thinkeuropa.dk/sites/default/files/notat_europol-udkast_afsloerer_nye_detaljer_om_dansk_saeraftale.pdf (last accessed 24 March 2017).

[54] Søren Pape Poulsen, 'Møde Nr 26. Om Konsekvenser Af Danmarks Udtrædelse Af Europol' (2016) http://www.ft.dk/samling/20161/forespoergsel/f5/beh1/forhandling.htm?startItem=4#nav.

[55] Zenia Stampe, 'Møde Nr 26. Om Konsekvenser Af Danmarks Udtrædelse Af Europol'. http://www.ft.dk/samling/20161/forespoergsel/f5/beh1/forhandling.htm?startItem=6#nav.

[56] See Lauridsen and Sørensen (n 53) 1.

[57] Agreement on Operational and Strategic Cooperation between the Kingdom of Denmark and the European Police Office, Article 10(6).

be excluded that Denmark as a voluntary outsider regarding Europol may in practice and informally be granted more liberal access to relevant data, also from other Member States, than its legal position would warrant.

3.3 Europol and a UK Tangle

The agreement between Europol and Denmark may be a template for the UK after Brexit, but many of the conditions imposed on Denmark, alone or together, may prove problematic for the UK in future arrangements with Europol. As highlighted by the European Union Committee of the UK House of Lords, the accountability of Europol to EU institutions, including the CJEU, is considered a major obstacle in the UK. Lord Kirkhope noted that many perceive Brexit to be advantageous as the UK will no longer be subject to the CJEU 'and its competence and control over us'.[58] A condition for future arrangements with Europol subjecting the UK to the jurisdiction of the CJEU may therefore prove problematic. Nevertheless, the NCA claims that the UK should not look at precedent but should look at 'something more than that'.[59] What this will entail is unknown at this point in time. One thing is certain: since the Europol Regulation entered into force on 1 May 2017, future agreements between Europol and third countries are formal 'international agreements' negotiated on the legal basis of Article 218 of the TFEU and entailing a veto power by the European Parliament. This is a quite different legal and political situation to that prevailing with Denmark, when it was (with considerable haste) entered onto the list of third countries with which Europol could make agreements.

The UK government has been asked to provide clarity on the matter. In a meeting of 22 February 2017, the House of Commons European Scrutiny Committee specifically asked the government to clarify how any conditions imposed on Denmark in establishing new operational arrangements with Europol may affect the scope and content of any new post-Brexit agreement between the UK and Europol.[60] The House of Commons Justice Committee stressed, moreover, the importance of these negotiations, given 'the seriousness of the matter and the degree of mutual interest give weight to the

[58] House of Lords, 'Brexit: Future UK-EU Security and Police Cooperation' (n 10) 62.
[59] ibid 60.
[60] House of Commons European Scrutiny Committee, 'Thirty-second Report of Session 2016–17, Documents Considered by the Committee on 22 February 2017' (2017) https://www.publications.parliament.uk/pa/cm201617/cmselect/cmeuleg/71-xxx/71-xxx.pdf (last accessed 3 March 2017).

suggestion that this aspect of negotiations be separated firmly from others'.[61] The Justice Committee considers the security and safety of the UK's residents as 'too precious to be left vulnerable to tactical bargaining'.[62]

A further practical issue for negotiation concerns the actual time it may take for the UK to negotiate an agreement with Europol. The average negotiation time for operational agreements that allow for the exchange of data is around nine to twelve years.[63] The UK is unlikely to accept this lengthy period of negotiation, particularly as it has played such an 'active role in the development of EU policy on police cooperation and access to data for law enforcement purposes'.[64] Academics have furthermore highlighted a practical issue in negotiations, namely that EU Member States may not feel particularly inclined to offer flexibility in negotiations with the UK. It has been noted that: 'the UK's cherry-picking in combination with the then announced plan to hold a UK referendum on EU membership—have pushed some other Member States patience to breaking point'.[65]

4. Information Exchange and the Prüm Decisions: Below the Radar?

The Prüm decisions date back to the 2005 Prüm Convention,[66] which was signed by seven Member States as a means of achieving closer cooperation to combat terrorism, cross-border crime, and illegal immigration more effectively.[67] The Prüm Convention was an intergovernmental treaty adopted outside of the framework of the EU.[68] Following a proposal from the German

---

[61] House of Commons Justice Committee, 'Implications of Brexit for the Justice System: Ninth Report of Session 2016–2017' (2017) 11 https://www.publications.parliament.uk/pa/cm201617/cmselect/cmjust/750/750.pdf.

[62] ibid.

[63] House of Lords, 'Brexit: Future UK-EU Security and Police Cooperation' (n 10) 58.

[64] See Carrera, Guild, and Luk (n 12) 4.

[65] Ilke Adam and others, 'The UK in Justice and Home Affairs: The Engaged Outsider' (Institute for European Studies, Policy Brief Issue 2016/6 2016) http://www.ies.be/policy-brief/uk-justice-and-home-affairs-engaged-outsider (last accessed 25 January 2017).

[66] Cristina Blasi Casagran, *Global Data Protection in the Field of Law Enforcement: An EU Perspective* (Routledge 2017) 17.

[67] Prüm Convention on the stepping up of cross-border cooperation, particularly in combating terrorism, cross-border crime and illegal migration; see Note from the Council of the European Union on the Prüm Convention (2007) 3 https://ec.europa.eu/anti-fraud/sites/antifraud/files/docs/body/prumtr.pdf (last accessed 1 March 2017).

[68] European Parliament, 'Working Document on a Council Decision on the Stepping up of Cross-Border Cooperation, Particularly in Combating Terrorism and Cross-Border Crime' (2007)

Presidency of the Council,[69] Prüm was integrated into the EU legal framework by means of Council Decisions 2008/615/JHA and 2008/616/JHA.[70] The Prüm decisions essentially set up information exchange mechanisms for DNA, fingerprint, and vehicle registration data. The exchange mechanism for biometric data (DNA and fingerprint) operates on a 'hit/no-hit' basis, whereby a search is conducted with the result of whether the search is a match or not. The actual personal data is not exchanged and can only be provided following a separate follow-up request.[71] The UK exercised its block opt-out option during the Treaty of Lisbon negotiations and did not include the Prüm decisions in the opt-in that took place in 2004.[72] However, the UK government proposed to rejoin the Prüm decisions in 2015. This was accepted by the European Commission in May 2016.[73] According to a letter sent in October 2016 by the Minister of State for Policing and Fire Services, Brandon Lewis, the UK was due to implement Prüm fully and begin exchanging information in 2017.[74] In September 2016, the House of Lords Select Committee on the European Union considered the possibility of implementing Prüm following the Brexit referendum. Professor Steve Peers noted that a withdrawal agreement including the continuation of Prüm should be possible without too many issues, given the recent assessment conducted for UK membership of Prüm and that Prüm is not inherently linked to Schengen membership.[75]

   Whilst the UK government clearly wishes to stay connected in police and security cooperation, the Secretary of State for Exiting the European Union David Davis appeared ambiguous on Prüm. In a recent debate in the House of Commons, he responded to a question seeking clarification on the Prüm framework and whether he could ensure that personal data would no longer be subject to the CJEU. Mr Davis responded by first clarifying what data can

---

2 http://www.europarl.europa.eu/meetdocs/2004_2009/documents/dt/660/660824/660824en.pdf (last accessed 1 March 2017).

   [69] See Casagran (n 66) 17.   [70] OJ 2008 L 21012 (6 August 2008).   [71] ibid 18.

   [72] House of Lords, 'Brexit: Future UK-EU Security and Police Cooperation' (n 10) 104.

   [73] Commission Decision (EU) 2016/809, 20 May 2016 on the notification by the United Kingdom of Great Britain and Northern Ireland of its wish to participate in certain acts of the Union in the field of police cooperation adopted before the entry into force of the Treaty of Lisbon and which are not part of the Schengen acquis, OJ L 132/105 (21 May 2016).

   [74] Brandon Lewis, 'Letter from Brandon Lewis MP, Minister of State for Policing and Fire Services, to Lord Boswell of Aynho, Chairman of the House of Lords European Union Select Committee' (2016) https://www.parliament.uk/documents/lords-committees/eu-home-affairs-subcommittee/Implementation-of-Prum-19-Oct.pdf (last accessed 1 March 2017).

   [75] House of Lords and Select Committee on the European Union, 'Unrevised Transcript of Evidence Taken before the Select Committee on the European Union, Home Affairs Sub-Committee (14 September 2016)' (2016) http://data.parliament.uk/writtenevidence/committeeevidence.svc/evidencedocument/eu-home-affairs-subcommittee/brexit-future-ukeu-security-and-policing-cooperation/oral/39000.html (last accessed 1 March 2017).

be exchanged under Prüm and followed that by stating that the UK 'will be making new arrangements to keep terrorism, crime and so on under control'.[76] The UK government has not yet provided clarification on these 'new arrangements' and whether the intention to remain connected therefore also extends to the Prüm framework.

As regards the jurisdiction of the CJEU, the UK government has explicitly rejected its continued jurisdiction in a future relationship[77] and has highlighted 'taking control of our own laws' as a top priority in the negotiations. The UK government wants to 'bring an end to the jurisdiction of the Court of Justice of the European Union'.[78] It is unlikely, therefore, that the UK government will accept an international agreement with the EU on Prüm that subjects it to the jurisdiction of the CJEU. In the government's review of Prüm in 2015, it looked to the precedent set by Denmark with its agreements in this field and noted that: 'all agreements concluded to date require Denmark to submit to [CJEU] jurisdiction for both interpretation and to ensure compliance'. The Commission and Council considered CJEU jurisdiction as a 'red line' during the negotiations with Denmark'.[79] It is hard to see how the issue of CJEU jurisdiction can be ring-fenced in any way, nor indeed, from the perspective of the EU 27 and their citizens, why it should be.

5. Cooperation in 'Law and Order': A Spider's Web

On 19 September 2001, just a week after the 9/11 terrorist attacks,[80] the Commission submitted a proposal for a EAW[81] as a means of making it easier for justice to be administered across borders between Member States. The Council Framework Decision on the EAW officially entered into force in January 2004,[82] providing a legal basis for the extradition of individuals

---

[76] House of Commons, 'Debate: Exiting the EU: New Partnership (2 February 2017)' (2017) https://hansard.parliament.uk/commons/2017-02-02/debates/208B4D90-F003-4990-9F42-411631DC04BF/ExitingTheEUNewPartnership (last accessed 1 March 2017).

[77] Department for Exiting the European Union, *The United Kingdom's Exit from, and New Partnership with, the European Union* (Cm 9417, 2017) 7.

[78] ibid.

[79] Home Office, 'Prüm Business and Implementation Case' (2015) 80 https://www.gov.uk/government/uploads/system/uploads/attachment_data/file/480129/prum_business_and_implementation_case.pdf (last accessed 3 March 2017).

[80] Libor Klimek, *European Arrest Warrant* (Springer 2015) 23.

[81] Commission, 'Proposal for a Council Framework Decision on the European arrest warrant and the surrender procedures between the Member States' COM(2001) 522 final.

[82] Council Framework Decision 2002/584/JHA of 13 June 2002 on the European arrest warrant and the surrender procedures between Member States [2002] OJ L 190/1.

between EU Member States.[83] The extradition of individuals is based on the principle of mutual recognition of judicial decisions. The results of a decision taken in another EU Member State are thereby accepted as equivalent to decisions taken in one's own state.[84] The principle of mutual recognition allows for smooth coordination amongst Member States, rather than lengthy and complicated litigation procedures within the various national criminal systems.[85] The UK implemented the EAW in 2003[86] and rejoined the measures in December 2014 after having exercised its block opt-out option during the Treaty of Lisbon negotiations.[87] The UK government has considered whether to retain the EAW following its exit from the EU. It considered reverting to the 1957 Council of Europe Convention on Extradition[88] (which was the basis of EU legislation prior to the EAW Framework Decision)[89] but the extradition times under the Convention have been criticized as being 'slower' and 'potentially undermining public safety'.[90]

As Secretary of State for the Home Department, Theresa May joined a House of Commons debate in 2014 on whether to rejoin the EAW. Mrs May highlighted that the UK had to decide whether to accept the jurisdiction of the CJEU 'so that our law enforcement agencies can continue to use those powers to fight crime and keep us safe' or whether to 'reject those measures and accept the risk to public protection that that involves'. She characterized this as 'a vote about law and order, not a vote about Europe' and encouraged the rejoining of the smaller package of measures, which included the EAW. She argued that, whilst the 'CJEU should not have the final say over matters such as substantive criminal law', the government 'must act in the national interest to keep the British public safe' and transpose the 'measures in the national interest' into national law, including the EAW.[91]

The question whether to accept the CJEU jurisdiction is particularly important in the current Brexit context. As mentioned also with regard to the Prüm decision, it is uncertain whether an agreement between the UK

---

[83] House of Lords, 'Brexit: Future UK-EU Security and Police Cooperation' (n 10) 124.

[84] Libor Klimek, *Mutual Recognition of Judicial Decisions in European Criminal Law* (Springer 2017) 6.

[85] House of Lords, 'Brexit: Future UK-EU Security and Police Cooperation' (n 10) 6; Klimek, *Mutual Recognition of Judicial Decisions in European Criminal Law* (n 84).

[86] Extradition Act 2003.

[87] House of Lords, 'Brexit: Future UK-EU Security and Police Cooperation' (n 10) 124.

[88] Council of Europe, Convention on Extradition 1957.

[89] See Klimek, *European Arrest Warrant* (n 80).

[90] Theresa May, 'House of Commons Debate (10 November 2014)' (2014) https://www.publications.parliament.uk/pa/cm201415/cmhansrd/cm141110/debtext/141110-0002.htm (last accessed 2 March 2017).

[91] ibid.

and the EU on future cooperation in terms of the EAW would include a condition subjecting the UK to the CJEU. A possible precedent is the bilateral
agreement concluded with Iceland and Norway on the surrender procedure
between Member States of the EU and Iceland and Norway, where disputes
are resolved through a 'meeting of representatives of the governments', rather
than through recourse to the CJEU.[92] The bilateral agreement states that the
contracting parties shall consider 'the development of the case law of the
Court of Justice' as well as the development of the case law in Iceland and
Norway to achieve uniform application and interpretation of the agreement.[93]
In this way, the case law of the CJEU may play a role in the interpretation
of provisions. The practicalities of this influence are unclear as yet, particularly considering that the Norway/Iceland agreement has not yet entered into
force.[94]

The UK government may moreover consider the nationality exception as
problematic. The nationality exception in the Norway/Iceland Agreement
provides that the execution of an arrest warrant may be refused on the ground
that the person in question is a national of the executing state.[95] The government has also questioned whether the UK will be able to secure a similar
agreement *outside* the EU and outside Schengen, given that both Norway and
Iceland are members of the Schengen area.[96]

The Council Framework Decision on Joint Investigation Teams (JITs)[97]
was adopted on the same day as the Council Framework Decision on the
EAW. The Framework Decision was a response to the slow process of ratification of the 2000 Convention on Mutual Assistance in Criminal Matters.[98]
The Framework Decision will cease to apply once the Convention has been
ratified by all Member States and officially enters into force. JITs are set up
to carry out criminal investigations in one or more of the Member States
that set up the team. The competent authorities of two or more Member

---

[92] Council Decision 2006/697/EC of 27 June 2006 on the signing of the Agreement between
the European Union and the Republic of Iceland and the Kingdom of Norway on the surrender
procedure between the Member States of the European Union and Iceland and Norway OJ L 292/
1, Article 36.

[93] ibid, Article 37.   [94] See Hufnagel (n 37) 174.

[95] Agreement between the European Union and the Republic of Iceland and the Kingdom of
Norway on the surrender procedure, Article 7(1)(2)(3); Klimek, *European Arrest Warrant* (n 80).

[96] House of Lords, 'Brexit: Future UK-EU Security and Police Cooperation' (n 10) 130.

[97] Council Framework Decision 2002/465/JHA [2002] of 13 June 2002 on joint investigation
teams OJ L 162/1.

[98] Council Act of 29 May 2000 establishing in accordance with Article 34 of the Treaty on
European Union the Convention on Mutual Assistance in Criminal Matters between the Member
States of the European Union OJ C 197/1; Council of the European Union, 'Joint Investigation
Teams Manual' (2011) 4.

States negotiate a mutual agreement on the JITs, which are set up for a spe-cific purpose and a limited period.[99] The House of Lords EU Committee was optimistic on the possibilities for the UK to continue participating in JITs from outside the EU.[100] It considered that the UK could benefit from an arrangement similar to that of Norway, Iceland, and Switzerland. In hearing witnesses before the EU committee, Mr David Armond (the National Police Chiefs' Council) furthermore characterized JITs as mechanisms 'to enable not only EU Member States but other interested parties to join in an initiative'.[101] Hufnagel furthermore highlights that Article 13 of the 2000 Convention paves the way for Norway to participate in JITs and that therefore Article 8 of the Council of Europe Second Protocol to the European Convention on Mutual Assistance in Criminal Matters, which is very similar in its wording, may be a sufficient legal basis for the UK to participate in JITs.[102]

The potential practicalities are legion. Would the UK for example with-draw from JITs immediately, particularly the ones that it leads? Or would the cooperation simply be extended 'under the radar'? Given the levels of secrecy involved in this kind of cooperation, the latter is certainly a strong possibil-ity. A careful eye will need to be kept by the UK on the often invisible way that bits of the thirty-five police and criminal justice measures that the UK rejoined in 2014 fit together. This 'spider's web' entails the risk that 'if you start to dismantle even some of the more minor things, you run the risk of affecting others which are actually more important'.[103]

6. The UK and AFSJ: Bespoke Bits and Pieces?

In 2014, after extensive empirical research Adler-Nissen concluded that: 'the management of the British and Danish opt-outs highlights the strength of European integration and the difficulty of maintaining national sovereignty in the EU'.[104] Less than three years later, two referenda (a limited one on

[99] Council Framework Decision 2002/465/JHA of 13 June 2002 on joint investigation teams [2002] OJ L 162/1, Article 1.
[100] House of Lords, 'Brexit: Future UK-EU Security and Police Cooperation' (n 10) 85.
[101] David Armond, 'Home Affairs Sub-Committee Meeting of 12 October 2016: Corrected Oral Evidence: Brexit: Future UK-EU Security and Policing Co-Operation' (2016) http://data.parliament.uk/writtenevidence/committeeevidence.svc/evidencedocument/eu-home-affairs-sub-committee/brexit-future-ukeu-security-and-policing-cooperation/oral/41072.html (last accessed 2 March 2017).
[102] See Hufnagel (n 37) 173.
[103] House of Lords, 'Brexit: Future UK-EU Security and Police Cooperation' (n 10) para 144.
[104] See Adler-Nissen (n 38) 189.

Europol in Denmark and a general one in the UK on EU membership) have caused some tectonic shifts that belie that optimistic reading, at least from the perspective of European integration and its doxa of 'ever closer Union'. At the same time, Adler-Nissen's conclusions remain potentially valid for the future of the EU 27, given that it will inevitably include large dosages—and many faces—of differentiation across (sensitive) policy areas.[105]

The proof of the specific Danish Europol 'pudding' will be in the future 'eating'. Given the voluntary and non-temporary nature of the structural opt-out from Europol, it is hard to see how Danish officials will in practice manage quite as efficiently and effectively as they did to date the 'stigma' of their formal non-participation. The highly pragmatic solution adopted—at the very last moment before the new Europol Regulation enters into force on 1 May 2017—of being added in an unprecedented fashion as a Member State, to the list of 'third countries' with which Europol may conclude agreements, bears witness to the desire of the EU to find a solution that could enable some ongoing cooperation and access to databases, even if visibly at least not the same as full participation in Europol. But we should recall that that fundamental political willingness to engage in these kinds of legal and temporal gymnastics was for a 'full' Member State and not for a genuine 'third country' which is what the UK is about to become.

The likelihood of considerable 'bits and pieces' looms large, in particular as the UK struggles to maintain already existing levels and choices of cooperation. The reason may not only be the security and well-being of the citizens and residents of the UK but also the considerable sunk costs incurred by the UK in setting up the existing arrangements (eg on implementing the Prüm decisions) as well as the likely costs of replicating capabilities outside the EU (eg on the EAW or a Europol type agency or database). The content of these bits and pieces matters for the unity of the EU legal order of the EU 27, especially if pragmatic diplomatic solutions are reached which remove important areas of citizens'—and non-citizens'— rights and interests from the authority and jurisdiction of the CJEU. It matters too for the UK and the transparency and accountability of UK–EU security and police cooperation in the future. The UK clearly faces the future in a different position to its past one. It will move from being an engaged insider, which, even in areas where it enjoyed formal opt-outs in the AFSJ, to a disempowered outsider. It operated in practice as a leader—'a leading protagonist in driving and shaping the nature and direction of cooperation on police and security matters under the auspices of

---

[105] See, in particular, the Commission's recent White Paper, *The Future of Europe* (2017) https://ec.europa.eu/commission/sites/beta-political/files/white_paper_on_the_future_of_europe_en.pdf.

the European Union'.[106] The vista even beckons of the UK having formally to prove 'adequacy' arrangements prior to any data-sharing agreements, just like any other third country—a bitter pill indeed for the UK, given the manner in which its own personal data protection for law enforcement purposes preceded—and provided a model for—that of the EU itself.

Moving forward to the AFSJ for the EU 27, we are likely to see more of what we already have at the EU level in terms of actual integration and policy. The leadership role of the UK has undoubtedly been very instrumental in helping design the very foundations of AFSJ, as well as constructing some very important pillars (for example on data retention and recent EU rules on PNR). But emancipation is nigh for the EU 27. There is no reason to believe that we will see anything but further intensification of the role and powers of the agencies in this field and their steering 'management' of national administrations and actors on the ground. Information sharing and, in particular, the further development of the principle of interoperability across the supranational—national divide will gain ever more importance and accrued practical content. The role of the CJEU will be more and more pivotal in ensuring the balance with fundamental rights and the issue of access to justice for individuals will remain as challenged and difficult as it is today.

The UK as an exponentially stigmatized outsider will almost inevitably in the future be forced to 'mimic' rules and regulations without any democratic participation in their content nor in ongoing and at times fundamental debates on core issues before the CJEU. Mimicry of bits and pieces of AFSJ and continued application of the interpretation by the CJEU is, it seems, the bespoke Brexit antidote, in this field at any rate. The AFSJ is a space to be closely watched as the negotiations unfold—both in law and in actual and ongoing practices, which at times will be well below the political radar. In particular in the area of personal data processing—given its ubiquitous and unobserved nature in practice—it must be doubted whether custom-made, complex legal solutions will ever be implemented on the ground by data 'cops'. More than third country status in all its existent permutations may be required post-Brexit in order to avoid the impossible—the surgical severing of what is today 'an integral part of a living and functioning system'.[107] Otherwise, it may be an artery that is severed, cutting off a much needed relationship with a previously healthy and even essential part of the EU itself.

---

[106] House of Lords, 'Brexit: Future UK-EU Security and Police Cooperation' (n 10) para 27.

[107] Paul De Hert and Vagelis Papakonstantinou, "The Rich UK Contribution to the Field of EU Data Protection: Let's Not Go for 'Third Country' Status after Brexit" (2017) 33 *Computer Law and Security Review* 354, 360.

10

Brexit and the EU Internal Market

Catherine Barnard

The EU is too bureaucratic and too undemocratic. It interferes too much in our daily lives, and the scale of migration triggered by new members joining in recent years has had a real impact on local communities. We are clear about what we want from Europe. We say: yes to the Single Market. Yes to turbocharging free trade. Yes to working together where we are stronger together than alone. Yes to a family of nation states, all part of a European Union—but whose interests, crucially, are guaranteed whether inside the Euro or out. No to 'ever closer union'. No to a constant flow of power to Brussels. No to unnecessary interference. And no, of course, to the Euro, to participation in Eurozone bail-outs or notions like a European Army.

Conservative Party manifesto, 2015

1. Introduction

Nowhere can the UK's ambivalence towards the EU be seen more clearly than through its attitude to the single market. The UK has been a champion of the single market. The Conservative nominated Commissioner, Lord Cockfield, was the brains behind the 1992 programme launched by Jacques Delors. The 2015 Conservative party manifesto, which committed David Cameron to holding an in-out referendum should he win the election, also committed the UK to saying 'yes to the single market'. David Davis, the strongly Euro-sceptic Secretary of State for Exiting the EU, was found to have given a speech in 2012 where he conceded that the EU 'has enjoyed some successes, namely the single market'. On the customs union, he said: 'My preference would be that we should remain within the customs

Brexit and the EU Internal Market. First edition. Catherine Barnard © Catherine Barnard 2017. Published 2017 by Oxford University Press.

union of the EU [even though we would] give up some freedoms in terms of negotiating our trading arrangements with third countries: "The advantage would be that our manufacturers would not face complex and punitive rules-of-origin tariffs" '.[1]

Yet, by the time of her Lancaster house speech on 17 January 2017,[2] the UK Prime Minister Theresa May was clear: 'What I am proposing cannot mean membership of the single market. European leaders have said many times that membership means accepting the "4 freedoms" of goods, capital, services, and people. And being out of the EU but a member of the single market would mean complying with the EU's rules and regulations that implement those freedoms, without having a vote on what those rules and regulations are. It would mean accepting a role for the European Court of Justice that would see it still having direct legal authority in our country. It would to all intents and purposes mean not leaving the EU at all'. She also added that 'both sides in the referendum campaign made it clear that a vote to leave the EU would be a vote to leave the single market'. It was at this moment that hard Brexit apparently became a political reality. What the prime minister proposed instead was 'the greatest possible access to [the single market] through a new, comprehensive, bold, and ambitious free trade agreement'.

Given the uncertainty surrounding all aspects of the Brexit negotiations, this chapter will focus on three questions and paradoxes. First, it will consider why the four freedoms are seen to be so interconnected. It will suggest that in fact they are less connected than would first appear and had this been realized sooner the outcome of the Brussels negotiations in February 2016, and subsequently the referendum, might have been different. Further, it will argue that this view of the indivisibility of the four freedoms will make negotiating any future deal more difficult (section 2).

Secondly, the chapter considers the evolution of a new single market, this time within the UK itself. It notes the paradoxes and lessons that the UK has learned from its membership of the EU single market and considers how they might impact on the UK's own single market (section 3).

Thirdly, it will consider the effect of the UK's departure on the future development of the EU's single market (section 4). Section 5 concludes with a certain number of 'what ifs'.

---

[1] http://www.dailymail.co.uk/news/article-4415434/The-day-Brexit-Secretary-praised-EU-s-single-market.html#ixzz4eUQ7Wxjy (last accessed 30 July 2017).
[2] https://www.gov.uk/government/speeches/the-governments-negotiating-objectives-for-exiting-the-eu-pm-speech (last accessed 30 July 2017).

2. The Interconnectivity of the Four Freedoms

2.1 Divisible or Indivisible?

It is now sacrosanct in EU parlance that the four freedoms are one. As the European Council put it in the guidelines for negotiating Article 50: '[it] welcomes the recognition by the British government that the four freedoms are indivisible and that there can be no "cherry picking" '.[3] Guardians of the faith have long espoused this.[4] Certain books give that impression.[5] The Treaty itself even gives a steer in this direction. Article 26 provides that 'The internal market shall comprise an area without internal frontiers in which the free movement of goods, persons, services, and capital is ensured in accordance with the provisions of the Treaties.'[6]

But at no point does the Treaty say the four freedoms are, in fact, indivisible. Rumour has it that it was a last minute addition to a European Council communiqué by the Maltese prime minister that made the four freedoms 'indivisible'. I would like to argue that the four freedoms are—and should be—less inter-connected than currently considered. I would like to suggest that there are four reasons why the four freedoms are, in fact, divisible. None of the reasons is determinative but, taken together, they suggest that the four freedoms are not, in fact, mutually interdependent, especially for those countries not in the Eurozone.

The first reason is historical. When the Treaty of Rome was drafted, there were transitional periods for, eg, the removal of customs duties (there was a twelve-year timetable, which was in fact completed eighteen months ahead of schedule) and for the liberalization of free movement of service providers.[7] Free movement of capital was not liberalized until the single currency project was properly launched.[8] At no stage was there a suggestion that the four freedoms were intimately linked and interconnected and so could not be liberalized in different stages. Rather, the EU took a vertical approach, working through the liberalization process freedom by freedom. A look at the Internal

---

[3] Special meeting of the European Council (Article 50) (29 April 2017).

[4] 'The power brokers behind Brexit: Nick Timothy and Martin Selmayr' *Financial Times* (13 April 2017) https://www.ft.com/content/8027f188-1f03-11e7-a454-ab04428977f9 (last accessed 31 July 2017). Nick Timothy resigned as the Prime Minister's co-Chief of Staff after the election on 8 June 2017.

[5] See eg C Barnard, *The Substantive Law of the EU: the Four Freedoms* (OUP 2016).

[6] Article 26(2) TFEU.   [7] See EEC, Article 8.

[8] See L Flynn, 'Free Movement of Capital' in C Barnard and S Peers, *European Union Law* (OUP 2017).

Market White paper of 1985 is instructive.[9] It focused on the removal of physical, technical, and fiscal barriers to trade—but it was still very much focused on goods. The tariff barriers had been successfully removed but non-tariff barriers (NTBs) had proliferated in their place and much of the 1992 programme was about addressing these barriers. It took until the mid-2000s for a serious attempt to be made at the liberalization of services. The Services Directive 2006/123[10] has, in fact, had only modest success and in a limited range of sectors.[11] Yet at no point has the argument been made that without the liberalization of services the single market has not been achieved.

The second reason why I would argue that the four freedoms are divisible is organizational: other free trade organizations do not depend on the four freedoms operating concurrently. Take the WTO. First and foremost, GATT 1947 was about removing tariff barriers to trade. The WTO agreements subsequently expanded the WTO's remit to include NTBs and, somewhat grudgingly, free movement of people but only in the very narrow confines of Mode 2 (consumption abroad such as tourism) and Mode 4 services (natural persons supplying services in another country). At no point are the issues of the limited rights to movement of people and the more ambitious approach to goods, interconnected. Of course, the level of integration in the WTO is much less than in the EU and the objectives of the WTO much less ambitious but it still shows that trading arrangements are not dependent on all four freedoms operating concurrently.

The third reason is legal. It comes from looking at the EU's Brussels renegotiation of February 2016.[12] The agreement did recognize that: 'Free movement of *workers* within the Union is an integral part of the internal market which entails, among others, the right for workers of the Member States to accept offers of employment anywhere within the Union'. This suggests some idea of indivisibility of the four freedoms. Yet the Brussels agreement also recognized that the purity of free movement law was less pure than many had thought. It noted that different levels of remuneration among the Member States made some offers of employment more attractive than others and that the social security systems of the Member States, which Union law coordinates but does not harmonize, were diversely structured and this could, in itself, attract workers to certain Member States. Therefore, it was legitimate to take this situation into account and to provide for measures 'limiting flows of workers of such a scale that they have negative effects both for the Member

---

[9] COM(85) 310.   [10] OJ [2006] L376/76.
[11] C Barnard, 'Unravelling the Services Directive' (2008) (45) *Common Market Law Review* 323.
[12] European Council Conclusions of 18–19 February 2016.

States of origin and for the Member States of destination'. Subsequently, the agreement acknowledged that restrictions on the free movement of workers under Article 45 TFEU could be justified not only by the express derogations but also by proportionate overriding reasons of public interest, including encouraging recruitment, reducing unemployment, and protecting vulnerable workers. Contrary to the orthodoxy, this could be read as giving a green light for directly discriminatory restrictions on free movement of *persons* (not goods, services, and capital) being allowed where circumstances so justified (in other words some kind of emergency brake on migration), thus suggesting that free movement of persons is different from the other freedoms and that different rules apply. However, the possibility of some kind of emergency brake on migration was, surprisingly, not highlighted in the referendum campaign and was ultimately insufficient to persuade the waverers in the referendum that the EU had done enough to listen to their concerns. I return to this point below.

The fourth reason why the four freedoms are, in my view, divisible is economic. Economic theory suggests that in an optimum currency area, free movement of people is a necessary component; it acts as a safety valve for regions in difficulty.[13] To an extent, this is what we have already been witnessing in the EU. The large influx of Spanish, Italian, and Portuguese workers into the UK in recent years can be explained in part by the lack of opportunities in those countries while their economies are struggling following the Eurozone crisis. However, since the UK is not in the Eurozone economic theory would suggest that EU free movement of persons rules are not an integral part of delivering on a currency area and so the UK could legitimately argue that it could impose restraints on free movement of people.[14]

That said, the UK itself recognized that it had a moral obligation to open up its labour market to EU 8 migration in 2004 and not impose transitional arrangements when a number of other states, in particular Germany, did just that. The UK government knew that UK goods and services would have access to the markets in the EU 8 states. In return, their people should have access to the labour market in the UK.[15] In fact, the evidence indicates that the UK has benefited from the arrival of this pool of talent.[16] There was

---

[13] For a summary of the work of Mundell and others, see J Jager and K Hafner, 'The Optimum Currency Area Theory and the EMU: An Assessment in the Context of the Eurozone Crisis' (2013) 5 *Intereconomics* 315.

[14] For useful summary of some of the economic arguments see https://www.cer.org.uk/sites/default/files/ditchley_2016_report_12dec16.pdf (last accessed 31 July 2017).

[15] http://www.telegraph.co.uk/news/politics/tony-blair/11473737/Tony-Blair-insists-EU-immigration-was-not-a-mistake.html (last accessed 31 July 2017).

[16] See eg C Dustmann and T Frattini, 'The Fiscal Effects of Immigration to the UK' (2014) *The Economic Journal* 1.

a political argument too. Sir Stephen Wall, a former diplomat and EU adviser to Tony Blair, said that '[T]he primary argument [to opening up the UK's labour market to EU-8 nationals] was the political one—this was the right thing to do, we attached a lot of importance to them as democratic countries and keeping our position as the number one friend of eastern and central Europeans.[17] But the arguments in favour of opening the UK's markets are moral and political, not economic. The four freedoms are not necessarily interconnected – economically—for countries outside the Eurozone.

2.2 Why Does It Matter?

2.2.1 *Obstructing the Search to Finding a Solution to a Rise in Anti-migrant Sentiment*

Why is the question of the divisibility of the four freedoms significant? The answer lies in that such fundamental beliefs obstructed creative and dynamic thinking about how to manage the growing rise of Euroscepticism in the UK (and beyond). It is becoming increasingly clear that many people voted to Leave the EU because of their concerns about the lack of control over migration.[18] It is also clear that other states, such as Austria but also France and Germany, have political parties that are responding to populist pressure to limit migration, albeit in their cases mainly from non-EU countries. The failure to consider the effects (or perceived effects of migration) is serious. The political scientist Matthew Goodwin puts it this way: [19]

Brexit ... owed less to the personal charisma of Boris Johnson [a leading Leave campaigner], the failings of David Cameron or the ambivalence of Jeremy Corbyn [Leader of the Opposition Labour party] than to a much deeper sense of angst, alienation and resentment among more financially disadvantaged, less well-educated and older Britons who are often only one financial crisis away from disaster. They are the voters of former industrial strongholds, like the northern towns of Barnsley, Mansfield, Stoke and Doncaster, Welsh towns like Merthyr Tydfil that once fuelled the industrial revolution, fading coastal towns such as Blackpool, Great Yarmouth and Castle Point, or blue-collar but aspirational places like Basildon, Havering and Thurrock.

---

[17] Quote taken from https://www.theguardian.com/news/2015/mar/24/how-immigration-came-to-haunt-labour-inside-story (last accessed 31 July 2017).

[18] Ashcroft found that approximately 80 per cent of those who thought that immigration was mostly a force for good voted to Remain, while a similar proportion of those who thought of it as a force for ill voted to Leave; see http://lordashcroftpolls.com/2016/06/how-the-united-kingdom-voted-and-why/ (last accessed 31 July 2017).

[19] M Goodwin, 'Inequality, Not Personalities Drove Britain to Brexit' *Politico.eu* (28 June 2016) http://www.politico.eu/article/inequality-not-personalities-drove-britain-to-brexit/(last accessed 31 July 2017).

He contrasted two communities, Boston, a small, east coast port where 76 per cent voted to leave the EU, and Lambeth in London, the area that returned the strongest vote for Remain (79 per cent).[20] Boston, which has experienced significant migration from Central and Eastern Europe, is 'noticeable for economic deprivation. The median income in Boston is less than £17,000 and one in three people have no formal qualifications at all'. It is also 'Filled with disadvantaged, working-class Britons who do not feel as though they have been winning from European integration, immigration, and globalization'. Life is remarkably different in Lambeth: 'Compared to Boston, there are more than twice as many professionals, nearly twice as many 18–30-year-olds and fewer than half as many working-class voters, pensioners and people with no qualifications. The average voter in Lambeth earns nearly £10,000 more each year than the average voter in Boston'.[21]

The totem of the indivisibility of the four freedoms was an impediment to constructing an imaginative solution to address the concerns of people in Boston, Barnsley, and Blackpool who do not feel they have benefited from the EU project. Yes, the Brussels agreement did give a nod to those concerns: as we have seen, it appeared to allow direct discrimination to be justified and thus a potential emergency brake on migration; it certainly expressly allowed for restrictions on migrants' access to benefits.[22] For a number of Member States this was already a bridge too far. But, in fact, concern about migrants' access to benefits proved a distraction from the main issue facing voters in the UK, which was the sudden influx of a large number of EU migrants into small towns. As the *Economist* noted, where foreign-born populations increased by more than 200 per cent between 2001 and 2014, a Leave vote followed in 94 per cent of cases.[23] The proportion of migrants might be relatively low in Leave strongholds such as Boston in Lincolnshire (where 15.4 per cent of the population are foreign-born) But it had grown precipitously in a short period of time (by 479 per cent, in Boston's case). The *Economist* concluded: 'High

---

[20] ibid.

[21] ibid. See also A Persaud, 'Brexit and Other Harbingers of a Return to the Dangers of the 1930s' *Vox* (26 August 2016) http://voxeu.org/article/brexit-and-other-harbingers-return-dangers-1930s): the data reveal that there was an 'unusually positive correlation (+0.60) between the percentage of those who voted to leave in a Local Authority and the percentage of non-graduates in that Local Authority' and that 'The much-touted correlation between age and the Brexit vote was also positive, but more modestly so at +0.15. Young graduates voted heavily to remain and elder workers who didn't go to university voted heavily to leave'.

[22] C Barnard, 'The Benefit of Benefits: the Changing Face of Free Movement in the European Union' in M Ronnmar and J Votinius (eds), *Festschrift Till Ann Numhuaser-Hennig* (Juristforlaget I Lund 2017) 43.

[23] http://www.economist.com/news/britain/21701950-areas-lots-migrants-voted-mainly-remain-or-did-they-britains-immigration-paradox (last accessed 31 July 2017).

levels of immigration don't seem to bother Britons; high rates of change do'. This suggests that it was the sudden (and unplanned?) influx of migrants, creating pressure on public services (such as access to schools, doctors' surgeries, and housing), that may have been the reason why these groups voted to leave.[24] And it wasn't just public services but a loss of local identity. In big cities, where there was a high vote to remain, the identity of their inhabitants may well be constructed around a cosmopolitan, international culture. In small towns, this is not the case.[25]

Therefore, had the February 2016 agreement introduced a clearly articulated emergency brake on migration this might have shown that, despite the problems this would cause to the integrity of the four freedoms and to the indivisibility of the integration project, the EU understood the concerns of those communities where the numbers of migrants had increased rapidly in a short space of time. The brake could have been modelled on Article 112 EEA (and the procedural safeguards in Article 113 EEA). Article 112 EEA provides:

1. If serious economic, societal or environmental difficulties of a sectorial or regional nature liable to persist are arising, a Contracting Party may unilaterally take appropriate measures under the conditions and procedures laid down in Article 113.
2. Such safeguard measures shall be restricted with regard to their scope and duration to what is strictly necessary in order to remedy the situation. Priority shall be given to such measures as will least disturb the functioning of this Agreement.
3. The safeguard measures shall apply with regard to all Contracting Parties.

The Article 112 EEA power has never been used by Norway and Iceland (the tiny state of Liechtenstein has a special arrangement) but it provides reassurance. The introduction of such a power would undoubtedly have meant a Treaty change—but that could have been promised to be delivered at a time of a future Treaty change. Crucially, however, it would have shown that the EU was listening.

---

[24] By contrast in Scotland, as Deakin argues, which has also undergone significant deindustrialization in the same period, the protest found an outlet in the rise of nationalism and the election to office of the predominantly social democratic Scottish National Party, which has held a controlling bloc of seats in the Scottish Parliament continuously since 2011. Every Scottish region voted by a majority for Remain and the overall vote in Scotland was over 60% for rejecting Brexit (S Deakin, 'Brexit, Labour Rights and Migration: Why Wisbech Matters to Brussels' (2016) 17(Brexit Supplement) *German Law Journal* 13 https://static1.squarespace.com/static/56330ad3e4b0733d-cc0c8495/t/5776e3fe6a49632d6e6e2007/1467409407368/04+PDF_Vol_17_Brexit+_Deakin.pdf.

[25] E Kaufmann, 'It's not the economy, stupid: Brexit as a story of personal values' http://blogs.lse.ac.uk/politicsandpolicy/personal-values-brexit-vote/. See also Nicolaïdis in this volume.

2.2.2 Obstructing the Path to a 'Deep and Special Partnership' with the EU

The insistence on the indivisibility of the four freedoms also stands in the way of a forging a future 'deep and special relationship' with the EU. As we have seen, the EU is determined that the UK cannot 'cherry pick' the bits of the single market it likes. So, this already appears to rule out the so-called 'Norway' option in the longer term, namely the UK reapplying to join EFTA and then joining the EEA as an independent state. The EEA agreement gives access to and membership of the single market. [26] 'Doing a Norway' was the 'soft' Brexit option, which some of the leading proponents of the Vote to Leave, including Daniel Hannan, had appeared to call for in the run up to the referendum. Granted, this model would have been unpopular with the majority of those voting to Leave: it would have required continued respect of EU rules without having a say on those rules, the continuation of free movement of people, and continued scrutiny by the EFTA Court. For these reasons the prime minister rejected the Norway model as a possibility in her Lancaster house speech. It is, however, still being mooted as a vehicle for agreement in the transitional period to soften the hard edge of Brexit.

Another possibility would be to follow the Swiss model. Switzerland is a member of EFTA. The EFTA agreement is primarily about goods and its provisions broadly replicate those of Articles 28, 34–36, and 110 TFEU. As a consequence of the rejection of the EEA membership in 1992,[27] Switzerland and the EU agreed on a package of seven sectoral agreements signed in 1999 including: free movement of people, technical trade barriers, public procurement, agriculture, and air and land transport. In addition, a scientific research agreement fully associated Switzerland into the EU's framework research programmes. A further set of sectoral agreements was signed in 2004, covering, inter alia, Switzerland's participation in Schengen and Dublin, and agreements on taxation of savings, processed agricultural products, statistics, combating fraud, participation in the EU Media Programme, the Environment Agency, and Swiss financial contributions to economic and social cohesion in the new EU Member States. The Swiss do not enjoy full free movement of services (which would also be damaging for the UK), although this does show that the four freedoms are not always indivisible. These bilateral agreements

[26] The EEA states are not in the customs union and so there would still need to be a border between the North and South of Ireland.
[27] The following summary draws on http://ec.europa.eu/trade/policy/countries-and-regions/countries/switzerland/index_en.htm.

have proved difficult to manage and for that reason the Swiss solution is unpopular with the European Commission.

So, the UK's 'new deep and special partnership' may in fact mean entering into some sort of arrangement similar to the one the EU has with Canada or Ukraine. The Canadian CETA agreement, which has been so painstakingly negotiated over the last five or so years, is the most comprehensive free trade agreement entered into by the EU. It covers not only goods but also people. However, free movement of people is still subject to national immigration law. The right to work is connected with Mode 4 services. Further, the agreement does not address the issues of natural persons seeking access to employment market of a contracting party; nor to measures regarding citizenship, residence, or employment on a permanent basis.

The EU's deal with Ukraine is, according to the Commission 'the most extensive form of co-operation offered by the EU to its non-candidate neighbours to date. [It] foresee[s] far reaching political and economic integration with the EU by significantly deepening political and economic ties'. The political and cooperation provisions of the Association Agreement (AA) with Ukraine have been provisionally applied since November 2014. The AA also contains a Deep and Comprehensive Free Trade Agreement (DCFTA), which the EU and Ukraine have provisionally applied since 1 January 2016. However, such agreements often involve the partner country accepting most of the EU's *acquis communautaire*, ie most rules concerning the single market and other parts of the EU legal order. As far as free movement of people is concerned, the AA envisages the introduction of visa free travel regime for citizens of Ukraine in 'due course' provided that conditions for well-managed and secure mobility are in place.

If all else fails the UK will 'fall back on the WTO' in its dealings with the EU.[28] This is less attractive than some of its proponents would have the public believe. While it is thought that the UK will not need to apply to join, and in the interests of efficiency it could rectify the EU's schedules and make them its own, it is thought that UK exports could face significant most-favoured-nation (MFN) tariffs on 58 per cent of goods that go to the EU and the 51 countries the EU has an FTA with (ie markets where UK currently has tariff free access) and the UK could end up levying tariffs on the 65 per cent of imports that originate from EU and other preferential partners (currently zero tariff).[29] Of more substantive concern, is how existing EU tariff quotas

---

[28] See also the chapter by G Sacerdoti in this volume.
[29] https://www.sussex.ac.uk/webteam/gateway/file.php?name=briefing-paper-1.pdf&site=18 (last accessed 31 July 2017).

on products such as lamb and chicken will be divided up between the EU 27 and the UK. Tariffs represent only one part of the process of free trade. This overlooks the serious problems with NTBs, which the WTO has not proved sufficiently effective in dealing with. Further, the WTO enforcement mechanisms are much weaker than those in the other agreements.[30]

It is quite clear that, from a single market perspective, the alternatives to single market membership outlined above are much less palatable and effective in terms of unrestricted access to the single market than the UK currently enjoys. This was noted bluntly by one very experienced senior civil servant:[31]

Lord Kerr said leaving the EU will mean that Britain's economic relationship with Europe will be less advantageous than it is now; that its relationship with the rest of the world will be more difficult economically; that trade halves as the distance doubles and that customs cause delays that damage modern global supply chains.

Furthermore, it is inevitable that UK goods will continue to have to comply with EU technical standards for so long as manufacturers want to trade in the EU. From this point of view, the prime minister will not be able to live up to the claim in her Lancaster House speech that the UK can avoid 'complying with the EU's rules and regulations that implement those freedoms, without having a vote on what those rules and regulations are'.[32] Chinese and American firms trading in the EU must respect those rules; so must the UK.

2.3 The paradoxes of indivisibility

Thus, the rigid insistence on indivisibility of the four freedoms resulted in a deal in Brussels in February 2016 that failed to address the UK's concerns, caused deep anxiety elsewhere in the EU, and resulted (in part) in a vote for the UK to leave the EU, thereby delivering a fundamental blow to the integrity of the EU and its project. Further, the paradox of indivisibility is that the UK may end up, eventually, with a deal which is closer to a highly divisible model that the EU had not wanted to offer the UK in February 2016 but not, of course, full membership.

There is a further paradox. The White Paper on the Great Repeal Bill reveals just how closely the UK wishes to stick to EU rules in the name of

---

[30] A Armstrong and C Barnard, 'How Will We Enforce Post-Brexit Trade Deals' *Prospect* (28 October 2016).

[31] https://www.ft.com/content/bbd70038-f8f8-11e6-bd4e-68d53499ed71 (last accessed 31 July 2017).

[32] https://www.gov.uk/government/speeches/the-governments-negotiating-objectives-for-exiting-the-eu-pm-speech (last accessed 31 July 2017).

certainty and consistency. In her introduction to the Great Repeal Bill White Paper, Prime Minister May said that:

The Government's first objective as we negotiate a new deep and special partnership with the European Union is to provide business, the public sector, and everybody in our country with as much certainty as possible as we move through the process.

...

Our decision to convert the 'acquis'—the body of European legislation—into UK law at the moment we repeal the European Communities Act is an essential part of this plan. This approach will provide maximum certainty as we leave the EU. The same rules and laws will apply on the day after exit as on the day before. It will then be for democratically elected representatives in the UK to decide on any changes to that law, after full scrutiny and proper debate.

There is one further paradox which became apparent as part of my Economic and Social Research Council (ESRC)-funded public engagement work conducted under the non-partisan UK in a Changing Europe (UKCE) think tank. Together with my colleague, Amy Ludlow, I spent early 2017 canvassing opinion from hundreds of people across the east of England through a series of debates and workshops in schools, community centres, and even a prison, as well as gathering views in streets and town squares. This fieldwork was conducted in locations ranging from the strongly pro-Brexit, including the Lincolnshire town of Boston, to Remain strongholds such as the city of Cambridge itself, which voted 73.8 per cent to stay. Compatible with the public engagement objectives of the UKCE, we asked people what they wanted from the Brexit negotiations and talked to them about the alternatives. It became increasingly clear that people recognized the need for compromise, and an overall consensus that a deal closer to the EEA 'Norway model' might be best, at least in the short term.[33] Other studies have reached similar conclusions.[34] Remodelling the UK's relationship along lines similar to the EEA was frequently described as a 'rebalancing', rather than pulling up the drawbridge to the world. Although the prime minister appears to have rejected this as a

[33] C Barnard and A Ludlow, 'Unravelling and reimagining the UK's relationship with the EU: Public engagement about Brexit in the East of England' (May 2017). The methodology used is explained at http://www.cam.ac.uk/sites/www.cam.ac.uk/files/73732_camb_unravelling_reimagining_the_uk.pdf (last accessed 30 July 2017).

[34] See also research by Rand, which reached similar conclusions: https://www.rand.org/blog/2017/07/finding-the-common-ground-building-a-brexit-around.html. It is reported that the majority of labour party members also want to stay in the single market: https://www.theguardian.com/politics/2017/jul/17/most-labour-members-want-uk-to-remain-in-single-market (last accessed 30 July 2017), and a majority of those voting leave would also accept free movement in return for greater access to the single market https://www.theguardian.com/politics/2017/jul/17/majority-of-brexiters-would-swap-free-movement-for-eu-market-access (last accessed 31 July 2017).

possibility in the longer term, as we have seen, the EEA might be a stepping stone towards departure during the transitional period and those we talked to showed some support for this.

3. What Effect Will Brexit Have on the EU's Single Market?

So, at a time when the UK is leaving the EU, the EU is celebrating the 60th anniversary of being a Union of states. Inevitably this means it is contemplating its future direction of travel, including the future of the EU's single market. With the departure of the UK, the EU is losing its most important supporter of an open, free-trading single market. The benefits of the single market were considered as part of the UK's Balance of Competence Review, launched in July 2012, which was in essence 'an audit of what the EU does and how it affects the UK'. [35] As the single market report put it, 'In this area the UK has been broadly successful in enshrining its more liberal economic model into at least some of the DNA of the Single Market'.[36]

Most commentators accept that the UK has punched above its weight in respect of shaping the single market. As we have seen, Lord Cockfield was the brains and principal mover behind the 1992 programme. UK ideas underpinned some of the key developments in other areas, in particular the free movement of services. The Services Directive 2006/123[37] was enthusiastically supported by the UK, even though its content fell far short of the full deregulation that the UK had wanted. The UK was used as a testing ground for the implementation of the Services Directive. Further, the refit process[38] has been modelled on the UK's red tape challenge. The 2014 public procurement package[39] was heavily influenced by the UK—so much so that the UK was able to copy and paste whole tracts of the directive straight into UK law, even down to using the same Article numbers, and bringing the implementing Regulations into force more than a year ahead of the deadline. Similarly, the UK has been

---

[35] https://www.gov.uk/guidance/review-of-the-balance-of-competences (last accessed 30 July 2017).

[36] https://www.gov.uk/government/uploads/system/uploads/attachment_data/file/227069/2901084_SingleMarket_acc.pdf para 3.44 (last accessed 31 July 2017).

[37] OJ [2006] L 376/36.

[38] http://ec.europa.eu/info/law/law-making-process/overview-law-making-process/evaluating-and-improving-existing-laws/reducing-burdens-and-simplifying-law/refit-making-eu-law-simpler-and-less-costly_en.

[39] See European Commission, 'EU Public Procurement reform: Less bureaucracy, higher efficiency. An overview of the new EU procurement and concession rules introduced on 18 April 2016'.

highly influential in ensuring the opening up of the market in audio-visual media services;[40] the current push towards a digital single market[41] also plays to the UK's strengths.

The paradox is that, at the time when the EU's single market is looking at its most British, the UK is going to leave. What will happen to the single market going forward? There has always been resistance in Continental Europe to the UK's push towards deregulation. While the UK has enjoyed support from like-minded states such as Sweden, Germany and France have always been resistant.[42] Many commentators think that the effect of the UK's exit will be a less ambitious, more regulatory, possibly more protectionist EU single market. And the UK will pay the price for this—UK manufacturers and service providers will have to comply with new rules over which the UK government will in future have no say. Even as a member of the EEA the UK would have some influence—not a vote but an ability to participate in working groups. Fully outside the EU as third country, the UK would not even have this. It would act as a recipient of rules, not as a rule-maker or shaper. And, as the Balance of Competence Review points out, the UK will be a loser:[43]

... integration has brought to the EU, and hence to the UK, in most if not all observers' opinions, appreciable economic benefits. It has also spread the UK's liberal model of policy-making more widely across the EU. But it has brought with it constraints on policy-making of varying kinds, and a regulatory framework which some find difficult to operate within or find burdensome, even if the obligations are not necessarily any greater than would have been imposed nationally. Is that trade-off, between cost and benefit, between economics and politics, of overall benefit to the UK? ... Most observers, and indeed most of the evidence received for this report, answer positively. They do so, not without qualifications or reservations, but with a focus on the economic benefits already achieved... and on those potentially available in the future.

4. The UK's Own Single Market

While acres of print have been devoted to the EU's single market, little attention has been paid to the UK's own single market. One of the most striking features of the recent documentation coming from the government on Brexit

---

[40] https://ec.europa.eu/digital-single-market/en/audiovisual-media-services-directive-avmsd.

[41] https://ec.europa.eu/commission/priorities/digital-single-market_en.

[42] See the chapter by Uwe Puetter in this volume.

[43] https://www.gov.uk/government/uploads/system/uploads/attachment_data/file/227069/2901084_SingleMarket_acc.pdf at 6 (last accessed 31 July 2017).

is the increasing reference to the UK's single market.[44] David Davis, in his foreword to the Great Repeal Bill White Paper,[45] said:

As we leave the EU, we have an opportunity to ensure that returning powers sit closer to the people of the United Kingdom than ever before. In some areas where the existence of common frameworks at EU level has also provided common UK frameworks, it will be important to ensure that this stability and certainty are not compromised

Examples of where common UK frameworks may be required include where they are necessary to protect the freedom of business to operate across the *UK single market.*

The issue of the UK's single market becomes crucial in respect of the very short section of the Great Repeal Bill White Paper on devolution.[46] As the white paper explains, in areas where the devolved administrations and legislatures have competence, such as agriculture, environment, and some transport issues, the devolved administrations and legislatures are responsible for implementing the common policy frameworks set by the EU. At EU level, the UK government represents the whole of the UK's interests in the process for setting those common frameworks and these also then provide common UK frameworks, including safeguarding the harmonious functioning of the UK's own single market. When the UK leaves the EU, the powers which the EU currently exercises in relation to the common frameworks will return to the UK. In other words, devolution has worked (more or less) successfully within the framework and context of the EU. There have been problems where the wholly internal rule has operated, notably over student fees (Scotland gives free university education to Scottish and EU students but not to English and Welsh students) but generally the transition to greater devolved powers has functioned smoothly.

However, outside the EU the issue will become more relevant and Westminster will face some of the issues currently experienced by the EU (and criticized by those in favour of Leave), namely the need for centralized decision-making in some areas to ensure that the UK single market is preserved. As the white paper says:

As powers are repatriated from the EU, it will be important to ensure that stability and certainty is not compromised, and that the effective functioning of the UK single market is maintained. Examples of where common UK frameworks may be required include where they are necessary to protect the freedom of businesses to operate

[44] The language did start to be used during the Scottish referendum in 2014. See eg 'Scottish independence: Single energy market should continue, says report' http://www.bbc.co.uk/news/uk-scotland-scotland-politics-28237478. (last accessed 31 July 2017).

[45] https://www.gov.uk/government/publications/the-great-repeal-bill-white-paper (last accessed 31 July 2017).

[46] See the chapter by Douglas-Scott in this volume.

across the UK single market and to enable the UK to strike free trade deals with third countries. Our guiding principle will be to ensure that no new barriers to living and doing business within our own Union are created as we leave the EU.

Take the case of the minimum pricing of alcohol in Scotland at issue in the *Scottish Whisky* case.[47] The Scottish Parliament passed the Alcohol (Minimum Pricing) (Scotland) Act in 2012, providing for the imposition of a minimum price per unit (MPU) of alcohol and empowering the government to determine the MPU by secondary legislation. The Scottish government published a draft order setting the MPU at 50 pence. This was challenged as a disproportionate barrier to trade contrary to Article 34 of the TFEU and contrary to the EU rules on the common organization of the market in agricultural products, one of the objectives of which is to maintain effective competition in an open market. The Court of Justice of the European Union (CJEU) broadly agreed that the legislation was a barrier to trade but said it could be justified. The question was whether the Scottish rules were proportionate and this question was referred back to the Scottish courts. The Court of Session dismissed the appeal brought by the Scotch Whisky Association and found that the Scottish legislation was compatible with EU law.[48] Applying the necessity limb of the proportionality test, and relying on the parameters provided by the CJEU, the Court of Session concluded that a general increase in the taxation of alcohol might be less restrictive of trade but would not be 'as effective' as the introduction of a MPU in securing the primary objective of the legislation. In particular, it would not be able to target alcohol that was cheap in relation to its high strength.

In future, such legislation could not be challenged under EU rules but it could potentially create an obstacle to the functioning of the UK's own single market. How will the UK deal with this in the future? One answer would be to deny powers being devolved back to the Scottish, Welsh, and Northern Irish administrations. In other words, the repatriation of powers from Brussels will go to Westminster and stay there. This UK centralization approach would ensure problems of the sort that arose in *Scottish Whisky* did not arise in the UK's own single market but would not be compatible with the principle of subsidiarity/devolution. The government appears to recognize this:

This will be an opportunity to determine the level best placed to take decisions on these issues, ensuring power sits closer to the people of the UK than ever before. It is

---

[47] Case C-333/14 *The Scotch Whisky Association and Others v The Lord Advocate and The Advocate General for Scotland* ECLI: EU:C:2015:845, [2015] WLR (D) 544.
[48] [2016] CSIH 77.

the expectation of the Government that the outcome of this process will be a significant increase in the decision-making power of each devolved administration.

But if there is a significant increase in the decision-making powers of each devolved administration what will happen if they use these powers in such a way that results in the creation of obstacles to the free movement of goods or people in the UK? Will one of the unexpected effects of Brexit be a significant remodelling of the UK's own constitution?[49] Will there eventually be a need for a written constitution, which sets out the powers of the centre (Westminster) and those of the devolved administrations? Will that written constitution have provisions rather similar to those in the EU Treaties—on duties of cooperation and respect and on the free movement of goods, persons, services, and capital? In the meantime, will the UK courts be forced to forge common law principles, along the lines of a right to engage in economic activity, against which this devolved legislation can be challenged?[50] Is one of the paradoxes of the UK leaving the EU that it will make the UK more EU-like in its construction, at least in so far as the single market is concerned?

5. Conclusions

The single market is totemic in the minds of its proponents. It must remain untouched and defended at all costs. Such a purist view is wholly comprehensible when seen from the institutions in Brussels and Strasbourg. The real world is different. Some more substantial concessions on these key pillars might have changed the outcome of the EU referendum in the UK,[51] albeit creating yet more difficulties for its European partners.[52] And yet, as the 2015 Conservative party manifesto demonstrates, there was commitment to the UK's continued membership of the single market. In the world of what ifs, many things could have been different for David Cameron: if the public had understood that free movement of goods is more than about tariffs; if there had been better education as to what the EU was (and was not) trying to achieve; if people had understood that Brussels was not simply an overbearing

---

[49] See the chapter by Tierney in this volume.

[50] For very early signs of the courts using common law principles as a means of striking down secondary legislation see *R (on the application of UNISON) (Appellant) v Lord Chancellor (Respondent)* [2017] UKSC 51.

[51] See eg 'David Cameron's EU deal a "slap in the face for Britain" as PM admits it won't cut migration' http://www.telegraph.co.uk/news/newstopics/eureferendum/12135328/EU-referendum-draft-deal-revealed-by-Donald-Tusk-live.html (last accessed 31 July 2017).

[52] For a useful summary of the European press reaction to the Brussels deal see https://www.ft.com/content/767cbfa8-d880-11e5-a72f-1e7744c66818 (last accessed 31 July 2017).

bureaucracy but taking (usually) necessarily centralized powers to ensure that the EU's single market functioned properly, as the Balance of Competence review had showed; if the Leave and Remain campaigns had been required to have a manifesto setting out what they believed in and whether that included single market membership. The paradox is that the public knows more about the EU and its workings post-referendum than it ever did in the period running up to the referendum—and, as our ESRC research has shown, the public now recognizes that there is a need for give and take. This understanding may ultimately benefit the UK government in the inevitable compromises it will have to make to secure a free trade deal with the EU and in working out how to fashion a working UK single market.

With hindsight, the UK's integration into the EU should have stopped before Maastricht. Or at least there should have been a referendum in 1992 to validate the UK's continued deeper cooperation and integration into the EU project. Maastricht made explicit the political nature of the integration project, beyond the remit of the single market. It was at that moment that the EU's legitimacy in the eyes of many started to wear thin. The EU itself has recognized that for some Member States the level of integration now envisaged is too much. One of the five scenarios envisaged by the white paper on the future of Europe is 'Nothing but the Single Market', gradually 're-centring' the EU 27 on the single market. This is the final what if—what if the EU had realized this in February 2016. But for the UK this is too little, too late. The question now is what can be salvaged from the tattered remains of the UK's relationship with the EU.

PART 4

BEYOND BREXIT: RELAUNCHING THE EU?

11

Brexit and Euroskepticism

Will "Leaving Europe" be Emulated Elsewhere?

Marlene Wind*

The decision made by Britain to leave the EU and the political and economic consequences that will follow have made a measurable impact for citizens of other Member States: their support of the European Union has grown.[1]

1. Introduction

Foreign Affairs recently published an article with the title "The Reverse Domino Effect."[2] The article suggested that after the Dutch elections in March 2017, but also the election of Alexander van der Bellen in Austria in December 2016 and Mariano Rajoy in Spain in June 2016, all the doomsday preachers after Brexit and Trump were proven wrong and that Europe would now say goodbye to populism. After the landslide election of Emmanuel Macron

* I would like to thank Regitze Helene Frederiksen, Stine Resen and Emil Bønding Wichmann for research assistance for this contribution. I would also like to thank my colleagues at iCourts (the Center of Excellence for International Courts) at the Faculty of Law of the University of Copenhagen for commenting on a previous draft and Federico Fabbrini for many helpful suggestions. This research is funded by the Danish National Research Foundation Grant no. DNRF105 and conducted under the auspices of the Danish National Research Foundation's Centre of Excellence for International Courts (iCourts).

[1] Isabell Hoffmann and Catherine de Vries, 'Brexit has raised support for the European Union' Bertelsmann Stiftung (21 November 2016) https://www.bertelsmann-stiftung.de/en/publications/publication/did/flashlight-europe-022016-brexit-has-raised-support-for-the-european-union/

[2] Pierpaolo Barbieri, "Europe's Reverse Domino Effect: No One is Following Britain out of the EU," *Foreign Affairs* https://www.foreignaffairs.com/articles/western-europe/2017-03-16/europes-reverse-domino-effect?cid=int-now&pgtype=hpg°ion=br2.

Brexit and Euroscepticism: Will 'leaving Europe' be emulated elsewhere. First edition. Marlene Wind © Marlene Wind 2017. Published 2017 by Oxford University Press.

(66%) over Marine Le Pen (33%) on the May 7 presidential election, this hypothesis by *Foreign Affairs* seem further confirmed. In fact, we may now go as far as saying that *because* of Brexit and Trump, Europeans are now waking up and reacting against populism's easy answers to complicated questions. Or is this all wishful thinking? This chapter will try to ask what we can learn from Brexit and whether the UK's goodbye to the EU is likely to be emulated in other European countries in the near future. Is the EU falling apart or was the UK relationship with Europe so special that the domino thesis predicted by many after the Brexit vote and the election of Donald Trump in the US must be rejected? This chapter argues and seeks to demonstrate that Brexit most likely will be a unique endeavor.

As it is dangerous to predict about the future this will also not be attempted here. However, it will be suggested that the UK's historical past, uneasy relationship with Europe and in particular its obsession with sovereignty is and always has been special compared to most other Member States and that it may have influenced the decision to leave the EU and to hold a referendum in the first place. It is important here to emphasize that this chapter does not represent a thorough analysis of the UK's decision to leave or to hold a referendum. It is also not an in-depth comparison between the UK and other European countries. Rather, it looks at some specific but—I will argue—important traits and central issues related to the "domino" thesis presented by scholars and commentators after Brexit and the election of Trump. Apart from a look at the special British situation, the chapter will thus focus on the result of the national elections in Europe following Brexit and Trump, where populism and anti-European sentiments were expected to take hold. It will also use important opinion polls from European countries in the aftermath of Brexit and the election of Donald Trump as an indicator of the domino effect predicting an undermining of liberal institutions like the EU.

The chapter is structured in four parts. The first part discusses whether populism is an unstoppable global and European trend and argues that, no— it is a very crude narrative proposed by the media and certain commentators. Little in the data we have collected here suggests that populism is a coherent unstoppable wave that is taking all liberal institutions down. The second part argues that the British uneasy relationship with the EU has always been different and that their type of anti-Europeanism is of a sort that we do not find in most other European countries. What is scrutinized most in depth here is the British conception of sovereignty, which was at the core not only of the "leave campaign" but also in Theresa May's emphasis on "taking back control of our own laws" and escaping the Court of Justice of the European Union (CJEU). The third part looks closely at the opinion polls in other European countries. Here, it is documented that dissatisfaction with the establishment, with political elites and globalization, and the EU plays out differently in different European countries. The fourth part, finally, concludes and summarizes the findings.

2. Populism: An Irreversible Trend?

The big question in many EU capital cities but certainly also in Brussels after the British decision to leave the EU in the referendum of June 23, 2016 was exactly whether other countries would follow suit.[3] Would Brexit trigger an implosion by EU skeptic voters in other Member States demanding a similar vote? Would others—infused by the populism of the leave campaign and the exit-strategy of the May government, but also by the victory of Donald Trump on the other side of the Atlantic—want to follow in the British footsteps and free themselves from the so-called Brussels bureaucracy, the Luxembourg court, transnational regulators, and the world-leading single market?

This chapter argues that this is a very unlikely outcome. If we look at the available polls, it even seems as if Europe has been strengthened by Brexit and Trump after the very clear pro-Europe win by Emmanuel Macron as president of France. Moreover, the doomsday predictions result at least in part from a limited appreciation of the unique character of the British relationship with Europe and its special conception of sovereignty, combined with an understandable collective shock and media hype. One of the more noticeable warnings was made by Polish-American historian Anne Appelbaum in the *Washington Post* in April 2016: "Is this the end of the West as we know it?" suggesting that, if Brexit happens, Trump is elected and Le Pen becomes the next French president, the West will no longer constitute the same liberal order we used to know.[4] In April 2016, former European Parliament President and now German chancellor candidate Martin Schulz also warned that Brexit might trigger an implosion.[5] Much less sophisticated doomsday

---

[3] See Kate Lyons and Gordon Darroch, "Frexit, Nexit or Oexit? Who will be next to leave the EU?" *Guardian* (June 27, 2017). This brief article discusses the possibilities that Brexit will happen in either the Netherlands, France, Italy, Austria, Sweden, Germany, or Denmark. It includes, however, limited data on the support for such a referendum and the public support for the EU itself. Most countries are considered to be unlikely to issue a referendum. http://www-theguardian.com/politics/2016/jun/27/frexit-nexit-or-oexit-who-will-be-next-to-leave-the-eu.

[4] https://www.washingtonpost.com/opinions/donald-trump-and-the-end-of-nato/2016/03/04/e8c4b9ca-e146-11e5-8d98-4b3d9215ade1_story.html?utm_term=.2d7afaee1b2b.

[5] Cited from Z HYPERLINK http://www.faz.net/aktuell/politik/europaeische-union/martin-schulz-sieht-bedrohung-durch-europafeindliche-bewegungen-14173019.html.

stories than the one presented by Appelbaum and Schulz came from US observers in high numbers.[6]

Now that British Prime Minister Theresa May has handed over the divorce papers to European Council President Donald Tusk in Brussels, the British and American press are no less "[f]ull of alarm and excitement."[7] It is, of course, understandable that many broadcasters see the Brexit negotiations as an opportunity to speculate about the spread of the "Brexit disease."

However, as the Dutch parliamentary vote in March 2017—together with the Austrian presidential election in December 2016 and the very pro-European Macron win in May 2017—have demonstrated, the likelihood that one can easily deduce from Brexit and Trump the "fall of Europe" seems very superficial to say the least. While the agony with Europe and established parties and elites cannot of course be denied, political dynamics clearly play out differently in different countries. In fact, polls show that Le Pen has not even herself benefited from Brexit—not even in the short term. She landed on 21 percent in the first round—much lower than expected. As Lafitte and MacShane put it, this is even less than what the French Communist party (with very similar ideas of protectionism) received in the 1950s and 60s.[8] In the second round, she landed on 34 percent which—even though her party's best result ever—was far from what was predicted by pollsters and experts on populism. However, it would probably still be dangerous to discharge Le Pen and National Front entirely if Macron does not succeed with his overall reform program during the next five years.

Even though it is difficult at this stage to list the exact causes of the reactions to Brexit and Trump among ordinary Europeans, we can—as we shall see below—detect a certain reinvigoration of the European project in many European countries. Many of the recent polls thus show a steady and increasing support for Europe—a support which rose markedly right after the British people voted to leave the EU in June 2016. Whether other European countries will follow the UK with their own referenda in the coming years will probably in part depend on the final outcome of the Brexit negotiations

---

[6] See e.g. *The National Interest*, "Europe Will Implode" http://nationalinterest.org/feature/the-eu-will-likely-implode-15314. Just like during the financial crisis, where many American analysts and media people saw the end of not only the Eurozone but the EU as such, Brexit and Trump will now result in a meltdown of all liberal institutions—at least so it is predicted. However, as with the Eurozone, where as *Foreign Affairs* (n. 2) puts it: "[a] Spanish bailout came and went; a new Italian government restored confidence, as did European Central Bank President Mario Draghi," who pledged that he wanted to do "whatever it takes" to save the euro. Things did not, in other words, end as predicted in the newsrooms.

[7] See www.politico.eu/article/why-marine-le-pen-wont-win-trump-brexit/.

[8] www.politico.eu/article/why-marine-le-pen-wont-win-trump-brexit/.

and the deal that the UK eventually gets. If the outcome were to be too beneficial for the UK—getting access to the single market but with fewer strings attached than is the case under the current EU rules, this could animate anti-EU movements in other European countries to campaign for a similar exit route for their countries. Influential EU-skeptic parties in Denmark have thus explicitly announced that they will demand a referendum if the deal that the UK gets is more favorable to the UK than expected and thus to the one Norway already has. Nevertheless, at this stage the likelihood that the UK will be able to obtain a good deal seems rather limited, which suggests that it is unlikely that other EU Member States will seek to follow the same path.

3. Why the UK Is Special

It is hardly controversial to say that the UK is exceptional when it comes to its rather schizophrenic approach to the EU[9]. Moreover, defining British opposition to the EU as part of a British exceptionalism makes it possible to examine this specialness more thoroughly. For the British people, the EU has represented different possibilities. For some, the EU was a promise of peace and stability, for others the Single Market's promise of jobs and prosperity was at the center of attention. However, as pointed out by Leonard, none of these readings or possibilities seems seductive enough anymore.[10] The British people today understand the EU both as a heavy bureaucratic machinery and as the cause behind many of the negative changes in their society, like migration, rising housing costs, and inequality. A vote for Brexit, moreover, was for some also a way to reinvigorate the past British "grandeur"—with the UK becoming an economic powerhouse by itself. Thus, the opposition is deeper than just structural or institutional factors, which is highlighted by the more pragmatic and utilitarian approaches to the EU.[11]

The UK first applied to join the Common Market in 1963 but membership was vetoed by the French President Charles de Gaulle. In 1973, Britain—together with Denmark and Ireland—was finally admitted into European Economic Community (EEC) under Conservative Prime Minister

[9] http://www.telegraph.co.uk/news/2016/06/16/leave-or-remain-in-the-eu-the-arguments-for-and-against-brexit/.

[10] Mark Leonard, 'Europe Seen from the Outside—The British View,' European Council on Foreign Relations (2016). http://www.ecfr.eu/article/commentary_europe_seen_from_the_outside_the_british_view_7091.

[11] Andrew Glencross, *Why the UK Voted for Brexit: David Cameron's Great Miscalculation* (Palgrave Studies in European Union Politics 2016) 7 ff.

Edward Heath. As opposed to Denmark, the British government did not let a referendum decide whether to enter the EEC. Instead, in 1975—after having entered—it held a referendum asking: "Do you think the UK should stay in the European Community (Common Market)?" The referendum divided the Harold Wilson Labour government while the public endorsed membership with a huge margin. 67 percent voted to stay in. In the wording of James Callaghan the referendum moreover framed the EU as a "business arrangement" and played into the utilitarian idea that pooling sovereignty with other European Member States should be based on a calculation of the cost and benefits of doing so. Glencross argues that British Euroskepticism is born out of concerns about the costs in relation to both core principles of European integration and moves towards a greater political union. Thus, British opposition to the EU project, as catalyzed only two years after joining the Union, can be understood as a utilitarian question as to whether the UK really needed to be part of the project. The same attitude reoccurred over the years and can for sure also be found in the 2016 referendum, here premised on the belief, that the UK could quit the project, because it now has higher costs than benefits, with no deleterious consequences.[12]

In sum, whether the 1975 referendum was historic or not, fighting Brussels already began shortly after the 1975 referendum and in 1984, at a summit in Fontainebleau, the UK obtained its famous "rebate" from the EEC, after Margaret Thatcher threatened not to pay into the EU budget.[13] As Thatcher put it: "We are not asking the Community or anyone else for money. We are simply asking to have our own money back."[14]

The UK was at the time the third poorest member of the Community but ended up becoming the biggest net contributor to the EU budget. This was mainly because the UK had relatively little agriculture and thus a rather small share of farm subsidies, which at the time made up more than 70 percent of the EU budget.

In 1993 John Major had problems selling the Maastricht Treaty to his own backbenchers. The Treaty was voted down at a referendum in Denmark in 1992, resulting in the so-called Edinburgh-agreement where Denmark was given permanent opt-outs on (1) the euro; (2) defence; (3) Union

---

[12] See Glencross (n. 11) 8–9.

[13] Iain Begg and Friedrich Heinemann, "New Budget, Old Dilemmas," Centre for European Reform, Briefing Note (2006) http://83.143.248.39/faculty/didar/EUR324/briefing_new_budget_22Feb06.pdf.

[14] http://news.bbc.co.uk/2/hi/europe/4721307.stm.

citizenship—an opt-out that was later deleted as it was no longer relevant;[15] and (4) supranational cooperation in the Justice and Home Affairs area.[16] Based on these opt-outs Denmark, in a second referendum in 1993, approved the Maastricht Treaty. UK Prime Minister John Major did not call a referendum on the Maastricht Treaty but ended up opting out of the single currency and the treaty's "social chapter." Later, when Tony Blair took over as prime minister in 1997, the UK moved closer to Europe. Speaking to the European Parliament in 2005, in fact, Blair wore the clothes of a passionate pro-European, claiming that he wanted the UK to be in "the heart of Europe."

However, in 2005, the Dutch and the French voted the European constitution down and when its replacement, the Lisbon Treaty was finally adopted in 2009, the new British Prime Minister Gordon Brown did not show up for the ceremony. Brown moreover became famous for avoiding meetings in Brussels altogether whenever he could.[17]

The agony over Europe within the conservative party grew even more serious under Prime Minister David Cameron and he promised already when elected in 2010 to "bring back powers from Brussels." After Cameron came to power, several polls made it clear that in particular British conservative voters who were escaping the Tories being more attracted to the new anti-EU party UKIP (UK Independence Party), which had become famous for its leader Nigel Farage and his hard rhetoric against the EU.

Therefore, on January 23, 2011, Prime Minister Cameron delivered a major speech on Europe where he promised his voters and the British people to renegotiate the UK's EU membership. He also presented the UK Parliament for the EU Act 2011, which set a legal requirement for a referendum in case of any future EU treaty reform.[18] In 2014 Cameron, before the upcoming

[15] The reason why it was no longer relevant was that Denmark had only refused to accept Union citizenship if it were to replace national citizenship. In the Amsterdam Treaty some years later, it was written into the Treaty that Union citizenship was only a supplement and not a replacement of national citizenship.

[16] For an in-depth analysis of the Danish (and British) opt-outs see R Adler-Nissen, *Opting Out of Europe* (Cambridge University Press 2015).

[17] Tony Barber reporting for the *Financial Times*: "The UK prime minister's appearance at an EU summit of heads of state and government tomorrow will be his first visit to Brussels since he succeeded Tony Blair in June—a lengthy absence that has not gone unnoticed at the European Commission and among EU national embassies. Britain at the moment is 'more detached from the EU than at any time since the mid-1980s,' says an experienced western European ambassador, referring to the years when Margaret Thatcher, as UK premier, adopted a famously abrasive stance on Europe." http://www.ft.com/cms/s/0/697be030-a91e-11dc-ad9e-0000779fd2ac.html?ft_site=fa lcon&desktop=true#axzz4hEbwFMmQ

[18] See Paul Craig in this volume and his: "The European Union Act: Locks, Limits and Legality" (2011) 48(6) *Common Market Law Review* 1915.

general election, held yet another speech saying that EU migration was one of the biggest problems of EU membership, combined with the migrants' access to the British welfare benefit system. He also said that he would "rule nothing out" (including leaving the EU) if his attempt to "get a better deal for Britain" from his EU collaborators did not work. In the European Parliament election in 2014, UKIP was very successful and won twenty-four out of seventy-three seats (26.77% of the votes, with an increase of eleven mandates),[19] setting Europe firmly back on the British agenda. To the surprise of many, Cameron came out of the 2015 general election much stronger than expected and with a promise to take back power from Brussels through a new deal.

The repeated promise of an EU in-out referendum throughout the British history rests on two concerns. The first was that EU membership was too restrictive for the UK, here perceived as a more free trade and globally oriented player. The second was that membership lacked popular support. This feeds back to the utilitarian attitude, but also to a narrative, framed by UKIP, that the British people never got what they voted for back in 1975. A common argument within the Euroskeptical camp was that the EU had developed beyond the control of the UK and especially the British people.[20] It was, however, also a narrative about the EU or "Brussels taking decisions" on its own—decisions that fundamentally contradicted British interests and which the British delegates mostly voted against. While this description was far from the truth, it became the one that won in the British tabloids. Cameron was, moreover, good at playing this game in front of the national press, presenting his "victories" in Brussels as some he had won against all odds. The concessions that Cameron finally obtained from the UK's EU partners when negotiating "a new deal" in February 2016 were thus a hard sell. At the same time, the migrant crisis immediately following the Eurozone crisis did not contribute to make the EU look better in the eyes of the British public. In February 2016, a referendum on Britain's membership was eventually announced to be held on June 23 the same year. After a fierce campaign for and mainly against Europe, the "leavers" won the referendum by 51.9 percent against 48.1 percent for remain. A YouGov study[21] from 23–24 of June 2016 revealed a generational divide (see figure 11.1).

Citizens aged 50 years and above were in large majority in favor of leaving the EU. The younger generations largely voted "remain." Education also

---

[19] Election results found at www.europarl.europa.eu/elections2014-results/en/country-results-uk-2014.html and http://www.bbc.com/news/events/vote2014/eu-uk-results.

[20] See Glencross (n. 11) 10 ff.

[21] https://d25d2506sfb94s.cloudfront.net/cumulus_uploads/document/oxmidrr5wh/EUFinalCall_Reweighted.pdf.

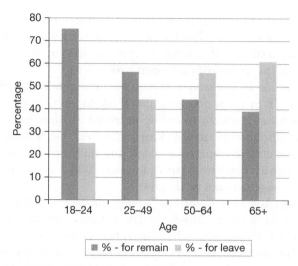

Figure 11.1 Vote in the EU referendum by age

Source: data from YouGov <https://d25d2506sfb94s.cloudfront.net/cumulus_uploads/document/oxmidrr5wh/EUFinalCall_Reweighted.pdf> (last accessed August 19, 2017) © 2016 YouGov plc.

played a role as 63 percent of the people with a "low attention to politics" voted "leave" and 62 percent of the people in the lowest income group voted "leave."

4. Taking Back Control or "The Allure of Sovereignty"

The UK has long been shorn of its empire; now it will be shorn of Europe, too.[22]

In her Lancaster House speech[23] but also during the leave campaign (of which Theresa May did not take part as she herself recommended to vote "remain") two central elements were recurring. The first was to "to take back control" of migration— not of asylum-seekers and refugees, who had hardly surfaced as a problem during the debate—but, rather, of EU migrants. The second was the wish to escape the CJEU jurisdiction and to "write and judge on our own laws," as May put it in her speech. So, we are in other words talking about

---

[22] https://www.project-syndicate.org/commentary/uk-post-brexit-small-economy-model-by-michael-o-sullivan-and-david-skilling-1-2017-03?barrier=accessreg.

[23] http://www.telegraph.co.uk/news/2017/01/17/theresa-mays-brexit-speech-full/.

the "reclamation of British sovereignty from technocrats in Brussels."[24] Or in Nigel Farage's own words: "Britain should reassert itself as a proud, patriotic country that has control of its borders, represents itself on the world stage and makes its own law in our own sovereign parliament."[25]

In her Lancaster House speech, Theresa May also launched a rather nostalgic vision of the UK as a new dominant player on the global stage—dominating the Commonwealth which, according to Ishaan Tharoor, some anonymous government officials even labeled "Empire 2.0." As Tom Whyman[26] puts it:

"Brexit is rooted in imperial nostalgia and myths of British exceptionalism, coming up as they have—especially since 2008—against the reality that Britain is no longer a major world power."

Moreover, a You Gov Eurotrack Survey[27] showed in February 2017 that most Britons think the EU needs the UK at least as much as the UK needs the EU. Indeed, 33 percent of the Britons here believe the EU needs Britain more than Britain needs the EU; 28 percent believe that they need each other equally. The data displays that Britons probably see themselves as a more important actor internationally than they maybe are (in contrast to the other countries' views of them).

Looking at May's speech but also at the "vote leave" campaign—not to mention the debate going on (for years) in the UK on leaving the European Convention on Human Rights (ECHR)[28]—the sovereignty issue is central. As argued by current British Foreign Secretary Boris Johnson: "you cannot express the sovereignty of parliament and accept the 1972 European Communities Act."[29] As is well known, EU law prevails over domestic law in cases of conflict. In the UK, the principle of the supremacy of EU law over national law was established in *Factortame* in 1991, when a British parliamentary Act on ship registration was set aside by the CJEU after complaints by Spanish fishermen.[30]

---

[24] Ishaan Tharoor, 'Brexit and Britain's delusions of empire' *Washington Post* https://www.washingtonpost.com/news/worldviews/wp/2017/03/31/brexit-and-britains-delusions-of-empire/?utm_term=.ad5dbeff2103.

[25] https://publiclawforeveryone.com/2014/10/15/1000-words-parliamentary-sovereignty/

[26] https://www.nytimes.com/2017/02/15/opinion/theresa-mays-empire-of-the-mind.html?_r=0.

[27] February 8, 2017. Fieldwork done January 19-24, 2017. See https://d25d2506sfb94s.cloudfront.net/cumulus_uploads/document/di1fktb0k8/January_Eurotrack_W.pdf.

[28] See J. Christoffersen and M. Rask Madsen, *The European Court of Human Rights between Law and Politics* (Oxford University Press 2011).

[29] Boris Johnson cited in Mark Elliot, "Brexit: Vote Leave, Take Control? Sovereignty and the Brexit Debate" *Frankfurter Allgemeine Zeitung* (June 23, 2016) https://publiclawforeveryone.com/2016/06/23/vote-leave-take-control-sovereignty-and-the-brexit-debate/.

[30] Case C-221/89 R *(Factortame Ltd) v Secretary of State for Transport* [1991] 3 All ER 769, [1991] ECR I-3905.

The question of sovereignty has, however, haunted the British EU debate for decades, if not centuries.[31] What parliamentary sovereignty implies, in its most conventional understanding, is as pointed out by Dicey: "Parliament can make whatever laws it wishes; that no 'higher' constitutional laws or principles constrain Parliaments legislative authority; and that other institutions, including the courts, must accept as valid laws duly enacted by Parliament."[32] According to this view, the fact that for instance the UK parliament respects fundamental rights is due not to a written constitution or supranational courts or conventions, but simply to a deliberate political choice made by parliament itself. This echoes Richard Bellamy's[33] definition of "political constitutionalism" in opposition to "legal constitutionalism" where the parliament is seen as limited by either a constitution, the courts (supranational or national) or international conventions.

According to Elliot,[34] the UK is fairly alone in this conception of sovereignty in the EU. Most countries after the Second World War adopted forms of *legal constitutionalism* (instead of political constitutionalism). Or to use Ronald Dworkin's version of the same typology: "constitutional" as opposed to "majoritarian democracy" emphasizes the sovereign majority in parliament as elevated above other balancing powers, including the courts.[35] That the UK should be entirely alone is, however, not quite true, as a similar conception of sovereignty, democracy and the role of Parliament can be found among the Scandinavian countries as I have demonstrated in much of my recent writings.[36] In Denmark, Sweden, and Finland (but to a much lesser extent Norway), unlimited majoritarian democracy for centuries trumped any conception of constitutionalism. In Scandinavia, there was either no tradition

---

[31] http://www.economist.com/news/britain/21695056-talk-taking-back-power-may-be-delusional-more-democracy-not-dreaming-sovereignty.

[32] Originally by A. V. Dicey, "The Law of the Constitution" 1885, here cited in Mark Elliot, "1,000 Words/Parliamentary Sovereignty" *Public Law for Everyone* (October 15, 2014) https://publiclawforeveryone.com/2014/10/15/1000-words-parliamentary-sovereignty/. See also R. Bellamy, *Political Constitutionalism: A Republican Defence of the Constitutionality of Democracy* (Cambridge University Press 2007).

[33] See Bellamy (n. 34).   [34] See Elliot (n. 31).

[35] R. Dworkin, *Freedom's Law: The Moral Reading of the American Constitution* (Harvard University Press 1996).

[36] M. Wind, "Who is Afraid of European Constitutionalism? The Nordic Distress with Judicial Review and Constitutional Democracy," in Claudio Franzius, Franz C. Mayer, and Jürgen Neyer (eds.), *Modelle des Parlamentarismus im 21. Jahrhundert. Neue Ordnungen von Recht und Politik; Recht und Politik in der Europäschen Union*, Band 4 (iCourts Working Paper Series No. 13 Nomos Verlag 2015) https://papers.ssrn.com/sol3/papers.cfm?abstract_id=2539045 http://cep.polsci.ku.dk/pdf/iCourts_Working_Paper_Series__No._13.pdf; see also M. Wind (2009), "When Parliament Comes First: The Danish Concept of Democracy Meets the European Union' (2009) 27(2) *Nordic Journal of Human Rights* 272–88.

for practicing judicial review at the national level or this was directly for-
bidden in the national constitutions until the beginning of the 2000s. As
I have explained elsewhere these anti-court sentiments are still strong and
have produced a reluctance towards supranational courts which is similar to
that of the UK. In particular, in Denmark and Sweden the aversion against
European constitutionalism has been so manifest, that only very few cases
have been referred to the ECJ,[37] and the ECJ case law is very rarely cited by
these countries' highest courts.[38] The UK is thus not alone in its ambivalent
relationship to the ECJ (or the European Court of Human Rights for that
matter). Countries based on majoritarian democracy will always find it hard
to merge into a political system like the European one based on constitutional
rather than majoritarian principles.

The question, however, is whether "unconstrained" majoritarian democracy is a very useful guide in a globalized world where sovereignty increasingly is something you pool rather than retain? In other words, do you
become more rather than less sovereign by leaving the EU? You may think
more. Yet, being outside the EU with no influence on the rules that will
limit and structure any states manoeuvring in a twenty-first century global
society will most likely make you much less sovereign. This is in fact confirmed by the UK government's "Great Repeal bill".[39] As the government
white paper makes clear, the bill will simply copy-paste EU law into UK law.
Moreover, if the UK wants to continue trading with the EU in the future
it will largely have to live up to and implement the exact same standards in
effect today among the EU Member States. Regardless of the details of the
withdrawal deal, the UK remains heavily dependent on the rules and regulations of one of the world's largest markets—just like the Norwegians and the
Swiss are. The British people may "believe" that they are more sovereign than
regular EU members by focusing merely on the formal rules but in reality
they end up being much less sovereign than if they had remained a member
exercising influence on its own future laws and regulations.[40] As McBride

[37] M. Wind, "The Nordic Reluctance Towards Supranational Judicial Review" (2010) 48(4)
Journal of Common Market Studies 1039–63; See also Wind *et al.*, "The Uneven Legal Push for
Europe" (2009) 10(1) *European Union Politics* 63–88.
[38] M. Wind, "Do Scandinavians Care about International Law?" (2016) 85 *Nordic Journal of
International Law* 281–302.
[39] https://www.gov.uk/government/publications/the-great-repeal-bill-white-paper. The government's White Paper on the Repeal Bill has no exact figures for the number of EU rules which will be
transferred into domestic law. However, it does note that there are currently more than 12,000 EU
regulations in force. The White Paper adds that Parliament has passed 7,900 statutory instruments
implementing EU legislation and 186 Acts which incorporate a degree of EU influence.
[40] J. Fossum and E. O. Eriksen, "Det norske paradoks: Om Norges forhold til Den europei-
ske union" (Universitetsforlaget 2014). The book *The Norwegian Paradox* deals with the impact

argues[41]—the UK when discussing to leave the EU had to decide about continuing to be a "rulemaker" or—if quitting—become merely a "ruletaker." The essential question was whether the UK wanted to continue being either inside influencing the law-making or turn into a "copy-paster," following those rules that the EU has made and which will shape the future.[42] As pointed out in an analysis on sovereignty and the Brexit debate in the *Economist*:[43]

"Many talk of being sovereign as if it were like being pregnant: one either is or is not. The truth is more complex. A country can be wholly sovereign yet have little influence. Britain has signed some 700 international treaties that impinge on sovereignty. Although the EU has the biggest impact, others count a lot: membership of NATO, for example, creates an obligation to go to war if another member country is attacked. It can be worth ceding this independence to gain influence.".

Apparently however, the understanding of what it means to be sovereign in the 21st century, and what it means to leave a collaboration like the EU based on the pooling of sovereignty hardly influenced the Brexit debate prior to the referendum. The question is now whether other EU Member States may embark on a similar journey as the UK—launching referenda on the EU and eventually leave. We saw above that in particular Denmark and other Scandinavian nations look at sovereignty and democracy very much in the same way as the UK does. Denmark entered the EU at the same time of the UK and has had a very pragmatic relationship to the EU.[44] However, Denmark has not—so far at least—drawn the same consequences from its majoritarian outlook. It may very well come down to the fact that Denmark is and perceives itself as a small open economy fundamentally dependent on a larger market to survive. The Danes surely love their "perceived" sovereignty as well and still do not like either judicial review or supranational courts setting aside their national parliamentary laws. However, as things look now overall pro-European sentiments have increased in Denmark after Brexit. Certainly, things may not stay that way and much will probably depend on the quality of the deal that the UK ends up getting with the EU, but polls show that so far the Danes stick to

of Norway's EU accession for democracy and asks if it affects the preconditions for constitutional democracy?

[41] J. McBride, "The Debate over Brexit" Council of Foreign Relations (2017) https://www.files.ethz.ch/isn/196540/The%20Debate%20Over%20%27Brexit%27%20-%20Council%20on%20Foreign%20Relations.pdf.

[42] K. Schaldemose, "Sovereignty in the 21st Century," Master's Thesis, Department of Political Science, University of Copenhagen.

[43] https://www.economist.com/news/britain/21695056-talk-taking-back-power-may-be-delusional-more-democracy-not-dreaming-sovereignty.

[44] M. Kelstrup, D. Martinsen and M. Wind, "Europa i Forandring", [Europe under Transformation: A Book on the EU's Political and Legal System] (Hans Reitzels Forlag 2017).

what they know and what they got. Let's now take a closer look at the surveys and results we have managed to collect so far. The general picture is also here that the UK is much more skeptical towards the EU construct than any of the other European Member States.

5. Will Other Countries Follow the UK Out? No So Likely …

"Should I stay or should I go?" asked the Clash back in 1982. "Stay" is certainly the answer if we look at public opinion polls and surveys from the months following the Brexit referendum. Two important insights can be taken home from the preliminary data, polls, and surveys we have collected. First, populism and attitudes towards Europe and European integration have different roots and causes in different EU Member States: According to the data, therefore, it is not possible to detect a general aligned anti-establishment or populist trend. Second, data reveal that also after the activation of Article 50 there continues to be a great split in attitude towards Europe between the UK and the continent.

After Brexit there was, however, as indicated earlier, much discussion on who would follow next. Even people in the new Trump administration saw Brexit and the UK's goodbye to the EU as the first sign of a genuine European split: According to different media reports the first question asked by the new Trump administration to European officials in Brussels was: "which country 'would leave next?' "[45]

It is in this light rather interesting to take a look at the first European surveys after the Brexit-vote. They may thus be able to tell us a little about where the attitudes in Europe are moving. The first survey we have consulted is the You Gov European Mega Survey from August–September 2016.[46] This survey, conducted right after the Brexit vote, confirmed that Britain is a special case when it comes to the public's approval of EU membership. The majority of the respondents in the other Member States have a much higher approval rating of their EU membership than UK respondents.

In another segment, being asked about EU immigration, the distribution shows, however, that France also has a large number of people seeing

[45] *Foreign Affairs* (n. 2).

[46] Fieldwork You Gov done August 31–September 9, 2016 http://d25d2506sfb94s.cloudfront. net/cumulus_uploads/document/smow6e2p43/MegaEurotrackerResults_AugustSeptember2016_ Toplines.pdf.

immigration from other EU countries as a bad thing. The other countries score lower. Moreover, being asked if it is likely that their country will leave the EU, of all countries other than Britain only one in five say that they believe their country will be next. The You Gov dataset goes into detail as regards many EU countries on some central issues. Relevant for our research here, however, is the overview of whether the populations would vote "remain" or "leave" if an "exit" referendum were to be held (see figure 11.2).

The data above shows that in August 2016—after the "real" referendum— 45 percent of Britons would vote to leave the EU, which is slightly higher than the percentage (43%) who would remain. In contrast, the populations of the Netherlands, Denmark, France, and Germany would all vote to stay in the EU, with a confident margin (see figure 11.3).

A study with similar results comes from the Bertelsmann Stiftung.[47] The data here shows that, since Britain voted to leave the EU, there have been signs of a more positive approach in other countries to the EU. This is something that might be explained by the many uncertainties surrounding the UK situation after the referendum. It thus suggests—as we also will get back to below when analysing the national elections held in other European countries in 2017—that Brexit may in fact have had the opposite effect than expected by the domino theory and taken some of the air out of the populist movements in Europe.

To put it differently, not much of the data we have had the opportunity to look at supports the doomsdayers' prediction that other EU Member States will put Europe on the ballot not to mention leave the EU in the near future. If we look at data from the Pew Institute, we learn that: "Populism is not a coherent transatlantic trend."[48] It is, moreover, underlined that the populism that can be detected is a much more plural movement with local roots.[49] Both in the US and EU it may be anti-establishment and anti-globalization, but the things that really matter are by and large peoples' own national problems. And these differ. So, what this study concludes is that populism needs to be understood in the context of each country. This may sound self-evident but does nevertheless counter those many post-Brexit (and Trump) narratives who foresaw a uniform flood of disenchanted voters overhauling and crushing not only the political establishment but all liberal institutions.

---

[47] http://www.bertelsmann-stiftung.de/en/topics/aktuelle-meldungen/2016/november/brexit-boosts-eu-survey-results/.

[48] https://euobserver.com/opinion/136454.

[49] It is thus telling that in Spain the radical party Podemos's ratings went significantly down after Brexit, while the pro-European Mariano Rajoy gained momentum. At the moment and despite youth unemployment still being too high, the Spanish economy is one of the fastest growing.

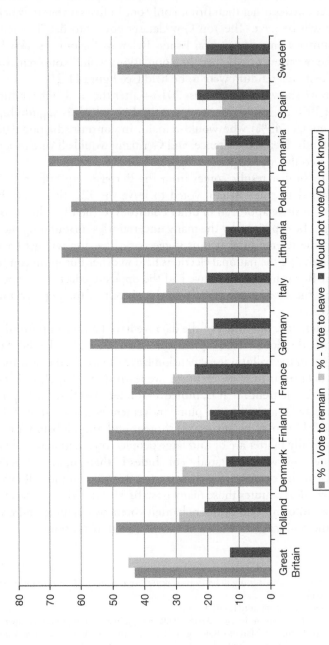

Figure 11.2 Vote in potential EU membership referendum by country

Source: data from YouGov <http://d25d2506sfb94s.cloudfront.net/cumulus_uploads/document/smow6e2p43/MegaEurotrackerResults_AugustSeptember 2016_Toplines.pdf> (last accessed August 19, 2017) © 2016 YouGov plc.

	Netherlands	GB	Germany	France	Italy	DK
Strongly approve or approve	56 %	41 %	59%	54 %	54 %	61 %
Strongly disapprove or disapprove	30 %	46%	26%	34 %	35 %	29 %
Don't know	14 %	14%	15%	12 %	12 %	10%

Figure 11.3 Approval level of EU membership by country

Source: data from YouGov <http://d25d2506sfb94s.cloudfront.net/cumulus_uploads/document/smow6e2p43/MegaEurotracker Results_AugustSeptember2016_Toplines.pdf> (last accessed August 19, 2017) © 2016 YouGov plc.

Let us therefore take a closer look at some of the elections in Europe in 2016–2017—what did they in fact show us?

The first national election, which could have given an indication of whether a general populist trend was emerging and were foreseen with great anxiety by the rest of the EU, was the presidential election in Austria in December 2016. In that election, the choice was between the green candidate Van der Bellen and the right-wing nationalist leader of the Austrian Freedom Party FPO Nobert Hofer. Hofer was at first a highly supported presidential candidate in the 2016 election, receiving 35 percent of the vote in the first round as opposed to only 21 percent of his rival the "Green" Alexander Van der Bellen. In the second round of voting, however, Van der Bellen came out as the winner (49.7:50.3%) but the election was annulled by the Constitutional Court owing to voting irregularities. In the rerun on December 4, 2016 (after Trump had just been elected) Hofer received only 46 percent of the vote and Van der Bellen became president. Had Nobert Hofer won, it would no doubt have shaken the EU and been considered a victory for populism. Nevertheless, Norbert Hofer has recently (Spring 2017) stated that he is now committed to the EU and that he has no intentions of either calling a referendum nor leaving the common currency were he at some point in the future to be elected President or joining government.[50]

The next test of populism and anti-European sentiments was the election in the Netherlands in March 2017. Here, much international media hype predicted a great victory in terms of votes for the anti-immigration and anti-Europe candidate Geert Wilders from the Freedom Party. He promised Dutch voters that they would get an EU referendum concerning their membership if he was voted into government. Prior to the Dutch election, polls indicated

[50] http://www.reuters.com/article/us-austria-politics-fpo-idUSKBN17R232.

that there was a significant chance the Freedom Party could become the largest party in the Dutch Parliament, but as no other party wanted to form a government with Wilders, his possible success in terms of governmental posts was slim and never truly considered among national experts.[51] However, here too the predictions and polls were wrong in foreseeing Wilders' victory. Thus the incumbent, Prime Minister Mark Rutte was re-elected, referring to himself as representing "good populism" as opposed to the "bad" version of Geert Wilders.[52] Much less noted in the international media was the fall of the socialist party in the Netherlands[53] and the concurrent rise of several smaller but very pro-European parties with young party leaders. For instance, Jesse Klaver from the Green Party and D66 both experienced a leap in support for their green and pro-EU agenda. The election winners were also more moderate, e.g. Christian Democratic Appeal (CDA) who acquired nineteen seats (gaining seven). Democrats 66 got nineteen (gaining six), and the Green Links (Klaver's party) landed at fourteen (gaining ten). Both the D66 and GL are not only pro-European but also progressive on social themes.[54]

While many experts had warned against a Wilders victory in the Netherlands an even greater media hype was connected to the second round of the French election on May 7, 2017. This election demonstrated more than any of the others that we may indeed have been dealing—not with a domino—but a reverse-domino effect in Europe after Brexit and Trump. The second round of the French election thus revealed that a large majority chose Europe alongside the young Emmanuel Macron. In the second round, 66 percent voted for Macron against the nationalist and anti-EU candidate Marine Le Pen who gained 34 percent of the vote.[55] Moreover, Macron's march to Europe's anthem on election night in front of the Louvre "said more than words," according to several observers.[56]

Hence the French people ended up neglecting the Front Nationale and Le Pen's promise of an EU referendum and a goodbye to the Eurozone. Instead, they opted for more Europe and enforced cooperation in the Eurozone which are among Macron's big aspirations. The French election was special in the

[51] http://www.telegraph.co.uk/news/2017/03/15/dutch-election-results-geert-wilders-andmark-rutte-vie-power/.

[52] https://www.theguardian.com/world/2017/mar/19/dutch-election-rutte-wilders-good-populism-bad-.

[53] The labour party PvDA was severely defeated as they lost 19.1% of their voters and are now down at 5.7%, losing 29 seats.

[54] https://www.brookings.edu/blog/order-from-chaos/2017/03/20/the-netherlands-complicated-election-result-explained/.

[55] https://www.ft.com/content/62d782d6-31a7-11e7-9555-23ef563ecf9a.

[56] https://www.theguardian.com/commentisfree/2017/may/08/macron-europe-president-nationalism.

sense that Emmanuel Macron gained more support from the other candidates' voters in the second round than Marine Le Pen. It seems as if Le Pen was only able to mobilize some of the right-wing voters from the republican Francois Fillon.[57] One of Le Pen's most unpopular promises was in fact her wanting to ditch the euro and go for an EU referendum. However, Le Pen's own supporters feared for their own, as well as the French economy in case of an exit. Thus, Le Pen voters as well as some of the right and left wing supporters from the established parties may not have endorsed Macron's very pro-EU program but they clearly feared that less than a goodbye to the European Union.[58]

The Austrian, Dutch, and now French election have thus all worked against the theory of a domino effect following from Brexit and Trump—or perhaps even confirmed the anti-domino thesis suggested by *Foreign Affairs*. It is nevertheless interesting to note the great difference in voter turnout in the three elections. Whereas the French at 66.6 percent was the lowest since 1969,[59] the voter turnout in the Dutch election was relatively high.

Moving on from the presidential election to the election of the national assembly in France, this too showed great support for the pro-EU agenda. Emmanuel Macron's centrist party En Marche! won the majority in the parliament with 351 out of 577 seats,[60] giving him the best possibilities to follow through on his plans to reform the EU, and a result that can be seen as a cementation of the public will, which was illustrated in the presidential election. The last major European election that now awaits is the German general election.

The German election in September 2017 is far from as exciting as the previous ones as we here have two very pro-EU establishment candidates competing against each other, current chancellor Angela Merkel and her socialist contender Martin Schulz. Moreover, as Alternative für Deutschland (AfD), once a rising factor in German politics, has gone down at an all-time low of

---

[57] https://www.ft.com/content/62d782d6-31a7-11e7-9555-23ef563ecf9a.

[58] https://www.bertelsmann-stiftung.de/fileadmin/files/user_upload/EZ_eupinions_2017_02_ENG.pdf. This study by the Bertelsmann Stiftung conducted on May 5, 2017 stresses that even the extreme right has a problem with their voters when being too anti-European. Norbert Hofer had exactly the same problem with his voters in the Austrian presidential election, which may be the reason that he has now retreated, being anti-European.

[59] https://www.nytimes.com/interactive/2017/05/07/world/europe/france-election-results-maps.html?_r=0; http://edition.cnn.com/2017/05/08/europe/french-voters-spoiled-ballots-abstained/index.html; http://www.electionguide.org/elections/id/2968/; http://www.politico.eu/article/lesson-from-the-low-country-fear-is-good-netherlands-election-result-mark-rutte-geert-wilders/.

[60] https://www.theguardian.com/world/2017/jun/18/emmanuel-macron-marches-on-majority-french-parliament.

8 percent in the polls this suggests that populism and Brexit certainly will not spread to Germany either. If we look at the elections in several European countries, the cases of Brexit and Trump may thus—quite paradoxically and against the expectations, trigger more—and not less—integration in the future. Without Great Britain as "the awkward partner"[61] and with Macron in the Élysée Palace and Merkel or Schulz in the Kansler Amt in Berlin, Europe may thus experience a new momentum. The chaotic process of leaving the EU that Great Britain is going through at the moment certainly seems only to have strengthened this motion. A large poll by Bertelsmann's Stiftung[62] completed in the six largest Member States (Germany, France, Great Britain, Italy, Spain, and Poland) show that the average support for the EU has gone from 57 percent before the British referendum to 62 percent after the referendum. The polls show that the support has risen in all of the six countries except Spain, where it fell from 71 percent to 69 percent. Hence, the support also rose in Great Britain.

The driving force in the populism narrative that has been dominant throughout the European media is the polarized people. A survey by Bertelsmann Stiftung looks at exactly this phenomenon, finding that one in five French people consider themselves far-right or far-left. However, as the study also concludes, it is nevertheless a big mistake to take the polarized population as per se anti-European. One should thus be careful not always to interpret fear of globalization as implying anti-Europeanism. Many in fact view the EU as the best protection against unconstrained market forces.[63] That being said, the French, with a more pessimistic worldview, were more likely to vote Le Pen.[64] Therefore, the vital battle for the future direction of the EU probably lies in whether or not it can facilitate and help improve the economic situation for that part of the population who feel they have not gained from either European integration in the past ten to fifteen years nor from globalization as such. If jobs are not created, it is certainly possible that the far-right populist narrative may facilitate more anti-EU mobilization in the future.

What concerns many Europeans at the moment is, however, exactly, but perhaps also paradoxically, the rise in (right wing) protest parties. In a future of Europe survey (Eurobarometer), an in-depth study asked the public about

---

[61] S. George, *An Awkward Partner: Britain in the European Community* (Oxford University Press 1998). See also *Eurobarometer* (2016) 83

[62] https://www.bertelsmann-stiftung.de/fileadmin/files/user_upload/EZ_flashlight_europe_02_2016_EN.pdf.

[63] https://www.bertelsmann-stiftung.de/fileadmin/files/user_upload/EZ_eupinions_2017_02_ENG.pdf.

[64] https://www.ft.com/content/62d782d6-31a7-11e7-9555-23ef563ecf9a.

the central concerns facing the EU right now, and how they see the Union in the future.

The survey concluded:[65] "[t]hat the majority of respondents agree the rise of political parties protesting against the traditional political elites in various European countries is a matter of concern (59%), with 21 percent totally agreeing with this statement. Overall, three in ten disagree with this statement (30%), with 9 percent saying they totally disagree. 11 percent do not know" (Eurobarometer, 2016: 83). See figure 11.4.

The chart shows that there is generally great concern about the rise of anti-establishment parties such as AfD, Front Nationale, and Geert Wilders's Freedom Party. Germany scores the highest on the chart when it comes to agreeing that the rise of anti-establishment parties is a matter of concern.

The survey was undertaken soon after the UK voted to leave the EU. Here it was also found that: "The majority of respondents have a positive view of the European Union, and agree it embodies peace, social equality and solidarity, and tolerance and openness to others. Moreover, [...] Most respondents support more European-level decision-making in a range of key policy areas, including fighting terrorism, promoting democracy and peace, protecting the environment and dealing with migration issues. Since 2014, there have been large increases in the proportions who think there should be more EU level decision-making about health and social security issues and migration issues from outside the EU. Although most agree more decision-making should take place at the EU level, respondents' opinions are divided over a "two-speed Europe.". And Finally, a large majority of respondents consider that the European Union project offers a future perspective for Europe's youth."[66]

Just to supplement the study about the anxiety concerning the rise of anti-establishment parties, we have done a study of the number of right-wing parties in selected EU countries. In particular, Hungary and Poland give rise to concern (see figure 11.5).

The graph illustrates the development in right-wing and far-right parties in Denmark, France, the Netherlands, Poland, Germany, and Hungary. In countries where there are more than one right- or far-right party, the vote share is summarized. This is, e.g. the case in Hungary, where there have been four different parties, and where there were two in the latest election in 2014. The development in percentage of votes stems from national election results and in cases where there have been an upper and lower house of Parliament, the result is taken from the lower house. The French regional election from

---

[65] http://ec.europa.eu/COMMFrontOffice/publicopinion/index.cfm/Survey/getSurveyDetail/instruments/SPECIAL/surveyKy/2131.

[66] ibid 137–38.

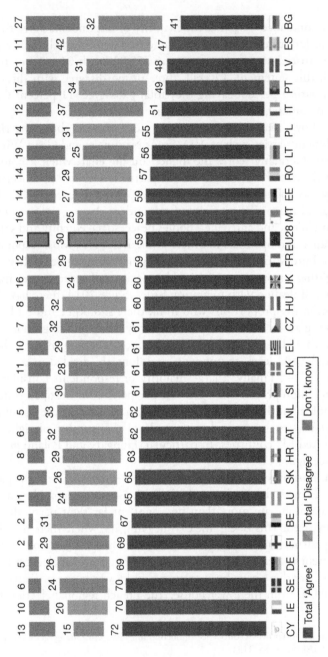

Figure 11.4 Concern on rise of political parties protesting against traditional political elites by country

Source: Special Eurobarometer 451, "Future of Europe" <http://ec.europa.eu/COMMFrontOffice/publicopinion/index.cfm/Survey/getSurveyDetail/instruments/SPECIAL/surveyKy/2131> (last accessed August 19, 2017) © European Union, 2016

2015 is included to show a more up-to-date picture. The vote share of Geert Wilders's Freedom Party from the newly held election is also included.[67]

The data is taken from a *New York Times* article, which made an overview of the European right-wing parties' development using European Election Database, Inter-Parliamentary Union, and electionguide.org.

While the graph above shows that the right-wing parties of Europe have largely upheld the *status quo*, concern for the rise of anti-European right-wing parties has actually increased, which suggests growing popular opposition toward political forces that advocate for populism and their states' withdrawal from the EU.

6. Conclusions

This chapter has examined and discussed whether Brexit will be emulated in other Member States in the near future. The answer to this question has been a solid no: this is not very likely. In fact, to the contrary, several things today suggest that *because* of Brexit and Trump, Europeans are moving closer together, not farther apart. As it is obviously impossible and risky to predict the future, the analysis here has been based on a critical examination of the projections made about populism as a general Western phenomenon fostered by anti-establishment sentiments following on from the Brexit referendum in June 2016 and the election of Trump in November 2016. It was then discussed how the special British relationship to Europe might tell us something about how the UK is different in terms of wanting to risk its access to the world's greatest market in a yes/no referendum. Finally, the chapter investigated the past three national/presidential elections in Europe to try to find evidence of a populist surge among Europeans and in fact found the opposite. This tendency was further confirmed by investigating recent opinion polls and surveys documenting that the rise in right-wing populism in Europe has indeed been decreasing, together with a stabilization in the support for right-wing parties. It was also shown that the largest fear among Europeans today is in fact not globalization or more power to Brussels but almost the contrary: a rise and increasing empowerment of right-wing populism.

The main finding when it comes to the British goodbye to the EU was the country's conception of sovereignty as a zero sum game. The obsession with 'taking back control' and retrieving some kind of formal sovereignty is to a large extent shared with in particular the Scandinavian countries, who also

---

[67] The graph has been updated after the French presidential election.

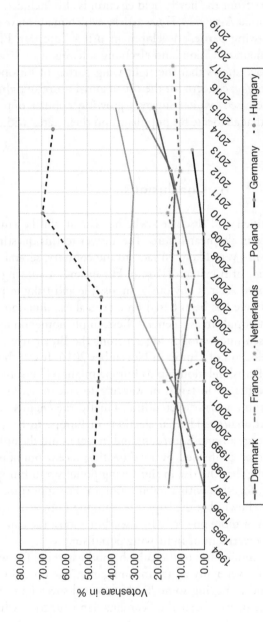

Figure 11.5 Vote share of right and far-right parties by country (for countries with multiple right and far-right parties, the vote share is summarized)*

Source: data from Gregor Aisch, Adam Pearce, and Bryant Rousseau, 'How Far Is Europe Swinging to the Right?' *New York Times* (March 20, 2017) <https://www.nytimes.com/interactive/2016/05/22/world/europe/europe-right-wing-austria-hungary.html?smid=fb-nytimes&smtyp=cur&_r=2> (last accessed August 19, 2017)

* See also European Election Database, Inter-Parliamentary Union, ElectionGuide.

have a majoritarian outlook and view European integration in a very formalist fashion. More Europe is in this light always conflated with less national sovereignty, instead of for instance seeing a stronger EU as a precondition for the ability of individual nations to continue influencing the world. Solving problems jointly with other nations should thus not – as the present author sees it – be equated with a loss of impact on one's own future but as a unique opportunity actually to form one's own destiny by influencing the European rules of the game. Whether other countries will follow in the UK's footsteps is therefore highly unlikely. However, much will probably depend on the deal that the UK manages to negotiate with Brussels. Denmark in particular has previously on many occasions used the UK as a negotiating shield and as a copycat for deals that Denmark wanted to obtain for itself. It is therefore also quite clear that should the British get a deal that—when seen from an equally sovereignty obsessed nation's perspective—is too tempting another referenda on Europe cannot be entirely excluded.

12

Brexit and EU Institutional Balance

How Member States and Institutions Adapt Decision-making

*Uwe Puetter**

1. Introduction

The departure of one of the Union's biggest Member States raises immediate questions about the future relations between smaller and larger Member States, the formation of coalitions, and the consequences for the functioning of individual EU institutions, notably the Council and the European Parliament. The difficulties in determining and adjusting the EU's formula for qualified majority voting, which was subject to several intergovernmental conferences in relation to the EU's own expansion, document this. Next to France, Germany, and Italy, the United Kingdom (UK) is among the EU's four most populated Member States. Under the double-majority rule of the Treaty of Lisbon it carries significant weight, as it did under the previously existing voting rules.[1] The UK is—next to France—the only EU Member State that has a permanent seat in the United Nations Security Council. Together with France, Germany, and Italy, it is a member of the G7 and plays lead roles in international forums such as the International Monetary Fund (IMF), the World Bank, and the G20. Because of its international roles and its military and diplomatic capabilities the UK is together with France and Germany referred to as the 'EU-3' in the domain of the Union's Common Foreign and Security Policy (CFSP). The negotiations about Iran's nuclear programme, which took place under the participation of the EU-3 and the

* The author would like to thank Federico Fabbrini and the participants of the conference 'The Law and Politics of Brexit' (Dublin City University, 20–21 April 2017) for comments and discussion.

[1] See TFEU, Articles 16 and 238, as well as Protocol No 36 on transitional provisions.

Brexit and the EU Institutional Balance: How Member States and Institutions Adapt Decision-Making. First edition. Uwe Puetter © Uwe Puetter 2017. Published 2017 by Oxford University Press.

EU's High Representative are an example for this influential coalition within the domain of CFSP. Another episode, which may illustrate the potential leadership role of the EU-3 as a coalition of the EU's most influential Member States, goes back to the time of the European Convention when the EU's current institutional architecture was significantly shaped. The British Prime Minister Tony Blair, the French President Jacques Chirac and the German Chancellor Gerhard Schröder were seen to have been instrumental in pushing for the office of an elected president of the European Council. This move was associated with an attempt to institutionalize intergovernmentalism and the de facto lead roles of the EU's three biggest Member States.[2] Ultimately, Tony Blair himself was traded as candidate for the new job, which became vacant for the first time in 2009.

The UK is also associated with determining the direction of particular EU policies and institutional choices. Notably, the country has been the prime opponent to the EU's Economic and Monetary Union (EMU) and the euro.[3] Only the granting of a formal opt-out from the final stage of EMU to the UK made progress on the implementation of EMU possible when the Treaty of Maastricht was signed in the early 1990s. Yet, this move triggered a number of institutional arrangements, which involved the establishment of two-tiered decision-making mechanisms.[4] These mechanisms make it possible for euro area Member States to decide without the UK and other Member States that are not part of the euro area. At Maastricht, the UK also blocked efforts to expand EU legislative powers in the field of social policy and again provoked the creation of parallel institutional structures.[5] Although this move was formally corrected by the New Labour government under Tony Blair in the second half of the 1990s and with the Treaty of Amsterdam, the UK remained reluctant to allow substantial progress in the social policy domain.[6]

At the same time, the UK under both Conservative and New Labour governments was seen to be in favour of the single market and a process of continuing liberalization across economic sectors.[7] In alliance with Germany, the Netherlands, the Scandinavian Member States and liberally minded

[2] See Y Devuyst, 'The European Union's Institutional Balance after the Treaty of Lisbon: "Community Method" and "Democratic Deficit" Reassessed' (2008) 39(2) *Georgetown Journal of International Law* 29; J Tallberg, *Leadership and Negotiation in the European Union* (Cambridge University Press 2006) 225; and U Puetter, *The European Council and the Council: New Intergovernmentalism and Institutional Change* (Oxford University Press 2014) 111–12.

[3] See Chapter 8 by Michele Chang in this book.   [4] See section 4.

[5] The relevant social policy provisions were included in the so-called Social Protocol and Social Agreement, which were both annexed to the Maastricht Treaty. They were signed by all Member States except the UK.

[6] See section 5.   [7] See Chapter 10 by Catherine Barnard in this book.

governments in the Czech Republic, Slovakia, and Poland, the UK was considered to have been pivotal in preventing efforts to establish more interventionist single market policies and to curtail competitive dynamics. Finally, various British governments were considered to have been in opposition to the supranational powers of the European Commission and the Court of Justice of the EU. While Margaret Thatcher's hostilities with Jacques Delors and her resistance to the size of financial transfers to the community budget became a synonym for British scepticism towards supranational empowerment, the new engagement with EU policies and politics on part of the Blair government was marked by the creation of alternative and more intergovernmental forms of EU governance, notably the open method of coordination and the Lisbon process.[8]

Brexit thus triggers the question of what may change with the departure of the UK from the Union. Will resistance against supranational empowerment reside? Will coalitions within the Council change? Are there new majorities possible in the Council, which may resolve deadlock with regard to certain policy dossiers such as social affairs? This chapter provides an overview of the respective roles of the EU's main political institutions and decision-making dynamics within them. While an exhaustive review of the consequences for institutional politics in relation to all policy domains is beyond the scope of this chapter, the cases referred to here are intended to help a better assessment of the consequences of Brexit for the EU's institutional balance. The main argument is that while Brexit certainly will trigger new institutional dynamics, its impact on core EU institutions should not be overstated. The main reason for this is that the EU has already witnessed prior to Brexit a prolonged period of growing British disengagement with specific EU policies. Moreover, an informal practice of decision-making without the UK has been established already. Next to Brexit, the Union is undergoing a number of significant challenges. The future of the Eurozone after the crisis and the refugee crises are the most pressing issues. It is telling that in relation to none of these two issues there was prominent involvement of the UK. If there was, then it was negative. The British veto of Treaty changes at the peak of the euro crisis is a case in point.[9]

The chapter is structured as follows. The subsequent section 2 discusses the theoretical background of the following review of the core political institutions of the EU. Sections 3, 4, 5, and 6 review the implications of Brexit in

---

[8] An example is the so-called Cardiff process on economic reform, which was launched under the 1998 British EU presidency and later became a constituent element of the Lisbon process.
[9] See section 4.

relation to the Commission, the European Council, the Council, and the European Parliament respectively. Section 7 concludes by offering a number of broader expectations as regards the consequences of Brexit for further institutional development and the relatives roles of Member States within EU decision-making.

2. Institutional Balance and the Role of Member States

The literature on EU integration in general and theories on institutional dynamics more specifically provide no explicit guidance as to how to estimate the consequences of Brexit for EU inter-institutional relations, the further development of the institutional architecture or the role of individual Member States. Yet, more recent debates about the Union's development in the post-Maastricht period provide important insights into broader trends in institutional development, which need to be considered when assessing the consequences of Brexit. The theory of new intergovernmentalism emphasizes that since Maastricht Member States in general have opted against further supranational empowerment. Yet, governments pursued further integration based on intergovernmental policy coordination in new areas of EU activity such as EMU and CFSP, as well as social and employment policy.[10] Intergovernmental forums for joint decision-making, such as the European Council, the Council, and the Eurogroup, acquired a central role in the policy-making process. Policy coordination and intergovernmental agreement are key methods of governance. In this set-up consensus has become the guiding norm of decision-making, as sanctioning mechanisms in cases of non-compliance are lacking. Given the significant expansion of the scope of EU policy-making since Maastricht, the Commission has benefited comparatively less than the EU's most prominent intergovernmental forums. It is within these forums where ultimate decision-making powers within the above quoted policy domains are concentrated. Even the expansion of the Commission's surveillance powers under the most recent institutional reforms within the context of the euro crisis do not correct the apparent loss in the body's political standing.[11] Moreover, new intergovernmentalism sees the EU

[10] Cf C J Bickerton, D Hodson, and U Puetter, 'The New Intergovernmentalism: European Integration in the Post-Maastricht Era' (2015) 53(4) *Journal of Common Market Studies* 703.
[11] Cf M W Bauer and S Becker, 'The Unexpected Winner of the Crisis: The European Commission's Strenghtened Role in Economic Governance' (2014) 36(3) *Journal of European Integration* 217; and E da Conceição-Heldt, 'Why the European Commission Is Not the "Unexpected Winner" of the Euro Crisis: A Comment on Bauer and Becker' (2016) 38(1) *Journal of European Integration* 1.

in a state of disequilibrium. There are tensions surrounding the Union's mode of integration, which are difficult to dissolve. While national governments insist on exercising tight control over the integration process, they themselves undermine the legitimacy of supranational authority where it already exists. While national governments nonetheless pursue further integration, they remain reluctant to formally concede further ultimate decision-making competences to the EU level.

There are a number of take-aways from new intergovernmentalism as a theoretical perspective that structure the discussion of the consequences of Brexit in this chapter. First, although the UK acted as the prime opponent of EMU at Maastricht, it was by far not the only proponent of what is referred to here as the new post-Maastricht intergovernmentalism. Quite to the contrary, intergovernmental policy coordination became an important method of integration in prominent new areas of EU activity. Economic governance under EMU and CFSP are the leading examples. The stance of the Commission has been a difficult one in the post-Maastricht EU until today. Despite Thatcher's prominent spats with Jacques Delors, British prime ministers were by far not the only ones who sought to curtail the Commission's traditional role as a policy initiator. Rather, Tony Blair was seen to be in ensemble action with Gerhard Schröder and Jacques Chirac—as much as their successors were—to establish political leadership at the level of the European Council. Secondly, new intergovernmentalism shows that collective decision-making among Member States is not only about the relative influence of smaller and bigger Member States but also about the mode of decision-making as such. Consensus politics are deeply enshrined as a method of decision-making in the EU's key forums for intergovernmental decision-making.[12] Thirdly, it is a key assumption of the new intergovernmentalism that those who are involved in consensus politics are committed to integration more generally and the development of individual policy areas more specifically. As the UK moved further and further away from this commitment in the more recent past, the readiness of the European Council to take decisions without the British prime minister increased.[13] This general willingness was first revealed with the creation of the informal Eurogroup as early as in the late 1990s.[14]

Finally, the new intergovernmentalism's claim that the EU is in disequilibrium implies that expectations that the departure of the UK would free the Union from its major institutional dilemmas are unfounded. What is important here is that the notion of disequilibrium advanced by new

---

[12] See Puetter, *The European Council and the Council* (n 3). [13] See section 4.
[14] See section 5.

intergovernmentalism is broader than the idea that there may be an imbalance of influence with regard to the respective roles of individual Member States in EU decision-making. This is not say that Franco-German dominance cannot constitute a serious problem for the EU and notably its smaller Member States. Yet, also the reverse may the case. In the latter scenario, however, the duo is more positively referred to as an 'engine'. Rather the notion of disequilibrium refers to a state of integration in which by and large all Member States—large and small ones—cannot escape a paradoxical attitude towards integration, namely that they seek closer integration without supranational empowerment.

3. The European Commission

While the Commission generally found it difficult to defend its central role in EU politics in the post-Maastricht period, notably with regard to the new areas of EU activity, it was the predominant player in one of the biggest EU projects during the same period—the substantive enlargement of the EU. In 1995, 2004, 2007, and 2013, the Union expanded from twelve to twenty-eight Member States. In particular, the EU's 2004 and 2007 enlargements were accompanied by a prolonged period of political reform and legislative change in the new Member States of Central and Eastern Europe. The Commission was the main interlocutor for national governments and the guardian of EU conditionality. With the prospects for further EU expansion being slim after the accession of Croatia in 2013, the role of the Commission as the central enforcing agent of the EU's *acquis* in relation to new members was diminished.

Somewhat ironically, the Brexit negotiation process and the establishment of future relations between the EU and the UK are likely to lead to a temporal (re-)empowerment of the Commission in a domain within which it had established profound political leadership throughout the 1990s and the first decade of the new millennium. The Commission received a political mandate from the European Council to act as the EU negotiator in the Brexit process.[15] This mandate is underpinned by a Council decision and more specific Council directives, which provide further guidance on specific negotiation subjects and which are issued following a recommendation

---

[15] See European Council, *Guidelines for Brexit Negotiations (Article 50)* (29 April 2017) http://www.consilium.europa.eu/en/meetings/european-council/2017/04/29-euco-guidelines_pdf/ (last accessed 11 May 2017).

from the Council.[16] The Commission's leading role is further underpinned by the choice of its chief negotiator, the former French commissioner Michel Barnier. Barnier heads up the Commission's so-called Article 50 Task Force and works directly with Commission President Jean-Claude Juncker.

The Commission possesses important competences and administrative resources, which make it a crucial actor in the Brexit process. Those domains of EU activity in which the Commission enjoys its greatest range of decision-making competences are at the heart of the Brexit process. Within the new areas of EU activity, in which intergovernmental policy coordination prevails as the main governance mechanism, divorce is relatively easy in organizational terms. The UK is already an outsider to the single currency and a partial outsider to the Area of Freedom, Security, and Justice. The departure from the CFSP will instead not remain without consequences for both parties. Notably, it implies a number of challenges as regards the development of future cooperation between the EU and the UK. Yet, these issues are less complex and do not necessarily require immediate solutions. In fact, the scenario of the UK's departure from CFSP is more comparable to previous case of coordination failure and lacking collective action.

Instead, the centrality of the Commission in the Brexit process is derived from the importance of the most central domain of supranational integration for the UK's ties with the Union: the single market and the so-called four freedoms. There is nonetheless an important caveat to the Commission's central role in the Brexit process. While it remains the only actor who has the knowledge and bureaucratic resources to represent the Union on the full spectrum of single market issues, it lacks the capacity to make ultimate decisions as regards the distribution of costs and benefits that are associated with Brexit for both parties. In short, overall political guidance on the EU's position in Brexit negotiations, its readiness to compromise or to resist cannot be delivered by the Commission.

This is also reflected in the organizational set-up of the Brexit negotiations. Next to the political and formal negotiation mandates, which the Commission obtained and will continue to obtain from the European Council and the Council, the process is overseen and co-managed by a special Task Force on the UK, which is located at the General Secretariat of the Council and mirrors the Article 50 Task Force of the Commission. The Task Force's director Didier Seeuws was appointed by European Council President Donald Tusk. Seeuws previously served as the head of cabinet of former European

---

[16] TFEU, Article 50 requires that the negotiation process is conducted in accordance with TFEU, Article 218(3), which gives the Council the right to appoint an EU negotiator.

Council President Herman van Rompuy and as a director in the General Secretariat of the Council. Seeuws acts as the right hand of European Council President Donald Tusk and coordinates Member States' positions within the Council. He is the key interlocutor for the Commission's chief negotiator Michel Barnier. The set-up shows that Brexit is not without political risks for the Commission. It either closely aligns itself with the European Council on this matter and pre-coordinates its policy decisions or risks being even more tightly controlled.

Brexit may lead to a limited although more lasting political (re-)empower-ment of the Commission when it comes to the relations with the EU's imme-diate neighbourhood after prospects for further EU enlargement declined substantially. In particular issues of common trade and the mobility of citi-zens will be important to EU-UK relations. Again, it is unlikely that the Commission will solely determine the evolving future relationship with the UK, yet in tandem with the European Council and the Council it will be able to mobilize its political and administrative resources and will act as an interlocutor.

4. The European Council and the Heads

The European Council's central role in EU policy-making is reaffirmed with Brexit—both in terms of the actual process of negotiating the exit of the UK and the long-term future role of the institution. As in the case of the Commission, the general role of the European Council in contemporary EU politics has been significantly shaped by the broader institutional dynamics of the post-Maastricht period of EU integration. The event of Brexit has not changed these fundamentals. Moreover, the European Council has already pre-empted Brexit in several ways that allow the detection of some conse-quences at an early stage in the separation process.

Developments in two key policy areas of EU integration in which the European Council is important for regular decision-making illustrate this particularly well: economic governance under EMU and the CFSP. The New Labour governments, especially under Tony Blair, sought to compensate for the lack of British membership in the Eurozone through engagement within the European Council on EU-wide economic policy coordination, includ-ing structural reforms, and the CFSP, including British-Franco cooperation on defence matters. Yet, later on the UK kept a much lower profile on these matters. The role of David Cameron within the European Council first became overshadowed by the euro crisis and later by his increasing focus on renegotiating aspects of the UK's EU membership. Both developments prevented him from playing a central role in the European Council. Instead, the Franco-German tandem represented by Merkel and Nicolas Sarkozy, as well as Merkel and François Hollande gained ever greater prominence within the European Council. Franco-German leadership in the European Council during the euro crisis was, for example, documented by the practice that Hollande and Merkel had restricted meetings with Greek Syriza Prime Minister Alexis Tsipras at the fringes of European Council meetings in order to secure agreements or to address particularly contested matters. Even though the European Council president was present at these meetings, this practice can be seen as indicative of the relative influence of these two heads.

However, the euro crisis not only consolidated Franco-German leadership but also the lead role of Eurozone countries in setting the pace and direction of integration more generally. With the economic crisis turning into an outright sovereign debt and euro crisis, the eagerness of Eurozone countries in general to move ahead unilaterally with financial assistance and institutional reforms increased.[17] First in the context of informal meetings and then under the label 'Euro Summit', the first full-time president of the European Council Herman van Rompuy convened a series of meetings for the heads of the euro area only. Moreover, the process of institutional reform received broader political support within the European Council. British Prime Minister Cameron found himself isolated when he vetoed Treaty change within the European Council in December 2011.[18] The other twenty-six heads moved immediately to circumvent Cameron's veto and instead brought forward an agreement outside the EU Treaties. The Treaty on Stability, Coordination and Governance in EMU—also known as the Fiscal Treaty—was signed in March 2012 in a ceremony presided over by European Council president Herman van Rompuy.

In a similar vein, the European Council's reactions to the confrontation between Russia and Ukraine and the annexation of Crimea played out. The beginning of this crisis coincided with Cameron's increasing focus on a Brexit referendum in the UK. Following the June 2014 European Parliament elections, and in connection with the appointment of the new Commission, Cameron documented his departure from the core European Council consensus by remaining next to Hungary's Viktor Orbán the only head of government not endorsing the new Commission president Juncker. Instead of

---

[17] Cf D Hodson and U Puetter, 'The Euro Crisis and European Integration' in M Cini and N Pérez-Solórzano Borragán (eds), *European Union Politics* (Oxford University Press 2016).

[18] Cf 'David Cameron blocks EU treaty with veto, casting Britain adrift in Europe' *The Guardian* (9 December 2011) https://www.theguardian.com/world/2011/dec/09/david-cameron-blocks-eu-treaty (last accessed 11 May 2017).

playing a key role in the process as one of the potential EU lead actors in CFSP, Cameron was almost absent from the diplomatic scene. Stripped of more decisive British domestic political backing the EU's outgoing High Representative and Labour appointee Catherine Ashton kept a low profile too. Instead, Merkel and Hollande acted as the EU's de facto representatives. They established the so-called Normandy Quartet in June 2014 for dialogue between and with Russia and Ukraine. Hollande and Merkel also negotiated the so-called Minsk Agreement in February 2015 with the presidents of Russia and Ukraine. In March 2016 Angela Merkel and Dutch Prime Minister Mark Rutte, who represented the rotating presidency of the Council of the EU allegedly pre-negotiated the EU-Turkey refugee deal ahead of the actual EU-Turkey summit on the next day.[19] Again, one of the EU's greatest policy challenges in its more recent past was addressed without any significant leadership on the part of the British prime minister as a member of the European Council.

The European Council ultimately went into Brexit mode when its second full-time president Donald Tusk—who had taken office in December 2014—was brokering a coordinated response by the other twenty-seven Member States to Cameron's requests to provide an offer to the British electorate regarding the conditions of British EU membership. The episode can be seen as a test run for what became a new informal routine format of the European Council since Theresa May took office as British prime minister after the Brexit referendum in July 2016: meetings without the British prime minister. With Brexit the European Council and its president assume a central role. The process is far from technical but involves important political decisions about potential costs and compromises. The Commission alone is not able to deliver these decisions despite its crucial role in the actual negotiations. Not coincidentally, European Council president Donald Tusk publicly called for moderation and goodwill when the rhetoric between Juncker and May had become tense following a dinner meeting in May 2017.[20]

The political oversight role of the European Council was formally documented by the Special European Council meeting on 29 April 2017. Article 50 of the TFEU empowers the European Council to issue guidelines on negotiating an agreement with the country leaving the Union.[21] The European

---

[19] 'Merkel machte Türkei konkrete Zusagen bei Flüchtlingszahl' *Die Welt* (13 March 2016) https://www.welt.de/politik/deutschland/article162778752/Merkel-machte-Tuerkei-konkrete-Zusage-bei-Fluechtlingszahl.html (last accessed 11 May 2017).

[20] 'EU's Tusk says Brexit talks will be "impossible" if emotions unchecked' *Reuters* (4 May 2017) http://www.reuters.com/article/us-britain-eu-tusk-idUSKBN18020F?il=0 (last accessed 11 May 2017).

[21] See Chapter 3 by Paul Craig in this book.

Council guidelines notably included the verdict 'that the four freedoms of the Single Market are indivisible and that there can be no "cherry picking" '.[22] Next to this, the unity of the remaining Member States is asserted. Both affirmations are indicative of the trade-offs the Union is facing. As in previous instances of decision-making that had major repercussions for the future of the Union, the European Council is the only institution which can engineer a consensus among the Member States and align the Commission with them. Notions that the future relations with UK should be close and that at the same time a price should be paid for leaving the Union are not trivial but require a concrete agreement by the Member States' heads of state or government.

While the Commission's role may be crucial for negotiating future trade relationships with the EU, such negotiations remain likely to be overseen if not directly mandated by the European Council. The question of the UK's relationship with the Union will continue to be an issue of existential importance for the latter. The European Council will play a central role regarding these issues for the reasons stated above . Brexit will certainly revive debates about differentiated integration.[23] With the UK leaving the Union, an important veto player will be removed from the European Council. In particular, Member States outside the euro area will find it difficult to resist the tendency that the euro area will determine the overall direction and scope of EU integration. Yet, this is not entirely new. The euro crisis had already revealed that at moments when decision-making pressure is particularly strong a coalition of the willing, which is constituted by the euro area members and those Member States who are generally affirmative of stronger economic policy coordination, will move ahead, even if this requires leaving a Member State behind and circumventing potential constitutional obstacles, as was the case with the Fiscal Treaty.

5. The Council

Similar to the Commission and the European Council the direct impact of Brexit on the functioning of the Council has to be assessed against broader institutional dynamics during the post-Maastricht period. Moreover, the effects of Brexit in several ways precede the actual departure of the UK from the Union. For example, the calendar of the rotating presidency of the Council

---

[22] European Council, *Guidelines for Brexit Negotiations (Article 50)* (n 15).
[23] See Chapter 13 by Fédérico Fabbrini in this book.

has already been adjusted by removing the UK as the holder of the second semester of the 2017 Council presidency. The Council is a diverse setting as it operates in different ministerial configurations. Each configuration deals with a particular policy portfolio or a set of grouped portfolios. The impact of Brexit thus will vary across Council formations. Even though according to the formal rules of Council decision-making the qualified majority voting procedure would make the formation of blocking coalitions possible, it is impossible to associate the UK with such behaviour. Except for the more recent controversies about Brexit, British representatives by and large subscribed to the consensus politics approach that applies in Council decision-making more generally.[24]

Where British ministers cast a negative vote, it was to express opposition publicly. Yet, these votes did not derail individual Council decisions.[25] This is not to say that British opposition did not slow down progress within some legislative portfolios. The country has been associated with pro-market positions under different governments. It has been reluctant to embrace developments on many aspects of justice and home affairs issues and it has been in more or less radical opposition to new social policy legislation.[26] In short, after Brexit individual legislative issues may move forward more easily or may move into a different direction. Yet, as the UK has not been in a stable coalition with other countries across policy areas, the impact of Brexit on the functioning of the Council thus varies.

Three examples may illustrate that some variation across policy areas and thus different Council formations should be expected. The first case refers to the Economic and Financial Affairs (ECOFIN) Council, which was the first, and until the event of Brexit, the only Council formation which moved to exclude the UK from decision-making. As early as 1998 when the transition of the first Member States to the single currency became imminent, the finance ministers of the new Eurozone created their own informal meeting format with the explicit aim to exclude the British not only from voting but also from ministerial deliberations altogether.[27] Ever since then the so-called Eurogroup has been at the centre of Eurozone economic governance. It is one

---

[24] Cf J Lewis, 'The European Council and the Council of the European Union' in M Cini and N Pérez-Solórzano Borragán (eds), *European Union Politics* (5th edn.Oxford University Press 2015) 148–50.

[25] Cf the VoteWatch Europe database for detailed information on British voting behaviour in the Council http://www.votewatch.eu/en/term8-council-votes-term8-united-kingdom.html (last accessed 11 May 2017).

[26] See Chapter 9 by Deirdre Curtin in this book.

[27] Cf U Puetter, *The Eurogroup: How a Secretive Circle of Finance Ministers Shape European Economic Governance* (Manchester University Press 2006).

of the most frequently convened and most influential ministerial groupings in EU governance. It received formal recognition through the Lisbon Treaty and the institutional reforms that were adopted in the context of the euro crisis.[28] The Eurogroup's centrality mitigates the impact of Brexit on euro area economic governance. Yet, the leading role of the Eurogroup itself is not going to change with Brexit for the foreseeable future. Future Eurozone reforms are rather likely to lead to its further empowerment. As long as there is a sizeable number of Member States that remain outside the Eurozone, the EU will have a two-tier EU system for decision-making on economic governance issues.

What is more important, therefore, is the role of the full ECOFIN Council in matters of general EU economic governance and the coordination of joint EU positions in international forums for financial and economic governance, notably the G20, the IMF, and the G7. With regard to general EU economic governance the euro crisis already did its part to shift the political focus on those countries which are within the euro area. Nevertheless, the so-called European Semester process extends to all EU Member States. As mentioned earlier the launch of the Lisbon process, as its predecessor, was accompanied by British engagement with the EU-wide economic policy coordination agenda. The then British finance minister Gordon Brown was a key actor within the ECOFIN Council at that time. Yet, this period of British engagement is long gone. What is practically more relevant during the Brexit period and thereafter is the departure of Britain from EU-wide coordination on global economic and financial matters. While with regard to other policy issues British engagement has been in steady decline, there is evidence that ECOFIN Council coordination during the euro crisis with regard to this portfolio included Britain.[29]

The solution for a future format or practice of British-EU coordination formally does not have to be resolved in the context of the Brexit negotiations. It could be pragmatically implemented at any point in time. The professional and informal contacts between Member States' finance ministries and the British Treasury are likely to remain close. As with finance ministers from other countries or representatives of the IMF, the ECOFIN Council could invite the British finance minister to attend specific parts of ECOFIN Council meetings as a guest. Moreover, the president of the Eurogroup may act as an interlocutor with the UK.

---

[28] See TFEU, Protocol No 14 on the Euro Group.
[29] Cf D Hodson, *Governing the Euro Area in Good Times and Bad* (Oxford University Press 2011).

The second example, which can help to assess the consequences of Brexit for the operation of the Council, is the Foreign Affairs Council. This Council formation assembles the foreign ministers of the Member States and is in charge of the Union's CFSP and external relations more generally. It is chaired by the EU's High Representative. Next to the Eurogroup and the ECOFIN Council it is among the most frequently convened Council formations. The High Representative also convenes meetings of the Foreign Affairs Council on defence and trade, which are respectively attended by Member States' ministers of defence and trade. As highlighted in the beginning of this chapter the domains of foreign affairs, security, and defence policy but also trade constitute domains of British engagement under the New Labour cabinets of Tony Blair and Gordon Brown. The Union's first High Representative who was to act in double capacity as chair of the Foreign Affairs Council and Vice-President of the Commission was Labour appointee Catherine Ashton. She held the post from 2009 until 2014. The EU's trade portfolio within the Commission was prominently headed by Peter Mandelson from 2004 until 2008, who was one of the pro-EU architects of New Labour. The personnel politics within the EU's external affairs domain reveal the British ambition under the New Labour governments to compensate for the UK's absence from the single currency through playing a lead role in EU external affairs. This ambition also reflected the UK's resources in diplomacy, defence, and global trade and development policies. The EU thus loses an important Member State which provided key resources to the decentralized CFSP and the EU's defence policy framework as well to the EU's development policy.

Quite directly, the European External Action Service (EEAS), which operates under the supervision of the High Representative and the Foreign Affairs Council will lose important resources. Yet, it is also true that the UK has been a reluctant supporter of independent EEAS resources, which it feared would give ground to supranationalization dynamics. Similarly, the UK was reluctant to support greater independence of the EU's defence policy coordination outside the NATO framework. Yet, British military resources were, next to those of France and Germany, central to the EU's general capacity to deliver collective military action. At a political level, the central role of the UK was reflected in the role of the above mentioned EU-3 coalition. Informal pre-coordination among Britain, France, and Germany was a key feature of internal Foreign Affairs Council dynamics and was reflected in the operation of the EU's Political and Security Committee, the standing preparatory arm of the Foreign Affairs Council.

The departure of the UK from the Union thus will undoubtedly be felt within the external affairs domain of Council activity. As outlined above in relation to the European Council, high-level Franco-German coordination activities may be indicative of the duo playing a similar dominating role just without Britain in the external affairs domain. Certainly, British engagement in this domain has been gradually declining for years now. Yet, it is not clear whether other groupings, which are similar to the EU-3, will emerge. The appointment of the former Italian foreign minister Federica Mogherini as the new High Representative and Vice-President of the Commission and thus chair of the Foreign Affairs Council in 2014 certainly documented the ambition of other larger Member States to play a key role in the external affairs domain. Poland has made repeated attempts to play a more important role in CFSP. It has engaged in trilateral consultations with France and Germany in the context of the so-called Weimar Triangle. Yet, despite Poland's embracement of EU action against Russia and the EU's defence policy ambitions, these efforts have been hampered by the outlier position the governing Polish PiS party government maintains in EU politics. Progress on defence policy coordination and coordinated procurement, which appears to have accelerated with Britain retreating from direct engagement with this policy portfolio during the transition period, however, may also help pluralism.

The third and final example is the social and employment policy portfolio of the Employment, Social Policy, Health, and Consumer Affairs Council (EPSCO). This Council formation meets in different compositions depending on the policy portfolio that is to be discussed. The Council formation was the scene of numerous controversies. As highlighted at the beginning of this chapter the UK had fiercely opposed new legislative competences within the social policy domain at Maastricht. The Social Protocol and the Social Agreement indeed allowed the other Member States to agree on new legislation even though innovation remained limited to a short period immediately after the adoption of the Maastricht Treaty. A good example is the EU working time directive.[30] It was first adopted in 1993 and was intended to prevent downward competition between Member States within the single market. With the New Labour government of Tony Blair coming to power, Britain joined the full social policy acquis again and transposed the working time directive in 1998. However, the Blair government used exceptions, which were foreseen within the directive, to the full extent. For Britain, the directive regulated several aspects of the labour market which so far had not been subject to regulation at all. Negotiations within the EPSCO Council about a reformed directive, which reflected the results of various

---

[30] Council Directive (EC) 104/93 concerning certain aspects of the organization of working time [1993] OJ L 307/18.

judicial and political controversies, were divisive and lengthy.[31] It was only in November 2003 that, jointly with the European Parliament, a new directive was adopted.[32]

Even though the UK had rejoined the full EU social policy *acquis*, it was traded as a reluctant partner against whom socially minded Member States had to organize majorities within the EPSCO Council. Overall progress on EU social policy legislation has been sluggish throughout the 2000s. The UK is an important although not the only factor in this. The general reluctance to create new regulatory powers at the EU-level within this policy field is another important aspect and so is the EU's expansion, which has increased gaps between different degrees and models of social protection. Under the Juncker Commission, the EPSCO Council has lost its legislative role altogether because of a total lack of legislative initiatives.[33] This in itself makes the role of the UK much less relevant than was the case in the past. Instead, the EPSCO Council has sought to re-establish itself through closer engagement in European Semester policy coordination. Again, this shift in focus comes at a time when the days of stronger British engagement with EU-wide socio-economic policy coordination are long over. If the EU manages to return to renewing and potentially expanding the legislative social policy *acquis* in response to its ongoing legitimacy challenges, then it will not be because of Brexit but because a large majority of other EU Member States managing to forge a new political consensus on the EU's role in this policy domain. Such a scenario is currently not in sight.

6. The European Parliament

The European Parliament has been the scene of some of the hardest Brexit rhetoric over the past years. British euro-scepticism has in many ways shaped European Parliament politics during recent electoral terms. The leader of the UK Independence Party (UKIP) Nigel Farage used the

---

[31] See on the importance of and controversies around the working time directive R Geyer, A Mackintosh, and K Lehmann, *Integrating UK and European Social Policy: The Complexity of Europeanisation* (Radcliffe 2005) 130–3 and J Shaw, J Hunt, and C Wallace, *Economic and Social Law of the European Union* (Palgrave Macmillan 2007) 408–409.

[32] Council Directive (EC) 88/2003 concerning certain aspects of the organization of working time [2003] OJ L 299/9.

[33] Cf A Maricut and U Puetter, 'Deciding on the European Semester: The European Council, the Council and the Enduring Asymmetry between Economic and Social Policy Issues' (2017) *Journal of European Public Policy*, forthcoming.

European Parliament as a stage for his attacks on the EU. UKIP's growing electoral successes in European Parliament elections since the end of the 1990s impacted on the development of euro-sceptic party groupings within the parliament. In the current European Parliament UKIP, as one of the largest national euro-sceptic delegations, forms a larger euro-sceptic grouping with Italy's Movimento 5 Stelle (the Five Star Movement), called Europe of Freedom and Direct Democracy. This grouping is separate from the Europe of Nations and Freedom political group, which is the other major euro-sceptic and far-right grouping and which includes the French Front National and the Dutch PVV.

Moreover, the British Conservative Party played a major role in opening up possibilities for group building of like-minded political forces that are decisively euro-sceptic, even though not as extreme as the previously mentioned party groupings. In a sign of opposition to the mainstream centre-right pro-EU integration stance of the European Peoples Party (EPP), British Prime Minister David Cameron withdrew his MEPs from the European Parliament's largest political group in 2009. Together with the then governing Czech Civic Democratic Party and the Polish Law and Justice Party (PiS), Cameron established a separate pan-European political platform for reforming the EU and for preventing federalization. Their European Parliament political group, the European Conservatives and Reformist Group (ECR), is currently the third largest political group within the European Parliament and also includes decidedly anti-EU parties such as the Danish People's Party and the Finns Party. However, the British Conservatives and Poland's governing PiS are the only sizeable national delegations within the ECR, which assembles numerous individual MEPs from various different national parties.

Brexit, thus will have a considerable impact on the organization of euro-sceptic and right-wing parties in the next European Parliament. Moreover, Brexit may also have implications for the EU's mainstream pro-integration groups. The Group of the Progressive Alliance of Socialists and Democrats (S&D), the mainstream social-democratic political group, will lose their twenty Labour Party MEPs. This is particularly important as the S&D's main rival, the EPP group, will not lose individual members because of Brexit. This loss was pre-empted with the above outlined departure by British Conservative MEPs in 2009. Provided that other factors influencing the relative group size of EPP and S&D remain similar in the next European parliamentary elections, Brexit is likely to expand the EPP's lead as the largest political group within the European Parliament over the S&D to a comfortable margin. This prospect could, for example, make it more likely that the EPP group expels the Hungarian Fidesz, which repeatedly caused deep controversies within the

EPP group, yet represents an important national delegation of thirteen MEPs in the current pre-Brexit European Parliament.[34]

With regard to the overall role of the European Parliament in EU politics the impact of Brexit will be limited. Even though the parliament was under particular attack as a supranational institution the key factors determining the European Parliament's future role are not chiefly determined by British EU membership. The European Parliament's major institutional dilemma is not resolved by Brexit, even though the UK is a heartland of euro-scepticism. This dilemma is that the European Parliament, on the one hand, received ever greater decision-making power in the traditional domains of EU legislative governance and yet, on the other hand, still lacks the degree of legitimacy and recognition among EU citizens that would be necessary to push up the EU's overall approval ratings. Brexit may make general institutional reform easier, yet neither has the UK been the only obstacle to Treaty changes, nor is it certain that the cure of the EU's legitimacy problems can be found in Treaty change. The public rhetoric used by Member State governments in relation to EU decision-making may be a much more decisive factor in this regard. A small and indirect relief for the European Parliament could be that Brexit renders ideas about a separate parliament for the Eurozone less compelling and thus increases the chances for an enhancement of European Parliament oversight powers in this domain.

7. Conclusions

Brexit raises immediate questions for the functioning of the EU's core political institutions as well as for the relationship between individual Member States within EU decision-making and their relative influence. A key observation that informs the review of all institutions within this chapter, except for the European Parliament, is that a number of consequences of Brexit have already emerged prior to the actual event of the formal departure from the Union. It is not only after the formal exit that core institutional dynamics will change. Most importantly, the continuous and, indeed, growing disengagement with EU politics and policy-making on the part of the UK has been detectable in a number of policy areas. Moreover, many key institutional developments of the more recent past have been informed by broader post-Maastricht trends of institutional development and are not a direct consequence of Brexit. The

[34] See on EPP and Fidesz relations R D Kelemen, 'Europe's Other Democratic Deficit: National Authoritarianism in Europe's Democratic Union' (2017) 52(2) *Government and Opposition* 211.

preference for intergovernmental policy coordination and the empowerment of the European Council are important examples in this regard.

With the UK leaving the EU, there is undoubtedly the question of how this may affect the role of other larger Member States in decision-making. There is little doubt that France and Germany played key roles in more recent EU development and external relations. Notably, their leaders who are members of the European Council have been at the forefront of policy action and acted as quasi external representatives of the Union on several occasions. What is important here is that this dominant role of the Franco-German couple, and in addition of German Chancellor Merkel individually, occurred well before Brexit. Such lead roles are also consistent with earlier periods in which there was British disengagement with certain EU policies and/or massive opposition from London. The only major exception in this regard is British engagement with EU-wide economic policy coordination and in particular the Union's CFSP under Tony Blair. There is little doubt that a large Member State like the UK had the potential to act as a counterbalance to the Franco-German couple and, indeed, also as a third member of this leadership group, as the history of CFSP shows.

As regards the future development of the EU, it is less clear whether the British role as a member of the EU-3 is going to be directly replaced by one or several of the other larger Member States. This is also far from certain, because none of them commands resources which are similar to those of the UK. This does not necessarily mean Franco-German dominance. The UK's departure also gives potentially more room for plurality. Italy clearly seeks to play a key role in external affairs as the EU's southern border is key to contemporary policy challenges. Poland plays a similar role with regard to Eastern Europe. In both cases, domestic politics will also determine how successful these Member States are in playing leading roles in the EU's broadening external affairs portfolio. Countries such as Spain matter in this regard too. Spanish finance minister Luis de Guindos, for example, has been repeatedly touted as a candidate for the Eurogroup presidency in recent years. The backing from his government underlined the Spanish ambition to play a key role in Eurozone politics. Moreover, some of the smaller EU Member States will miss Britain as a coalition partner in some areas when it comes to offsetting Franco-German influence but with Britain having already played a less central role in recent years, this development does not come with the event of Brexit alone.

13

Brexit and EU Treaty Reform

A Window of Opportunity for Constitutional Change?

Federico Fabbrini

1. Introduction

The decision by the United Kingdom (UK) to leave the European Union (EU) represents a profound shock for the project of European integration. Since its creation with the Treaty of Paris of 1951 and the Treaties of Rome in 1957, the EU has been inspired by the idea that Member States committed to a process of "ever closer Union."[1] Historical developments seemed to vindicate that view: in sixty years, EU membership had widened from six to twenty-eight Member States, and EU competences have deepened, increasingly absorbing hallmarks of state sovereignty. The EU gradually tied Member States and their citizens closer together and succeeded in transforming a continent of warring states into a *Rechstgemeinschaft*. Scholars conceptualized this state of affairs by describing the EU as a project of integration through law.[2] Although integration has over time increasingly accommodated differentiation among Member States, the idea that all countries of the EU proceeded in the same direction has remained a defining assumption in the EU. Brexit shattered all that: the UK's departure from the EU has revealed the deep flaws that cut through the EU constitutional fabric, and challenged consolidated understandings on the *finalité* of the European project.

Nevertheless, the decision by the UK to leave the EU may also represent a timely window of opportunity for the EU to seriously re-think its foundations. Even the most ardent pro-European would not deny that, today, the state of the EU is not strong. During the last decade, the EU has been

---

[1] TEU, Preamble.
[2] See Mauro Cappelletti et al. (eds.), *Integration Through Law*, Vol. 1 (de Gruyter 1986).

Brexit and EU Treaty Reform: A Window of Opportunity for Constitutional Change. First edition. Federico Fabbrini © Federico Fabbrini 2017. Published 2017 by Oxford University Press.

bumping from a crisis to the next—at the very risk of its own survival. While since 2009 the euro-crisis has challenged the stability of Europe's Economic and Monetary Union (EMU), the migration-crisis has put under pressure the Schengen internal border-free zone, and additional challenges, from internal security to external defense, trade, and the changing transatlantic relations have strained the EU on other fronts too. These challenges have dramatically exposed the limits of the current EU constitutional set-up. In fact, in recent years top policy-makers at national and EU level have increasingly called for reforming the EU powers and institutional architecture, with the aim of strengthening the Union and relaunching the integration project. By catalyzing the centrifugal dynamics at play in the EU, Brexit represents a dramatic wake-up call, but simultaneously a welcome chance to restructure the EU legal and institutional foundations.

The core argument of this chapter is that the decision of the UK to withdraw from the EU increases the urge—and at the same time creates the possibility—to improve the constitutional architecture of the EU. Brexit, in fact, compels the EU and its (remaining) Member States to engage in some significant legal and institutional reforms in order to adapt the EU constitutional framework to the new normal of a Union at twenty-seven. As this chapter shows, after the UK leaves the EU—by default in March 2019, two years after the notification of Article 50 TEU—the remaining Member States will need to amend several provisions of the EU treaties. Moreover, the EU institutions and its Member States will need to pass other key legal acts— such as a new decision concerning the allocation of the seats for the European Parliament (EP), and new rules on the funding of the EU—which have essentially a constitutional status, and in fact require unanimity in the Council, EP consent, and ratification by the Member States according to their respective constitutional requirements. In other words, Brexit will call for significant constitutional reforms in the EU—whether the Member States and the EU institutions like it or not.

The EU institutions and Member States could limit constitutional engineering to addressing the issues caused by Brexit. However, the chapter suggests that the reforms compelled by the UK withdrawal offer a window of opportunity that should be seized to fix several other problems of the current EU constitutional order, and to rethink the powers and institutional architecture of the EU for the future. There is no lack of proposals on how this should be done. During the euro-crisis several high-level blueprints have outlined a roadmap to enhance the EU and democratize EMU: among others, in December 2012 the President of the European Council, in cooperation with the Presidents of the European Commission, Eurogroup, and European Central Bank (ECB), produced a report toward a deeper and more genuine EMU;[3] and, in June 2015, the President of the European Commission, in coordination with the Presidents of the European Council, Eurogroup, ECB, and also the EP published a report to complete Europe's EMU.[4] Moreover, in the context of the celebrations for the 60th anniversary of the Treaties of Rome and the activation by the UK of Article 50 TEU, a whitepaper by the Commission,[5] several resolutions of the EP,[6] and a solemn declaration by the twenty-seven heads of state and government and leaders of the European Council, European Commission, and EP have re-started the debate on the future of the EU, proposing alternative scenarios.[7]

The chapter examines these reform projects, and considers how they may become part of a grand bargain among EU Member States and institutions, as they inevitably engage in reform after Brexit. While the chapter acknowledges that changing the treaties opens a Pandora's box, it claims that this step is necessary to improve the EU effectiveness and legitimacy. At the same time, while the chapter emphasizes some well-known difficulties that treaty reform would meet in the EU—due to either legal obstacles or political opposition in several Member States—it seeks optimistically to contextualize them. On the one hand, it claims that the current EU constitutional set-up is a one size fits none, with no Member State satisfied with the status quo: this situation opens the door for attempts to reform the EU constitutional settlement in a Pareto-optimal way. On the other, it suggests that the recent high-level talks in favor of multi-speed integration may work as a disciplinary factor, pushing recalcitrant Member States to go along plans of constitutional revision: because no state wants to be left behind when a core group vanguards forward, the likelihood that change will occur if a majority of countries so desires increases. With that said, the chapter concludes noting that multi-speed integration remains a distinctive possibility in case the efforts to reform the EU constitutional system after Brexit were to falter due to idiosyncratic national reasons.

The chapter is structured as follows. Section 2 analyzes the *constitutional changes* necessary after the UK abandons the EU, and underlines that the EU institutions and Member States will need to amend at the minimum

---

[3] President of the European Council, final report "Towards a Genuine EMU" (December 5, 2012).

[4] President of the European Commission, report "Completing Europe's EMU" (June 22, 2015).

[5] See European Commission, white paper "The Future of Europe" (March 1, 2017).

[6] See *e.g.* European Parliament resolution of 5 April 2017 on negotiations with the UK following its notification that it intends to withdraw from the EU, P8_TA(2017)0102.

[7] Rome Declaration of the leaders of twenty-seven Member States and of the European Council, the European Parliament and the European Commission (March 25, 2017).

several provisions of the EU treaties, the European Council decision establishing the composition of the EP and the rules on the financing of the EU: As I explain, given the nature of these changes, major interstate and interinstitutional bargaining and negotiations are to be expected. Section 3 summarizes the leading *constitutional proposals* for reform in the EU articulated during the euro-crisis, and more recently in the context of the celebrations for the 60th anniversary of the Treaties of Rome: Here, I emphasize how these blueprints could be implemented as part of a grand bargain. Section 4 finally, considers the *constitutional challenges* that still pave the way toward treaty reforms, identifying legal and political obstacles in some Member States: As I suggest, however, the prospect of constitutional revisions at twenty-seven is shaped by the ever more realistic alternative that a core group of Member States may decide to opt for a multispeed solution, preceding in integration on its own, outside the EU legal order. Section 5 briefly concludes.

2. Constitutional Changes

The departure of the UK compels the EU institutions and the remaining Member States to change a number of key EU law measures.[8] Several provisions of the treaties require amendment. Moreover, revisions are necessary to the European Council decision on the allocation of seats in the EP, as well as the rules on the financing of the EU. These legal acts are formally not treaty amendments, since there is no need to use the procedure of Article 48 TEU to change them. And yet, they have a quasi-constitutional status: substantively, because they deal with crucial aspect of the (institutional and financial) functioning of the EU; and procedurally, because their approval is subject to special legislative procedures which are akin for all practical purposes to a treaty revision. Modifying the decision on the EP composition and the rules on the EU own resources requires Member State unanimity, EP involvement, as well as ratification by each Member State according to its respective constitutional requirements. The necessity to re-adopt these crucial EU legal acts to adapt the EU to the departure of the UK will thus compel the Member State to engage in the broad and complex bargaining, proper of major constitutional reforms.

---

[8] See Federico Fabbrini, "How Brexit Opens a Window of Opportunity for Treaty Reform in the EU" Bertelsmann Stiftung & Jacques Delors Institute Berlin, Spotlight Europe No. 01/2016.

2.1 EU treaties

The most glaring treaty change that will have to be made as a result of Brexit concerns Article 52 TEU. This provision—which is then further specified by Article 355 TFEU—lists the Member States of the EU, including the UK. Article 52 TEU has been updated over time to account for EU enlargement. The last amendment occurred in 2013, when Croatia joined the EU. On that occasion, Article 13 of the Act concerning the conditions of accession of the Republic of Croatia—annexed to the Treaty between the twenty-seven EU Member States and Croatia—modified Article 52 TEU to include Croatia among the states of the Union.[9] After the UK exits from the EU, Article 52 TEU will necessarily have to be modified to remove the UK from the list of Member States to which the EU treaties apply. However, an important point must be underlined. Article 49 TEU (which regulates enlargement) explicitly authorizes "adjustments to the Treaties on which the Union is founded" to be made in the accession agreement between the Member States and the applicant state. Hence, formal modifications of the EU treaties which result from the accession of a new Member State can be dealt with in the accession treaty and accompanying documents—without the need for a revision of the EU treaties according to the rules of Article 48 TEU.

On the contrary, Article 50 TEU (which regulates withdrawal) does not mention an equal rule, and only states that the EU shall "conclude an agreement with [the withdrawing] State, setting out the arrangement for its withdrawal, taking account of the framework for its future relationship with the Union." Since the agreement with the withdrawing state is negotiated by the EU as any normal international pact pursuant to Article 218(3) TFEU—and is thus a legal act hierarchically inferior to the EU treaties[10]—this implies that in order to modify Article 52 TEU and remove the name of the UK from the list of EU Member States, resort should be made to normal amendment procedure of Article 48 TEU. An international agreement concluded by the EU, in fact, cannot modify EU primary law.[11] In other words, while in the case of enlargement the accession agreement suffices to introduce formal amendments to the EU treaties (such as a change to Article 52 TEU), in the case of withdrawal the secession agreement cannot do: even a banal and formal

---

[9] See Act concerning the conditions of accession of the Republic of Croatia and the adjustments to the Treaty on European Union and the Treaty on the Functioning of the European Union, Article 13 OJ [2012] L 112/25.

[10] See TFEU, Article 218(11).

[11] See Paul Craig, *The Treaty of Lisbon: Law, Politics and Treaty Reform* (OUP 2010) 401.

adjustment to the EU treaties such as the one under discussion here needs to be undertaken through the revision procedure disciplined in Article 48 TEU.

As is well known, Article 48 TEU outlines two revision procedures to amend the EU treaties: a simplified, and an ordinary one. However, according to Article 48(6) TEU the simplified revision procedure can only be used to "revise all or part of the provisions of Part Three of the TFEU" and at the condition that the amendment "shall not increase the competences conferred on the Union in the Treaties." In order to modify Article 52 TEU, therefore, resort has to be made to the ordinary revision procedure. This procedure requires the European Council to "convene a Convention composed of representatives of the national Parliaments, of the Heads of State or Government of the Member States, of the [EP] and of the Commission" and charged to "adopt by consensus a recommendation [to amend the treaties] to a conference of representatives of the governments of the Member States." Pursuant to Article 48(3) TEU, the European Council may decide by a simple majority "not to convene a Convention should this not be justified by the extent of the proposed amendments"—but it must obtain EP consent to do so: hence the EP can insist on calling a Convention to examine proposals for revisions to the EU treaties.[12] Finally, amendments to the treaties have to be agreed by common accord by a conference of representatives of the Member States and "shall enter into force after being ratified by all the Member States in accordance with their respective constitutional requirements."

In sum, when the UK has withdrawn from the EU, Article 52 TEU (and, relatedly, Article 355 TFEU) will need to be amended. As explained, the withdrawal agreement cannot introduce a modification to Article 52 TEU, since an international treaty concluded by the EU under Article 218 TFEU cannot modify EU primary law. Moreover, a simplified treaty amendment procedure cannot be used to change Article 52 TEU, so an ordinary treaty amendment procedure is required in this context. It is quite possible that the remaining twenty-seven Member States in the European Council will quickly settle to modify Article 52 TEU and decide that a Convention is not worth for such a formal amendment. However, Article 48 TEU gives to the EP a right to insist on convening a Convention. Considering that the EP has on multiple occasions called for setting up a new Convention,[13] it cannot be excluded that the EP will exploit the opportunity created by Brexit to force the European Council to eventually set in motion a broader project of revisions and updates of the EU treaties.

---

[12] See Jean-Claude Piris, *The Lisbon Treaty: A Legal and Political Analysis* (CUP 2010) 104.
[13] See section 3.

2.2 Composition of the European Parliament

Besides the treaty amendment discussed above, when the UK withdraws from the EU, the composition of the EP will have to be modified to account for the secession of one of its (most populous) Member States. Whereas the EU treaties provisions dealing with the European Council, the Council, the European Commission and the European Court of Justice (ECJ) can be applied without much ado to a Union of twenty-seven, institutional engineering is needed to adapt the EP to the new reality. According to Article 14(2) TEU, in fact, the EP shall be composed of maximum 750 members, plus the President—hence, for a total of 751 MEPs, to be elected in the various Member States according to the principle of degressive proportionality "with a minimum threshold of six members per Member State. No Member State shall be allocated more than ninety-six seats." As Article 14(2) TEU clarifies the specific allocation of EP seats in the various Member States is determined in a European Council decision, "adopted by unanimity, on the initiative of the [EP] and with its consent."

Currently, the EP composition is set in a European Council decision adopted in June 2013.[14] This decision—the first passed since the entry into force of the Lisbon Treaty—determined the apportionment of seats in the 8th EP elections in June 2014 and was the result of a long wrangling among the Member States.[15] In fact, concerns about the allocation of EP seats among the states played out in the negotiations leading to the Lisbon Treaty and are reflected in the fact that Declarations No. 4 and No. 5, annexed to the EU treaties, address specifically this issue. Declaration No. 4, in particular, indicates that "the additional seats in the [EP]" (*i.e.* the 751st seat) will be attributed to Italy, and Declaration No. 5 states that the European Council "will give its political agreement on the revised draft Decision on the composition of the [EP] for the legislative period 2009–2014, based on the proposal from the [EP]." These declarations—which technically are not binding, and do not have the same legal values as the EU treaties—testify, however, to the difficulties of finding an acceptable interstate and interinstitutional compromise, on an issue which is regarded by national governments as a proxy for the status of their countries within the EU.

[14] European Council Decision of 28 June 2013 establishing the composition of the European Parliament, 2013/312/EU, OJ [2013] L 181/57.
[15] See further Federico Fabbrini, "Representation in the European Parliament: of False Problems and Real Challenges" (2015) 75 *Zeitschrift für ausländisches öffentliches Recht und Völkerrecht* 823.

Following the departure of the UK, the European Council and the EP will have to agree on a new decision on the allocation of EP seats. In fact, the June 2013 European Council decisions already anticipated that a new formula for the allocation of seats had to be agreed upon in view of the 9th EP elections in 2019,[16] and the EP is expected to come up with a proposal shortly. Yet, it is clear that the withdrawal of the UK creates space for major new demands by several Member States, and potentially for a heavy reshuffling of seats. In fact, the current European Council decision assigns to the UK 73 seats in the EP—the third largest delegation (after Germany and France, and on a par with Italy).[17] Considering that the new decision will have to be proposed by the EP, approved unanimously by the European Council, voted by the EP— and then de facto ratified domestically by all Member States, since national legislation will have to be put in place to regulate the specific modalities for electing the number of MEPs assigned to each Member State by the EU decision—it is clear that much will be at stake during the negotiations. After all, comparative studies reveal that choices on the allocation of seats in federal systems are often taken within the framework of broader constitutional bargains, when units which may be losing out in terms of corporate representation can be compensated with other payoffs.[18]

In sum, the need to adopt a new decision on the composition of the EP after Brexit seems to create another window of opportunity for significant updates and revisions to the EU institutional set-up. As amending this European Council decision is—in terms of complexity—almost tantamount to a treaty revision, it cannot be excluded that the opportunity will be exploited to call for a more fully-fledged change to the EU institutional architecture, or at least to some other specific amendments to EU primary law, which may be part of a package-deal on how to assign seats among the various Member States within the EP.

2.3 Financial provisions

In addition to the new rules on the allocation of EP seats, another legal area where major reforms will be necessitated in the EU by Brexit concerns the rules on the financing of the EU. The EU treaties provisions regulating the financing of the EU set up a highly technical and complex system, which can be summarized as follows. First, under Article 312 TFEU, the Council, acting

---

[16] See European Council Decision 2013/312/EU, Article 5.   [17] ibid Article 3.

[18] See Jonathan Rodden, "Strength in Numbers? Representation and Redistribution in the European Union" (2002) 3 *European Union Politics* 151.

unanimously and with the consent of the EP shall adopt a regulation laying down the multiannual financial framework (MFF) of the EU: this regulation, usually adopted for a seven-year time-span, "shall ensure that Union expenditure develops in an orderly manner." Second, under Article 311 TFEU, the Council, acting unanimously and after consulting the EP shall adopt a decision laying down the system of own resources of the Union: this decision—which "shall not enter into force until it is approved by the Member States in accordance with their respective constitutional requirements"—defines the *revenues*-side of the EU financing, and thus complements the MFF regulation which instead sets the *expenditures*. Third, based on the funding prospect set in the own resources decision and in light of the expenditure plan sketched in the MFF regulation, the EP and the Council adopt every year the annual budget of the EU according to Article 314 TFEU.

The current rules on the financing of the EU were set in a package of legal measures adopted after the entry into force of the Lisbon Treaty. In particular, on the revenue-side, the own resources of the EU are set in a Council decision adopted in May 2014.[19] On the expenditure side, instead, rules are condensed in a Council regulation adopted in December 2013, which sets the MFF for 2014–2020.[20] Both these legal measures were the result of highly complex political negotiations. A proposal for a new own resources decision was tabled by the Commission in 2011,[21] and it took three years to approve it in the Council: in fact, the own resources decision is still subject to parliamentary ratification in several Member States (but will apply retroactively as from 1st January 2014, when national ratification will be completed).[22] At the same time, negotiations for the MFF 2014–2020 broke down on several occasions, and the intervention of the European Council (in place of the Council) was necessary in order to find a compromise among the Member States.[23]

As is well-known, the difficulties in negotiating the own resources decision and the MFF regulation are a result of the way in which the EU is currently funded.[24] Since, despite the letter and the spirit of the EU treaties, today resources are mostly transferred to the EU from Member States' coffers, EU

[19] Council Decision of 26 May 2014 on the system of own resources of the European Union, 2014/335/EU, Euratom, OJ [2014] L 168/105.

[20] Council Regulation (EU, Euratom) No. 1311/2013 of 2 December 2013 laying down the multiannual financial framework for the years 2014–2020, OJ [2013] L 347/884.

[21] See Commission proposal for a Council Decision on the system of own resources of the European Union (June 29, 2011) COM(2011)510 final.

[22] See Council Decision 2014/335/EU, Euratom, Article 11.

[23] See European Council Meeting (November 22–23, 2012).

[24] See Federico Fabbrini, "Taxing and Spending in the Eurozone" (2014) 39 *European Law Review* 155.

countries consider the contributions they make to the EU budget as *their* money, and aggressively measure the difference between their contributions to, and their receipts from, the EU budget. As a result of this state of affairs, the decision-making process about the EU budget has been captured by endless negotiations among the Member States about the precise costs and benefits that each Member States would incur. Because no Member State is willing to transfer *its* money to the EU budget for the benefit of *other* Member States, the discussion about the EU funding have become increasingly costly and decreasingly effective—every Member State having a veto power on how much resources the EU should raise and how it should spend them.

Given this situation, it is to be expected that after Brexit the negotiations of the new EU financial framework will be highly contentious. Although the UK enjoys a famous rebate (obtained in 1984, and preserved ever since) which allows it to pay less than it should, it still remains one of the major contributors to the EU budget—the fourth total net payer into the EU coffers (after Germany, France, and Italy).[25] Hence, when the UK will pull out of the EU the question will arise of how to handle the loss of UK contributions to the EU budget. In principle, the EU could reduce expenditure in proportion to the UK quota—but it seems unlikely that states which are net beneficiaries of EU spending would endorse such an outcome. Alternatively, the states which are net contributors to the EU budget could increase their contributions to wind-up the shortfall—but again it seems unlikely that countries that are already paying into the EU budget more than they receive in return would endorse this option. In this context, therefore, Brexit may create a window of opportunity for a more significant constitutional re-thinking of the EU financing system.[26]

In sum, the need to adopt new legal rules for EU revenues and expenditures for the post-2020 financial framework attains a new meaning as a consequence of the UK departure from the EU. Given the complexities already characterizing the negotiations of the EU financing system, it is to be expected that the withdrawal of one of the (richest) Member States will further heat up the tone of the future negotiations, both between Member States and among EU institutions. Since the adoption of the MFF regulation, and even more so of the own resources decision, are practically tantamount to a treaty revision—as reflected in the need of state ratifications according to

[25] See European Commission, "EU Expenditure and Revenue 2014–2020," interactive chart available at http://ec.europa.eu/budget/figures/interactive/index_en.cfm.

[26] See Edoardo Traversa and Alexander Maitrot de la Motte, "Le fédéralisme économique et la fiscalité dans l'Union européenne," in Stéphane De la Rosa et al. (eds.), *L'Union européen et le fédéralisme économique* (Bruylant 2015) 343.

national constitutional requirements—major challenges are to be expected. Brexit changes the stakes in the negotiations, tipping the balance in favor of some kind of reform. Although until now Member State governments have been lukewarm at initiatives to endow the EU with adequate taxing and spending powers—independent from Member States' financial transfers—in the aftermath of Brexit these ideas may acquire a new attractiveness as a way to provide adequate funding to the EU.

3. Constitutional Proposals

As the previous section has shown, Brexit opens windows of opportunity for wider constitutional changes in the EU. Resort to Article 48 TEU could be exploited by the EP to push further other revisions to EU primary law. Moreover, since the UK is one of the most populous and richest Member State of the EU, its withdrawal from the EU will significantly change the stakes of the renegotiation of the decision on the composition of the EP and the financing of the EU: while these acts were already scheduled to be renewed before 2019 (for the new EP elections) and 2020 (for the new MFF), it seems clear that without the UK the other Member States and the EU institutions will need to engage in a much more significant grand bargain, both to re-apportion seats and to re-think the revenues and expenditures of the EU for a post-Brexit era. In this context, several of the proposals for constitutional reform that had been brought forward by EU institutions and Member States' government may acquire a new relevance. In fact, in the midst of the euro-crisis, and then at the occasion of the celebrations for the 60th anniversary of the Treaties of Rome, multiple blueprints have been outlined to re-launch the project of European integration: and these may become part of a package-deal of constitutional reforms post-Brexit.

3.1 The euro-crisis and EMU

The euro-crisis, which challenged the functioning of EMU since 2009, prompted a wide set of legal and institutional reforms.[27] Nevertheless, additional proposals have been articulated over time at the highest EU institutional level to improve further the effectiveness and the legitimacy of EMU. Following an explicit mandate of the European Council, the President of the European Council, jointly with the Presidents of the European Commission, the Eurogroup, and the ECB, delivered in December 2012 a report entitled

---

[27] See Federico Fabbrini, *Economic Governance in Europe* (OUP 2016).

"Towards a Genuine EMU,"[28] which outlined a road-map of EMU reforms, including deeper economic, banking, and fiscal union, coupled with a new framework of democratic legitimacy and accountability. And following the EP election in May 2014, and the appointment of a new European Commission in October 2014, the heads of state and government of the Eurozone entrusted the President of the European Commission, in close cooperation with the Presidents of the European Council, the Eurogroup, and the ECB, with the task to bring forward the work on the future of EMU[29]—an effort which resulted in the publication in June 2015 of a report, signed also by the President of the EP, on "Completing Europe's EMU."[30]

The European Commission, the ECB, and the EP have then also been individually active to push for further changes in the functioning of EMU. In November 2012 the European Commission unveiled a blueprint for a deep and genuine EMU, opening a debate on future reforms,[31] and in October 2015 it charted its proposed steps to complete EMU.[32] The ECB President has on multiple occasions underlined the importance of overcoming the asymmetry of EMU, by complementing monetary policy with a real supranational economic policy.[33] And the EP has repeatedly expressed its desire that constitutional changes be brought back on the agenda of the EU institutions, including by reviving the Convention method to re-discuss the architecture of EMU.[34] In particular, the EP has made the case in favor of endowing the Eurozone with a fiscal capacity—that is, a counter-cyclical stabilization mechanism, funded by real EU taxes, that can be used to ensure the proper functioning of EMU—and has called for greater parliamentary scrutiny in the framework of EU economic governance.[35] At the same time, the EP has stated that action should be taken to re-incorporate within EU

[28] President of the European Council, final report (n. 3).

[29] Euro Summit Statement (October 24, 2014,) para 2.

[30] President of the European Commission, report (n. 4).

[31] European Commission Communication, "A Blueprint for a Deep and Genuine EMU. Launching a European Debate" (November 28, 2012) COM(2012) 777 final.

[32] See European Commission Communication, "On Steps Toward Completing Economic and Monetary Union" (October 21, 2015) COM(2015) 600 final.

[33] See *e.g.* ECB President Mario Draghi, "Introductory Statement in Front of the EP", Brussels (June 15, 2015) (expressing its support for "a quantum leap towards a stronger, more efficient institutional architecture" for EMU).

[34] See European Parliament Resolution of 20 November 2012 towards a Genuine EMU, P7_TA(2012)0430 para. 6; and European Parliament Resolution of 12 December 2013 on the constitutional problems of multi-tier governance in the European Union, P7_TA(2013)0598 paras. 67–9.

[35] See European Parliament Resolution of 23 May 2013 on future legislative proposals for EMU, P7_TA(2013)0222; and European Parliament Resolution of 24 June 2015 on the review of economic governance framework: stock-tacking and challenges, P8_TA(2015)0238.

law the EMU-related intergovernmental treaties concluded outside the EU legal order, using that opportunity for a broader overhaul of the EMU constitutional system.[36]

Moreover, several national governments have made the case for further legal and institutional reforms in EMU aimed at enhancing the Eurozone effectiveness and legitimacy. Among others, the former French President brought forward the idea to create a Eurozone presidency and endorsed the call for an EMU fiscal capacity.[37] The Italian Minister of Finance proposed the creation of a European funded unemployment insurance scheme.[38] And the then French and German Ministers of the Economy argued that the EU needs institutional changes to handle its democratic and executive deficit.[39] In fact, although the European Council as a whole has so far shied clear of endorsing any major blueprint for constitutional change in the EU, proposals for legal and institutional reforms have been supported by several national governments, including Spain[40] and Belgium.[41] And the German government too—despite the comfortable dominant position it has come to play in EMU governance during the euro-crisis[42]—has emphasized the need to change the treaties, to either reform the institutions,[43] or improve the rules.[44]

---

[36] See European Parliament Resolution of 2 February 2012 on the European Council meeting of 30 January 2012, P7_TA(2012)0023, para. 7.

[37] See French President François Hollande, "Intervention liminaire de lors de la conférence de presse" Paris (May 16, 2013) 6 (speaking of "un gouvernement économique qui se réunirait, tous les mois, autour d'un véritable Président.").

[38] See Italian Minister of Finance Pier-Carlo Padoan, "European Unemployment Insurance Scheme" (October 2015).

[39] See French Minister of the Economy Emmanuel Macron and German Minister of the Economy Sigmar Gabriel, Op-Ed, "Europe Cannot Wait Any Longer" *The Guardian* (June 3, 2015) (stating that "to make its institutions work ... Europe will need to address its democratic deficit as well as its executive one.").

[40] See Government of Spain, "Better Economic Governance in the Euro Area: Spanish Contribution" (May 2015) 7, and "Spanish Position on the Future of Europe" (February 2017)

[41] See Government of Belgium, "Report on Preparing for Next Steps in Better Economic Governance in the Euro Area" (April 27, 2015) 3.

[42] See Federico Fabbrini, "States' Equality v States' Power: the Euro-Crisis, Inter-State Relations and the Paradox of Domination" (2015) 17 *Cambridge Yearbook of European Legal Studies* 3.

[43] See Berlin Group, Final Report of the Future of Europe Group of the Foreign Ministers of Austria, Belgium, Denmark, France, Italy, Germany, Luxembourg, the Netherlands, Poland, Portugal and Spain (September 17, 2012).

[44] See German Finance Minister Wolfgang Schäuble, "Strategy for a European Recovery", Keynote speech at the 5th Bruges European Business Conference (March 27, 2014) (speaking in favor of a "European budget commissioner, who would be able to reject national budgets if they don't correspond to the rules we have jointly agreed.").

3.2 The 60th anniversary of the Rome Treaties and the EU

The debate on EU constitutional reform has then received a further boost on the occasion of the celebrations of the 60th anniversary of the Treaties of Rome in March 2017. As this historic moment arrived exactly at the time when the UK triggered Article 50 TEU, the EU institutions and the Member States sought to reflect on how to absorb the loss of the UK while charting a new way forward. The results of these reflections go beyond the EMU-focused debate that took place during the euro-crisis, but the blueprints produced on the road to Rome reflect variable levels of ambition. The European Commission published in March 2017 a white paper aimed at opening a debate on the future of the EU of twenty-seven.[45] The white paper, which was then integrated by several sector-specific contributions,[46] outlines five alternative scenarios: (1) carrying on; (2) nothing but the single market; (3) those who want more do more; (4) doing less more efficiently; and (5) doing much more together. These scenarios are presented by the Commission to the Member States for consideration, but the Commission has not itself outlined its preferences for the way forward.

While the initiative of the Commission lacked a clear vision, the EP has been more consistent in advancing proposals for constitutional reforms in the EU after Brexit. The EP has recently approved a set of resolutions which combine calls for a greater exploitation of the legal and institutional mechanisms currently available under the Treaty of Lisbon, while outlining a roadmap for treaty reforms in the mid-term. On the one hand, the EP has claimed that the action should be taken *à traité constant*, with further integration in the area of economic governance, social policy, and defense.[47] Moreover, the EP has reaffirmed its intention to set up a fiscal capacity for the EU, based on real EU taxes,[48] as recently indicated also in the final report of the High Level Group on Own Resources chaired by former Italian Prime Minister and European Commissioner Mario Monti.[49] On the other hand, however, the EP has also

---

[45] European Commission white paper (n 5).

[46] See *e.g.* European Commission reflection paper on "The Social Dimension of Europe" (April 26, 2017), European Commission reflection paper on "The Deepening of Economic and Monetary Union" (May 31, 2017) and European Commission reflection paper on "The Future of European Defence" (June 7, 2017).

[47] See European Parliament resolution of 16 February 2017 on improving the functioning of the European Union building on the potential of the Lisbon Treaty, P8_TA(2017)0049.

[48] See European Parliament resolution of 16 February 2017 on budgetary capacity for the Eurozone, P8_TA(2017)0050.

[49] See Mario Monti, High Level Group on Own Resources, final report and recommendations "Future Financing of the EU" (December 2016). See also European Commission reflection paper on "The Future of EU Finances" (June 28, 2017).

unveiled its plans for constitutional changes beyond the Treaty of Lisbon, aimed at overhauling more fundamentally the EU institutional architecture,[50] and it has emphasized how Brexit should be used to this end.[51]

Heads of state and government, finally, have also debated the future of the EU, first in a declaration signed in Bratislava in September 2016,[52] and then in a declaration signed in Rome—together with the Presidents of the European Council, European Commission, and the EP—in March 2017.[53] While this declaration is mostly focused on celebrating the achievements of sixty years of European unity, it indicates space for future interstate cooperation in the field of internal security, economic growth, social protection as well as foreign policy and defense—an area where rapid changes have occurred since the election of the new US administration.[54] The declaration avoids any discussion on the legal and institutional mechanisms to achieve these objectives, and contents itself with proclaiming that the EU Member States and institutions will "promote a democratic, effective and transparent decision-making process and better delivery." Nevertheless, the minimalist compromise reached in Rome has not obfuscated the calls—notably by the Italian President,[55] and the speakers of parliaments of fourteen EU Member States[56]—for immediate treaty changes to establish a federal union endowed with adequate powers and democratic legitimacy. In fact, a major *élan* in favor of treaty reform has followed the French presidential elections in Spring 2017: with the victory of Emmanuel Macron, who had long argued for strengthening EMU with a Eurozone Treasury subject to adequate democratic controls, the topic of constitutional change has squarely returned on the EU agenda.[57]

---

[50] See European Parliament resolution of 16 February 2017 on possible evolutions of and adjustments to the current institutional set-up of the European Union, P8_TA(2017)0048.

[51] See also European Parliament resolution of 28 June 2016 on the decision to leave the EU resulting from the UK referendum, P8_TA(2016)0294.

[52] See Bratislava Declaration (September 16, 2016).

[53] See Rome Declaration (n. 7).

[54] See High Representative of the EU for Foreign Affairs and Security Policy, "A Global Strategy for the EU Foreign & Security Policy" (June 2016); European Parliament resolution of 22 November 2016 on the European Defense Union, P8_TA(2016)0435; Foreign Affairs Council Conclusions (March 6, 2017) Annex—Concept Note: Operational Planning and Conduct Capabilities for CSDP Missions and Operations; and European Council Conclusions (June 23, 2017) EUCO 8/17, para 8.

[55] See Italian President Sergio Mattarella, "I valori dell'Europa", intervento in occasione della seduta congiunta delle Camere per il 60° anniversario dei Trattati di Roma, Rome (March 22, 2017) (speaking of the need to relaunch "la riforma dei Trattati").

[56] See President of the French Assemblé Nationale Claude Bertolone, President of the Italian Camera dei Deputati Laura Boldrini, President of the German Bundestag Norbert Lammert *et al.*, "Un patto per l'Unione federale," *La Stampa* (February 26, 2012).

[57] See French President Emmanuel Macron, Interview, *Les Temps* (June 21, 2017) (saying that "il faut avoir une intégration plus forte au sein de la zone euro. D'où l'idée, que je défends avec vigueur,

3.3 Grand bargain?

During the last decade, many proposals for reform have been advanced in the EU and EMU. While several of the blueprints openly speak about treaty amendments and the revision of other EU basic acts, others are instead more modest and rather seek to bring about change within the framework of the current treaties. Nevertheless, all proposals reveal unease for the way how the EU currently functions and thus call for reforms of the system, by tackling several legal or institutional problems in the EU, and EMU specifically. In particular, all the reform projects by the EU institutions as well as by national governments identify two main areas for action. First, calls are being made for changes to the EU *institutional* architecture—*e.g.* to enhance the legitimacy of decision-making, or to improve the effectiveness of executive action, if it may be through the creation of new institutions. Secondly, reform proposals persistently focus on *substantive* issues, and notably on the problems of EMU stability, fiscal capacity, and EU own resources to finance the growing set of policies that the EU is expected to carry out.

As section 2 has pointed out, Brexit will compel the EU institutions and the twenty-seven Member States to engage in constitutional reforms *precisely* in the areas of the institutions and the finances of the EU. As such, Brexit opens a window of opportunity for implementing a number of constitutional proposals which had been discussed at the highest level for several years—but so far never put into practice. Constitutional change is a serious business and Member States and EU institutions understandably engage reluctantly with it. But since after Brexit the EU treaties and other quasi-constitutional acts will have to be changed anyway, entrepreneurial EU institutions and Member States now have greater margin of maneuver to push for constitutional change. In this context, therefore, the reform proposals debated during the last decade may be taken seriously as part of a grand constitutional bargain between EU Member States and institutions.

As scholars of constitution-making have emphasized,[58] changes to the legal foundations of a political regime hardly ever occur in good times: rather, they tend to occur in moments of crisis, when there is a window of opportunity to exploit. Moreover, constitutions are never ideal documents: rather, they are

---

d'un budget de la zone euro, doté d'une gouvernance démocratique") and Interview, *Ouest France* (July 13, 2017) (saying that "il faudra à un moment des changements de traités, parce que cette Europe est incomplete; la question n'est pas de savoir si ces changements seront nécessaires, mais quand et comment").

[58] See Tom Ginsburg *et al.*, "Does the Process of Constitution-Making Matter?" (2009) 5 *Annual Review of Law and Social Science* 201 and Sujit Choudhry and Tom Ginsburg (eds.), *Constitution Making* (Elgar 2016).

the result of compromise between competing interests. In order to succeed processes of constitution-making must ensure that each player around the negotiating table obtains some net gain from the end result. Given the far-reaching adaptations to the EU legal order that the EU institutions and the Member States will need to make as a result of Brexit, however, the need for a grand bargain significantly increases, and proposals which have been thus far only discussed in the abstract may become real. In fact, more far-reaching institutional and substantive changes to the EU regime could become indispensable for reaching the inter-state and inter-institutional compromises necessary to adapt the EU to the reality of a Union of twenty-seven. By compelling treaty reforms, therefore Brexit offers an opportunity which can—and, in my view, should—be seized to strike a new grand bargain to improve the EU constitutional architecture.

4. Constitutional Challenges

The previous section summarized the multiple proposals recently advanced for constitutional reform in the EU, and discussed how these could be part of a grand bargain after Brexit. However, it is clear that any major initiative to reform the EU—even one exploiting the window of opportunity created by the need to adapt the EU to the new reality of twenty-seven—would meet important challenges. There are in fact legal constraints and political obstacles in a number of Member States that complicate any major project of constitutional revision. Yet, while not being unaware of these difficulties, I want to submit that there are relevant incentives that still push in the direction of a constitutional change. On the one hand, although the Member States bear collective responsibility for the existing EU architecture, the EU seems to have increasingly become one size fits none, which may spur efforts to change the status quo. On the other, the growing calls in favor of a multi-speed Europe may pressure recalcitrant states to go along, as a least-worst alternative to a scenario where a core group of Member States decides to move forward outside the EU legal order.

4.1 Obstacles

Needless to say, the key impediment toward a major reform of the EU is the unanimity requirement: as pointed out in Section 2, amendments to the EU treaties and to several other quasi-constitutional acts of the EU require the unanimous consent of the (soon twenty-seven) EU Member States. In this context, of course, every EU Member State wields a veto power on any constitutional change in the EU.[59] Even if unanimous agreement were to be reached among the governments of the Member States congressed in an intergovernmental conference (or other intergovernmental settings), moreover, domestic constraints may still limit the states' scope of action. These constraints may be legal or political—depending on the Member States' constitutional systems.

In Germany, for example, the Constitutional Court, the *Bundesverfassungsgericht* (BVerfG) has drawn over time a number of red-lines on possible future steps in European integration: while the BVerfG has never prevented the ratification of an EU treaty so far, its case law has restricted the room of negotiation for the German government on EU affairs.[60] In its *Lissabon Urteil*, the BVerfG has identified a core set of competences which belong to the heart of state sovereignty and which cannot be transferred to the EU.[61] In reviewing the German law for the election of the EP, the BVerfG has reaffirmed its view that the EP is not a real parliamentary assembly, as it does not elect a government.[62] And in its judgments related to the legal measures adopted to respond to the euro-crisis, the BVerfG has been adamant in claiming that efforts to stabilize the EMU should not undermine the budgetary sovereignty of the German Parliament, or the right to democracy.[63] In fact, in referring its first preliminary reference to the ECJ in 2014 the BVerfG has affirmed that action by the ECB consisting in the purchase of government bonds would be in breach of Germany's constitutional identity[64]—a view it later retracted.[65]

Although the position of the BVerfG is in many ways exceptional,[66] other national constitutional courts, particularly in Central and Eastern Europe, have taken similar stands. At the same time, while any treaty change would need to pass muster before national courts in some EU Member States, other

[59] See Steve Peers, "The Future of EU Treaty Amendments" (2012) 31 *Yearbook of European Law* 17.

[60] See Sabino Cassese, "L'Unione europea e il guinzaglio tedesco" [2009] *Giornale di diritto amministrativo* 1003.

[61] See BVerfG 123, 267 (2009).

[62] See BverfG 2 BvE 2/13, judgment of February 26, 2014.

[63] See BverfG 2 BvR 1390/12 et al, judgment (preliminary measures) of September 12, 2012.

[64] See BverfG 2 BvR 2728/13 et al, order of February 7, 2014.

[65] See Case C-62/14 *Gauweiler*, ECLI:EU:C:2015:400 and BverfG 2 BvR 2728/13 *et al.*, judgment of June 21, 2016.

[66] See Monica Claes, "The Validity and Primacy of EU Law and the 'Cooperative Relationship' between National Constitutional Courts and the CJEU" in Federico Fabbrini (ed.), *The European Court of Justice, the European Central Bank and the Supremacy of EU Law* (2016) 23 Special Issue *Maastricht Journal of European & Comparative Law* 151.

countries are facing different kinds of constitutional constraints on the path toward greater integration. In Ireland, for instance, under the *Crotty* doctrine of the Supreme Court, every EU treaty that entails a transfer of power from the national to the European level requires to be approved through a constitutional referendum.[67] As is well known, however, Irish voters rejected the last two EU reform treaties. In 2001, Ireland voted down the Treaty of Nice; and in 2007 the Treaty of Lisbon.[68] On both occasions, the European Council took stock of the decision of the Irish voters and at the request of the Irish government produced official declarations aimed at reassuring Ireland of the fact that, among others, the EU treaties would not undermine the principle of Irish military neutrality.[69] Based on these reassurances, the Nice and Lisbon Treaties were put to a second vote, and eventually approved in 2002 and 2008 respectively.

Even in countries where there is no constitutional requirement for referendum on treaty changes, moreover, political expediency may make such a step inevitable. As the recent examples of Denmark and the Netherland highlight, however, the popular mood may be strongly against any further step in European integration. Hence, in December 2015 the Danish citizens voted against the proposal endorsed by the nation's government to abandon Denmark's opt-out on several measures in the field of criminal justice and police cooperation,[70] limiting the possibility of cooperation between the law enforcement agencies of Denmark and the other EU Member States. And in consultative referendum in April 2016 the Dutch citizens voted against the Ukraine Association Agreement,[71] complicating the possibility for the EU to strengthen its economic ties with Ukraine. If one considers also the maverick July 2015 Greek referendum, where a majority of voters rejected the terms of the draft third memorandum of understanding between Greece and its EU creditors,[72] a picture of increasing popular wariness against the EU seems to emerge.

---

[67] See *Crotty v An Taoiseach* [1987] IESC 4.

[68] See Grainne de Búrca, "If at First You Don't Succeed: Vote, Vote Again: Analyzing the 'Second Referendum' Phenomenon in EU Treaty Change" (2010) 33 *Fordham International Law Journal* 1472.

[69] See Presidency Conclusions, European Council, (December 11–12, 2008) EU Doc. 17271/08.

[70] See Danish Parliament, *Resultat af folkeafstemning: Nej* http://retsforbehold.eu.dk/da/nyheder/2015/resultat.

[71] See Dutch Election Council, *Uitslag referendum Associatieovereenkomst met Oekraïne* https://www.kiesraad.nl/actueel/nieuws/2016/04/12/uitslag-referendum-associatieovereenkomst-met-oekraine.

[72] See Greek Government, *Euroelections* http://ekloges.ypes.gr/current/e/public/#{%22cls%22:%22main%22,%22params%22:{}}.

4.2 Incentives

All the above notwithstanding, however, the prospect of constitutional change in the EU remains a possible outcome. First, history thus far has shown that national legal obstacles to integration are not ultimately insurmountable. During the last twenty-five years, the EU treaties have been subject to a "semi-permanent treaty revision process."[73] Four major overhauls have occurred in short sequence, even excluding the failed attempt to adopt a Treaty Establishing the European Constitution: the Treaty of Maastricht of 1992, the Treaty of Amsterdam of 1996, the Treaty of Nice of 2001, and the Treaty of Lisbon of 2007 have all introduced relevant changes to the architecture of the EU—and they were all eventually approved despite the difficulties of national ratifications. Moreover, the ink of the Lisbon Treaty text was barely dried when the EU Member States exploited the newly introduced simplified treaty revision procedure of Article 48(6) TEU to rewrite Article 136 TFEU and allow for the establishment of a permanent stability mechanism for the Eurozone:[74] the European Stability Mechanism.[75]

Second, also recent electoral opposition to the EU must be contextualized. To start with, as political scientists have explained through empirical data, popular support in favor of the EU has increased in the aftermath of Brexit, even in traditionally Eurosceptic countries—confirming that membership is regarded by most EU citizen as a valuable asset.[76] Moreover, in my view the dissatisfaction of European citizens toward the EU should not be interpreted as an opposition to European integration as such. Rather, discontent vis-à-vis the EU should be seen as the product of an unsatisfactory functioning of the EU.[77] Electoral disapproval for the EU is largely the result of a system of governance which is unresponsive to citizens' preferences—and when voice is

---

[73] Bruno De Witte, "The Closest Thing to a Constitutional Conversation in Europe: The Semi-Permanent Treaty Revision Process," in Neil Walker *et al.* (eds.), *Convergence and Divergence in European Public Law* (Hart Publishing 2002) 39.

[74] See European Council Decision of 25 March 2011, amending Article 136 TFEU with regard to a stability mechanism for Member States whose currency is the euro, 2011/199/EU, OJ [2011] L 91/1.

[75] See Treaty Establishing the European Stability Mechanism (February 2, 2012) http://www.european-council.europa.eu/media/582311/05-tesm2.en12.pdf.

[76] See Marlene Wind in this book, as well as Isabell Hoffmann, "Brexit has Raised Support for the European Union" Bertelsmann Stiftung, Eupinions trends (November 21, 2016).

[77] See Joseph H. H. Weiler, "Europa: 'Nous Coalisons des Etats, Nous N'Unissons pas des Hommes,'" in Marta Cartabia and Andrea Simoncini (eds.), *La sostenibilità della democrazia nel XXI secolo* (Il Mulino 2009) 51, 62 (stating that the system of EMU governance contributes to the political and democratic deficit of the EU).

limited, exit becomes an option.[78] Hence, if EU constitutional reforms were to address more fundamentally the current disconnect between the European citizens and the project of European integration, creating channels of legitimacy from the citizens toward the institutions, they may ultimately revert the tide, and win the support of the people.

In fact, relevant incentives play in favor of an overhaul of the EU constitutional system. On the one hand, the EU appears to be in a state of unstable equilibrium, and the *status quo* does not seem to be satisfactory for any Member State.[79] The euro-crisis has exposed the weaknesses of the EMU, and states, notably in the South (but also in the West), have suffered from a constitutional regime that prioritizes fiscal stability at the price of growth and employment. The migration-crisis, otherwise, has revealed the EU deficiencies in the field of Schengen and immigration, displeasing states particularly in the North, which have had to shoulder a greater burden in the management of asylum claims. At the same time, states in the East have been concerned that the current EU is not able to sufficiently protect them from external military threats, particularly in the face of a resurgent Russia and a US administration which appears less concerned with EU defense. In sum, the current EU set-up is being criticized by states across the EU, albeit for different reasons in different places: in this situation, it is not implausible for push toward Pareto-optimality to succeed.

On the other hand, however, a major pressure toward a new settlement in the EU constitutional architecture may derive from the growing calls for a multi-speed Europe. This occurs when not all Member States are willing to move forward in integration, and those who want to do so do it on their own, through forms of special cooperation. In fact, at a time when the EU is facing multiple challenges, the idea voiced by several Member States that they may decide to act independently as a sub-group to the side of the EU works as a powerful incentive for outlier states to re-align themselves toward the median view. Despite national differences, no one of the twenty-seven EU Member States today openly wishes to be excluded from the project of integration, so even the simple threat of such a scenario materializing operates as a disciplinary factor on recalcitrant members. Considering that Brexit forces the EU Member States and institutions to engage in forms of constitutional change, the desire to remain part of the club may be a powerful incentive even for the

---

[78] See Albert Hirschman, *Exit, Voice, Loyalty: Responses to Decline in Firms, Organizations and States* (Harvard University Press 1970).

[79] See Kalypso Nicolaïdis in this book, as well as Sergio Fabbrini, *Which European Union?* (CUP 2015).

lukewarm Member States to move along with the majority in updating the
EU regime.

4.3 Multispeed Europe?

Yet, the idea of multi-speed Europe does remain on the table in case the
efforts to reform the constitutional architecture of the EU after Brexit were
to falter for idiosyncratic national reasons. The idea of a multi-speed Europe
is nothing new. Legally speaking, it has existed for twenty-five years. Since
the Maastricht Treaty of 1992, EU law has introduced opt-outs, exempting
some Member States from participating in some EU project. And since the
Amsterdam Treaty of 1996, EU law created the enhanced cooperation procedure, allowing those Member States that are willing to move forward to
do so within the EU legal order. As a result of that, Europe has developed in
variable geometry: two countries (the UK and Denmark) have a derogation
from adopting the common currency;[80] two countries (the UK and Ireland)
have an opt-out from Schengen;[81] and three countries (the UK, Poland, and
the Czech Republic) have obtained a protocol that seeks to exempt them
from the application of the EU Charter of Fundamental Rights.[82] Moreover,
twenty-five Member States have embarked in the process of enhanced cooperation to set up a Unitary Patent court,[83] and ten Eurozone countries are
discussing the introduction of a financial transaction tax.[84]

Nevertheless, since Brexit several national governments have re-invoked
the idea of multi-speed integration with a new streak, namely as a way to
overcome deadlock in the EU system. In the run-up to the celebrations of the
60th anniversary of the Treaties of Rome, the Benelux countries (Belgium,
Luxembourg, and the Netherlands) indicated in a joint document that
"[d]ifferent paths of integration and enhanced cooperation could provide
for effective responses to challenges that affect Member States in different
ways."[85] The European Commission white paper identifies multi-speed integration as the third possible scenario for the future of the EU.[86] And the four
largest countries of the Eurozone—Germany, France, Italy, and Spain—have
expressed their wish "qu'il y ait de nouvelle formes de coopération pour de

[80] See Protocol No. 15 and Protocol No. 16.   [81] See Protocol No. 20.
[82] See Protocol No. 30.
[83] See Regulation (EU) No. 1257/2012 of the European Parliament and of the Council of 17
December 2012 implementing enhanced cooperation in the area of the creation of unitary patent
protection, OJ [2012] L 361/1.
[84] See Economic & Financial Affairs Council Conclusions (December 6, 2016) Doc. 15205/16.
[85] See Benelux Vision on the Future of Europe (February 3, 2017).
[86] See Commission white paper (n. 5) 20.

nouveaux projets – ce que l'on appelle les coopération différenciées – qui fassent que quelques pays puissent aller plus vite, plus loin dans de domaines comme la défense, mais aussi la zone euro au travers l'approfondissement de l'Union économique et monétaire […] sans que d'autre ne puissent s'y opposer."[87]

Needless to say, the idea of a multi-speed Europe is controversial in many EU Member States. The government of Croatia has openly spoken against it,[88] and Poland—reflecting a widespread view in Central and Eastern Europe—has vigorously opposed it. In fact, the March 2017 Rome Declaration was until the last minute held hostage of the Polish government precisely on this point. While the draft text of the Declaration indicated that states would act together whenever possible and at different paces and intensity where necessary,[89] the final text affirms that the Member States "will act together, at different paces and intensity where necessary, while moving in the same direction, as we have done in the past, in line with the Treaties and keeping the door open to those who want to join later." Otherwise, although the President of the European Council has emphasized that the positive side-effect of Brexit has been to draw the twenty-seven remaining Member States closer together,[90] there are clear fissures within the Union—and nothing proves this better than the decision by the Polish government to vote (alone) against the re-appointment of Poland's Donald Tusk as President of the European Council for a second mandate in March 2017.[91] In fact, the clear authoritarian drift in countries like Poland and Hungary can only deepen the cleavage within the EU, raising question on the ability of the EU to reform itself at twenty-seven.

In this context, the possibility of taking the road of multi-speed integration outside the EU legal order to achieve greater political union remains an option for the states that want to do so. And a recent model exists. The Fiscal Compact, concluded in 2012 by twenty-five of the then twenty-seven EU Member States (all excluding the UK and the Czech Republic), strengthened budgetary constraints outside the EU legal order, while still foreseeing the involvement of the EU institutions in its functioning.[92] Moreover, in order to

---

[87] See Déclaration au Sommet informel Allemagne, Espagne, France, Italie à Versailles (March 6, 2017).

[88] See Croatian Prime Minister Andrej Plenkovic, "We Must Not Fall into the Trap of Multi-Speed Europe", Speech, Zagreb (March 22, 2017).

[89] Draft Rome Declaration (March 12, 2017).

[90] See European Council President Donald Tusk, statement (March 29, 2017) Doc. 160/17.

[91] See European Council, press release (March 9, 2017), Doc. 122/17.

[92] See Treaty on Stability, Coordination and Governance in the Economic and Monetary Union (March 2, 2012) http://www.eurozone.europa.eu/media/304649/st00tscg26_en12.pdf.

bypass national vetoes, the Fiscal Compact set the rule that the treaty would enter into force when ratified by only twelve contracting parties whose currency is the euro, although it would obviously apply only to the ratifying states.[93] By effectively requiring that only a minority of EU Member States approve the treaty, the Fiscal Compact shifted the cost of non-ratification to the hold-outs: a Member State unwilling or unable to ratify the treaty would be simply cut off, without preventing the others from moving forward.[94] Yet, the effect of this ratification rule has been to put pressures on all countries to join—a dynamic visible in Ireland where the Fiscal Compact was approved, albeit disgruntledly, in a referendum in 2013.[95]

If post-Brexit constitutional reform were to prove hopeless in the framework of the Union of twenty-seven, therefore, the possibility to resort to multi-speed integration along the model of the Fiscal Compact may re-emerge as an option to establish a political union, particularly among the 19 Eurozone countries.[96] Otherwise, the ECJ in *Pringle* has maintained that the Member States remain free to use inter-se intergovernmental agreements in cases where the EU treaties do not devolve a specific competence to the EU.[97] And because the creation of a federal-like union would certainly require going beyond the current constitutional set-up of the EU, it seems safe to argue that action by the Member States outside the EU legal order would also not unlawfully bypass the EP legislative powers.[98] In sum, while Brexit creates a window of opportunity to reform the EU constitutional architecture for the good of all twenty-seven Member States, the possibility of a multi-speed Europe remains available as a back-up: after all, if the American example can teach us anything, it is that at constitutional moment rules of the game can be unexpectedly changed—and that this is often the pre-condition for the success of a new constitutional endeavor.[99]

---

[93] See Fiscal Compact, Article 14.

[94] See Carlos Closa, *The Politics of Ratification of EU Treaties* (Routledge 2013).

[95] See Roderic O'Gorman, "An Analysis of the Method and Efficacy of Ireland's Incorporation of the Fiscal Compact," in Federico Fabbrini *et al.* (eds.), *The Constitutionalization of European Budgetary Constraints* (Hart Publishing 2014) 273.

[96] See Christian Calliess, "The Governance Framework of the Eurozone and the Need for a Treaty Reform," in Federico Fabbrini *et al.* (eds.), *What Form of Government for the European Union and the Eurozone?* (Hart Publishing 2015) 37.

[97] See Case C-370/12 *Pringle v. Ireland*, ECLI:EU:C:2012:756.

[98] See Federico Fabbrini, "A Principle in Need of Renewal? The Euro-Crisis and the Principle of Institutional Balance" (2016) 50 *Cahiers de droit européen* 285.

[99] See Michael Klarman, *The Framers' Coup. The Making of the United States Constitution* (OUP 2016) (explaining how the US Constitution entered into force because the framers set the rule that ratification by 9 states out of 13 would be sufficient for its validity, notwithstanding the fact that the Articles of Confederation, *i.e.* the 'old' US Constitution, required unanimous consent by the 13 states as a condition to approve amendments to the Articles themselves).

5. Conclusion

Brexit opens a window of opportunity for constitutional change in the EU. As this chapter argued the withdrawal of the UK from the EU compels the remaining Member States and the EU institutions to amend the EU treaties as well as several quasi-constitutional EU acts regulating the composition of the EP and the financing of the EU. In this context, wider proposals for constitutional reform could become part of a package-deal in which EU institutions and Member States reach consensus on how to adapt the EU to the new reality of a Union of twenty-seven. During the euro-crisis, and in the run-up to the 60th anniversary of the Rome Treaties, EU institutions and national governments have outlined several blueprints to improve the EU's effectiveness and legitimacy. Since Brexit requires action precisely in these areas, entrepreneurial policy-makers may now find the space to push change forward. Certainly, as this chapter has pointed out, several challenges have to be taken into account: legal obstacles and political opposition at national level constrain the scope for treaty revisions. Nevertheless, no state appears to be fond of the status quo. And the potential for differentiated integration by a core group of Member States may also function as an incentive for recalcitrant countries to go along with the prospect of amendments at twenty-seven. However, if efforts to reform the constitutional architecture of the EU after Brexit were to falter for idiosyncratic national reasons, innovative ideas should be explored to establish "a more perfect Union"[100] in Europe.

---

[100] US Constitution, Preamble.

Index

Schengen border control system
Danish participation 190–1
Gibraltar 122
impact of migration crisis 268, 287
multispeed Europe 175, 288
no inherent link with Prüm 194
Switzerland's participation 209
UK as point of entry for other Member
    States 41
UK opt-out 2, 39, 185
UK participation in AFSJ 185–6
UK participation in Europol 189
Scotland
Barnett formula 101–2
different levels of devolution 107
English votes for English laws
    (EVEL) 107–10
impact of devolution 99
independence referendum
    catalyst for change 103–4
    open-ended list of further devolved
        powers 104
    process towards the Scotland
        Act 2016 104–5
new challenges opened by Brexit 1–2
single market priority 56
special position in relation to Brexit
    continued single market membership for
        Scotland 123–4
    Great Repeal Bill 125–31
    impact of EU referendum 117–18
    legislative consent under Sewell
        convention 131–5
    overview 115–16
    possibility of 'Great Continuation
        Act' 133–4
    'reverse Greenland' option 121–3
    scope of negotiations after withdrawal
        letter 135–7
    Scotland's access to single market 118–20
    UK approach 120–1
    UK's own single market 216
services
future relations envisaged by Article 50(2) 61
post-Brexit trade regime 75
UK's ability to adapt 40
UK's strong interest in Financial services 18
Sewel Convention
impact of Miller judgment 7
Scotland's role in Brexit 17, 116,
    131–3, 135
single market
benefits of cooperation 34
Britain's early role 43

exclusion of UK from future
    participation 60
future relations envisaged by Article
    50(2) 59–60
impact of Brexit 213–14
impact of leaving single market on Northern
    Ireland 145–9
interconnectivity of four freedoms
    managing rise in Euroskepticism 206–8
    obstruction to 'deep and special
        partnership' 209–11
    paradoxes of indivisibility 211–13
    underlying reasons 203–6
key issue 217–18
post-Brexit new free trade and customs
    agreement 74–7
Scottish question
    continued single market membership for
        Scotland 123–4
    impact of Great Repeal Bill 128–9
    key question 118–20
    national priority 56
structure of state control 37
UK ambivalence 201–2
UK's own single market 214–17
withdrawal under Art 50 7
Single Resolution Mechanism (SRM) 166
**Social Democratic and Labour Party
    (SDLP)** 139, 142
sovereignty
formal exit clause in Lisbon Treaty 35
key referendum argument 5
request for re-negotiation 3
'taking back control'
    continuing trade-off between control and
        cooperation 26–7
    focus on 'control' 27–8
    'ideological crap' as one possible
        response 25–6
    lessons from the Brexit paradox 28–9
    power of mantra 25
    transformative challenge 28
    two key elements in referendum 229–34
Stability and Growth Pact (SGP) 170, 181
state succession principles 83–6

'taking back control'
continuing trade-off between control and
    cooperation 26–7
control of territorial borders
    Britain's island mentality 39
    importance of Britain's labour
        market 39–41
    movement of third-country nationals 41